The Shape of Data in the Digital Humanities

Data and its technologies now play a large and growing role in humanities research and teaching. This book addresses the needs of humanities scholars who seek deeper expertise in the area of data modeling and representation. The authors, all experts in digital humanities, offer a clear explanation of key technical principles, a grounded discussion of case studies, and an exploration of important theoretical concerns. The book opens with an orientation, giving the reader a history of data modeling in the humanities and a grounding in the technical concepts necessary to understand and engage with the second part of the book. The second part of the book is a wide-ranging exploration of topics central for a deeper understanding of data modeling in digital humanities. Chapters cover data modeling standards and the role they play in shaping digital humanities practice, traditional forms of modeling in the humanities and how they have been transformed by digital approaches, ontologies that seek to anchor meaning in digital humanities resources, and how data models inhabit the other analytical tools used in digital humanities research. It concludes with a Glossary that explains specific terms and concepts for data modeling in the digital humanities context. This book is a unique and invaluable resource for teaching and practising data modeling in a digital humanities context.

Julia Flanders is Professor of the Practice in the Northeastern University Department of English and the Director of the Digital Scholarship Group in the Northeastern University Library. She also directs the Women Writers Project and serves as editor in chief of *Digital Humanities Quarterly*, an open-access, peer-reviewed online journal of digital humanities. Her apprenticeship in digital humanities began at the Women Writers Project in the early 1990s and continued with work on the development of digital humanities organizations such as the Text Encoding Initiative, CenterNet, and the Alliance of Digital Humanities Organizations. She has served as chair of the TEI Consortium, as President of the Association for Computers and the Humanities, and as Secretary of ADHO. She has also taught a wide range of workshops on text encoding and served as a consultant and advisor on numerous digital humanities projects. Her research interests focus on data modeling, textual scholarship, humanities data curation, and the politics of digital scholarly work. She is the co-editor, with Neil Fraistat, of the *Cambridge Companion to Textual Scholarship*.

Fotis Jannidis is Professor for computational literary studies at the University of Würzburg in Germany. In the 1990s, he was mainly interested in digital editions and became co-editor of the digital edition *The Young Goethe in His Time* (1999) and of the critical edition of Goethe's *Faust* (beta 2016ff.). He was involved in the development of TextGrid, a framework for digital editions, and is involved in DARIAH, a large European infrastructure project for the digital humanities. His recent work focuses on a corpus-based history of the German novel, creating several corpora and creating, evaluating and applying computational methods for the analysis of collections of literary texts. He also manages a B.A.-/M.A.-program for Digital Humanities. His research interests focus on data modeling and computational literary history. He is co-editor, with Hubertus Kohle and Malte Rehbein, of *Digital Humanities: Eine Einführung* (2017).

Digital Research in the Arts and Humanities
Series Editors: Marilyn Deegan, Lorna Hughes,
Andrew Prescott and Harold Short

Digital technologies are increasingly important to arts and humanities research, expanding the horizons of research methods in all aspects of data capture, investigation, analysis, modeling, presentation and dissemination. This important series covers a wide range of disciplines with each volume focusing on a particular area, identifying the ways in which technology impacts on specific subjects. The aim is to provide an authoritative reflection of the "state of the art" in technology-enhanced research methods. The series is critical reading for those already engaged in the digital humanities, and of wider interest to all arts and humanities scholars.

A full list of titles in this series is available at: www.routledge.com/history/series/DRAH. Recently published titles:

The Shape of Data in the Digital Humanities

Modeling Texts and Text-based Resources

**Edited by Julia Flanders
and Fotis Jannidis**

Routledge
Taylor & Francis Group

LONDON AND NEW YORK

First published 2019
by Routledge
2 Park Square, Milton Park, Abingdon, Oxon OX14 4RN

and by Routledge
52 Vanderbilt Avenue, New York, NY 10017, USA

First issued in paperback 2020

Routledge is an imprint of the Taylor & Francis Group, an informa business

British Library Cataloguing-in-Publication Data
A catalogue record for this book is available from the British Library

Library of Congress Cataloging-in-Publication Data
Names: Flanders, Julia, editor. | Jannidis, Fotis, editor.
Title: The shape of data in the digital humanities : modeling texts and text-based resources / edited by Julia Flanders and Fotis Jannidis.
Description: Abingdon, Oxon ; New York, NY : Routledge, 2019. | Series: Digital research in the arts and humanities | Includes bibliographical references and index.
Identifiers: LCCN 2018013030| ISBN 9781472443243 (hardback : alk. paper) | ISBN 9781315552941 (e-book)
Subjects: LCSH: Digital humanities—Research—Methodology. | Information storage and retrieval systems—Humanities.
Classification: LCC AZ105 .S43 2019 | DDC 025.06/0013—dc23
LC record available at https://lccn.loc.gov/2018013030

ISBN 13: 978-0-367-58403-0 (pbk)
ISBN 13: 978-1-4724-4324-3 (hbk)

Typeset in Times New Roman
by Florence Production Ltd, Stoodleigh, Devon, UK

Julia dedicates this work to her parents, who are fascinated by data modeling under myriad other names.

Fotis dedicates this work to Simone and Matthias.

Contents

Figures

Tables

Contributors

Piotr Bański is a member of the Grammar Department and of the Research Infrastructure Group at the Institute for the German Language in Mannheim. His current research foci are linguistic and lexicographic modeling, annotation science, and standardization of language resources. Dr. Bański is a former member of the TEI Technical Council, and, together with Andreas Witt, a co-convener of the TEI Special Interest Group "TEI for Linguists" (LingSIG). He is also a DIN representative to ISO TC 37/SC 4 "Language resource management" and Chair of the CLARIN Standards Committee.

Lou Burnard is a graduate of Oxford University with a Masters in nineteenth-century English literature. He has been active in the application of IT to literary and linguistic research since the 1970s. At Oxford University Computing Services, he played a major role in establishing and developing several key initiatives and projects, including the Oxford Text Archive, the UK's Arts and Humanities Data Service, the British National Corpus, and, of course, the Text Encoding Initiative. Initially working in the field of database design and support, he has published widely, on "digital humanities," on database systems, and on corpus linguistics, as well as producing a range of teaching materials for numerous courses and workshops about the TEI, both introductory and advanced, in English and French. These include the annual TEI Summer Schools at Oxford, and (in collaboration with others) a number of similar training events in France and elsewhere in Europe. He took early retirement from Oxford in 2010, since when he has been working as a consultant, most notably with a French national infrastructural project (TGE Adonis) and others. He continues to provide training services about the TEI in France, as a part of the French contribution to the DARIAH initiative, and is also active on both the TEI Technical Council and its Board of Directors.

Christopher Donaldson is Lecturer in Regional History at Lancaster University, where he is also an investigator on the Leverhulme Trust-funded Geospatial Innovation in the Digital Humanities research project. He has recently published (with Drs. David Cooper and Patricia Murrieta-Flores) a collection entitled *Literary Mapping in the Digital Age* (Routledge, 2016); he co-edits (with Dr. Zoe Alker) the Digital Forum for the *Journal of Victorian Studies*.

Øyvind Eide is Professor of Digital Humanities at the University of Cologne in Germany. He holds a Ph.D. in Digital Humanities from King's College London (2013). He was an employee in various positions at the University of Oslo from 1995 to 2013, working on digital humanities and cultural heritage informatics. From 2013 to 2015 he was a lecturer and research associate at The University of Passau. He is the chair of the European Association for Digital Humanities (EADH) and is also actively engaged in several other international organizations such as the Alliance of Digital Humanities Organizations (ADHO), ICOM's International Committee for Documentation (CIDOC), and Cultural Literacy in Europe (CLE). His research interests are focused on transformative digital intermedia studies, using critical stepwise formalization as a method for conceptual modeling of cultural heritage information. This is used as a tool for critical engagement with media differences, especially the relationships between texts and maps as media of communication. He is also engaged in theoretical studies of modeling in the humanities as well as beyond.

Peter Fankhauser is senior researcher at IDS (*Institut für Deutsche Sprache*), Mannheim, Germany. He currently works on long-term archival of language resources and text analytics. In the 25 years of his academic career he has worked at various research institutions in Germany. His expertise and interests include database and repository technologies, XML, and data and text mining with applications to language corpora. Peter Fankhauser was coeditor of the XQuery formal semantics (W3C), and has published over 70 peer-reviewed papers.

Ian Gregory is Professor of Digital Humanities in the Department of History at Lancaster University, UK. His research is concerned with the use of geographical information systems (GIS) to study the past. Originally, this was concerned with using quantitative data to study modern British history. However, more recently he has been researching how textual sources can be incorporated into GIS in a range of disciplines across the humanities from the history of public health to Lake District literature. He was Principal Investigator on the European Research Council-funded Spatial Humanities: Texts, GIS, Places project that explored this topic along with a range of other topics. He has published five books and over 70 journal articles and book chapters.

Andrew Hardie is a Reader in Linguistics at Lancaster University. His main research interests are the theory and methodology of corpus linguistics; the descriptive and theoretical study of grammar using corpus data; the languages of Asia; and applications of corpus methods in the humanities and social sciences. He is one of the lead developers of the Corpus Workbench software for indexing and analysing corpus data, and the creator of its online interface, CQPweb. He is co-author, with Tony McEnery, of the book *Corpus Linguistics: Method, Theory and Practice* (Cambridge University Press, 2012).

Willard McCarty, Ph.D., FRAI, is Professor Emeritus, King's College London, and Fellow of the Royal Anthropological Institute. He has been Editor of the online seminar Humanist since 1987, of *Interdisciplinary Science Reviews* since 2008, recipient of the Roberto Busa Award in 2013 and the 2017 Besterman Lecturer at Oxford. His current book project is an historical study of the relation between computing and the humanities. See www.mccarty. org.uk/

Isabel Meirelles is a Professor in the Faculty of Design at OCAD University in Toronto, Canada. In addition to collaborating with scientists and humanists in the development of visualization systems, Isabel's research focuses on the theoretical and experimental examination of how information is structured and communicated in different media. She is the author of *Design for Information: An Introduction to the Histories, Theories, and Best Practices Behind Effective Information Visualizations* (Rockport Publishers, 2013).

Christian-Emil Smith Ore is an Associate Professor and Head of Unit for Digital Documentation (EDD) at the University of Oslo, and has worked with digital methods in the humanities for 25 years. Ore works along three main lines: Methods for cultural heritage documentation, lexicography and corpus, and electronic text editions (medieval charters). An important issue in Ore's work is how to make the information in memory institutions electronically available: Standards like TEI for text encoding and common core ontologies like CIDOC-CRM for data interchange. Standards must not be straitjackets choking new research. Without them, however, we can never interlink our research data meaningfully, making it harder to argue for the usefulness of digital methods. Ore has been the principal investigator for several large-scale national database and digitalization projects for the university museums and cultural heritage collections in Norway and was one of the two founders of the Medieval Nordic Text Archive (menota.org). He has participated in and coordinated long-term language documentation projects in Southern Africa, served on scientific and advisory boards in the US, Germany and Scandinavia, chaired ICOM-CIDOC (2004–10), co-chaired TEI ontology SIG, and has participated in the development of CIDOC-CRM and FRBoo since 2002 and is one of the international editors of the standard.

Elena Pierazzo is Professor of Italian Studies and Digital Humanities at the University of Grenoble-Alpes; formerly, she was lecturer at the Department of Digital Humanities at King's College London where she was the coordinator of the MA in Digital Humanities. She has a Ph.D. in Italian Philology: her specialism is Italian Renaissance texts, digital edition of early modern and modern draft manuscripts, digital editing and text encoding. She has been the Chair of the Text Encoding Initiative and involved in the TEI user-community, with a special interest in the transcription of modern and medieval manuscripts. She co-chairs the working group on digital editions of the European Network NeDiMAH and is one of the scientists in chief for the ITN DiXiT.

Wendell Piez grew up in Asia (including the Philippines and Japan) and the United States and attended school at Yale College and Rutgers University.

Interested from early years in computers and logical contraptions of all kinds, he nonetheless sought out and received a humanistic education, specializing in Classics (Ancient Greek literature and philosophy) and English Literature and literary theory. In years directly following receiving his degree in 1991, Dr. Piez became immersed in digital technologies (this time, in an archive), culminating in a post at the Center for Electronic Texts in the Humanities, an early "DH text center" (*avant la lettre*) where pioneering work was done with and in support of emerging text encoding standards. In 1998 Dr. Piez took a position in the private sector, developing technology and working with leading technologists in XML document and data modeling to support initiatives in several sectors and vertical markets including journal and book publishing in electronic media. Dr. Piez contributes to open source software development initiatives and produces papers and presentations reflecting theoretical work in markup languages and data modeling. Since 2012 he has been an independent consultant working in Rockville, Maryland.

Stephen Ramsay is Susan J. Rosowski Associate University Professor of English and a Fellow at the Center for Digital Research in the Humanities at the University of Nebraska-Lincoln. He has written and lectured widely on subjects related to digital humanities, teaching humanities majors to program, and designing and building text technologies for humanist scholars. He is the author of *Reading Machines: Toward an Algorithmic Criticism* (University of Illinois Press, 2011).

Paul Rayson is a Reader in Computer Science at Lancaster University, UK. He is director of the UCREL interdisciplinary research centre which carries out research in corpus linguistics and natural language processing (NLP). A long-term focus of his work is the application of semantic-based NLP in extreme circumstances where language is noisy—e.g. in historical, learner, speech, email, txt and other CMC varieties. His applied research is in the areas of online child protection, learner dictionaries, and text mining of historical corpora and annual financial reports. He is a co-investigator of the five-year ESRC Centre for Corpus Approaches to Social Science (CASS) which is designed to bring the corpus approach to bear on a range of social sciences.

Benjamin Schmidt is an assistant professor of history at Northeastern University and core faculty at the NuLab for Texts, Maps, and Networks. His research interests are in the digital humanities and the intellectual and cultural history of the United States in the nineteenth and twentieth centuries. His digital humanities research focuses on large-scale text analysis, humanities data visualization, and the challenges and opportunities of reading data itself as a historical source. His current project, *Creating Data,* focuses on re-analyzing the data collected by the nineteenth-century American state. He also contributes to popular conversations on topics, including higher education in the United States, computational detection of anachronisms in historical fiction, and the "crisis" of the humanities.

C.M. Sperberg-McQueen (Black Mesa Technologies LLC) is a consultant specializing in the use of descriptive markup to help memory institutions preserve cultural heritage information. He co-edited the Guidelines of the Text Encoding Initiative, the XML 1.0 specification, and the XML Schema Definition Language (XSDL) 1.1 specification.

Elke Teich is a full professor of English Linguistics and Translation Studies at Universität des Saarlandes, Saarbrücken, and principal investigator in the Cluster of Excellence Multimodal Computing and Interaction (MMCI: www. mmci.uni-saarland.de/) and the German CLARIN project (Common Language Resources and Technology Infrastructure: http://de.clarin.eu/de/). Since October 2014, she has been the head of the Saarbrücken Collaborative Research Center (SFB 1102) Information Density and Linguistic Encoding funded by the German Research Foundation (DFG) with 15 projects (www.sfb1102.uni-saarland.de). Teich's expertise ranges from descriptive grammar of English and German over (multilingual) register analysis (with a special focus on scientific registers) to translatology. In terms of research fields, she has worked in machine translation, automatic text generation, corpus linguistics as well as digital humanities. She has published two monographs and over 50 peer-reviewed papers.

Ted Underwood is Professor of Information Sciences and English at the University of Illinois, Urbana-Champaign. He is the author of two books, including *Why Literary Periods Mattered* (Stanford, 2013), and of articles in journals ranging from *PMLA* to *Big Data and Society*.

Andreas Witt is Professor for Digital Humanities and Linguistic Information Processing at the University of Cologne in Germany. He also heads the research infrastructure group at the Institute for the German Language in Mannheim and is Honorary Professor of Digital Humanities at the Institute for Computational Linguistics at Heidelberg University. His research is situated in the field of annotation science. Andreas Witt is an active member of standards bodies: he chairs an ISO working group on linguistic annotation and, together with Piotr Bański, co-chairs the TEI Special Interest Group, TEI for Linguists. For the 2016–2018 academic years he has been selected by the iSchool of the University of Illinois at Urbana-Champaign as a research fellow.

Preface

This book is a quintessential product of the digital humanities community of the past decade. At the 2008 TEI conference held at King's College London, the editors had the kind of enthusiastic conversation that is so common at conferences, and that so often produces a feeling that there is a good book to be written if one only had the time. We were each seized with a sense of how important data modeling was to digital humanities research, and how little had been written on the topic for a humanities audience. A great opportunity. Someone should definitely do it. We both filed the meeting away with the other events of the conference and went back to our other commitments.

But something durable must have been set in motion, because the following year at the TEI meeting in Ann Arbor, we resumed the conversation and (somewhat to our mutual astonishment) agreed to start planning a book. We started with a mapping exercise: a workshop in March 2012, funded by the NEH and the DFG under a program designed to foster international collaboration on key research problems in digital humanities. This event brought together an international group of experts from a range of disciplines to think about what might be meant by "data modeling in digital humanities." The record of that event is available at the Women Writers Project website,[1] and the resulting white paper summarized the overall contours of the domain of interest and the salient research questions. The workshop served as a crucial catalyst for our thinking: it demonstrated the richness of the topic and its centrality in binding together strands of theory and practice from widely differing areas of digital humanities: scholarly editions, art history, geospatial information, digital repositories, text markup, data representation standards, virtual worlds, digital pedagogy. The resulting book reflects a good deal of that richness but for reasons of space has to be selective, and the transcriptions and other materials from the workshop remain a distinctively valuable resource.

During the years between our initial conversation and the completion of the book, our thinking about the scope and orientation of the problem has evolved and matured, and the field itself has changed. With the enormous global rise of interest in digital humanities, the need we originally identified for reflection on data modeling and its intersections with scholarship has magnified considerably. And the emergence of graduate and undergraduate degree programs in digital humanities and related fields means that the need for an introductory text in this area is even greater than before. The global nature of the field now also fore-grounds both the cultural specificity of modeling and its political and ideological significance. Being critical participants in global digital humanities means being aware of models and the power they exert—often invisibly—over data, systems, and the conceptual framing of research.

We hope this volume will be valuable to several different audiences. First, for anyone teaching digital humanities, it provides a varied set of entry points into the challenges of data modeling, and offers a strong introductory grounding in the key concepts and questions. For those new to the field, the contributions to this volume represent a good sampling of theoretical and practical approaches and offer insight into a range of different kinds of digital humanities scholarship. And finally, we hope the book will serve as a provocation for those who are already deeply engaged with this topic: the contributions suggest new research directions, unanswered questions, and technical challenges.

The volume is divided into three major sections. The two introductory chapters by the editors provide an orientation in the problem space and a grounding in essential concepts. In the first chapter, we discuss the significance of data modeling to digital humanities and to twenty-first-century humanities research more generally. The second chapter provides a thorough introduction to the funda-mentals of data modeling and to the most significant digital meta models, explaining their roots in logic and mathematics and their applicability to different kinds of data. The main section of the book includes contributions by twenty-one experts who explore specific theoretical and practical topics in detail. The con-cluding keywords section provides glosses of key terms and explains essential technical concepts.

The editors offer warm thanks to the contributors to this volume and also to the participants in the original workshop for bringing such thoughtful energy to this research area. Our especially warm thanks go to Kristina Schmidt for her care with the manuscript. In particular, we would also like to thank Piotr Bański, Sina Bock, Øyvind Eide, Willard McCarty, Stephan Moser, Christof Schöch, and Thorsten Vitt for their very insightful comments on draft versions of the volume. We are excited by the future possibilities and hope the book will inspire readers to join in the work.

Julia Flanders and Fotis Jannidis

Note

1   www.wwp.northeastern.edu/outreach/conference/kodm2012/.

Part I
Orientation

1 Data modeling in a digital humanities context

An introduction

Julia Flanders and Fotis Jannidis

1 Modeling in the humanities

Despite persistent ambivalence about the concept of "data" in humanities research,[1] there is a long and rich tradition of gathering and modeling information as part of humanities research practice. From the perspective of the digital humanities, that tradition now appears in retrospect like important prehistory for an understanding of data modeling. And that prehistory is significant not only because it shows how integral such activities have been to humanities research, but also because it reminds us of the distinctive complexities and challenges that humanities data poses. While the terms "data" and "modeling" may be new, many of the activities and intellectual frameworks they entail are familiar and deep-rooted. In a general sense, we understand intuitively that specific theoretical approaches rely on concepts and terms that divide the universe of ideas in specific ways. For instance, literary periodization constitutes a model of history in which spans of time are associated with distinct stylistic patterns and, indirectly, with cultural, economic, and historical phenomena that are presumed to influence those patterns and their evolution. The literary-historical approach is in itself a kind of general model, within whose terms more specific models could be framed and debated (for instance, concerning whether and how one might distinguish the medieval and Renaissance periods, and where the boundary falls in different national traditions). And we might reject the literary-historical way of modeling culture altogether, in favor of a model that disregards periodization, or that is uninterested in historical change, or that denies the existence of "literature" as a category. Debates about method are ultimately debates about our models.

In a more specific sense, our models represent the shaping choices we make in representing and analyzing the materials we study. As Michael Sperberg-McQueen put it in his keynote to the 2012 workshop on Knowledge Organization and Data Modeling, "modeling is a way to make explicit our assumptions about the nature of a text/artefact," and this statement is importantly agnostic with respect to medium. Although the digital medium has brought these choices and representational systems into heightened visibility, they have been at the heart of scholarship since the beginning. A classic example is the critical apparatus in a scholarly edition, a form of knowledge management that might be said to originate with humanism itself. As pure content, the critical apparatus is simply an account of the variations among the witnesses to a particular text, which could be communicated through a footnote or a prose essay. As information, however, the critical apparatus has taken its current structured shape through two closely related processes. The first of these is the formalization of the information it contains, placing it under regulation so that all of the components are verifiably present: the lemma or base reading, the variant readings and their sources, and so forth. The second, and closely related, is the development of standard notation systems that enable that formalized information to be processed efficiently and consistently. The use of punctuation, standardized abbreviations, and other notational conventions to group, delimit, and document each variant makes it possible for a reader to process this information quickly and systematically, and to perceive patterns—in effect, to do with the human mind what we now consider the hallmark outcome of good data modeling in digital systems. Digital scholarly editions emerged so early in the history of humanities computing in part because they were able to build on a clear existing model deriving from a long-standing tradition of practice.

The more recent history of data modeling builds on this trajectory. It draws on the insights generated by *informal models* (such as the difference between types of variant readings), which offer a descriptive language and an underlying set of ideas, but not at a level of precision that would support the creation of a formal model. It realizes the informational potential represented by existing *formalizable models*, such as the critical apparatus, or the structure of a dictionary entry, or the organization of a financial ledger, which possess all of the qualities requisite for formalization: a clearly defined set of informational items with clearly defined relationships. Research on data modeling has sought to express this information in ways that support computational reasoning, as a *formal model*: one that rests on a logical or mathematical basis, whose definitions are expressed using some formal constraint notation (such as a schema), such that the information being modeled can be processed and analyzed with reference to the model.

This chapter will explore the significance of this shift for our research methods, for the tools of scholarship, and for our understanding of the relationship between our models and our theories of the world. We will first consider in more detail what the digital turn has done for modeling approaches in the humanities and digital humanities. Then we will discuss the kinds of intellectual traction formal modeling can provide for researchers—a point that is picked up more fully in the next chapter, and in Michael Sperberg-McQueen's contribution to this volume—and the complex relationship between those formal models and the tools through which we express and work with them. Next we will consider the relationship between our models and the intellectual scenarios they seek to represent, the relationship between models and the tools we use to manipulate and process humanities data, the tension between models and data, and the forms of critical engagement we must exercise in using digital models in a humanities context. We'll conclude this chapter with some proposals for a research and pedagogical agenda in the domain of data modeling in digital humanities.

1.1 The digital turn: modeling in digital humanities

It is often assumed that the affordances of the digital medium have brought into being new ways of thinking about data and new kinds of questions that were not previously thinkable. But in fact historical examples reveal a long tradition of attempts to analyze and represent data, often representing great ingenuity in the face of limitations in the medium of print. A regularly cited example is the attempt by Teena Rochfort Smith in 1883 to present a four-column edition of *Hamlet*, in which the Folio and the first and second Quartos are shown in parallel, together with a conflated text, with complex typography through which the reader can apprehend the specific passages that differ between versions.[2] Isabel Meirelles's *Design for Information* (2013) offers numerous samples of complex visualizations representing analysis by hand of mortality data, historical imports and exports, agricultural production, and attendance at the Paris Universal Exhibition. The members of the New Shakspeare (*sic*) Society in the 1870s developed notation systems for displaying metrical patterns in poetry, aimed at supporting a large-scale analysis of prosody to assist in dating Shakespeare's plays. And concordances were a common form of humanities research data (and one of the earliest forms of digital humanities data) until they gave way to widespread use of dynamic searching.

Although more or less formal information models can be found in a variety of humanities contexts, there are some environments in which their operation is particularly visible to humanities scholarship. One of these is (naturally enough) in the domain of information science, where it impinges on humanities research practice: in the controlled vocabularies and information systems of the research library. Reference works such as dictionaries, bibliographies, concordances, and catalogues represent another long tradition of strongly modeled information. Still another is to be found in certain kinds of paratexts: title pages, colophons, footnotes, indexes, tables of contents, running heads, and other systematic apparatus through which publishers frame the cultural intelligibility of the text. These are particularly interesting examples since some of these formal systems exist not as an aid to the reader, but as an artifact of the work processes of publication itself: for instance, the printed signatures that assist in the ordering and assembly of the book, or the verbal formulae associated with the license to publish ("Cum privilegio" and equivalents), which are a standard component of title pages during periods when this kind of oversight was in place.

With this long history in mind, what does data modeling mean in a digital humanities context? The landscape is characterized by complexity and challenge. We inherit from the humanistic tradition a set of modeling practices and concepts that, while foundational, are often unsystematic, poorly understood by non-specialists, and invisible through their very familiarity. Complicating this relationship is the fact that, as Scott Weingart observes, "humanists care more about the differences than the regularities";[3] even in the domains where formalisms and "regularities" are well-established, we are inclined to treat exceptions and variations as the phenomena of greatest interest. Furthermore, humanistic data is strongly layered: the artifacts modeled in digital humanities are created with a purpose by identifiable agents and have a history that is part of their identity, and they then undergo further processes of curation whose intentions and methods need to be kept visible. Museum and cultural heritage institutions have developed ontologies—notably the CIDOC Conceptual Reference Model (CRM)—in which concepts like provenance and purpose are explicitly represented. Our models thus in many cases need to represent not only the history of the artifact itself, but also the history of the ways in which it has been described and contextualized. Alongside this humanistic legacy we also inherit from the history of digital technology a deep, thoroughly elaborated understanding of data modeling that has found a home in some specific domains of the digital humanities: notably, in areas including markup languages, network analysis, ontologies, and game studies. These are all spaces in which an understanding of the models themselves, and a critical and theoretical attention to their design consequences, has been central to (and tightly coupled with) the use of models in practical research.

That kind of tight coupling and its attendant expertise are now, ironically, being made scarcer by the interfaces and tools that have popularized the digital humanities to a new generation of scholars. Where early humanities computing engaged intimately with its data models—through the development of standards like the TEI Guidelines, tools like TUSTEP, resources like the British National Corpus—the great rise of digital humanities in the twenty-first century coincides, not coincidentally, with forms of digital scholarship in which contact with the model is at a remove and in which the technical expertise necessary to uncover and intervene in the modeling that animates our digital systems is increasingly rare. Our goal in this volume is to bring data modeling back into visibility and to demonstrate its centrality to all forms of digital scholarship. In order to do this, we need to re-examine our modeling activities—those that are already familiar to us and those that arise in the digital medium—in light of the more rigorous conceptual framework afforded by traditions of formal data modeling arising in fields like formal logic and mathematics, whose foundational relevance is suggested in the following chapter on the essentials of data modeling. Bringing these domains to bear may open up opportunities for greater formalism, greater clarity of expression, and a clearer understanding of the edge domains where formal modeling is not possible. We can also benefit from a detailed examination of specific modeling practices as they apply to specific kinds of information and specific forms of analysis: text, geospatial information, temporal information, visual information. And lastly, we need to understand the social, intellectual, and political contexts in which data modeling takes place: the circumstances that shape our data standards, the operations of constraint systems such as schemas and encoding languages, the role that ideology and discipline play in our modeling strategies. The chapters that follow explore all of these things. As a starting point, Chapter 2, A Gentle Introduction to Data Modeling, provides a foundational discussion of essential terminology and concepts, starting with the concept of the "model" and the distinctive intellectual work it performs. Subsequent chapters explore specific types of modeling and specific conceptual areas, and explore some of the politics and open research questions attendant on this work.

1.2 Gaining traction from models

The conceptual shift that digital humanities brings to the humanities is nowhere more visible or consequential than in the opportunity to formalize and exploit information models. As we have seen, humanities scholarship already makes extensive use of structured information: the digital medium adds several important dimensions to this structuring. First, in the digital medium it is possible to create a formal specification of the rules governing a given type of data: a model of the data. This model can be used as a kind of template for the data set, in abstract terms: it tells us the set of constraints within which the data operates. It can also be used to test whether a given set of data obeys these constraints. As Wendell Piez has shown (Piez, 2001), this kind of test has its roots in the history of manufacturing, with the emergence of interchangeable parts. The use of gauges and testing mechanisms that could verify the specifications of parts manufactured independently made it possible to ensure that they would fit together properly when assembled. In the digital environment, this kind of validation and testing is valuable for similar reasons: it enables data to be created independently of specific tools and contexts of usage. In specialized cases, it may also provide additional ways of learning about the data set, since it shows immediately the possible patterns the data can assume and also may reveal some of the assumptions underlying the data design. This kind of data modeling also facilitates collaboration by allowing communities to formalize standards that can be used as the basis for shared tools, and it serves a pedagogical role as well, by supporting systems that can prompt novice creators of data towards shared practice.

In addition to its practical value in relation to the data it governs, the formal data model (represented through a schema or other specification) becomes an object of study in itself. Scholars studying the history of critical editing can examine the apparatus of specific editions and learn inductively about how their editors thought about the critical apparatus and its components. If we wish to extend that study into the age of the digital edition, we can examine the editions themselves empirically, but we can also examine their data models to learn what formal categories the editors sought to impose (for instance, a distinction between orthographic and substantive variants). We can also compare the actual data to the data model (using validation tools) to discover whether these categories were used in practice. In effect, modeling processes write our knowledge about the content and semantics of our data into that data in formal terms, giving the data a kind of intelligence and self-awareness.

This "intelligence" in the data represents a crucial theoretical and practical asset. It is now commonplace to observe that computational processing offers advantages of speed and scale that can move formerly challenging tasks—such as concordancing or rapid statistical analysis—into the realm of the trivial. We can also observe that even within the digital realm, formal modeling creates opportunities for processing and analysis that are not possible with data whose modeling is less explicit. A stream of undifferentiated text—words and spaces— may express a novel, a collection of oral histories, a set of personnel records, but however apparent those differences may be to a human reader, they are inaccessible to computation until their structural model has been communicated in some way to the computer. That modeling might be represented through explicit structures in the data: for instance, as records and fields in a database, or through markup that writes concepts like "chapter" and "dialogue" and "speaker" and "date" into the text in ways that we will explore in the next chapter. However, it might also be represented in an algorithm that can read the unmarked data and infer the structure of an oral history interview from notational cues. Either way, the structure we assign to or infer from the data forms the basis of everything else we can do with it: small practical tasks we take for granted, such as sorting personnel records by postcode and surname for a mailing, or complex research tasks such as analyzing the gender dynamics of dramatic dialogue in early American plays.

If we approach the task of modeling in a purely decontextualized way, as an intellectual problem, it is tempting to let our ingenuity run away with us: working at ever-increasing levels of detail to create models of ever-greater complexity. Strong data modeling creates intellectual opportunities, but it also represents several added costs. One obvious cost is the extra labor of creating the data: both the amount of work, and the expertise it entails, will be greater the more detailed the modeling and the finer distinctions being represented. Identifying all of the names in a document can be done nearly automatically; distinguishing between the names of persons, places, organizations, and other entities requires human intervention and subject expertise to achieve with accuracy; identifying the individual parts of each name and associating the name with a specific named entity may require significant research effort. A less obvious cost is the work of developing and maintaining the model itself. In the case of an ontology like CIDOC-CRM, or a text encoding language like the Text Encoding Initiative Guidelines, or a metadata standard like METS, the model results from years of work by large numbers of experts, and the additional involvement of thousands of other contributors whose data and user requirements have shaped the model. And finally, there is the least visible cost of all: the cost of the extra complexity of documentation, training methods, and knowledge preservation over time that arises from maintaining a more complex data set. The point here is not that these costs are prohibitive or unjustified, but rather that good strategic planning involves balancing the costs and benefits, and focusing the effort in areas that offer a clear advantage. Strong, costly modeling of data that will be treated as ephemeral is as short-sighted as using poorly modeled data in a context where its limitations will impoverish research opportunities for years to come.

1.3 Data modeling in tension with modeling systems

We have been discussing the modeling of humanities data in ways that emphasize the intellectual contours of the information itself, and these contours are of great importance because they represent what the data means to us, the way it operates in our own minds. Within that sphere, we can readily conceptualize a scholarly edition as a transcription of a document that has a certain structure, to which we have added annotations that comment on specific passages, together with an apparatus that supplies variant readings for individual words and phrases. But when we undertake to architect a digital artifact representing this information, we need to work within specific modeling systems that have their own structural properties. As we will see, relational databases emphasize repeatable structures that assume a fundamental similarity of records across the data set, while XML emphasizes a grammar-based structure that is more open-ended and documentary, but requires that the document be conceptualized as a tree. Each of these approaches might offer certain kinds of informational advantages: a database would naturally enforce the regular structure of the annotations and variant readings, and would provide excellent tools for querying and analyzing the results, but that record-based regularity would feel less natural as a way to represent the documentary details of the base text. XML would offer better provision for open-ended documentary structures (including the representation of areas where individual words and phrases need to be marked or annotated in some way), but its prohibition of overlapping elements might prove awkward in cases where several different annotations or bits of textual apparatus apply to overlapping passages of the base text.[4] A non-XML-based markup language like COCOA or, more recently, LMNL would make it possible to freely annotate arbitrary segments of text without concern for overlap, but would sacrifice the informational value of the explicit containment and demarcation of data elements offered by databases and XML. Pragmatically speaking, each of these disadvantages can be overcome, albeit inelegantly. LMNL can be transformed into XML, restoring the explicitness of element boundaries; one can represent overlapping spans in XML using empty elements and pointers; one can represent mixed content in a database through various workarounds. And at some level, these models are isomorphic: given sufficient effort, each of these information formats can be converted into the others. But each approach has a certain natural logic that maps more elegantly onto some kinds of information than others.

These systems are evolving steadily, driven by dissatisfaction with their limitations and by a desire for more expressive models that are more congruent with current research methods and ways of understanding the objects being modeled. Even if a document is *like* a tree (or a file cabinet, or a network), or can be represented *as if it were* one of these things, in truth it is none of these and there are many situations where pretending otherwise becomes awkward and restrictive. Experimental systems like LMNL have come into being precisely as efforts to demonstrate the existence of alternative possibilities, and to explore the expanded potential they may offer. At the same time, our usage practices are also evolving and becoming more pragmatic, in part as a result of tools that mediate the data creation process and allow more complex processing that can overcome inelegances in the underlying modeling. In the days when every pointer had to be entered and checked by hand, creating a workaround for overlapping XML structures was cumbersome in ways that accentuated the mismatch between the encoding and the "real" information being represented. With the advent of tools that make help to automate this work (as well as tools that can process the resulting markup to yield useful results), the feeling of philosophical wrongness is a little milder.

When do these differences actually matter, and how? Are our data modeling systems simply tools to be understood and used pragmatically, or do they carry cultural significance that informs the data we create with them? In the early days of SGML, its tree structure seemed deeply consequential, whether one understood it as a form of intellectual tyranny (with its suggestions of hierarchy and patriarchalism) or as a statement about the orderliness and intelligibility of documents. Thirty years later, we remain aware of the tree primarily as a technical commitment that XML makes, and our decisions concerning whether or not to use XML are typically made not because of its rightness or wrongness with respect to the nature of texts, but because of its practical properties or inconveniences. But has familiarity inured us to philosophical questions that should be more vividly in our minds? And are such questions—if they do matter—issues of aesthetics or do they carry an ethical dimension as well? These questions are difficult to answer fully in the context of this discussion, although readers will find relevant discussion throughout the volume, but a few points are worth noting here by way of orientation. First, in many contexts it is possible to identify a principle of elegance or "good fit" in the modeling of data. This can be characterized by lack of redundancy in the data, use of data structures that correspond to our intuitions about the intellectual organization of the data (for instance, using a network structure with explicit linkages between nodes to represent a community of letter-writers), data elements whose level of abstraction and granularity matches that of our domain analysis, and an overall architecture in which making the information connections required for analysis is simple and direct rather than requiring elaborate or extremely indirect traversals. Data modeled in this way is likely to be easier to document, to explain, and to program for.

But further, it is worth bearing in mind that pragmatic considerations are often the strongest determinants of the shape of data, and these considerations often militate against elegance or a natural homology between the data modeling and the object being modeled. Database software was for a long time far ahead of XML software in its power and level of engineering sophistication, with the result that many projects used relational databases even for data that was arguably an extremely poor fit in modeling terms, purely for the sake of the advantage it offered in speed and ease of development. Conversely, a project whose practitioners are very familiar with XML might choose to represent what is essentially tabular data using an XML structure, because the effort and cost of creating a simple schema and display system were less than that of either acquiring a database program or developing a database application using a tool like MySQL. As a more extreme example, one often encounters projects using word-processing formats to capture data that is clearly tabular—and that could benefit from representation as a spreadsheet or an XML document—only because the project's editors are unfamiliar with other tools. The differences between these cases are instructive. In the first two scenarios, despite the arguably poor fit between data structure and modeling tool, the actual modeling of the data may be perfectly appropriate. As long as the identification of relevant data elements, the expression of their relationships, and the constraints on data types (numbers, dates, controlled vocabularies, and so forth) are intelligent and strategically appropriate, the most important goals of the modeling work have been met. With some effort, the data from one system can be exported and imported into another to take advantage of practical differences in speed, convenience, or specialized processing options. However, in the case of the word-processor, the problem lies in the fact that important aspects of the modeling are simply not taking place: the tool does not possess the capacity to formally constrain or validate the data, so the "modeling" is only taking place in the transcriber's mind. As a purely practical accommodation, creating data in this way is a reasonable first step (if there really are no alternatives), but only if there is an equally practical pathway to get the data into a more usable format. But as Michael Sperberg-McQueen observes in his contribution to this volume, this kind of non-formalized modeling also risks "vagueness and ambiguity": non-formal models "make it easy for modelers to deceive themselves as to the completeness, explicitness, and correctness of a model."

1.4 Modeling and the digital humanities tool set

For the digital humanities, data modeling is an essential part of our evolving relationship with tools. Within this relationship, formal modeling becomes a necessity, imposed by the tools; we're always making models (of some kind) whether we intend to do so or not. All digital tools operate upon some form of modeled data, whether or not they fully expose that model to us, so if nothing else, we are creating information that corresponds to our tool's way of modeling information. When we create a spreadsheet using a spreadsheet program such as Excel or Google Sheets, the data we create is modeled within the program as a set of rows and columns that are understood as computable objects: if we want to compute the total of items in a column or row, the spreadsheet software is able to do this. If we use a word-processing program to represent tabular data, we can get the same visual effect of rows and columns, but we can't perform computation on them; the software does not model the data as a set of computable values but simply as a set of text segments to be positioned on the page.

These days, people are creating data all the time: making travel reservations, doing online banking, wearing mobile fitness devices, sending text messages, writing Amazon reviews. The modeling of this data has only a practical significance for most people: they expect the systems that use it to work, but they don't have an intellectual stake in the way it is shaped. The decisions about how best to model this information are made by those who manage it: airlines, banks, app developers, and so forth. As data creators, academics have a different, more knowing relationship to their data: they create data that is going to be a persistent part of the research environment, and they act as both its creators, managers, and consumers. The stakes of the modeling decisions for research data are thus much higher, and to the extent that these decisions are mediated through tools, there is significant value—even a burden of responsibility—in understanding that mediation. And within the academy, the stakes for digital humanists are highest of all, since their research concerns not only the knowing and critical *use* of data models, media, and tools, but also their critical *creation*.

There are several different ways in which tools operate in relation to models. For one thing, they can control our creation and editing of data, by constraining our options and by providing feedback when we make an error or a correct choice. The model here is significant because it represents our level of control over the data and our intentions towards it. If our intentions align with those of the tool—for instance, using a drawing tool to create vector images—then the tool can assist us and serve as an ally. It can also serve to express the model and make it visible to us for inspection: for example, database tools often provide a structural view of the tables, fields, and relationships so that we can see how they are organized. XML editing tools similarly offer various structural views of XML documents and schemas through which we can inspect their architecture. If our intentions run counter to those of the tool, or if we're simply unaware of how the tool aligns with those intentions, then the outcome may be surprising or unsatisfying. For instance, if we use an XML-aware editor to create XML data, it can assist us by preventing us from inserting markup that is ill-formed or invalid. Conversely, if we use a word processor to author the textual notes for a critical edition, the word-processing software has no knowledge of the specific components of such notes (witnesses, lemmas, variant readings, and so forth): its model of the data is purely oriented towards page formatting. As a result, the "data" we create in the word processor can only model what lies within the conceptual model provided by that tool.

Furthermore, tools can also interact with our models through processes like interoperation and conversion: for example, when a tool like Microsoft Word ingests an HTML file, the ingestion process involves mapping the HTML data structures (elements for headings, paragraphs, hyperlinks, metadata, and so forth) onto Word's own internal data modeling, which includes many but not all of the same concepts. The conversion may involve a down-mapping (e.g. the elision of the distinction between "list inside paragraph" and "list in between paragraphs") or a shift in semantics (e.g. a mapping of "block quotation" onto "indented block of text"), or a simple loss of data. The more fully aware we are of these underlying models and the mapping logic different tools employ, the more control we can exercise over our data during its entire life cycle.

It is also useful to consider how different types of tools assist our modeling efforts, at different stages of our work. Some data creation tools invite or even require their users to do good modeling by foregrounding and enforcing the model. An XML editor can enforce the rules of well-formedness actively by providing tag completion, and passively by highlighting errors; an XML editor that is also schema-aware can prompt the users with valid element and attribute options. Similarly, database systems often have user interfaces for data entry that provide access to controlled value lists, enforce the use of appropriate data types, and report inappropriate or missing required values. But tools don't need to expose their models directly to do a good job of supporting them. For instance, an XML editor can offer users a formatted view of their data in which the formatting of specific elements (color, italicization, indentation, and so forth) provides a visual reinforcement of their correct usage. Proofreaders might not know that the author's name in a bibliographic record should be encoded with <author>, but they know that when the text is encoded correctly, the author's name shows up in green. Some word-processing programs attempt to reinforce consistent modeling of documents by offering users the ability to create styles that associate semantic categories (such as headings, quotations, lists, and the like) with formatting features (bold or italic text, indentation, bullets).

Tools for manipulating and analyzing data also draw attention to our models, and here the model is significant because it represents the horizon of possibility for the data in relation to the tool. The model is in effect the data's way (and the data creator's way) of communicating with the tool about what the data "knows": its potential to reward analysis. For example, the Juxta Commons is designed so that it can accept both plain text and XML input: it "understands" XML to the extent that it can ingest it successfully. But it does not take any advantage of the XML data structures in performing its tokenization and collation analysis, so XML data is handled as a benign but not advantageous form of modeling (whereas a data format like RTF or JPEG would be entirely unintelligible to this system). In a more fully XML-aware version of this tool, XML could offer positive advantages: for instance, by allowing the tool to ignore metadata, or enabling the user to identify specific components of the text for exclusion (such as page numbers or running heads) from the collation. To take another example: the Gephi network visualization tool is not only designed to read in predefined graph formats, but it can also take in and make sense of any tabular data (in the sense that it can parse such data as a structure). However, in the latter it needs help in determining which columns in the data are intended as nodes, and which are attributes of nodes. Gephi makes no assumptions about the tabular data model, which means that the person providing the data has more options, and also more responsibility for the success of the analysis, than if the input format was more precisely and exclusively aimed at producing network graphs.

In a very similar way, the publication tools and interfaces through which data is published for general consumption reflect their own underlying models in the opportunities they offer, or fail to offer, to their users. Here we are considering the large-scale publications—thematic research collections, digital editions, electronic research databases, online journals, and the like—that frame our access to a large portion of the available research data. These publications typically expose their underlying data modeling very selectively and not very explicitly through components such as metadata fields in a search interface, sorting options in a results list, or the formatting of a reading display. For instance, if a digital edition gives us the ability to see a manuscript transcription with or without authorial revision, we can infer that revisions are something that is explicitly modeled in the data; if we can sort a bibliography by publisher, we can infer that the publisher is explicitly modeled in the data. As above, the model is significant here because it represents the upper horizon of opportunity for our work with the data, the limits on what we can expect the resource to do. However, that horizon as practically realized in the resource may be much lower: our access to that modeling is limited to the places where the publisher chooses to expose it. So we may be able to view authorial revisions in the reading interface, but the search interface might not give us the option of searching for words that appear only in those revisions.

Such limitations are sometimes the result of deliberate design choices, arising either from usability concerns (since most users want only basic searching, why clutter the interface with rarely used options?) or from a need to limit costs. But they can also arise from limitations in the tools themselves. Digital publishing systems (including XML databases, digital repository systems, and content management systems) are designed around a set of the most common user needs and expectations: the ability to search on basic bibliographic metadata (author, title, publication date), the ability to browse and read items, the ability to use metadata facets to identify similar items in the collection. These systems offer simple configuration options (akin to the "dashboard" in WordPress) which make it very easy to develop publications organized around these features. But to offer more idiosyncratic options—which might take advantage of something very specific in a given data set, such as authorial revisions—requires that one intervene in the workings of the tool at a much deeper level. For instance, many TEI-aware publishing systems (such as XTF or Philologic) automatically index a limited set of TEI metadata elements that are needed for basic searching and display. But if one wants to index other data elements—such as markup representing textual revisions, or dramatic dialogue—so that these can be used to nuance a search, some custom configuration of the tool may be required. Some tools (tending towards the more complex and expensive) anticipate this customization and provide straightforward mechanisms for accomplishing it, while others may permit it only as a species of hacking, in some cases so as to effectively rewrite the tool itself.

These are important critical considerations, with impact not only on how our data is published and used but also—in a self-reinforcing way—on the expectations that users bring to these research tools and hence on how they frame their research in response. But there are also strategic and practical considerations that affect our design of the relationship between tools and data. An oversimplified version of these would state that data should always be modeled in a manner that is completely independent of specific tools, and indeed of all considerations concerning specific tools that might process it. The motivations for this statement are partly based on experience: the early history of digital humanities was populated by horror stories about research data trapped in formats only readable by specific word processors, or only usable on specific pieces of hardware. They are also partly curatorial: whatever our own intended purposes for our data, we understand that it may have potential research value for others that we cannot foresee, and that potential is heightened when we design our data without tool dependencies. The creation of meta-models like SGML and the relational model was strongly motivated by a desire to pull the modeling of data away from consideration of specific tools: to enable the same data to be used in many different contexts, and to abstract the essential processing of data structures (for instance, XML parsing) away from more tool-specific actions such as formatting or editing. The philosophical urgency underlying this position (which originated in economic considerations) draws as well on a sense of the importance of open data in the research community. The use of browser-specific HTML tags as a competitive weapon between browser manufacturers during the 1990s illustrated clearly how poorly the entanglement of data with a specific tool serves the creators and users of that data, and how tool-specific data could risk sabotaging the potential of a public data resource like the then-emergent World Wide Web. Similarly, early HTML modeled textual information in a way that was strongly aimed at web browser software aimed at displaying "web pages" on full-size computer screens, but the dissemination of web-based data has broadened to include other devices and other uses of the data. HTML has had to evolve in a way that abstracts it away from specific tools and separates data modeling from presentation, making it a more powerful and flexible language. Tool agnosticism thus enforces a kind of imaginative discipline, asking us to model our data to be as pure as possible an expression of the information we care about.

That discipline is a first and necessary move in a modeling process that does take tools into account, but resists situating them in positions of power or intellectual primacy. If we have in mind a specific form of output for our data— a printed monograph, a network visualization, an interactive hypertextual narrative—our vision for its distinctive functions will necessarily be shaped by the genre of tool through which those functions will be realized. The specification we write for that output will include considerations of the data's shape and specifications as well: for instance, the need to distinguish between different kinds of annotations so that they can be handled separately in the output interface (e.g. some as linked endnotes, some as marginal annotations that appear on mouse-over). A tool-dependent approach would be to have the data itself indicate how each note should behave in the output; a tool-agnostic approach would be to identify the underlying functional and semantic distinctions motivating the different behaviors (authorial vs. editorial notes, biographical notes vs. word glossing, and so forth) and build these distinctions into the modeling of the data. This approach provides a level of indirection between that modeling (reflecting durable scholarly categories) and the behaviors that are available or desired within a specific tool context, with the latter being controlled by a stylesheet or configuration file that can vary from tool to tool.

Other pragmatic factors also play a role. There are often multiple approaches we might take to modeling the same data, with equivalent intellectual results. For instance, the following are two acceptable ways of representing a personal name in TEI:

```
<persName>John Stuart Mill</persName>
<persName>Mill, John Stuart</persName>
```

Given this equivalence, it would be reasonable to choose between them based on what our intended output software will handle most easily. For instance, if these names are going to be used to generate an author list (which will be alphabetized by surname), then the second option is preferable to the first, but if they are going to be used as the heading for a biographical annotation, the first might be better. If we need to support both options (let alone a more open-ended set of functions), a more explicit modeling would be best of all:

```
<persName>
  <forename>John</forename>
  <forename>Stuart</forename>
  <surname>Mill</surname>
</persName>
```

There may also be cases where it is practically beneficial, and theoretically harmless, to include information that will be useful for a specific tool, even though that information plays no role in the deeper scholarly modeling of the data. It is in this spirit that one might propagate identifiers to all <div> elements in a TEI document, anticipating that a particular publishing tool will rely on them in generating a table of contents. Similarly, it may be useful to have our data contain a record of the tools it expects. The only cost of this information is the added burden of maintaining and documenting it.

For the tool-agnostic purist, these pragmatic considerations might seem like a dangerous concession, the first step on the road to sacrificing the independence of our data. But in the encounter between our data and our tools, there is an important heuristic element in play that should not be undervalued. Every digital practitioner knows that the quickest way to discover flaws in one's data is to load it into a tool—any tool—preferably as part of a public demonstration. This is humorous lore but also expresses an important fact: our data may exist apart from tools, but it reaches its fullest realization through enactment, through an active exploration of the patterns and ideas it enables. In this sense "the tool" constitutes a realization (albeit perhaps only partial) of our intentions for the data, and a test of the coherence of those intentions. Mobilizing our data through a set of different tools—even "the wrong tools"—can reveal omissions and inconsistencies in the data, areas where our modeling is too sparse or too detailed, and cases where our modeling fails to support the analysis we are seeking. Particularly for the novice practitioner, good data modeling is something to be done iteratively, interrogating and refining the model through a dialogue with both the source material and the operational context of tools.

2 The eternal struggle between models and data

As we have seen, data modeling is an attempt to create abstract, formal representations of the real world, and any model is in some sense a compromise or accommodation between two very different things: the quiddity and contingency of the material universe, and the clarity and computability of a formal abstraction.

How in practice we reach that accommodation, and what we sacrifice in reaching it, will depend significantly on the goals of the exercise and the work process we employ.

One approach to model creation is to first consider our existing theories. A scholar developing an XML schema to represent poetry might start from the position that she already knows something about this genre: poems include lines that possess qualities of meter and length; these lines may be grouped and those groupings may contain patterns of rhyme; larger groupings of lines may have formal names (like "sonnet" or "villanelle"). From these reflections the scholar can create a schema representing her theory of poetry. As soon as she begins transcribing actual poems and encoding them using the schema, she will discover that her actual documents diverge from the model, and she will be forced into one of two positions: either refine and extend the schema (for instance, to accommodate omitted genres, or to permit additional structures such as stanza headings and annotations), or omit any data that cannot be accommodated within it. In other words, she must decide whether her theory is useful to her on its own (as a way of identifying the class of poems that match it), or whether her project is really to arrive at a theory of poetry (a schema) that reflects the true diversity of poetry in the world. That latter position may feel more sympathetic, but it is also dangerous, since it precipitates a process of refinement that can only conclude when every poem has been examined and every possible nuance accommodated— a process that can be infinitely prolonged. And it does not really simplify anything, since she will still need to decide which texts are to be considered "poems" for purposes of testing the schema; in other words, she will need to admit at some point that she does have a theory of poetry that is a priori rather than purely derived from the actual world of documents.

Another approach would be to start from the bottom and work up: to decide what documents we are interested in considering and observe their behavior, and derive a schema empirically from what we observe. In this approach, we might not even be starting with the idea of a "poem," but might simply be examining all documents to see what structural phenomena they contain. As part of this process we might discover that some documents contain segments of text that are rhythmic in nature and contain rhyming patterns, sometimes grouped into regular structures, sometimes with descriptive or numeric headings. After encoding a certain number of these, we might find that our schema had more or less stabilized, and that the phenomenon of the "poem" was emerging as a distinct form of text with its own internal variation but also some general patterns. The schema would express both the general pattern and the potential for variation, and an examination of the encoded documents would show us how those variations are combined in practice and how widespread they are in the overall population of documents. We might at that point start to feel that we had a "theory of poetry," though we would remain prepared to adjust it based on further examples.

Of course, in practice things are never so clear-cut, and modelers of both types being illustrated here will in fact probably work iteratively with both documents and schemas; the ready availability of existing schemas like the TEI means that one rarely begins the exploratory process from a position of complete agnosticism. What these imaginary narratives illustrate is not two different literal workflows but two different intellectual scenarios in which an abstraction either is refined and tested by, or emerges from, a sampling of the world. In this narration, these two processes appear to converge at the moment where the modeler decides to stop working: either because the theory is satisfactory or because she has run out of documents, or because she is too exhausted to continue. But in fact the stopping point looks very different depending on whether one arrives there "from the top" or "from the bottom." For a modeler who begins the process with an interest in the data, the stopping point can be understood as a practical decision: one has considered all of the data that is relevant to a particular research problem (e.g. a particular collection, the work of a particular author, etc.), or one has reached a point of diminishing returns where the appearance of new variations is very rare. For a modeler who starts from the top, on the other hand, the stopping point has more to do with how much complexity one is willing to tolerate in the model—in other words, what kind of theory one is trying to develop. From this perspective, it becomes less interesting to list exhaustively all possible variations (which may not reveal anything essential about the genre) than to discover the patterns that are taken as *characteristic of* the model rather than merely *associated with* it. This kind of top-down modeling is aimed rather at developing a blueprint for poetry (which might be used to generate a new poem) than at developing an inventory of things that have been called poems.

The difference between the two approaches also becomes clear when the data takes its place in a workflow. During the prototyping process in a digital project, sample data and draft schemas may stand in for the eventual mature versions as developers and project analysts design things like search and display interfaces. If the schema is being designed from the top down—in other words, if a draft schema can be assumed to represent the essentials of a document genre, with only minor refinements expected from further document sampling—then design decisions can be made based on that draft with reasonable confidence that they will not be overturned by discoveries arising from further inspection of the document set. On the other hand, if the schema is being designed from the bottom up, with the possibility that new documents might offer an entirely new perspective on the genre, then the stakes of completing a survey of the document set would be much greater and the status of a draft schema much more tentative.

3 Engaging our models critically

As already noted, our relationship with digital tools is developing in the direction of higher and more seamless function. One challenge that digital humanists face is that of keeping our models visible, both to ourselves and to others. For those who are simply pragmatic users of tools—driven purely by outcomes and unconcerned with how those outcomes are achieved—the disappearance or inaccessibility of the model may pose no problems and indeed offers many conveniences, much as the evolution of the automobile has reached the point where drivers are relieved of the responsibility for knowing how their engines work or being competent to explain or repair or improve them. However, when humanities scholars use or create digital resources that operate as research contributions in their field, the stakes are different. For one thing, the modeling decisions in play have a direct relevance to the research being undertaken. The question of whether to create a synthetic edition of Hamlet that draws on both quarto and folio versions, or to treat the quarto and folio versions of the play as separate entities that can be compared, or to treat each individual copy of the quarto as a distinct text (as the Shakespeare Quartos Archive does), will profoundly influence how the play can be studied, and reflects the editor's beliefs about the nature of texts and documents and the role of the editor in mediating them. The editorial leader of these projects needs a detailed understanding of how these approaches work in practice, arising from deep competence with editorial theory and practice, and familiarity with the texts in question. And although the users of such materials don't need to be able to intervene in these kinds of modeling decisions, they do need to understand their stakes enough to assess what sort of edition is appropriate for the research they wish to undertake.

For editors of Shakespeare, their research field is scholarly editing and its concerns include the handling of textual sources, their variations, and the historical and textual causes that account for them. Digital humanities is also a research field whose concerns include the representation systems through which research artifacts become usable data, and the tools through which we manipulate and think with that data. As we see in Chapter 2, these systems and tools represent an evolving body of knowledge with a challenging research agenda of its own. And where digital humanities engages specific humanities subject domains (such as art history, scholarly editing, biblical studies, and so forth), it also takes on additional, specific questions arising from those domains, such as how to model scholarly editions as digital information systems. The stakes for understanding our models are thus highest of all for digital humanists, who are responsible for understanding and explaining not just how a given model applies in a given situation, but how modeling systems themselves are designed and make meaning. This domain of expertise also involves being able to critique the ways in which specific research materials are represented in specific models.

As humanists, we are trained to see symbolic or ideological significance in representational structure. So while the aesthetics or "elegance" of our data models—which as described above is rooted in functional properties—may lead us to seek a deeper meaning in our data structures, the problem of how to understand the cultural meaning of such structures is a methodological question that still awaits a rigorously framed response. The work of critical code studies[5] has demonstrated that program code and data can be read as a cultural text, but it is clear that the mapping of cultural structures onto data structures—for instance, reading the hierarchies of XML as representing a commitment to social hierarchy, or the rhizome of hypertext as a radical departure therefrom—does not work in any straightforward way. In particular, such readings need to provide an account of how conflicting ideologies might animate the same structural paradigm:

for instance, reconciling the rhizomatic nature of the internet with its origins in industrial-military research.

The ability to use tools and modeling systems critically is of clear importance to humanists and digital humanists. But for the latter group, the domain of expertise being described here also involves the ability to intervene in this ecology by designing more expressive modeling systems, more effective tools, and a compelling pedagogy through which colleagues and new scholars can gain an expert purchase on these questions as well. The revision and improvement of our models is an especially crucial part of the digital humanities research agenda. As these examples illustrate, models are situational, perspectival, and strategic. As artifacts of scholarship, they are necessarily always adapting, and this adaptation is an important research topic for digital humanists. One of these is changes to the technologies of modeling—that is, to the underlying representational systems through which digital information is shaped (which we discuss in more detail in Chapter 2). For example, the emergence of linked open data over the past decade has been supported both by the establishment of effective standards for modeling and disseminating such data, and the growth of practices and social expectations supporting its creation. These developments have meant that expertly modeled data from specific domains can be accessed and combined flexibly, rather than remaining in isolation or striving for self-sufficiency. Another example is the emergence of microformats such as hash tags, which can be included in social media such as blog posts and online communication systems like Twitter: because they are created by users in the very act of communication, they represent a genuinely bottom-up approach to modeling, but at the same time they permit a degree of formalization for entities (such as people and events), concepts (such as the expressions of political support represented through hashtags like #blacklivesmatter), and strands of shared activity (such as the discussion of keywords and contested terms tracked through #curateteaching).

4 A research and teaching agenda for data modeling in digital humanities

This book is the first, to our knowledge, to treat the domain of digital humanities data modeling as a cohesive field, but that treatment is only possible because of substantial prior work in more specific domains. These include large-scale, sustained research efforts by organizations like the TEI and CIDOC, which have not only resulted in widely used standards, but have also produced a legacy of sophisticated methods and insights. They also include foundational theoretical research in domains like network analysis, databases, and logic, and the thoughtful exploration of narrative and textual structures in domains like hypertext and game studies. Also deeply relevant is the work done in human-computer interaction and interface design that explores how people work with information and with the tools that expose information for our use. The digital humanities draws on all of these strands and more in an attempt to understand how the shaping of data shapes our research questions, activities, and discourse.

Our goal with this volume is to bring data modeling into greater visibility, in greater detail, for a new generation of digital humanists. The contributions to this volume help to illuminate the landscape and show the work that has already been done, the modeling approaches that are in use, and the complexities we encounter in applying them. They also help mark out a research agenda for future work.

One crucial item in such a research agenda is a history of data modeling. Some of the chapters in this volume make a start on this project—notably Lou Burnard's chapter on standards—and Willard McCarty's earlier work on modeling offers background as well. Isabel Meirelles's *Design for Information* provides numerous valuable historical examples of visualizations that illustrate the evolution of the modeling activities they represent. However, because of the rapid growth of the digital humanities as a field—and ironically, given that the field now has a history going back at least fifty years—there is generally too little awareness of the history of current debates and research questions, and of the separate disciplinary strands that contributed to the early shaping of the field. Historicizing digital humanities methods is a crucial priority, and a history of data modeling in the fields where its key terms and processes originate would be a significant contribution to this work.

Another area of urgent interest is the challenge of associating semantics with our models, and aligning the semantics of different models, which is becoming a more acute and practical need as linked open data becomes more central to digital humanities research and practice. A second area of importance, highlighted in Michael Sperberg-McQueen's contribution to this volume, is the question of how we can usefully model scholarly debate as an informational layer with the same degree of formality (and hence the same tractability to formal processing) as the representation of research materials themselves. For example, as scholarly communities form around research aggregations such as digital archives, how can data modeling help us identify significant strands of discussion, points of disagreement, and divergences or convergences of practice?

A critical related domain, and one whose importance is already fully acknowledged, is the exploration of how to model uncertainty and ambiguity. Some of the major data representation systems (such as the TEI Guidelines and CIDOC CRM) include provision for modeling uncertainty and ambiguity in specific domains, notably the representation of transcriptional and editorial uncertainty, but most modeling systems at their core require uncertainty to be represented in the content (e.g. through qualifying notations) rather than in the modeling itself. We also need further exploration of how to use information about uncertainty in the context of retrieval, display, and analysis.

A less obvious research area concerns the extension of our data modeling to include the modeling of processes. Some notable existing examples come from tools that support user-configurable workflows, such as WebLicht[6] (whose representation of a set of data analysis modules requires that their individual actions and interconnections be modeled, albeit at a high level of abstraction) or the now-obsolete Yahoo Pipes, which operated on similar lines. Data curation protocols for digitization and data cleanup are another area of process modeling that is highly relevant (if not precisely central) to digital humanities. But in all of these cases, the level of modeling for the process itself is under-generalized, even if the interconnections between steps use standard protocols and formats, and in many cases it is under-formalized as well: while data curation protocols may be well documented, they are not represented with anything approaching a formal model. There may be much to be learned here from other disciplines, particularly the social sciences and natural sciences, which have had success in modeling processes: for example, psychologists modeling the reading process, or physicists modeling processes like the fall of objects. As tools and workflows for complex data analysis become more central to humanities scholarship, it will become increasingly important to bring the underlying processes to visibility and to express them in ways that support formal comparison.

A further segment of the research agenda concerns tools. Of primary concern is the development of modeling and publishing tools that put more intelligent and complex modeling decisions into the hands of scholars, acting both as publishers and as consumers of data. But in addition, a fuller study of data modeling tools could yield important historiographic and theoretical insight. How have the tools we use for data modeling evolved over time? How do they express existing assumptions and practices? And how do they affect the way we approach the modeling process?

Among the most enduring and challenging sectors of the research domain is the problem of how to document the underlying meaning of data models in such a way that we can start to align different data models with one another and create crosswalks between them. Early approaches to interoperability have tended to focus on simplification and constraint, on the principle that only very strictly regulated data can be reliably converted into another modeling system. However, with the proliferation of scholarly data of higher complexity and nuance, the stakes are high for exploring methods of intermodel mapping that are more supple. Furthermore, when we broaden our view to consider the modeling not of individual objects but of systems of objects, we encounter a new set of challenges involving the management of variation and the balance between goals of systemwide consistency and representational accuracy. For example, in a publication like *Scholarly Editing* (the journal of the Association for Documentary Editing), the accommodation of editions that use somewhat different customizations of the TEI Guidelines entails the development of systems of stylesheets that can handle different encoding approaches. These challenges have significance for publishing workflows and for large-scale systems that aggregate digital resources, such as institutional repositories and digital publishing frameworks, and they raise additional research questions concerning methods for managing the differences between variant schemas and the varying data they govern. In the long term, these questions also concern data curation and the development of mechanisms for documenting and maintaining the integrity of data and systems over time. Ontologies may offer a possible avenue for mapping and documentation of this kind.

Spanning across all of the other items in this research agenda is a need for attention to the politics of data modeling: not only the ideological and cultural dimensions that inform all modeling activities (whether acknowledged or not), but also the issues of power and information access that determine who participates in the creation of reference models and standards, and hence determine the shape of those models and standards. This is an area of strong recent attention, for instance in the library community where metadata standards and formal descriptive practices are being reviewed with attention to their cultural politics.

And finally, we need general theory of data modeling, which treats modeling in the digital realm as a set of activities that share common features, which are embedded into cultural contexts in a similar way and which can be evaluated in similar terms even though the models (relational databases, XML) are markedly different and are based on different mathematical concepts.

Accompanying this research agenda is a complementary pedagogical agenda through which we can also continue to shape the digital humanities field. We need to teach literacy in the basic modeling systems and tools early on, ideally even before students reach university. We need to emphasize the scholarly importance of modeling decisions even as we teach our students how to create and publish digital materials, whether those are games or research data, or digital archives or creative works. The "how" of digital humanities needs to be accompanied by an equally compelling "why" that expresses the motivations and ideologies that animate these digital materials. And in a complementary way, we need to teach students to attend to the modeling decisions our tools are making for us, or preventing us from making, and teach them to be resourceful about keeping their data from being too closely entrapped by specific tools.

Notes

1   For discussion, see for instance Christof Schöch's "Big? Smart? Clean? Messy? Data in the Humanities" (http://journalofdigitalhumanities.org/2-3/big-smart-clean-messy-data-in-the-humanities/) or Miriam Posner's "Humanities Data: A Necessary Contradiction" (http://miriamposner.com/blog/humanities-data-a-necessary-contradiction/).
2   Alan Galey, "Floating Academy: Teena Rochfort Smith: The Ada Lovelace of the Digital Humanities." *Victorian Review: An Interdisciplinary Journal of Victorian Studies,* blog post (January 26, 2015). Available at: https://floatingacademy.wordpress. com/2015/01/23/teena-rochfort-smith-the-ada-lovelace-of-the-digital-humanities/. See also Alan Galey, *The Shakespearean Archive: Experiments in New Media from the Renaissance to Postmodernity* (Cambridge University Press, 2014), pp. 20–29.
3   Scott Weingart, "Demystifying Networks," The Scottbot Irregular, December 14, 2011. Available at: www.scottbot.net/HIAL/?p=6279.
4   A fuller discussion of the challenge of overlapping hierarchies in XML is given in Chapter 11. This problem has played a significant role in the research history on digital humanities data modeling, serving as a focal point for discussions of the homologies between the structure of data representation and the structure of the objects or concepts being represented. Early treatments of this problem (such as the seminal "What is Text, Really?" by DeRose et al. (1990)) sought to show that the hierarchical nature of SGML markup reflected a deeper truth about the nature of text as an "ordered hierarchy of content objects," and subsequent challenges to that position often retain the

philosophical significance while reversing its polarity, arguing that SGML and related markup systems fail to represent text precisely because they uncritically adopt theories of text arising from the print tradition and its formalization of language as an information system; see, for instance, Jerome McGann, *Radiant Textuality* (2001). A more pragmatic tradition, represented by standards such as the TEI, treats the SGML/XML data hierarchy as a practical feature whose chief significance has to do with processing convenience, possessing tradeoffs that can be compared with those of other data representation standards.

5   For instance, Mark Marino, "Critical Code Studies" (Electronic Book Review, December 4, 2006); Noah Wardrip-Fruin, *Expressive Processing* (MIT Press, 2009); Nick Montfort et al., *10 PRINT CHR$(205.5+RND(1));: GOTO 10* (MIT Press, 2012).

6   Available at: https://weblicht.sfs.uni-tuebingen.de/weblichtwiki/.

Further reading

Folsom, E., 2007. Database as Genre: The Epic Transformation of Archive, and responses: Stallybrass, P. (Against Thinking), McGann, J. (Database, Interface, and Archival Fever), McGill, M. (Remediating Whitman), Freedman, J. (Whitman, Database, Information Culture), Hayles, N.K. (Narrative and Database: Natural Symbionts), Folsom, E. (Reply), *PMLA (Publications of the Modern Language Association)*, 122(5, Special Topic: Remapping Genre), pp. 1571–612.

McCarty, W., 2004. Modeling: A Study in Words and Meanings. In: S. Schreibman, R. Siemens, and J. Unsworth (Eds.) 2004. *A Companion to Digital Humanities*. Oxford: Blackwell, Ch. 19.

Olson, H.A., 2002. *The Power to Name: Locating the Limits of Subject Representation in Libraries*. Dordrecht: Springer Science+Business Media.

Ramsay, S., 2004. Databases. In: S. Schreibman, R. Siemens, and J. Unsworth (Eds.) 2004. *A Companion to Digital Humanities*. Oxford: Blackwell, Ch. 15.

Svenonius, E., 2000. *Intellectual Foundation of Information Organization*. Cambridge, MA: MIT Press.

DeRose, S.J., Durand, D., Mylonas, E., and Renear, A.H., 1990. What is Text Really? *Journal of Computing in Higher Education*, 1(2), pp. 3–26.

Galey, A., 2015. Floating Academy: Teena Rochfort Smith: The Ada Lovelace of the Digital Humanities. *Victorian Review: An Interdisciplinary Journal of Victorian Studies* (blog) January 26. Available at: https://floatingacademy.wordpress.com/2015/01/23/teena-rochfort-smith-the-ada-lovelace-of-the-digital-humanities/.

Marino, M., 2006. Critical Code Studies. *Electronic Book Review*. Available at: www.electronicbookreview.com/thread/electropoetics/codology.

McGann, J., 2001. Radiant Textuality: Literature after the World Wide Web. New York: Palgrave.

Meirelles, I., 2013. *Design for Information: An Introduction to the Histories, Theories, and Best Practices Behind Effective Information Visualizations*. Beverly, MA: Rockport.

Montfort, N., Baudoin, P., Bell, J., Bogost, I., Douglass, J., Marino, M.C., Mateas, M., Reas, C., Sample, M., and Vawter, N., 2012. *10 PRINT CHR$(205.5+RND(1));: GOTO 10*. Cambridge, MA: MIT Press.

Piez, W., 2001. Beyond the "Descriptive vs. Procedural" Distinction. *Markup Languages*, 3(2), pp. 141–172.

Posner, M., 2015. Humanities Data: A Necessary Contradiction. *Miriam Posner's Blog* (blog) June 25. Available at: http://miriamposner.com/blog/humanities-data-a-necessary-contradiction/.

Schöch, C., 2013. Big? Smart? Clean? Messy? Data in the Humanities. *Journal of Digital Humanities*. Available at: http://journalofdigitalhumanities.org/2-3/big-smart-clean-messy-data-in-the-humanities/.

Wardrip-Fruin, N., 2009. *Expressive Processing*. Cambridge, MA: MIT Press.

Weingart, S., 2011. Demystifying Networks. *The Scottbot Irregular* (blog) December 14. Available at: www.scottbot.net/HIAL/?p=6279.

2 A gentle introduction to data modeling

Fotis Jannidis and Julia Flanders

1 What is data modeling?

Imagine you find a handwritten note beginning with the following text:[1]

```
1867
Albany May 24th

Mr Walt Whitman.
  You may
be surprised in receiving
this from me but seeing
your name in the paper the
other day I could not
resist the temptation of
writing to you.
```

You would be able to understand immediately that the text belongs to a specific text type or genre: it is a letter. A letter—today typically a personal communication between individuals—shows some specific features. Many letters bear a date and contain an indication of where they were written. They typically begin with the name of the person who is addressed, and the text is a direct communication making often use of the pronouns "I" and "you." Based on this knowledge, one can identify the text type of our example and also identify certain groupings of information within the text: "1867" belongs with "May 24th" as part of the date, while "Albany" is obviously the place of writing—or at least, obvious to us humans. To machines, the whole text is an undifferentiated sequence of alphanumeric characters and whitespace. If we want the computer to "understand" the text—for instance, to extract all dates from a collection of letters automatically, or sort the collection chronologically—we must either mark all occurrences of dates in a way that allows the computer to search for our marks and collect the text, or we need to describe the phenomenon of "date" with a series of rules (or train the computer to recognize dates through a process of machine learning) which allow the computer to identify specific parts of the text as dates. In other words, we have a choice between an algorithmic approach (which will be explored in more detail in several of the contributions to this volume, below) or what we might call a "metatextual" approach, in which information is added to the text in some explicit form that enables it to be processed intelligently. This latter approach will be our focus in the remainder of this chapter.

In short, to make information accessible to the machine in a processable way, we have to provide a general model for this type of information and to apply this model to the instance in question. Applied to our example, this means that we have to provide a model for dates in general and apply it to our specific date. A very simple model could look like this: we identify the boundaries of the "date" information in the text using explicit markers, and we provide a regularized version of the date in the form year-month-day. Applying it to our text could look like this:

```
1867 Albany [date-start]May 24th[date-end 1867-05-24]
```

Now we can search for all sequences beginning with "[date-end" and ending with "]" and extract the ten characters before the final bracket which represent the regularized date. We also know that the two numbers after the first dash are the month, since this was specified in the model. This is a start, but a simple model like this shows its limitations quickly: for example, how would it handle a date before the year 0, or dates in which only the month or the year are given and the rest is missing? How would we handle dates that use different calendar systems? These contingencies all require additional provisions in the data model. In what follows we will introduce some basic concepts of data modeling (section 2) before we outline some foundations for all forms of data modeling: logic, set theory and formal descriptions of sequences (section 3). On this basis, we can talk about some of the basic concepts of established approaches in data modeling like relational databases, XML, and graphs (section 4). Although these processes are quite different, we can describe some common aspects of the modeling process (section 5) and the evaluation of data models (section 6). We conclude with the discussion of some of the perspectives of and challenges for data modeling (section 7).

Before we delve into these topics, we should have a closer look at the term "model." We already used it because we all have some understanding of it. At the basis of our understanding of the term *model* is probably a class of physical objects such as a "model of a plane" or a "model of a house," which can be defined as "a small copy of a building, vehicle, machine, etc., especially one that can be put together from separate parts."[2] But we can also use the term to mean an abstract concept and its relation to other concepts, as in a sentence like "each model of a modern state has to include institutions for the executive, the legislative and the judiciary." We will be talking about models in this more abstract sense in the following. With Stachowiak, we can distinguish three basic properties of a model:

1. A model is a model *of something*. A model is always a kind of mapping. It represents something, an object, a concept, and so on, by representing it using something else like clay, words, images, and so forth.
2. A model is *not the original* and it is not a *copy of the original*. Unlike a copy, a model doesn't capture all features of the entity it represents, only some of them. The choice of features selected to be present in the model is usually based on assumptions by the creator of the model concerning which features are relevant for the intended use of the model.
3. A model is meant to be used *by someone for something*. As we already mentioned, a model has a use for someone who can do something with it. The model can be used as a substitute for the original at least for some operations and at least for some time.[3]

So one could say that a model is a representation of something by someone for some purpose at a specific point in time. It is a representation that concentrates on some aspects—features and their relations—and disregards others. The selection of these aspects is not random but functional: it serves a specific function for an individual or a group. And a model is usually only useful and only makes sense in the context of these functions and for the time that they are needed.

Models are not intrinsically computer-processable. In order to operate meaningfully in a digital context, a model must be represented in language that is unambiguous and explicit, and that represents the salient features of the model in a processable way. In the following, we will be talking about *formal models*. These are models that use a specified set of rules that explicitly and exhaustively define the model's syntax and semantics. This explicit and formal specification allows this kind of model to be processed automatically. But the relation between models and formal models is intricate. In one view, a model can be understood as the rich, conceptually expressed context of a formal model, framed as a communication among humans but containing all of the intellectual work necessary to establish a formal model. On the other hand, a model can also be understood as a looser precursor to a formal model, one whose expression in human language necessarily entails vagueness and indeterminacies that will need to be clarified in the formal model. The first of these views tends to focus on how the concept of the "model" is itself embedded in more general concepts like theory and how they, theories and models determine or at least interact with the formal model. The latter view places greater emphasis on formal modeling itself, its mechanisms and dependencies, and treats the more general "model" as a kind of natural preliminary. Our approach in this volume leans more toward the latter.

Formal models can be expressed as a set of logical expressions or mathematical functions, but often there are specific notation systems that have been developed for specific types of models—for example, the Entity-Relationship notation for the conceptual level of relational databases, or tables for the logical level, or XML schemas to describe the model for a group of XML documents.

When we talk about a formal model, we refer to a specific structure or a set of structures defined by the model; quite often, we also imply that the components of this structure have to conform to specific data types defined in the data model. For example, a simple data model for a date could stipulate that a date is a sequence of three components, either [day][month][year] or [month][day][year] and that the data type for day is an integer between 1 and 31.

Formal models which are defined by this application of logical/mathematical descriptions enable two functions: data constraints and data queries. During data entry or data creation, the model can be used to express constraints. For example, we might include in our model for a date of birth some constraints to ensure that only plausible information is entered (for instance, that the value entered is a date and that it is earlier than the date of death). The structure of the model can also enable us to query the data more precisely and intelligently: for instance, if the data "knows" that a specific string is a date, we can request search results that fall within a specific date range. Relational databases can be queried using relational logic (described in more detail further down), which is the foundation of the model; SQL (the Structured Query Language, which can be regarded as "an engineering approximation to the relational model" (Wikipedia, 2015)) is used as a query language for relational databases. XQuery, which can be used as a query language for XML documents, makes use of the formal structure of XML documents and enables much more complex retrievals than those based solely on an untagged string representation of the same texts. If we include one further function present in most models—that they enable and support communication between humans—we have the three main functions of formal models: adding constraints to improve data quality, enabling more complex and semantically rich queries, and supporting communication between humans and machines about data.

In computer science there are three main areas known for the application of formal models: *data modeling, process modeling* (including simulation) and *system modeling*, the design of software systems. Data modeling is concerned with the modeling of entities: documents, events, information systems, agents, data sets, and so forth. Process modeling is concerned with the modeling of events in time: for example, the amount of water passing through a river bed in a given time, the change of employment resulting from specific events, or the spread of a new scientific concept in scientific texts. For the modeling of more complex processes, *simulation* has become an important tool. *System* or *software modeling* is the design of software systems, usually an abstract view of the design of a piece of software, nowadays usually taking an object-oriented approach. An established tool in software modeling is the use of the Unified Modeling Language (UML) as a visual design instrument. As UML has a very abstract definition, its use in the other two fields has been proposed but is not very common. In the following and in this book in general we will talk mostly about data modeling. This form of modeling has a long history in the digital humanities; modeling has a long history in the humanities in general, and data modeling in the humanities builds on many earlier attempts to define concepts and their relations in a clear and unequivocal way, such as, for example, classification schemes in library science like the Dewey Decimal Classification or Ranganathan's Colon System.

There is also another use of the term "modeling" which is closely related to the data modeling we are chiefly talking about in this book—namely, the modeling of data using mathematical functions. For example, if we are studying the rent of flats in a city and the size of the flats in square meters, we can plot this data using x for the size and y for the rent, which would reveal that in general rent increases as the size of the flat increases. We can approximate this relation using a line, described by a mathematical function of the form $f(x) = ax + b$, and although none of the data points has to be exactly on the line, the line will provide a rough model of the relation between the two pieces of information. If we now add a new flat to our data set and look only at the size, we can make a rough prediction about the rent. (We may also observe that there are other factors influencing the rent, such as location, and we could expand the model to include these additional factors.) The mathematical function with its specific values for a and b is a model for the data. Both forms of modeling—data modeling and mathematical models— add information about the data, but they allow very different operations on the data. Data modeling using a metamodel like XML is usually adding descriptive information about the data; typical operations are querying the data for specific subsets. Mathematical models are usually used to make predictions about new data or answer questions such as whether specific factors correlate with one another.

2 Some basic concepts

Let us come back to our example of the letter, and let us talk about one of the alternatives mentioned above, the manual entry of information. The date of a letter is an interesting case: on one hand, any letter is written on a specific date (or a series of dates), and this date is a piece of information *about* the letter. On the other hand, very often dates may be found in the letter *as part of the text* (for instance, in references to events or discussion of future plans). In order for the date of the letter itself to function as a way of managing the digital item—for instance, to find letters written near a given date, or to sort a collection of letters by date—we need to treat that particular date in a specialized way: as *metadata*, or data *about* an entity. Typical metadata might include information about the entity being represented by the digital resource: the name of the creator(s), a title, a date of creation or publication. Metadata may also include information about the process of digitization, such as the name of the person who created the digital resource, the means of digitization—for example, OCR or manual transcription— the editorial methods used, and so forth. In order to be useful for discovery, metadata is highly structured information, and hence it may often be kept in databases or in some other format separated from the data. Another approach is to keep the metadata bundled together with the original data but clearly distinguishable from it, through markup or some other mechanism.

Metadata's explicit information modeling permits us to query and manage the digital object in very precise ways: it tells us that "this information component is the creation date." Without it, we might be able to infer that the first four-digit number we encounter in a letter is probably the creation date, but there might be many cases where that assumption was false. Similarly, if we want to query the content of our digital letter, we can also add information to the text of the letter to make explicit what kind of information a word or a series of words contains. Information added to some part of a digital object like a text is called *annotation* or *markup*, and it permits the computer to extract information precisely, without relying on inference.[4] For example, using our earlier imaginary data modeling scheme we could add the information that "Albany" is a place name as follows:

```
[placename-start]Albany[placename-end] May 24th
```

When we added the date to the text above we already added an annotation:

```
[date-start]May 24th[date-end 1867-05-24]
```

In both cases, we have added a new layer to the text: now we have the text of the original letter and another text (aimed at the computer) consisting of the annotations. In order for the computer to distinguish the two, we need a clear signal that delimits the annotations. In our example we used the character "[" while the character "]" signals a switch back to the normal text. The character used to indicate these switches is completely arbitrary and depends only on the standard you use. XML—for example, uses the characters "<" and ">" and shortens the -start/-end syntax used above like this:

```
<placename>Albany</placename>
```

This kind of annotation is also called *inline annotation* or *inline markup*, because it is added to the data file containing the original data. Another method would be to use *stand-off annotations* (see Chapter 11) that leave the original data intact and—using some addressing schema like the character offset—refer to the start and end of the data annotated (please see Table 2.1).

As inline annotations can always be converted to stand-off annotations and vice versa, it is more a matter of convenience which to use; stand-off annotation is most commonly used in cases where the annotations will be generated by a machine process, whereas inline annotation is more common in cases where the annotations are being added or edited by hand.

The example we offer here is a text, but actually all kinds of digital objects can be annotated; with non-textual media, it is most common to use stand-off

Table 2.1 Stand-off annotations

Beginning offset	Ending offset	Annotation
6	12	placename
14	21	date

Table 2.2 Metadata of Rubens's "The Judgment of Paris"

painter	title	year	id
Peter Paul Rubens	The Judgment of Paris	1606	21436

annotation. The metadata for an image like Rubens' "The Judgment of Paris" could be stored like this (please see Table 2.2).

The column "id" provides a *unique identifier*: that is, a name that is guaranteed to be unique among all other identifiers and can be used to reference this object. This identifier could be the common name of the object like "The Judgment of Paris," but since it is possible that more than one object with this name may exist, it is more common to use arbitrarily constructed identifiers that can be guaranteed to be unique.

A simple system to annotate images, for example, would allow to specify two points that mark the upper left and the lower right corner of a rectangle in the image. Here, the annotation as it could be depicted by a graphical user interface (please see Figure 2.1).

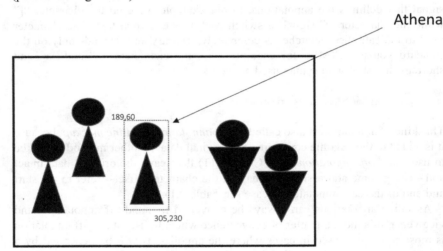

Figure 2.1 Image annotation.

And Table 2.3 shows a simple data model for this annotation.

Table 2.3 Data model of a basic image annotation

image id	upper-left-x	upper-left-y	lower-right-x	lower-right-y	annotation
21436	189	60	305	230	Athena

More complex annotation schemas would allow us to delineate any kind of form and add semantically more complex annotations like interactions.

Most of our examples in the following will be talking about the annotation of texts, which is mostly done by using *markup*: embedded notations that can be read and parsed by computational tools to assist in the analysis and processing of the text. Markup in this sense includes both metadata and the annotation of content, and in fact the distinction may not always be clear-cut. In addition, markup may be used to create data structures within the text that are not, strictly speaking, "annotation of content": for instance, we might use markup to create a timeline representing the events that occur in the letter. But for our purposes at the moment, we can set the more difficult cases aside and focus on the basic concepts.

Until now we have used the term "data model" rather loosely and have not distinguished between the different components of formal modeling: the *modeled instance*, the *data model* and the *metamodel*. The modeled instance is a digital model of a specific entity: for instance, a document, an art object, an event. All the metadata and the annotations related to the image example above are part of the modeled instance of this one image. The specific organization of the tables, their names and the column headings, constitute the data model which is used for all images in this collection. The concept of the *table itself*—a structure of rows and columns—as an organizational construct is the metamodel. We could also model this information in other ways: we might use a different model (a different organization of tables). But we might also use a different metamodel: for instance, instead of using a relational database with tables we could use XML. In the case of the letter example above, this might entail adding metadata and annotations to the text of the letter in the form of inline markup. The data model for our markup would be represented by a schema: for example, we might choose to use the TEI Guidelines and its schema, or we might choose to use HTML, or some other model. Here, the encoded letter is the modeled instance, the TEI (or HTML) is the data model, and XML is the metamodel. There are only a few metamodels widely used; we have already mentioned the relational model and XML. RDF, the Resource Description Framework, is used especially by cultural heritage communities. And the modeling of data in software, using for example an object oriented approach, is also very common.

On all three levels *data types* can play a crucial role. The term "data type" refers to the form in which one data point is stored, and it specifies the manner in which that data point will be interpreted: for example, as a date, or an integer, or a sequence of characters (string). In our image annotation table, the row labeled "image id" only stores integers, and the row labeled "annotation" only stores strings. Basic or "primitive" data types include different forms of numbers, such as integers (1, 2, 3) or floating point numbers (1.654, –23.91), Boolean values (True, False), characters ("a", "#") and strings ("history"). More complex data types, such as dates (2012-07-23), can be constructed out of these basic types. A data model usually also includes information concerning which kind of data type is allowed for a specific data element. Metamodels often include a list of predefined data types and also a way to define additional data types. In the world of relational databases—for example, the specification for the data management and query language—SQL also contains data types that include numeric types, character strings, Boolean and datetime types, intervals, and XML types.

A *data structure* is the organization of data values (possessing specific data types) into a more complex form, which also defines a set of operations on the data in the data structure. Most programming languages offer some predefined data structures like "list" or "dictionary" and also mechanisms to construct more complex data structures together with their accompanying operations—for example, object-oriented modeling. A list offers a structure that allows us to address each of its elements by its position in the list. Here we have a list of country names:

```
countries = ["France", "Germany", "Japan", "Syria",
        "USA"]
```

Given this structure, we can address the first element of the list ("France") using a syntax which could look like this (most programming languages start to count with 0):

```
countries[0]
```

Programming languages usually also provide operations for modifying a list: to append or delete elements, and so on.

Somewhat confusingly, the term "data type" is also used in statistics to describe another quite different but important aspect of data modeling that affects the processing of data: the system or scale which confers significance upon the data and hence determines its behavior in contexts like statistical analysis. One very common distinction is between *discrete* and *continuous* data. We speak of "discrete data" if a data point can only have a value from a set of possible values: for example, the "country of birth" field can only have one value (such as "Canada" or "USA" or "Japan" or "Germany," and so forth) from a list of possible values. Similarly, "marital status" is usually defined using a closed list containing values like "married," "single," "divorced," or "widowed." The possible values for discrete data are either finite (as in the examples above) or infinite but countable. Examples of continuous data include information like height or weight, which can be measured to an arbitrary level of exactness. Another important dimension of statistical data is the characteristics of the underlying scale used for the data. In the classification of scales, "scale types are individuated by the families of transformations they can undergo without loss of empirical information" (Tal, 2015). By "transformations," here we mean things like changing the order of values, making comparisons, or performing computations. So, for instance, values for data such as country of birth or marital status simply divide the space of possible values into different segments, but without stipulating an order for the segments. These values have meaning only insofar as they can be distinguished from one another, and hence can be transformed without loss of information: instead of "divorced" and "married" one could substitute "D" and

"M" (or "1" and "2") without losing anything. This kind of scale of measure is called *nominal*; it simply names the values. If the values are ordered in some way, they constitute an *ordinal* scale, as with the possible results of some form of test: "failed," "passed," "passed with merit," "passed with distinction." An *interval* scale has even more information: the distance between different values can be known and interpreted. Temperature measured in Celsius is an example for an interval scale. Its zero point is defined by the freezing point of water and the value 100 is defined by the boiling point of water. The scale between these two points has been divided by 100. In an interval scale, certain kinds of computation are possible: for instance, we can say that the difference between 10 and 20 degrees Celsius is the same as the difference between 40 and 50 degrees Celsius. However, because the zero point is arbitrary, we cannot make other kinds of calculations; a statement like "this water at 60 degrees is twice as hot as this water at 30 degrees" is not meaningful. A *ratio* scale uses values with a meaningful non arbitrary zero point which allows values to compared to each other in the form of ratios like "this house is double the height of that house." The temperature measured in Kelvin (which starts at absolute zero) is an example of a ratio scale.

Table 2.4 shows some additional examples of data using the classification described above.

Continuous data like yearly income in dollars can always be converted to discrete data by creating so-called "bins" representing ranges of values: "less than 20,000," "20,000–100,000," "more than 100,000."

An important aspect of data and scale types is their direct influence on the type of operations which can be meaningfully done with the data. It doesn't make any sense to perform arithmetic on the numbers on football shirts, or to calculate the ratio of Cartesian coordinates. But you can sort numbers that express the choice on a rating scale from 1 to 5, or you can look at the differences between the hours measured using a 12-hour clock. This understanding of "data type" is rather specific to statistics, but the underlying concepts affect all kinds of data modeling because all kind of digitally stored data can and will be used for data analytics. But thus far the data type (in a statistical sense) of some types of data still has to be inferred from the label of the data—for example, the column headings of a table—and is not annotated in a machine-readable way.

Table 2.4   Examples of statistical data with different data types

	discrete	*continuous*
nominal	type of car, political party, number on a football shirt	n.a.
ordinal	choice on a rating scale from 1 to 5, sequence of cars reaching the goal in a race, sick vs. healthy	n.a.
interval	n.a.	time of day on a 12-hour clock, location in Cartesian coordinates
ratio	n.a.	income, mass

Finally, we should clarify one other aspect: Where does a data model live? In what concrete format is the data model expressed? We are talking here not about the data model as an abstract rule set (expressed, for instance, in an external schema), but about the shaping of the data itself. To answer this question, we can look at the different ways our digital data can exist—as a byte stream on some storage device, as a data structure in some memory cells in a computer's memory, as a serialized format meant to be read by machines and humans. The data model can determine the structure of all of these, but sometimes it is also only an abstract layer of communication between realizations of the data which—for some pragmatic reason—use another model. XML data, for example, are sometimes stored in relational databases where a piece of middleware translates all XML-related structures into a relational structure. Especially for the long-term preservation of data though, it is preferable to express the data in a serialized format that is readable by humans and is a direct representation of the data model.

3 Foundations

Before we take a closer look at some established approaches to data modeling, we want to review the foundations of *formal* modeling. Above, we said that a formal model is a model that can be expressed as a set of logical expressions or mathematical functions. And even if the data is expressed using specific notations (such as relational databases, XML, etc.), the underlying concepts of logic, set theory, sequences, and the rest form the deeper basis for the processability of the model. So, in the following sections we will offer a short overview of these concepts. A treatment in depth can be found, for example, in introductions into discrete mathematics. (Rosen, 2013), for example, is a very readable introduction for non-mathematicians.

3.1 Logic

Reasoning is an important way to produce new insights, and controlling reasoning to make sure it is valid has a long history; traces of its beginnings can be found in Classical Greece, China and India. For formal modeling, logic is important because the circuitry of a computer processor can be described using logic, and mathematical statements can be seen as logical statements, so the underlying mathematical structure of formal models can be represented as a system of logical propositions. Logic is still a thriving field of research and, as with all other material presented in this chapter, we will only be able to outline some of the very basic concepts. But this should be enough to give readers an idea how this approach works in general and to get started with more specialized literature if the need arises.

3.1.1 Propositional logic

Logic is divided in many subfields. The most basic one is propositional logic, which covers the truth values of simple combinations of propositions. The starting point of this kind of logic is an abstraction: when considering combinations of statements, we can disregard the specific content of the statement and simply assume that it has a truth value (it is either True or False). The decision whether a specific basic statement is true or false falls outside of the realm of propositional logic, but once its truth value has been decided, logic can describe how it can be combined with other statements and what the truth value of these compound statements looks like. So, focusing purely on truth value, instead of statements like "the road is wet" or "In the year 2015 Obama was the president of the USA" or "The planet earth has one moon" (let's hope the truth value of this sentence does not change) we use variables like p or q.

Let us start with the first operator on propositions, the *negation*, which takes the proposition and states its negative; if the statement is "Today the sun is shining," then the negation is something like "It is not the case that the sun is shining today." If the initial proposition is represented with a variable "p" the negation is represented with an operator: ¬p ("not p").

To express the truth values of basic propositions and compound expressions in propositional logic, we create something called a truth table, which presents this information in an organized manner. Truth tables are an important instrument to describe the relation between the truth values of the basic propositions and the compound expressions, and, as we will see later on, we can use them to check whether two compound statements have the same truth values and are logically equivalent. A truth table for the negation operator looks like this (T = true, F = False).

p	¬*p*
T	F
F	T

This table shows that if we know that p is true, then we also know that the negation of p is not true. This is at least the case in a logic with two truth values (True, False). So if the proposition "Today the sun is shining" is not true, we can infer that its negation, "It is not the case that the sun is shining today" is true.

The next basic operator is the *conjunction*: p ∧ q (p and q); it combines two basic propositions into a compound proposition, which is only true if all the basic propositions are true.

The truth table for a conjunction looks like this:

p	*q*	*p* ∧ *q*
T	T	T
T	F	F
F	T	F
F	F	F

This table shows that if both p and q are true, then we also know that "p and q" is true, and that if one or both of p or q is false, the conjunction is also false.

The next operator is the *or* operator, which represents the disjunction, and it is a bit more complicated because there are two kinds of "or". One is the *inclusive or*, as in the following statement: "students who have taken the introduction to history class or the introduction to literary studies class can take the introduction to digital humanities course." It is enough that one statement is true for the compound statement to be true. This is the standard "or" and it is written like this: ∨.

The following shows the truth table of the inclusive or:

p	*q*	*p* ∨ *q*
T	T	T
T	F	T
F	T	T
F	F	F

Here, only one of the combinations of truth values of the basic propositions produces a false compound statement: if both p and q are false, the compound is also false. (Some say, if you have trouble remembering which symbol means what, you can use the following mnemonic: "and" (∧) in Latin is AUT while "or" (∨) is VEL; others say learning Latin to remember two symbols sounds like overkill).

The other kind of or is the *exclusive or*. If a restaurant menu offers as starters "soup or salad" it usually means you can have only one of them. Similarly, the exclusive or in a compound statement indicates that only one of the basic propositions can be true. There is no commonly used operator sign for the exclusive or, but a common notation is *xor*.

p	*q*	*p xor q*
T	T	F
T	F	T
F	T	T
F	F	F

Take, for example, the following propositions:

Proposition p: This car is blue.
Proposition q: This car is red.

The compound statement combining the basic statements with xor would be:

p xor q: Either this car is blue or this car is red.

If both sentences are true, the compound statement must be false. And if both propositions are false, the compound statement either must be false also.

The *material implication* is probably the most problematic operator and in some ways the most counter-intuitive. It expresses a relation between p and q which can be expressed in a number of ways in English, for example:

"if p, then q"
"p implies q"
"q when p"

So let us take two propositions like these:

p: John is at the party
q: Mary is at the party

Then we can construct a compound proposition like this:

p → q: If John is at the party, then Mary is at the party.

This expresses a relation that is obviously falsified if we find John at a party and Mary is not there. And if both are at the party—that is, both basic propositions are true—then it makes sense to attribute truth to the compound statement.

Now if John is not at the party but Mary is, what can we say about the truth value of the compound statement? In real life our answer would probably be: How should I know? But this does not work for propositional logic which must assign one of two values to a statement. The truth table for the conditional operator looks like this:

p	q	$p \rightarrow q$
T	T	T
T	F	F
F	T	T
F	F	T

There is long, intricate and controversial discussion in logic why and how the last two lines make sense (see Edgington, 2008). One of the better explanations points to the fact that if p is false and q is either true or false, then it still can be the case that the compound statement is not necessarily false and in a two-valued logic this means it must be true (see also Partee, ter Meulen, and Wall, 1990, pp. 104f.). One can add a pragmatic point: In the context of argument analysis, these values yield the best results and fit into the rest of the architecture of propositional logic.

There is a variant of the material implication, the biconditional. It constructs a closer relation between p and q: p if and only if q, sometimes abbreviated as "p iff q." The compound statement is only true if both basic propositions have the same truth value. For example:

> p: you can take the train.
> q: you bought a ticket.
> p ↔ q: you can take the train if and only if you bought a ticket.

The truth table for the biconditional looks like this:

p	q	$p \leftrightarrow q$
T	T	T
T	F	F
F	T	F
F	F	T

The biconditional can be found very often in more formal definitions in logic or mathematics.

As mentioned before, the truth tables can be used to check whether two compound statements are equivalent. This may seem a trivial exercise, but even simple logical statements can be demanding to understand without them.

For example, if one tries to see whether two logical statements, ¬p ∨ q and p → q, have the same truth values, it definitely helps to look at the truth table. It shows for the statements the same truth values, so these statements are logically equivalent.

p	q	$\neg p$	$\neg p \lor q$	$p \rightarrow q$
T	T	F	T	T
T	F	F	F	F
F	T	T	T	T
F	F	T	T	T

Thus, truth tables can be a powerful tool, even if they are restricted to propositional logic.

3.1.2 Predicate logic

Predicate logic extends propositional logic by adding two new concepts: predicates and quantifiers. While in the last section we only looked at self-contained statements in propositional logic (each of them having a truth value), here we are considering general expressions that have no truth value, but which constitute systems of potential truth value with variables representing the conditions we are interested in testing. For example, "x is president of the USA." This kind of expression is called a propositional function. It consists of a variable x and a predicate which is attributed to x, in our example "is president of the USA." The propositional function can also be written as $P(x)$. With different values for x, this function has different truth values.

To take a simple example, let $P(x)$ denote the statement "x is born in the year 1812" where x is the subject and "born in the year 1812" is the predicate. What are the truth values of P(Charles Dickens) and P(Friedrich Schiller)? We can check their values by substituting x with the specific names:

"Charles Dickens is born in the year 1812" is true
"Friedrich Schiller is born in the year 1812" is false

A propositional function can also have more than one variable, for example:

Let $A(x1, x2)$ denote the statement "x1 + x2 = 10"

If $x_1 = 2$ and $x_2 = 8$, then we get the proposition

$2 + 8 = 10$

This proposition is true. If $x_1 = 1$ and $x_2 = 4$, we get the statement $1 + 4 = 10$ which is false.

Until now, we looked at statements with one variable ("x is born in the year 1812") and with two variables ("$x_1 + x_2 = 10$") and we used $P(x_1)$ or $A(x_1, x_2)$ as a notation for an expression with one and two variables respectively. We can add more variables in the form $A(x_1, x_2, x_3, \ldots x_n)$, in which case A is also called a n-ary predicate.

Those familiar with the basics of programming will recognize the propositional function as a part of the conditional "if then" statement which can be found in most programming languages:

```
if x > 80 then print("Warning: Line too long; more than
   80 characters.")
```

The call to the print function—which issues a warning—will only be executed when the condition "x > 80" is true. For example, if x equals 87, the statement "87 > 80" is true and the function call will be executed.

3.1.3 Quantification

Up to this point the propositional functions we have looked at consist of a simple schema: one or more variables are combined with one or more predicates.

Quantifiers allow us to express additional information about the functions; they allow us to specify whether something is the case for one, some or all members of a domain. In predicate calculus, two quantifiers are commonly used:

1. the universal quantifier ∀x (for every x) and
2. the existential quantifier ∃x (there is at least one x).

The quantifiers cannot stand alone; they have to be combined with a propositional function (or a proposition) like this:

∀xP(x): P(x) is true for every x

For example, let P(x) denote the statement $x - 0 = x$. The quantification ∀xP(x) is true, because for all numbers this statement is true. Although the quantifier is called "universal," it is actually used in relation to a domain: in other words, the statement is true in a specific domain of discourse or universe of discourse. So the universal quantifier ∀x applied to P(x) has to be understood to express something like

P(x) for all values of x in the domain.

A domain can be any kind of set—for example, all natural numbers or all people who are afraid of flying. The definition of the domain is up to the person using the quantification—and it is important because the domain often decides whether a quantification is true or not.

The quantification ∀xP(x) is false, when there is a value of x in the domain which will produce a false P(x). For example, let P(x) be the statement "$x^2 > x$" and let the domain be ℕ (natural numbers 1, 2, 3 . . .) then ∀xP(x) seems to be true, because P(2) is true and P(10) is true, but we can find one counterexample: P(1) is false, and therefore ∀xP(x) is false.

The existential quantifier expresses that the quantification is true for at least one element of a specific domain. ∃xP(x) means:

There is an element x in the domain such that P(x) is true.

∃xP(x) is false, if there is no such element. For example, let P(x) be the statement "$5 - x > 3$" and let the domain be ℕ then ∃xP(x) is true, because P(1) is true ($5-1 > 3$).

These two quantifiers are quite important for logic and mathematics, but there are many more and we could even define our own. In logic, the quantifier ∃!x means that there is exactly one x such that P(x) is true. As we will see later on, in some parts of computer science there are some other commonly used quantifiers: for example, in regular expressions and schema languages we find specific quantifiers for "zero or one" occurrence, "zero or more" occurrences and "one or more" occurrences, all of which are useful in the context of searching and schema design.

3.2 Sets

Set theory was introduced by Georg Kantor in the nineteenth century as a way of thinking about the infinity of numbers, and it is now often seen as a foundation for mathematics in general (Pollard, 2015). Its concepts are also the basis for any data modeling, not least because it defines concepts like "set" and "tuple," which will play a role in most of our descriptions of data modeling approaches. This does not imply that set theory is especially deep or complex; general set theory is fairly straightforward, but it provides a very illuminating basis for the fundamental concepts of data modeling we want to introduce here.

A set, in the most general sense, can be informally understood as a collection of different objects. Anything can be part of a set: a word, a number, an idea, a real object, even a set. Usually, the members of a set have something in common, but that is not necessarily so. We call these objects the elements of a set. The elements in a set are not ordered. To express the information that a set A contains the element a, we write: a ∈ A (a is an element of the set A), while a ∉ A tells us that a is not a member of A.

There are two ways used to define a specific set. One way, the list notation, is to enumerate its members:[5]

A = {John, Mary, lamb}
B = {2, 4, 6, 8, 10}

Even if the list contains the same element more than once, only the distinct elements are counted and considered to be part of the set. We can also use a notation like this, if the list is very long:

C = {1, 2, 3, ... 99, 100}

Sets do not have to contain a finite number of elements. The following defines the set of the natural numbers:

ℕ = {0, 1, 2, ...}

All the members of a set, taken together, are called its *extension*. So we can describe a set by enumerating all its members and we can think of this method of defining a set as being data-driven: we define the set by making note of its actual members.

The other way to define a set is by defining the conditions under which an entity is an element of the set; this is called the *intension*. By contrast with the previous method, this approach could be thought of as being theory-driven, or pattern-driven: it defines a set by establishing a logical set of conditions that governs the members of the set. Very often the "set builder" notation is used, which allows us to specify the common properties of the set. So, if we want to specify a set with all even numbers between (and including) 2 and 10, we could write it like this:

A = {x | x is an even number larger or equal to 2 and smaller or equal to 10}

We might read this as "A is the set of values x where x is an even number larger . . . " Usually, set-builder notation is much more formal and compact. For example, we used the term "number," but what kind of number did we mean? Numbers like –2, 1.232 or the square root of 2? Or only natural numbers? To be more precise, we can use clearly defined notions and use the logical "and" we have seen above:

$$A = \{x \mid x \in \mathbb{N} \wedge 2 \leq x \leq 10 \wedge x \text{ modulo } 2 = 0\}^6$$

We can see here how set theory and logic come together in the set-builder notation. The part after the | is a predicate and states that x is part of the set A only if x is substituted by something in such a way that the resulting proposition is true. Any predicate defines two sets in relation to a domain: one whose members will, if inserted into the propositional function, create true propositions and one whose members will create false propositions. So, it makes sense that the first set, in our example A, is also called the *truth set* of the predicate.

There is also a specific set that can be thought of as the zero of the sets, the empty set: Ø. The empty set is a set without elements, so we also could refer to it like this: { }. Sometimes, we describe the intension of a set, only to discover that it defines an empty set—for example:

D = {x | x is president of the US ∧ x is chancellor of Germany}

The concept of data types, which is so important for programming languages and data modeling, can be understood in terms of set theory: a data type is a set and there is also a set of operations that can be performed on this data type. For example, in many programming languages there is a data type called "string" and the members of this set are all character sequences. The set of operations on strings usually includes the plus operator (+), which concatenates elements of the set string and creates a new element of this set.

Many endeavors in data modeling can be understood as seeking an exact description of the intension of a set such that all potential elements will be included as intended, even those we haven't yet seen. This becomes a crucial element of schema design, in cases where the goal is to create a schema that can anticipate and accommodate the structure of a large set of documents whose full extent and nature cannot be known in advance, such as the articles to be published in a journal, or the documents contained in an unfamiliar archive. The description of the intension doesn't have to be and often is not short; it can be and often is a specification that describes in formal terms the rules by which an element of this specific set—for example, the set of well-formed XML-documents—is defined. We will explore this in more detail below.

Let's now consider some of the ways in which two sets can be related: equality, subset/superset, and disjoint sets. Two sets are equal if they have the same elements: for example, these three sets are all equal:

A = {2, 3, 5, 7}
B = {7, 2, 3, 5, 2, 3, 7}
C = {x | x is a prime number ∧ x < 10}

A = B, because the repeated items only count once for the purposes of determining the set membership, and the sequence of the elements is also not important for the definition of a set. C uses the set-builder notation, but this does not affect the assessment of the set's contents.

We say that a set A is a subset of a set B, if all elements of A are also elements of B. This can be written using the following notation:

A ⊂ B

This defines a *true* subset, where B also contains elements that are not members of A. If A could be equal to B, the following notation is used: A ⊆ B. It means that A is either a subset of or equal to B. As mentioned before, sets can be elements of sets. The empty set is a subset of all non-empty sets, so the statement

Ø ⊂ A

is always true, if A is not empty. And because the definition says that if all elements of A are also elements of B, then A is a subset of B, it follows that B is a subset of B too, because all elements of B are also elements of B:

B ⊆ B

If A ⊂ B, then B in turn is called the superset to A:

B ⊃ A

Obviously, there are many sets that do not have any elements in common, and these are described as *disjoint* sets.

There is a subtle but important difference between A ∈ B and A ⊂ B. The first expression can only be true if the set B has an element that is the set A, while any set can be a subset of B. An example can clear this up:

Given the sets A = {1, 2} and B = {1, 2, 3, 4}

A is a subset of B because all its members are also elements of B. But the set A is not an element of the set B. That would be only the case if B looked like this: {1, 2, 3, 4, {1, 2}}.

Sets can be combined in many ways. The most common are the set operations *union*, *intersection* and *difference*. The union of the sets A and B creates a new set containing all elements that appear in either A or B or in both. To use a more formal notation:

$$A \cup B = \{x \mid x \in A \vee x \in B\}$$

Probably more interesting is the intersection. The intersection of the sets A and B creates a new set containing all elements that are in A and also in B. Here the formal notation is helpful to avoid ambiguities:

$$A \cap B = \{x \mid x \in A \wedge x \in B\}$$

And finally, the difference between the sets A and B creates a new set containing all elements of A which are not in B:

$$A - B = \{x \mid x \in A \wedge x \notin B\}$$

The difference is sometimes also written as A\B.

Our final set operation will seem a bit more unusual, but if we understand that we often want to understand something about all possible subsets of a set, it is clear that we need a shortcut to express this collection. The *power set* offers just that. The power set of a set A, usually written $P(A)$ or $\wp(A)$, creates a new set consisting of all the subsets of A including the empty set and A. So, if A = {1, 2, 3} then $P(A)$ = {Ø, {1}, {2}, {3}, {1, 2}, {1, 3}, {2, 3}, {1, 2, 3}}. It is generally the case that if A has n elements, then $P(A)$ has 2^n elements.

Relations between sets—like equality, subset/superset or disjoint—and also set operations such as union and intersection can be visualized using diagrams. There are two slightly different forms, called Euler diagrams and Venn diagrams, but in the following we will draw on features of both to express our concepts as clearly as possible.

Figure 2.2 visualizes the case where A ⊂ B (A is a subset of B). Figure 2.3 visualizes the three basic set operations: union, intersection, and difference.

We emphasized above that sets are unordered collections of items. However, as we will see shortly, order is a crucial aspect of data modeling: for instance, one of the key differences between XML nodes and database fields is that XML nodes are explicitly ordered. We can add the concept of order to set theory using the set theoretic primitive *ordered pair*. An ordered pair is usually written with parentheses: (a, b); a is the first *entry* (or *coordinate*) of the pair and b the second.

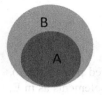

Figure 2.2 A set operation diagram: set A as a subset of set B.

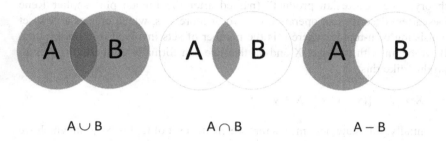

$$A \cup B \qquad\qquad A \cap B \qquad\qquad A - B$$

Figure 2.3 A diagram of the basic set operations: union, intersection, and difference.

The pair (a, b) is not equal to (b, a) unless a = b. But how can we derive this notion from the concepts we have seen thus far? We can express this ordered pair using our set notation thus:

(b, a) = {{b}, {a, b}}

The set {{b}, {a, b}} includes all those sets that are defined by going through the ordered entries from left to right and at each stage enumerating which elements we have seen, including the new element under focus. It is important to note here that the order of elements within this set—for instance, the fact that {b} comes first—is not significant and does not affect how this set expresses the order we are seeking to represent. Instead, the order is represented by the number of elements in each element of this set. The two-item set {a, b} represents the second item in the original ordered pair, and the item "a" that it adds (when the two-item set is compared with the one-item set {b}) is thereby identified as the second item in the original ordered pair. For a fuller and more formal explanation, see Halmos, 1960, Section 6.

In mathematics, an ordered pair is also called a 2-tuple, a special case of the more general concept of a *tuple* or an *n-tuple*, where n can be any positive integer and refers to the number of members. All of the following are tuples:

A = (1, 2)
B = ("a", "b", "c")

C = ("John," "Mary")
D = ("Mary," "John")
E = (32, "Mary," 1.3, "a", ⋈)

A is an ordered pair. Because order is significant for an ordered pair (2-tuple), C is not identical with D. Tuples can contain different kinds of elements as in E; we will see more of this when we talk about relations and relational databases below.

Now we have all the concepts needed to introduce the next term of set theory. The "Cartesian product" (named after the French philosopher René Descartes) describes an operation on two or more sets, which creates a new set consisting of n-tuples, where n is the number of sets involved in the operation. If we begin with two sets X and Y, then we can formally define the Cartesian product like this:

$$X \times Y = \{(x, y) \mid x \in X \wedge y \in Y\}$$

Essentially, this statement means that we create a set of tuples (x, y) in which we take each member of set X in turn and pair it with each member of set Y. The result set will contain all possible combination of elements. So, if we use the sets A and B we described above, the Cartesian product looks like this:

$$A \times B = \{(1, \text{``a''}), (1, \text{``b''}), (1, \text{``c''}), (2, \text{``a''}), (2, \text{``b''}), (2, \text{``c''})\}$$

Remember that the sequence of our elements in a list notation of a set is irrelevant, but the sequence of elements in a tuple is relevant. So, while the inputs to the Cartesian product are unordered, the outputs are ordered. Therefore, A × B is not the same as B × A, because it would create different tuples:

$$B \times A = \{(\text{``a''}, 1), (\text{``b''}, 1), (\text{``c''}, 1), (\text{``a''}, 2), (\text{``b''}, 2), (\text{``c''}, 2)\}$$

It is also possible to create the Cartesian product on a single set: A × A, also written as A^2:

$$A \times A = \{(1, 1), (1, 2), (2, 1), (2, 2)\}$$

Descartes introduced this concept of a product to represent each point on a geometric plane as a tuple of x and y coordinates, and because they are usually real numbers this is often written like this: R^2. But a Cartesian product isn't limited to two sets. It can combine n sets and each of its resulting tuples will then have n elements. If we combine our three sets A, B, C defined above into a product set A × B × C, its tuples look like this:

$$A \times B \times C = \{(1, \text{``a''}, \text{``John''}), (1, \text{``b''}, \text{``John''}), \ldots (2, \text{``c''}, \text{``Mary''})\}$$

In the context of data modeling, the Cartesian product is important because it provides the basis for one of our core concepts: the *relation*. A relation is formally defined as a subset of a Cartesian product—in other words, any subset of the Cartesian product of one or more sets is a relation:

$R \subseteq A \times B$ with $(x,y) \in R$

And we can now say that x is related to y by R (short form: x R y).

To explain this in more detail, let us define two new sets:

N = {"Tina", "Tom", "Alex"}
T = {55523, 66619}
T × N = {("Tina", 55523), ("Tina", 66619),
("Tom", 55523), ("Tom", 66619),
("Alex", 55523), ("Alex", 66619)}

Now let us define another set,

M = {("Tina", 55523), ("Tom", 66619), ("Alex", 66619)}.

M is a subset of T × N; it is one of many possible subsets and there is nothing special about this subset in comparison to all the other possible subsets. Because M is one of the possible subsets of T × N, we can say M is a relation from N to T. And we can say "Tina" is related to 55523 or (more compactly) "Tina" R 55523. Looking at it in this way allows us to apply all operators which can be applied to sets in general and also a specific operator—the operator "join"—which can only be applied to relations. We will discuss this in more detail below in the section on the relational model.

The meaning of this relation could be anything—for example, extension numbers in an office, or tax identification numbers. There are different ways to visualize a relation. We can use a table:

Or we can use a graph (please see Figure 2.4).

Table 2.5 A relation, represented as a table

	55523	66619
Tina	x	
Tom		x
Alex		x

Or we could use an adjacency matrix, which we will discuss below in the section on graphs. Relations on two sets are also called binary relations to distinguish them from n-ary relations (that is, relations based on n sets). An n-ary relation is a subset of $A_1 \times A_2 \times \ldots A_n$. We will have a closer look at them below in the section on relational models and databases.

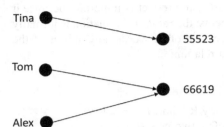

Figure 2.4 A relation between sets, represented as a graph.

Set theory as presented here is a powerful tool that allows to understand very different approaches in data modeling as doing basically the same thing—that is, offering a formal way to define sets and operations on sets. Even without any prior familiarity with formal set theory, most of it will seem intuitively plausible, an expression of common-sense concepts. The same is true for logic: it simply formalizes concepts that we use every day. The formal notation helps to avoid ambiguities and offers a compact way to express even complex relations clearly and precisely. On the other hand, we should point out that the version of set theory presented here is also called the "naive" set theory, in contrast to axiomatic set theory, which is more abstract. Axiomatic set theory came into being because naive set theory allows us to produce some rather baffling paradoxes. Probably the most well known is Bertrand Russell's famous paradox about the set of all sets that are not members of themselves. The intension of this set X is that all its members are sets and all of them are not an element of themselves. Now, if X is not a member of itself, then it clearly falls under its description: it is a set and not a member of itself. But if we say that X is a member of itself, it obviously doesn't fit the description of its members any longer. It is like the story about the difficult situation of a barber who only shaves those who don't shave themselves— if he does not shave himself, then by rule he ought to shave himself, but if he shaves himself, then he violates this rule. Axiomatic set theories like the one by Zermelo-Fraenkel define their premises in such a way that paradoxes like Russell's are avoided. But for our purposes, the naive set theory is good enough in most cases.

3.3 Sequences

Intellectual tools like logic and set theory allow us to specify sets and talk about the properties of these sets in a formal way. The concept of n-tuples extends the properties of sets by enabling us to describe an ordered collection or sequence. But tuples have their limits as a way of describing sequences, because in a typical set of n-tuples (as in the case of a relational database) all of the tuples are the same length. We can also generate open-ended sequences in a formal manner—

or instance, with a function that takes each element x_n as input and creates the next element x_{n+1}. But many of the types of sequences digital humanists must work with require open-endedness of a different kind. Humanities data is full of sequences that differ in length and form, but for which we can nonetheless identify a set of underlying rules or governing structures. For computer science, this area is of specific importance, because programming languages are a prominent example of this kind of formal communication. There are two common ways to specify this kind of sequence in a formal way: *regular expressions* and *grammars*. After outlining some of the basic concepts of regular expressions we will talk about one approach to describing a grammar, the extended Backus-Naur Form. A full coverage of regular languages or context-free grammars (which provide the theoretical background of regular expressions and grammars) is out of scope for this book, but will be helpful for anyone interested in a deeper understanding of the topic; see (Hopcroft, Motwani, and Ullmann, 2013) for a detailed introduction.

Regular expressions are a powerful tool to describe sets of strings. Essentially, they consist of a set of specially defined symbols that allow us to describe sets of characters and quantifiers. The following expressions describe one character and specify the set it belongs to:

. (i.e. a period)	any character
\d	any number
\s	any whitespace characters (space, tab, return, etc.)
\w	any word character plus numbers and underscore "_"
[xyz]	a self-defined set of characters consisting of the characters "x", "y" and "z". So [xyz] means one character, which is either x or y or z.

Quantifier operators indicate how many of the designated characters or sequences should be present. If there is no quantifier, it is assumed that the character or class in question appears only once. Quantifiers usually refer to the character or character class immediately preceding the quantifier. Examples of quantifiers are:

?	occurs 0 or 1 time
+	occurs 1 or more times
*	occurs 0 or more times

The notation takes a while to get used to; it is very compact but longer expressions can be hard to read. And it is not entirely standardized, although the syntax used by the scripting language Perl has been picked up by many other languages. Modern versions of regular expression engines usually work with Unicode; in early versions of regular expressions, the expression "\w" (any word character) referred to A-Z and a-z, but it now refers to all Unicode characters which are marked as word characters. The or-bar or pipe character (|) means "or"—that is, either the symbols to the left or to the right must be part of the pattern. Here are some examples:

`[A-Z][a-z]+\s`   The first character is a capital letter between A and Z, followed by any combinations of lower-case letters, with any single whitespace character at the end.

This regular expression would match "House" or "Zug" but not "house" (no capital letter at the beginning) and not "Über" (while the first letter is capitalized, in Unicode the Ü does not fall between A and Z).

`U[Ss][Aa]?`   Matches "USA", "US", "Usa" but not "usa" and not "USsa" (only one "s" allowed at the second position).

We can also specify the number of occurrences using {n} or {n, m} where n is the minimal number of occurrences and m the optional maximum number. Take, for instance, a list of 4- and 5-digit numbers like this:

`0123 2134 2200 34232 5390 9939 12129 2014 3911 3141#`

We can extract with the following expression all 4-digit numbers, not including any number above 4:

`[0-4]{4}[ #]`

In the next example we are looking for all numbers not containing a 9 (the ^ denotes a negation). This expression says "any character except a 9, allowing 4 or 5 characters in a row":

`[^9 ]{4,5}[ #]`

All of these symbols (+, *, \, [], ^, etc.) can be classified as metacharacters, because they have a special operational meaning in the context of a regular expression. But what if we want to look for one of the metacharacters in the patterns we describe? In that case, we can use an escape character to signal that the next character is to be treated as a normal character in the pattern. This escape character in regular expressions is usually the backslash. So if we are looking for an international phone number, which usually starts with a "+", we could use a pattern like this:

`\+[0-9]+`

The first "+" has the escape character in front of it, so any number starting with + like +4955112345 will be found.

Regular expressions are part of most programming languages, of text editors, and of powerful Unix tools like grep, and they have even found their way to some degree into word processors.

Another way of describing sequences outlines a kind of grammar and views the rules of the grammar as productive or generative: they describe how valid structures—valid in the context of the language described by the grammar—can be produced. Regular expressions offer this generative quality in a very limited way: they permit us to express an open-ended set of possible patterns which the expression will match. But they do not provide a method for defining a grammar in the full sense: an interdependent and exhaustive set of rules by which a language may be defined and against which it may be tested. The system we are outlining in the following, extended Backus-Naur-Form (EBNF) was devised by two members of a committee working on the programming language Algol in the early 1960s and has been in use ever since. It describes a context-free language. A context-free language is a language in which all possible statements in the language can be described by a set of "production rules" or replacement statements: rules for replacing one symbol with another.

Ordinary language, the language of everyday life, depends heavily in its production and reception on context, and attempts to describe it with context-free grammars have been futile, so this approach works best in cases where we are processing very formalized communications without many implicit assumptions: in other words, when communicating with computers. The principal idea of the EBNF is easy. An EBNF grammar takes the form of a set of production rules that specify definitions or substitutions that may be performed to generate symbol sequences. Here is a sample:

A = B, C;

This production rule indicates that the symbol "A" may be replaced by the sequence "BC" (the comma indicates that the elements must appear in the order given). There are two kinds of symbols: non-terminal and terminal symbols. A non-terminal symbol may be replaced by its definition (i.e. the part that follows the equals sign) in any production rule. A terminal symbol defines any kind of string that cannot be replaced by something else (in other words, it terminates the definition or substitution process), so terminals cannot occupy the left side of a production rule, whereas non-terminals may appear on either side. The documents described by an EBNF consist only of terminal symbols, and the possible sequences of these symbols are fully described by the EBNF.

To generate expressions using an EBNF grammar, we take each production rule in turn and make the substitutions it stipulates, until we are left with only terminal symbols and the substitution process comes to an end. In some substitutions there will be only one possibility, but in others we may be given a choice. The following example defines a very simple language that allows you to produce sentences like "The dog bites the man".

```
sentence    = subject, predicate, object;
subject     = article, noun;
predicate   = "bites" | "loves";
object      = article, noun;
article     = "a" | "the"
noun        = "child" | "dog" | "cat" | "woman" | "man"
```

Everything in quotation marks is a terminal symbol. Everything not in quotation marks is either a metacharacter like the comma in the first line or a non-terminal symbol like "sentence." We can read the first line as follows: to produce a sentence you create a sequence beginning with a subject, then a predicate and then an object, all of them non-terminal symbols (the comma serves a concatenation symbol that also indicates sequence). The second line indicates that a subject is produced by an article followed by a noun. The predicate is created by either the string "bites" or the string "loves," both terminal symbols. We can also indicate optional elements using square brackets—for example, the following definition would also allow a sentence like "dog bites man":

```
subject     = [article], noun
```

Notice that this handling of optionality is quite similar to the "?" in regular expressions. In fact, there are also equivalents to the other elements of regular expressions: for example, with {} we can allow zero or more repetitions of the symbols between the brackets:

```
subject     = article, {adjective}, noun
adjective   = "small" | "big" | "cruel" | "beautiful"
```

These rules allow the production of sequences like "a small cruel man" and "a big beautiful small cat."

A complete description of the EBNF can be found in the ISO standard ISO/IEC 14977. It works well with any kind of context-free language which is linear, but it does not work with any other kind of patterns, such as electric circuit diagrams. And as usual, although EBNF is well defined, many variations can be found. The XML specification, for example, uses a simplified version which is actually an easy-to-read mix between EBNF and regular expressions.

4 Established approaches

From one perspective, it can appear that there exist infinite approaches to data modeling, since for each new data set there may be specific requirements for processing it, and also distinctive modeling requirements to foreground specific aspects of the data. But while this may be almost true on the level of the specific data model, at the level of the metamodel things are much simpler. For most practical purposes, there exist three main metamodels: the relational model, XML, and graphs (including RDF). Data that cannot be modeled using one of these approaches is typically handled by creating a data model specific to the situation (which will also typically require software written for this specific data)—for example, using an object-oriented approach.

Even apart from the questions of design involved, the practical requirements for a workable metamodel are very significant: it must be a standard, in order to provide a stable and dependable basis for specific modeling efforts, and in the current information ecology that means it must also be an international open standard in order to enjoy wide adoption. It must typically also be accompanied by a suite of other standards that describe processes such as data creation, data manipulation, and data retrieval. The family of XML-related standards is a good illustration of the many aspects involved, as is the SQL standard with all its subdivisions. Nonetheless, the field of metamodels is still evolving, albeit slowly. In the last few years, for example, the demands of processing terabytes of data at high speed has not only produced new buzzwords like "big data," but has also yielded new data modeling concepts that are the foundation of the NoSQL databases. These new techniques still lack new standardized metamodels and hence currently lock users into specific software environments, but over time those standard metamodels may emerge, together with the accompanying families of supporting standards.

In the following, we will give a short introduction into some approaches. Our introduction will not be a replacement for a more detailed introduction into the specific metamodels, but it should provide a fundamental understanding of some of their core concepts. In particular, we will try to highlight the underlying logical and mathematical concepts and the kinds of processing they enable. And we will also try to give some hints when a specific metamodel is useful and when not, even if in most cases pragmatic considerations will also come into play in the choice of a metamodel. A short introduction into relational databases is followed by sections on XML and on graphs and RDF.

4.1 Relational models and databases

The relational model is one of the oldest metamodels and is used practically everywhere where computers are used. Many programming languages provide modules to access relational databases, and software companies developing relational databases like Oracle or IBM are among the biggest players in the market. The introduction into data modeling with the relational model is standard fare for computer science students. The process of developing a relational data model is usually divided in two steps: first, the creation of a conceptual model, and then based on that the creation of a logical model.

A conceptual model for a relational database is usually described by an entity-relationship model. It identifies all important entities of the universe of discourse—that is, the segment of the world which is to be modeled—and the important attributes of these entities. The entity-relationship model (ERM) is a way to describe the structure and semantics of data which was first proposed in a now famous paper by Peter Chen (Chen, 1976) and since then developed—with some important changes and additions—into a design tool especially for relational databases. Its basic assumption is that "the real world consists of entities and relationships" (Chen, 1976, p. 9). To be exact: in the real world we identify entities like Charles Dickens or Frida Kahlo, which belong to a given entity type—for example, "artist." An entity type and each of its entities usually have one or more attributes—for example, the entity type "artist" could have the attributes "year of birth," "name," and "year of death." A relationship describes the relation between entities—for example, between artists and works of art. Chen also proposed a graphical representation for the ERM which has become very popular, because it provides a relatively easy and accessible way to visualize ERMs. Entities are referenced by rectangles and relationships by diamonds. The lines between these building blocks contain additional information—for example, the possible number of entities being part of the relationship. The relationship between artist and work of art would be modeled like this ("m" and "n" indicate any positive integer).

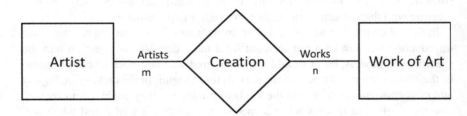

Figure 2.5 A sample entity-relationship model.

Modern variations of Chen's ER diagram often substitute the relationship symbol with a line. The so-called "crow-foot" notation, which is especially widespread, would describe the relationship in this way.

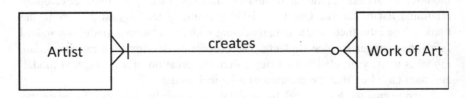

Figure 2.6 The same entity-relationship model, using "crow-foot" notation.

The vertical line indicates "at least one," the triangle with a middle line is the notation for "many," and the circle means "zero." So this diagrams says: "One or many artists create zero or more works of art." This aspect of ERMs is called the cardinality of a relation and it constrains the relation. For example, if we wish to model the relationship between the entity set "artist" and "place of birth," we would use cardinality to include the information that an artist can only have one birthplace.

There is no real standard for ER diagrams (the existing ISO standard has not established itself in practice as such) and there are many more or less similar implementations.

If one adds all attributes to this conceptual model, we have a visual representation of the logical model that can be transformed to a representation of the same model using tables. Every entity type in our ER diagram becomes a table on its own and every attribute of an entity becomes a column of the table. Now we can populate the table with entities described by their attributes (please see Table 2.6).

In 1970, E.F. Codd published a now famous paper outlining a mathematical model for this kind of information structure. At that time databases were ad hoc products with no coherent theoretical underpinnings; Codd's work provided a theoretical basis and an important field of application for a whole branch of mathematics, the *relational algebra* (Codd, 1970). Codd modeled the information in the column of a table as a set, so our table "Artists" would consist of three sets which are labeled Name, Year of birth and Year of death. And he conceptualized a row in a table as a tuple over these three sets: for example ("Charles Dickens", 1812, 1870). The table is thus a relation—that is, a set of tuples which are a subset to the Cartesian product of the three sets involved (Name × Year of birth × Year of death).

Table 2.6 A table with instances of an entity and its attributes

ARTISTS		
Name	Year of birth	Year of death
Charles Dickens	1812	1870
Frida Kahlo	1907	1954

The labels of the sets are called *attributes*—for example, the relation Artist has the attributes Name, Year of birth and Year of death. And for each attribute there is a set of possible values which are called the *domain* of this attribute. Each tuple represents a relationship between the elements of the tuple, in the context of a database we can also call them attribute values. At a given point in time, all tuples of a relation together specify all relationships.

We can view a table as a visualization of a relation, but it is important to remember that the ordering of the rows is of no consequence because a relation is simply a set (hence unordered) of tuples. These tuples can be visualized in the table as rows. Each tuple represents an ordered sequence of information (describing one entity) and the ordering of the columns is significant because it corresponds to the order of the sets Name, Year of birth and Year of death and therefore to the structure of the tuples. But in the tabular visual representation, the order of columns is insignificant.

Obviously, there are many mathematically possible tuples that don't make any sense from a semantic perspective—for instance, all of the dates on which Charles Dickens was *not* born. One can view the attributes also as a logical expression; something like this:

$$\exists(x,y,z)P(x,y,z) \text{ for } P(x,y,z): x \text{ is Name} \wedge y \text{ is Year of birth} \wedge z \text{ is}$$
Year of death

This translates to mean that there are elements x, y, z in the domain such that $P(x, y, z)$ is true, where x is a name, y is a year of birth and z is a year of death.

So the database represents the selection of mathematically possible tuples that also yield true statements, while all the other mathematically possible tuples (which do not result in true statements) are excluded from the database.

The relational model requires each tuple—each row in the table—to be unique. For many purposes we need to be able to identify each grouping of information (e.g. "Frida Kahlo -1907–1954"). We could use the field "name" as an identifier, but as mentioned above, entity names are often ambiguous (since there may exist in the world more than one entity of the same name), and therefore it is common either to use a combination of fields to construct a unique identifier or to introduce a new column with a unique identifier, the "primary key" (see Table 2.7).

Table 2.7 The same table with the addition of the primary key AID

AID	Name	Year of birth	Year of death
0	Charles Dickens	1812	1870
1	Frida Kahlo	1907	1954
2	John Smith	1662	1717
3	John Smith	1781	1852

If we have a table of works of art, we can now use the new identifier AID to refer unambiguously to the artist (and all information associated with that entity) instead of using the name (AID in the following table is called a "foreign key" in SQL) (see Table 2.8).

Because relations are sets, all set operations (such as intersection or union) may be used on relations as well. Additionally, the relational algebra allows powerful operations on the data and has become a core component of the Structured Query Language (SQL), the standard for relational databases. SQL describes

Table 2.8 Using a foreign key instead of the artists' names

WID	AID	Title	Year of publication
0	0	*A Christmas Carol*	1843
1	0	*Bleak House*	1852
2	1	*The Suicide of Dorothy Hale*	1938

how to query or manage data—for example, creating tables, adding or deleting information, retrieving information) in a declarative way: that is, it does not describe the procedure for achieving the results, but only the properties of the results. SQL provides a good example of the power of the separation of concerns: SQL offers an abstract data retrieval and data manipulation language, while the specific database systems take care of the way these instructions are implemented on the "physical" level of the model in the most efficient way—for example, the indexes that enable fast access to the information in the tables. From a data modeling perspective, this aspect is of no concern to us, so we can concentrate on the question how to work on conceptual and logical level. In the following, we will look at the way in which the relational algebra works and how this is realized in SQL.

The relational operator "join" allows us to combine two relations into a new one which contains all the columns of both input relations. An important prerequisite for a join is the existence of one attribute that is the same in both relations. We can join our two example relations because they share the attribute AID (the following describes what is called a "natural join," but other variants of join also exist). The resulting relation looks like this (Table 2.9).

Table 2.9 A natural join of the two relations

WID	AID	Name	Year of birth	Year of death	Title	Year of publication
0	0	Charles Dickens	1812	1870	*A Christmas Carol*	1843
1	0	Charles Dickens	1812	1870	*Bleak House*	1852
2	1	Frida Kahlo	1907	1954	*The Suicide of Dorothy Hale*	1938

Clearly, a lot of information in the resulting table is redundant. But often we need this kind of table for specific queries—for example, if we want to retrieve all works of art that were created when the artist was younger than 30. Entering and maintaining the data in this redundant format would be expensive and error prone, but performing a join between our two different tables enables the data to live in a non-redundant form and be combined only when needed for a specific query.

Because the relational algebra is such a powerful concept, a whole field has developed around how to model data in the most efficient way for a database.

Many SQL expressions can be reformulated as logical expressions (Date, 2011, Ch. 11). And logical expressions also play an important role as part of SQL expressions. For example, with the following expression we select those names from ARTIST who died before their 60th birthday:

```
SELECT Name
FROM ARTIST
WHERE Year_of_death - Year_of_birth < 60
```

As we have seen above, we can define a statement in predicate logic like this:

Let $A(x1, x2)$ denote the statement "$x2 - x1 < 60$"

Then we can create propositions with different values for x_1 and x_2, taking these values from our tuples in ARTIST. And each proposition has a specific truth value, which decides whether the name belonging to the dates is part of the output or not.

Relational databases are the best tool, if your data is well structured and you need efficient queries based on different views of the data. Because there are so many tools to design databases and the existing database systems are among the most solid software systems in existence, they are often the first choice if data has to be systematically organized. But they are not very well suited for partially structured data like texts, and we will turn in a moment to modeling systems that can accommodate these less systematically structured data sets.

The advent of NoSQL databases has loosened to some extent the belief that only data in a relational database could be understood as truly structured, but nevertheless the domain of relational databases has produced the deepest and most systematic literature analyzing the data modeling process and trying to make it smoother and less error prone.

Data modeling of relational databases has been refined over the last five decades to achieve the most compact and less redundant representations. The motivations for this process have been twofold: for one, a compact data model will save storage space. When storage was expensive this was a crucially important argument, while nowadays storage is just one factor to be balanced with others such as the complexity of queries (since reducing redundancy tends to increase that complexity). The second argument is the probability that a change to the database—for example, updating or deleting data—will leave the database in an invalid state. If there are many redundancies in a database structure, there is a higher probability that a change at some point will lead to inconsistencies by changing an attribute in one place but not in others. Let us assume our relation is as shown in Table 10.

Table 2.10 Redundancies in a database structure

WID	Name	Title	Year of publication
0	C. Dickens	*A Christmas Carol*	1843
1	C. Dickens	*Bleak House*	1852

If we now decide to update the name of the artist from "C. Dickens" to "Charles Dickens," or even to "Charles John Huffam Dickens," we have to make sure that we do this for each of the entries with his name. If there are many entries, the probability of missing some of them is higher. But if in these entries, instead of the name, there is only a number pointing to another relation where the number is associated with a full name, then we would only have to change the name in that one place.

The process of eliminating all redundancies is called database normalization and is usually described as taking at least three steps. We will only discuss the first step here, because a complete discussion of normalization is beyond the scope of this introduction.

In the first normal form, an attribute should only have atomic values (and no compound values that contain multiple pieces of information).

Let us assume our relation looks as in Table 2.11.

Table 2.11 Using compound values

AID	NAME	ACTIVITY
0	Charles Dickens	Writer, journalist
1	Johann Wolfgang Goethe	Writer, scientist, politician

Here, the attribute ACTIVITY has compound values: it designates more than one activity for each entity. If we would like to retrieve all tuples that describe writers, we would have to parse each entry to see whether it contains somewhere the information "writer". What the first normal form requires is an attribute value as shown in Table 2.12.

Table 2.12 An attempt at a solution for the compound values

AID	NAME	ART
0	Charles Dickens	Writer
1	Charles Dickens	Journalist

Table 2.13 Splitting of the two relations to eliminate the redundancy

AID	NAME
0	Charles Dickens
1	Johann Wolfgang Goethe

Table 2.14 Splitting of the two relations to eliminate the redundancy

AID	ART
0	Writer
0	Journalist
1	Writer
1	Scientist

This cannot be the final solution, because it creates another redundancy, but it is a first step in the right direction. Now we split the relation into two separate relations to eliminate the redundancy (please see Tables 2.13 and 2.14).

When pursued thoroughly, normalization expresses each relationship with a single formal relation, and results in data that is as economically and elegantly expressed as possible, not only in conceptual terms but in mathematical terms as well.

4.2 Trees and XML

Texts have structure, but typically not of the closely defined, repetitive form that we associate with a table. The structure of text is governed by pattern that permits more variation, allowing alternatives, omissions, repetitions, and recursions. Texts are sequences in the sense defined above, and a grammar-based instrument like the extensible Markup Language (XML) is the most effective approach to modeling this form of open-ended structure. At the very beginning of the research into this kind of structure, some believed that it would be possible to create one general model usable for all kinds of texts: a single grammar that could describe all of the features observed in texts of all kinds. But it quickly became clear that such a system would be much too large to be attractive and would still leave many requirements unfulfilled. So the task had to be redefined: to develop a common notation system (to enable the development of a shared tool set), but to leave the specifics of an annotation schema to be defined within particular contexts of usage. The solution was found quite early in a three-tiered system which matured into what we know now as SGML/XML.

1. The *metamodel* is essentially an agreement (expressed as a formal standard) about notation and syntax, and a protocol for defining descriptive systems or "languages" that use this syntax and for defining their vocabularies and grammars. The shared syntax and notation permits the creation of tools to process the data,

while the freedom to create individual languages supports the necessary diversity of descriptive approaches. XML, like its predecessor SGML, thus specifies the delimiters that distinguish the markup from the content, and also defines a notation and syntax via the rules of well-formedness: the markup must be delimited using the correct notation (described below), all elements must nest without overlap, and there must be a single root element that encloses the entire XML document. Finally, the XML metamodel also provides a way of defining a markup language through the mechanism of the schema: a set of rules describing the features of a genre or class of texts.

2. The *data model*, or schema, defines types of documents by specifying the data elements they may contain and the sequences and structures those elements may form: in other words, the "grammar" of the document. The most widely used schemas for humanities research data are the Text Encoding Initiative (TEI), XHTML, the Encoded Archival Description (EAD), and (to a more limited extent) DocBook. Because XML can be used to express any kind of grammar, it is also used to express other information structures besides documents—for example, vector graphics with SVG, or the Resource Description Framework triples (RDF) discussed below. There are several different languages in which the schema itself may be expressed—for example, DTDs (which are also used in the XML specification), XML Schema, and Relax NG.

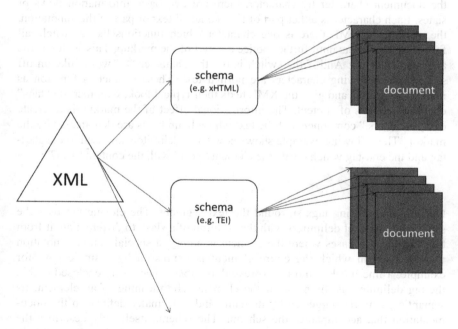

Figure 2.7 The relationship between the XML metamodel, a specific schema, and a schema-conformant document.

3. The modeled instance is the individual document, modeled using specific markup elements.

Figure 2.7 explains this relationship between the XML metamodel, a specific schema, and a document which has been marked up in conformity with that schema.

As noted above, XML data can also be created and used without a schema, and this approach makes sense in cases where some other constraint system is available (such as a data entry form), or where the data is simple and regular enough (or informal enough) that a schema is unnecessary. In the absence of a schema, XML documents must still follow the general rules of well-formedness (such as the nesting of elements), but there is no formal mechanism for describing and constraining the desired pattern of the data.

At the notational level, every XML document is identical—that is, it uses the same characters to delimit the markup, and it obeys the fundamental rules of well-formedness that are defined by the XML metamodel. Conformance with these rules is what enables XML software to operate on all XML data regardless of the specific schema. But at the level of vocabulary and grammar, every XML language—and the data it governs—is unique: this is what enables users of XML to accommodate the diversity of their data.

With this understanding of how XML is designed, we can now take a closer look at its building blocks. From the perspective of an XML parser, working through the document character by character, there are two basic information flows or states. Each character is either part of the "content" text or part of the annotation, the markup. In XML there is one character which functions like a switch: all following characters until further notice are part of the markup. This switch is the angle bracket "<". And if the switch is on, the character ">" works like an off switch: the following characters are normal text. These characters function as markup delimiters and give the XML texts their typical look, with markup "tags" enclosing chunks of content. The informational effect of the markup is to create data "elements," components of the text whose boundaries are demarcated by the markup. The following example shows how these delimiters are used in the start-tag and the end-tag which create the element "year" with the content "1867":

```
<year>1867</year>
```

Opening and closing tags surround the text segment. The closing tag uses the same angle bracket delimiters with the addition of a slash to differentiate it from the start-tag. (In cases where the element is empty, a special compact notation may be used in which the entire element is expressed by a single tag—for example, a line break could be expressed as <lb/>.) The string enclosed within the tag delimiters is the name of the element. The meaning of an element, its semantics, may be suggested by its name and is formally defined in the documentation that accompanies the schema. The schema itself only describes the structural context of an element: what elements can come before it or after it, what elements it may contain, and so on. Elements are the basic building blocks of an XML annotation.

The characters between a start-tag and an end-tag are called the *content of the element*. This content can consist of text or other elements or a mix of both. As noted above, the rules of XML well-formedness require that elements must nest completely inside one another, with a single outer element enclosing the entire XML document.

Let us look at a slightly more complex example bringing all the above-mentioned aspects together:

```
<letter>
  <year>1867</year><lb/>
  <place>Albany</place><lb/>
  <text>Mr <name>Walt Whitman</name> . . . </text>
</letter>
```

We can see here two important aspects of XML documents. First, their structure is hierarchical, because elements nested within another element can be understood to be at a level subordinate to the enclosing element. This relation is usually described using metaphors from family trees, so <year> in this example is called a "child" of <letter> and <letter> is a "parent" to <year>. The <year> and <place> elements are "siblings" and <letter> is an "ancestor" of the <name> element. Second, the elements are ordered and the order is significant: <year> is the first child of <letter>, <lb> the second, <place> the third, and so forth. Thus, an XML document can be visualized as a tree. The small document above would look as shown in Figure 2.8.

Any XML document can be understood as a tree similar to this one, even if most of them are much more complicated. When we say "tree," we mean a

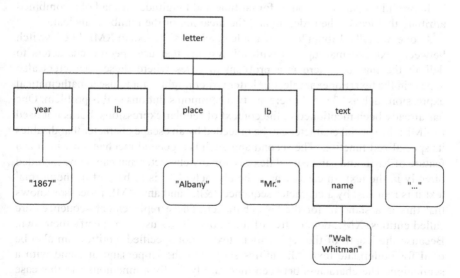

Figure 2.8 An XML document represented as a tree structure.

structure where all elements are part of one formation, and all components are either the root element or are connected with a parent component. And obviously the ordering of the branches of this tree is important, since it represents a text whose components are ordered. This structure enables a whole set of operations—for example, it allows us to restrict a search to specific parts of a tree, such as the part which contains the metadata, or the parts that are within footnotes. And it allows us to specify conditions for a search—for instance, to find only the <chapter> elements which contain a <quote> element.

Elements can be given further expressive power with *attributes*, which are a mechanism to attach name-value pairs to an element, providing additional descriptive detail. For example, here we specify the referent of a personal name by adding a reference to VIAF, the Virtual International Authority File, in the id attribute:

```
<name id="http://viaf.org/viaf/2478331">Walt
   Whitman</name>
```

An element can have multiple attributes, separated by white space. In the following example the <place> element has two attributes:

```
<place
gnis_id="977310"
coordinates="42.6525793 -73.7562317"/>
```

The attribute gnis_id refers to an authority file for place names, the Geographic Names Information System (http://geonames.usgs.gov) and the coordinates specify the latitude and longitude of the place. A more unambiguous approach would be to provide separate attributes for latitude and longitude, instead of a combined attribute that leaves the ordering and the meaning of the numbers unclear.

Above, we talked about how the angle bracket "<" works in XML like a switch between text and markup. As with all systems that use specific characters to delimit the markup, there is a problem in cases where these characters also appear in the text. For example, our letter writer might want to use a mathematical expression such as "3 < 5." There are two common solutions to this problem. One has already been mentioned in the context of regular expressions, but is not used in XML: the special character can be preceded by an escape character that disables its specialized function. The second approach is a general mechanism which is a feature of XML and can be used flexibly for any character that cannot be included directly in the text. In cases where the character "<" is to be part of the normal text it is replaced by a character sequence "<" and any XML processor knows that this is a stand-in for the "<" character. These replacement sequences are called entities. XML defines five of them, but allows users to specify their own. Because the length of the replacement text is not specified, entities can also be used for boilerplate text. All entities start with the ampersand and end with a semicolon. The characters between them are typically a mnemonic: in this case "lt" stands for the "less than" sign or angle bracket. Since the ampersand works as a metasymbol too—it signals the start of an entity—it is one of the other built-in entities and hence if we want to include a literal ampersand in the content of our text it must be expressed using an entity, as "&". The other three predefined entities are not strictly necessary, but sometimes help to avoid confusion: > (greater than: >), " (quotation mark: "), ' (apostrophe: '). A similar but more general mechanism, called a "numeric character reference," exists by which we can refer to any Unicode character using its numeric code point. For example, the Greek capital sigma (Σ) can be represented by the numeric character reference Σ. Numeric character references may use decimal notation (as in this example), or hexadecimal notation; in the latter case, the reference includes an x preceding the code point (e.g. Σ).

The notation for XML also provides ways for the XML file to be parsed, processed, and interpreted as data in the environments where it will be used. To indicate specific processing-related information, XML may contain processing instructions; like XML tags, these are delimited (with <? and ?>) so that the parser can distinguish them from other parts of the markup. The name of the processing instruction defines its target application; for instance, PHP (as in <?php ... >. In particular, processing by an XML stylesheet or schema is very common. The following instruction indicates that a Cascading Stylesheet (CSS) file named "common.css" is available to format the XML document:

```
<?xml-stylesheet href="common.css" type="text/css" ?>
```

Another crucial piece of information concerning the interpretation of the XML data is its character encoding: the mapping of the computer's internal data coding onto specific character sets. The standard character encoding of XML documents is Unicode, UTF-8, which is essential for the circulation of data in an international context and across hardware and software platforms, but other character encodings are permitted, in which case the character encoding must be specified. This is done in the XML declaration: the first line of the file (not in fact a processing instruction although it is similar in form), which also specifies the version of XML being used. The following line specifies that the document makes use of ISO-8859-1, which has been used to encode different characters from western European languages, and the XML version:

```
<?xml version="1.0" encoding="ISO-8859-1"
    standalone='yes' ?>
```

As we mentioned above, XML files can be linked to schema files that describe their permitted structures, and the schemas can be used to inform us whether a document is conforming to the data model as expressed in the schema. The XML specification describes two states of XML documents: well-formed and valid. As we have already observed, a document is well-formed if and only if it conforms to a small set of general rules stipulated by the XML specification: elements have to be nested and the syntax for elements, attributes, processing instructions and other XML structures must be correct. Data that is well-formed may be processed by XML-aware software, whether or not a schema is present. A document is additionally *valid* if there is a schema that specifies the grammar of the elements and attributes and the document conforms to this rule set as well. Software programs called XML parsers can be used to test whether an XML document is well-formed and valid, and XML editing software usually integrates such parsers to support authors in the process of data creation.

We can now look briefly at the schema itself. As mentioned above, there are different schema languages for XML and in the following examples we will use two in particular: the document type definition language (DTD), which is also used in the XML specification, and the RelaxNG format (RNG), because the latter is more modern and widely used and allows a tighter control of the schema. The following example shows the definition for an element called "place." It specifies that the content of a <place> element can only be text, with no internal markup allowed:

```
(DTD)   <!ELEMENT place (#PCDATA)>
(RNG)   <element name="place">
            <text/>
        </element>
```

It is easy to see that this is just a variant of the notation for grammars we looked at above. The #PCDATA (i.e. "parsed character data" or text) and <text/> components of the element definition can be understood as terminal symbols: when we process the grammar and make our substitutions, nothing further can be substituted for these patterns. The next example shows a very limited schema for a letter, which allows only a small set of elements and only one possible order in which they may appear:

```
(DTD)   <!ELEMENT letter (year, place, lettertext)>
        <!ELEMENT year (#PCDATA)>
        <!ELEMENT place (#PCDATA)>
        <!ELEMENT lettertext (#PCDATA)>
(RNG)   <element name="letter">
            <element name="year"><text/></element>
            <element name="place"><text/></element>
            <element name="lettertext"><text/></element>
        </element>
```

In EBNF this would be expressed as:

```
letter = year, place, text
```

For many transcriptional purposes, such a schema would be too minimal (because a typical letter contains other features) and also too strict (because many letters contain different sequences of date and place); the following structure accommodates these realities more flexibly, by allowing zero or more occurrences of <year> or <place> before <lettertext>:

```
(DTD)   <!ELEMENT letter ((year | place)*, lettertext)>
(RNG)   <element name="letter">
          <zeroOrMore>
            <choice>
              <element name="year"><text/></element>
              <element name="place"><text/></element>
            </choice>
          </zeroOrMore>
          <element name="lettertext"><text/></element>
        </element>
```

We can also define attributes for the elements. Here we specify the attributes @gnis_id and @coordinates for <place>:

```
(DTD)   <ATTLIST  place gnis_id CDATA #REQUIRED
                  coordinates  CDATA #REQUIRED>
(RNG)   <element name="place">
            <attribute name="gnis"><text/></attribute>
            <attribute name="coordinates"><text/>
            </attribute>
        </element>
```

(In the DTD language it must be made explicit if an attribute is required, while in RNG it must be made explicit if an attribute is optional.)

CDATA is one of ten different keywords to specify the content of the attribute. That sounds a large number, but in fact one of the weaknesses of DTDs (one of the earliest schema languages) is that they do not support the wide range of data types that have emerged with the rise of XML as a standard: for instance, URIs, floating-point numbers, and many others. More modern schema languages such as XML schemas or RelaxNG provide much greater power in this respect.

The schema is usually a stand-alone file because it is meant to be used by multiple documents, so we need a mechanism for linking the document to the schema or schemas against which it is to be validated. This is done by using a processing instruction:

```
<?xml-model href="[file-location]" ?>
```

File-location can either be a link to a web-accessible file or a reference to a local file.

It is possible for a document to be valid against more than one schema, either simultaneously or at different stages of the workflow. In the former case, there may be multiple sets of constraints in play: for instance, an internal schema representing the project's own constraints, and also a schema representing the data requirements of a collaborator or a repository to which the data will be submitted. In the latter case, there may be multiple schemas supporting different stages in a work process: the initial transcription with very basic structure, a later stage of annotation by content experts with more complex markup, a final publication stage in which metadata and details of publication are added. In these scenarios, the different schemas represent different perspectives on the same markup language: they each enforce or test for different subsets of the same language. In such cases we can simply reference all of the schemas in use at the top of the document, using the processing instruction mechanism we noted earlier. But there are also cases where a given document contains markup from two or more different markup languages, each with its own distinct vocabulary of elements. This is increasingly common as well-documented reference models are developed for specific domains: for instance, representing vector graphics, mathematical notation, music, or chemical formulas. A language like the TEI does not seek to duplicate those models, but rather assumes that a project needing to model such information will use the specialized languages developed and maintained by others. In these cases, we need a way to distinguish these languages and to indicate which elements in our markup come from which language.

To solve this problem, XML uses something called *namespaces*, which define distinct vocabularies of elements and allow them to be distinguished from one another. Usually they are declared in the root element of a document. Here we declare two namespaces, TEI and SVG, for our document:

```
<tei:TEI xmlns:tei="http://www.tei-c.org/ns/1.0"
         xmlns:svg="http://www.w3.org/2000/svg">
```

Each namespace declaration includes a prefix to be associated with elements in that namespace, so that in the document we can now explicitly state which namespace an element belongs to:

```
<tei:p>A rectangle looks like this:
<svg:svg x="100" y="100" width="500" height="200"/>
</p>
```

The namespace is especially crucial in cases where two XML languages use the same element name, but with a different meaning—for instance, the TEI language includes a <head> element which is used for section headings, and the XHTML language also includes a <head> element which is used for metadata. In a document that used both languages, the namespace prefix would make clear which element was being used in a given case, and hence how to assess its meaning.

Because one schema may predominate over others in our document, we can also specify this as the default namespace:

```
<TEI xmlns="http://www.tei-c.org/ns/1.0"
     xmlns:svg="http://www.w3.org/2000/svg">
   <p>A rectangle looks like this:
      <svg:svg x="100" y="100" width="500" height="200"/>
   </p>
```

Once a namespace has been declared for an XML document, it becomes an integral part of the XML language being used in that document, to the extent that a query without explicit reference to the TEI namespace (in the example above) would not show any results.

Thus far, we have considered XML mainly from a more technical perspective, focusing on its syntax and its implementation of the model of a context-free grammar. But XML and its predecessor SGML were invented to solve a very practical problem: the markup of text in all its variety and for many different purposes. In this process of developing SGML and XML (which have their beginnings in the 1960s), some basic concepts were introduced which are still important aspects of most models of digital text. One issue that emerged early on and has remained important is the question of how tightly the markup is aligned with specific tools and outcomes. In the early emergence of SGML, one of its important innovations was the fact that unlike many of its predecessors, its information was not aimed at instructing any specific application to produce a specific kind of output; instead, SGML focused on describing the structure and content of text in ways that could be used by a variety of applications for a variety of purposes. For this new role for markup, researchers developed the term "descriptive markup," used in contrast with "procedural markup" (e.g. PostScript or TeX), which communicates some directive to an application. Furthermore, in the context of descriptive markup, it became clear that if structural information is separated both from the procedural information that tells an application what to do, and also from renditional information that describes the intended output (e.g. a formatting stylesheet), the resulting data is exceptionally powerful. Markup languages like TEI take full advantage of both forms of separation, using XML's application independence to the fullest, placing their emphasis on structural and content features and allowing presentational details of output to be expressed as secondary information structures (in CSS or XSLT stylesheets, or more recently by embedding processing information in the TEI schema specification document).

Early articulations of this philosophy of descriptive markup (such as the line of debate stemming from DeRose et al. 1990) link the pragmatics of this scenario—the resulting ease of processing, flexibility of output—with its intellectual salience, arguing that descriptive markup necessarily focuses on what is informationally essential about the text. They take the point further to assert that texts always possess an identifiable informational essence that can be so represented and that hence serves as the natural pivot format from which other outputs can be derived. Languages like TEI have demonstrated quite thoroughly that our understanding of such an essence needs to be plural (to accommodate alternative ways of understanding the text as, for instance, a linguistic structure, an editorial structure, or an expository structure). But nonetheless, for many purposes there is substantial consensus about the core information components of documents that are recognizable regardless of specific formatting and that seem therefore to transcend specific instantiations: in the terms of the Functional Requirements for Bibliographic Records (FRBR),[7] operating at the level of the "manifestation" rather than the "expression." However, over time it has also become clear that there are also classes of documents within which the concept of structure is unknowable or meaningless—for instance, a single word on a manuscript page—or which deliberately seek to destabilize our collective literacy in conventional document structures, as in the case of artists' books. Similarly, editorial approaches in which agnosticism about authorial intentions (and hence document structure) is important at certain stages of the editorial process have caused the TEI to introduce new forms of encoding (such as the <sourceDoc> element and its contents) in which the markup represents documentary appearance as its primary structure.

These approaches have historically been presented as counterarguments to the theory of descriptive markup articulated above, because they treat the identification of an ideal document structure as the key aspect of descriptive markup, and they offer a critique in which something else—document appearance, documentary materiality—is given primacy. However, from a data modeling perspective, it may be more useful to understand a deeper homology between the two. Of the two key insights of SGML/XML, the first—that markup should be *declarative rather than procedural* (in other words, should not speak directly to specific applications)—is now universally uncontroversial and almost beside the point here. The second—that "presentational" information can and should be separated from structural information and handled as part of the output processing—is more complex because of the assumption that appearance and presentational details are necessarily secondary to informational structure. But if we reframe that separation to mean that markup should *model what really interests us rather than what we plan to do with it*, things become clearer. With this perspective, we can acknowledge that information about materiality or appearance is not "presentational"—that is, not aligned with "what we plan to do with it"—if it constitutes the primary scholarly and interpretive perspective on the document in question. As the TEI's <sourceDoc> markup demonstrates, information about the physical zones and marks on the page is at times the primary information construct we need for our research. And the much longer history of usage of the @rend attribute to capture important details of the source—data about font choices, alignment, use of specific delimiters, and the like—has been substantially motivated by similar research needs. The thinness of the line separating <hi rend="bold"> and <bold> (and the difficulty of explaining it using the terminology of "procedural" vs. "descriptive") has always been a small embarrassment for the classic theory of descriptive markup, but if we understand it as a question of *what is being modeled* and the scholarly motivations for that modeling, that distinction is no longer necessary to draw. The legitimacy of such markup can be assessed not by deciding whether it is "descriptive" (good) or "procedural" (bad), but rather by determining whether it successfully "models what really interests us" (a question of information design) and whether it successfully preserves our maneuverability with respect to the usage of the data (a question of workflow).

Like most strong metamodels, XML is surrounded by other standards that offer solutions for frequent tasks such as retrieval, conversion or rendering of documents. XPath provides a mechanism for navigating the XML tree structure and identifying sets of elements or other information nodes based on that structure. XQuery is a powerful and complex query language based on XPath with capabilities quite similar to SQL. XSLT is a programming language that can be used to transform and convert XML documents into other forms of XML or other data formats entirely; it is often used to convert XML documents into HTML. XSL-FO is a device-independent formatting language; XML documents can be converted to XSL-FO and rendered with an XSL-FO renderer to create a specific output, such as a PDF file. Most of these standards use XML internally as their own data format, and take advantage of its tree structure to support the identification and manipulation of document elements, using XPath.

XML is very widely used but has also received critiques, two of which are particularly prominent and are worth addressing here. First, XML is not only used for the markup of documents, but also has found a niche as an information exchange format in application programming interfaces. In these contexts some programmers prefer formats like JSON, as being less verbose than XML, and perhaps also because JSON more closely resembles data structures programmers are already familiar with like associative arrays (also called maps or dictionaries). Until recently, JSON had no provision for anything like a schema, giving XML an advantage in contexts where data constraint was needed, but the advent of JSON-schema may fill that gap: as formats for representing and interchanging highly structured data consisting of attribute-value pairs, JSON and XML may at some point be essentially equivalent. However, for representing semi-structured documentary data, JSON is inapplicable; it is not designed for this purpose and cannot be embedded into mixed-content contexts (where markup is embedded in text segments) in the way that XML can. Broad statements indicating that JSON renders XML obsolete tend to ignore this difference; XML and JSON should be understood as having specialized applicability.

The second common critique refers to the tree structure of XML, which some regard as a serious shortcoming; the most common version of this critique has to do with the difficulties arising around the representation of overlapping structures, which are common in humanities documentary contexts. This is a legitimate critique in an absolute sense: the hierarchical structure of XML poses design challenges for markup languages like TEI which are strongly document-oriented, although for more highly structured data this is generally not a significant concern. But as a comparison between XML and other possible data representation systems, the critique has less force. For one thing, an analogous limitation also exists in other systems. In databases, any content object can only be represented inside one data element at a time; XML provides greater flexibility here by permitting content objects to be nested inside one another, which databases do not. Formats like JSON suffer the same limitation as XML in this respect. The only data formats that permit the representation of overlapping structures are either highly experimental—for instance, LMNL, the Layered Markup and Annotation Language—or obsolete—for instance, COCOA. The reason such alternatives have not become more widely adopted is that they change not only the data model but the whole ecosystem of data entry, data serialization, data processing etc. An approach which uses XML for data entry and data representation but not for all forms of processing—allowing overlapping hierarchies in some processes— keeps the strengths of XML and works around its main weakness, and therefore seems far more promising.[8] For the time being, while the critique of XML at a philosophical level remains a useful impetus to that research, as a rationale for or against the use of XML it is not useful. In practice, in the contexts where this is a pragmatic problem, such as TEI, well-established workarounds exist that permit additional information structures to be represented and processed.

In this section we have covered the basics of XML and briefly mentioned some of its related standards. For those seeking more detail, there are many good books and websites explaining them in more detail—for example, Harold and Means, 2004).

4.3 Graphs and RDF

Recently, networks seem to be everywhere. But it took a while to develop this unified way of looking at society, at streets, at Facebook groups, at internet connections, at letter writers in the eighteenth century, and much more. Important figures in the development of what is now called *social network analysis* were Jacob Moreno who led a small working group in the 1930s, and Harrison White in the 1970s (Freeman, 2004). They paved the way for a relational view of society and they were involved in developing the mathematical tools to describe these networks. Nowadays, these concepts are also applied to other kind of networks, like telephone lines, neural networks, streets and many more (Newman, 2010). The complexity of networks often poses a challenge for the calculation of aspects like the shortest path between two nodes or the probability of two nodes being connected in a simplistic manner, so the invention of fast algorithms, new ways to characterize aspects of the network, or efficient ways to visualize them are still a lively research field. In the following we will introduce some of the very basic ideas of the field, including graph theory (the mathematical basis of network analysis), and then discuss two applications in the field of digital humanities.

Graph theory provides the logical model for any kind of network analysis. Its basic building blocks are *vertices*, also called nodes, and *edges*, also called links. The railway system of a country could be modeled as a graph, with the cities as the vertices and the railway connections between them as edges. In the following we will depend heavily on figures to visualize graphs, but it is important to under-stand graphs as abstractions and the figures as tools meant to help to understand them. Some properties of the following figures are informationally insignificant— for example, the size of the nodes or the length of the edges) but, as we will see later, these properties can be used to convey additional information.

A *simple* graph like the one in Figure 2.9 can be used to model relations which are reciprocal, like friend relationships. Its edges are *undirected*: the nodes are connected but no additional information about the direction of the connection is given. The length of the edges is just an effect of the chosen visualization and has no meaning. The information contained in this graph can be fully expressed by a list of the connected nodes.

There are different ways to add complexity to graphs. One is to include information concerning whether the edge is *directed*. Another step is to allow more than one connection between the vertices, which is called a *multigraph*, and a third step is to allow vertices to connect to themselves by loops. Figure 2.10 shows a) a directed graph and b) a directed multigraph with a loop at vertex 4.

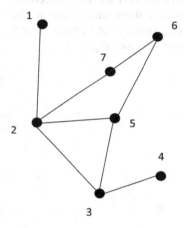

Figure 2.9 A simple network with 7 vertices and 8 edges.

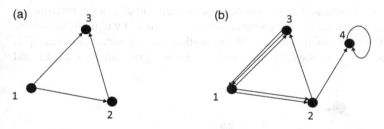

Figure 2.10 a) A directed graph, b) a *directed multigraph* with a loop.

What may look at first like a pedantic categorization—the labeling of a graph as a simple graph, a directed graph, and so forth—is important because behind each of these categories lies another formal definition of the graph, and each entails other operations on the graph. A directed graph D, for example, can be formally defined like this: D consists of a non-empty finite set V(D) of vertices and a finite set E(D) of ordered pairs of distinct vertices called edges. V(D) is the vertex set and E(D) the edge set of D. So a graph can be defined by these two sets: D = (V, E). The second set consists of ordered pairs of vertices to express the directedness; if we replace it by an unordered pair, we have a description of an undirected graph.

In many applications of graph theory it is assumed that all vertices represent the same kind of entity—for example, an individual twitter user or a neuron in the brain. But sometimes we want to model relations between different kinds of entities—for example, authors and the literary societies they belong to. To represent these more complex networks we can use *bipartite graphs*. A bipartite graph is a graph that consists of two independent sets of vertices, where each edge only connects a vertex from one set with a vertex in the other set. We can then infer relationships between entities in one set, based on their shared connections to entities in the other set—for example, a group of authors who belong to the same club. In the following bipartite graph we have two sets of vertices, U and V, and each edge only connects vertices in different sets (see Figure 2.11).

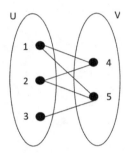

Figure 2.11 A bipartite graph with two sets of vertices.

Graphs can be used as data models because we can add additional information to this simple structure. A very common extension is to add weight to the edges. These weights can be used to indicate the strength of the connection. For example, in a network of people exchanging letters, the weights can be used to add

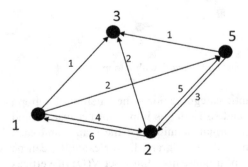

Figure 2.12 A directed multigraph with weighted edges.

information about how many letters have been exchanged. Figure 2.12 shows such a directed multigraph with weights.

So far, we have been assuming that the graph can represent different kinds of entities, but that information has not been an explicit part of our graph. We can add attributes to the vertices and edges to do exactly that. So we can add an attribute to a vertex with the name of a person or, even better, with a reference to an authority file like VIAF pointing to the name of a person.

There are many different kinds of graphs and many ways to classify graphs, but we will only mention a few specific graph attributes because they allow us to take a fresh look at something we already know. If we take a look at the three graphs in Figure 2.13, we can find many ways to describe how they are different from each other, but one aspect of particular interest is the path by which a vertex can be reached.

If you can find a path in a graph which starts at some vertex and then traverses a sequence of edges without using any edge a second time, coming back to the starting vertex, you have found a cycle. For example, in Figure 2.13a you can travel from 2 to 3, then to 4 and then back to 2. An acyclic graph is a graph without any cycles, like the graph in Figure 2.13b. If we use directed edges and allow only one root vertex we have a very special case of a rooted directed acyclic graph (Figure 2.13c). If, additionally, we claim that the ordering of the branches is important, we have an ordered, rooted, directed acyclic graph. This is the specific case of a tree we already know from our discussion of XML trees. Be aware that each feature we discussed in the context of graph theory usually only defines one specific attribute. The term "tree" in the context of XML is a compound statement implying a set of attributes like "having a root," "being ordered."[9] In other words, at this point we can connect our discussion of a tree as the logical structure of XML with the more general and more sophisticated discussion of graphs. Directed rooted trees are just a special case.

As useful as diagrams are for understanding graphs, they cannot be used as computational tools. So we must use some representational system which is computationally more tractable. A common representation of a network that serves this function well was developed before computers were used. It is an *adjacency matrix* which has a row and a column for each node. The number at

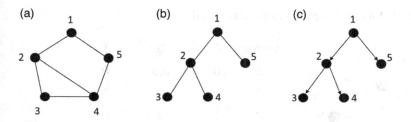

Figure 2.13 a) An undirected cyclic graph, b) an undirected acyclic graph, c) a directed acyclic graph.

the intersection indicates whether there is a connection between the nodes and optionally also gives information about the weight. For a simple graph— that is, a graph that is undirected and has no loops—the matrix contains a zero where the nodes are not connected and a one where they are connected. And because the edges are not directed in a simple graph, the matrix is symmetrical. The adjacency matrix for a simple graph like the following looks as shown in Figure 2.14.

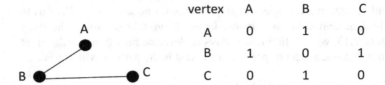

vertex	A	B	C
A	0	1	0
B	1	0	1
C	0	1	0

Figure 2.14 A simple graph and its adjacency matrix.

To describe an adjacency matrix a bit more abstractly: for a graph with n nodes, an adjacency matrix has n rows and n columns. An entry in the row *i* and the column *j* informs about the edge from vertex *i* to vertex *j*. So, in our example above, the row 2 and the column 3 show the edge between vertex 2 (B) and vertex 3 (C).

In an undirected graph, an edge connects vertices in both directions, so in our example A is adjacent to B and B is adjacent to A. In a directed graph, each node is only considered adjacent to the nodes you can reach by following the arrows, so the adjacency matrix shows fewer adjacencies; in the diagram below, A is adjacent to B, but B is not adjacent to A.

Figure 2.15 shows a directed graph and its adjacency matrix.

vertex	A	B	C
A	0	0	1
B	1	0	1
C	0	0	0

Figure 2.15 A directed graph and its adjacency matrix.

vertex	A	B	C
A	0	0,5	0
B	0,5	0	3
C	0	3	0

Figure 2.16 A weighted graph and its adjacency matrix.

The row determines the start of an edge and the column the end point, so row 2 connects to column 1 (B to A). As we saw above, a directed graph can also be used to represent a relation. And as the matrix represents the graph, we can also use it to represent a relation.

In a weighted graph, the matrix contains the weights instead of just the binary information that there is a relation (please see Figure 2.16).

Based on these very simple basic notions, a complex set of intellectual and computational tools has developed. Algorithms which can determine the shortest paths between two vertices are nowadays in use in all kinds of applications, such as navigation systems in cars where the map is represented as a network of cities linked by roads. In the digital humanities domain, an important application of network theory is the ability to model social networks and to use some of the available algorithms either to "describe" the network characteristics of specific vertices like persons or institutions, or to compare networks based on these characteristics. For example, *degree centrality* is one of the measures that enables us to express in formal terms our intuition concerning the most important nodes in a network: those that are most richly connected to others. It is essentially a count of the edges going to or coming from a specific vertex. In a network that models a group of letter writers, some people communicate with many, while others with only very few. One can, given the right circumstances, interpret those vertices with a higher degree centrality as being more important. In a simple graph, the *degree* is computed by counting all edges connected to a vertex. To permit comparison with other graphs, *degree centrality* is often normalized by dividing it by the number of possible connections, which is the number of all vertices minus one.

Other measures of centrality capture different aspects of the complex concept of importance. For example, *closeness* measures how close a vertex is to all other vertices, formalizing our intuitive understanding that a vertex is more important when it has many short connections—that is, when it has only few edges to traverse to connect to many other vertices. The Pagerank measure, made famous by Google, defines centrality for a vertex based on the importance of its neighbors; importance is based on the links to a vertex, but Pagerank also takes into account that a link from an important vertex is less important when it links to many other vertices at the same time.

The matrix notation is an important basis for these algorithms, not only because it allows fast computation of the results, but also because matrix techniques have been fruitful for the development of new network measures and algorithms.

We have given a very short outline of how graphs can be used as the underlying mathematical concept for networks. Even when the process of modeling networks as graphs seems sometimes almost natural, it is important to be aware that vertices and edges are abstract information units that can be used for any kind of modeling, and that any mapping from a conceptual entity and relation to a vertex or an edge is an intellectual activity by the modeler. A vertex has an obvious application for modeling self-contained entities like persons or neurons, but it can also be used to model any kind of concept—for example, events (such as the meeting of two persons), or pieces of text (as in a hypertext), or concepts (as in ontologies and linked data).

An important application of graphs is the Resource Description Framework (RDF) developed by the W3C consortium, which is also responsible for the specification for XML and XHTML. The purpose of RDF is to express information about any kind of entity in a way that is readable by both humans *and* machines. This is done through formal statements consisting of a subject, a predicate and an object. Together they form a structure called a *triple* (please see Figure 2.17).

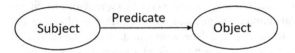

Figure 2.17 A graph representing an RDF triple.

Each statement is a small directed graph that ascribes one particular piece of information to the subject, for example:

```
[Walt Whitman]ₛ [is born on]ₚ [31.5.1819]ₒ
[Walt Whitman]ₛ [is creator of]ₚ [Leaves of Grass]ₒ
[Leaves of Grass]ₛ [is first published in]ₚ [1855]ₒ
```

The triples together form a labeled directed multigraph (please see Figure 2.18).

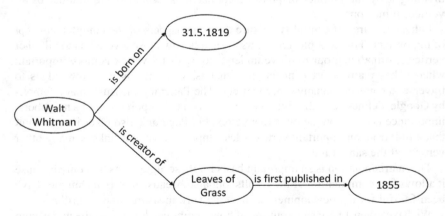

Figure 2.18 A graph representing the information in the three RDF triples about Whitman.

Because RDF is meant to be the language of a Semantic Web—that is, a collection of web resources which is not merely understandable by humans but can also be meaningfully processed by machines—the information about the subject, the predicate and the object is as far as possible expressed as an Internationalized Resource Identifier (IRI), an extension to URIs that extends the set of permitted characters to include all of Unicode. So, instead of the string "Walt Whitman," we can use a unique identifier based on an authority file. Instead of the string "is born on," which could vary in many ways across different encoders in different languages, we can use a defined predicate from a schema registry like schema.org that provides formal definitions of concepts like "birth" and "death." And instead of our free-form date which might look different depending on the country the encoder is living in, we can use a string and attach the information that it is a date following the structure and formatting specified in a particular schema. So, our original statement that "Walt Whitman was born on May 31, 1819" can be expressed in formal terms thus:

```
[http://viaf.org/viaf/2478331]ₛ [http://schema.org/
    birthDate]ₚ ["1819-5-31"^^<http://www.w3.org/2001/
    XMLSchema#date>]ₒ
```

Until now, for explanatory reasons, we have used our own system to notate the RDF triples, but the RDF specification by the W3C provides a series of formal systems, ranging from the very simple N-Triple's syntax up to rather verbose XML-serialization formats. The N-Triple is quite similar to what you have seen up to now. Re-expressed in that notation, our example would look like this (the triple would be on a single line in the file). The period at the end signals that the triple is complete:

```
<http://viaf.org/viaf/2478331><http://schema.org/birth
    Date> "1819-5-31"^^<http://www.w3.org/2001/
    XMLSchema#date>.
```

The vocabularies that provide the semantics of an RDF statement, such as birth or authorship, are not predefined; the RDF specification only defines a small set of information properties that specify abstract relationships between entities. So it is possible to express a given semantic concept in a variety of ways. But some vocabularies have been found to be especially useful—for example, Friend of a Friend (FOAF),[10] schema.org,[11] and the Simple Knowledge Organization System (SKOS),[12] which is also a W3C specification. RDF is meant to enable users to merge collections of RDF statements from different sources into one larger collection and mine this new collection for useful information, making use of simple inferences. There is also a retrieval language called SPARQL, which allows a user to query RDF data in a manner quite similar to SQL.[13] One of the largest RDF collections available is DBpedia, which extracts structured information from Wikipedia.[14] In particular, libraries have picked up the idea that their catalogues can be treated as a rich information set about books, and some have published these records as linked open data—that is, RDF data sets which are freely accessible on the web.[15]

An important further use of RDF, which extends and formalizes the establishment of specific vocabularies as described above, is in the description of ontologies. The term "ontology" has a long history in philosophy where it means something like "the study of what there is," including the discussion of "problems about the most general features and relations of the entities which do exist" (Hofweber, 2014). But since the 1990s, the term has been appropriated by computer science to refer to something different:

> an ontology defines a set of representational primitives with which to model a domain of knowledge or discourse. The representational primitives are typically classes (or sets), attributes (or properties), and relationships (or relations among class members). The definitions of the representational primitives include information about their meaning and constraints on their logically consistent application.
>
> (Gruber, 2009)

An important aspect of ontologies in this sense of the term is that they express an interdependent set of concepts that constitute the important aspects of some information domain, from the perspective of a specific community. An ontology provides a basis for sharing large collections of data within the community that subscribes to its definitions. However, precisely because they express a specific community perspective, they are also often challenged on grounds that they fail to accommodate individual or alternative views. In some cases, they may also be quite complicated to use because community processes can produce specifications that integrate many different points of views in more or less elegant ways.

The above is not meant as a complete introduction to RDF, but is supposed to outline some of the basic ideas behind RDF with an emphasis on their relation to the underlying graph model. A good introduction into the details of RDF can be found in the W3C tutorial on RDF.[16]

5 The modeling process

When we turn our attention to the modeling process itself, we can view it as a series of steps with the ultimate goal of meeting a set of requirements specified by future users of the data, or people who act on their behalf. These steps have been formalized early on in the domain of relational database design, but they also apply more generally. The first step is *conceptual data modeling*: the identification and description of the entities that make up the model and their relationship in the "universe of discourse"—i.e. that part of the world a modeler is modeling—and notation of the findings, for example in an entity-relationship diagram. So, for instance, if we are developing a data model for a database of letters, the entities in question might be the document, its creator, its creation date, the repository that holds the source document, and the country in which that repository is located. The entity-relationship diagram might describe these relationships by showing that every letter has a creator, a date of creation, and a source repository, and that the repository in turn is related to its country of location. The second is *logical data modeling*: defining the tables of a database according to the underlying relational model. Following our simple example, we might have one table representing the letters themselves (with their creation dates, creators, and repositories), and a second table might represent the repositories (with their locations and perhaps other information). The third is *physical data modeling*: optimization of the database for performance, in an actual implementation. There seems to be a consensus that this third step is usually done not by the data modeler but by an expert in database design. Ideally, both the conceptual and the logical model should be designed without any reference to the implementation, so that the implementation can be optimized or even replaced at a later time.

Although the distinction between the logical and the conceptual level may to some extent arise from specific database modeling techniques, it captures an important general aspect of data modeling. The logical model provides a structure for the data which allows the user to use a set of algorithms to answer questions of interest in relation to the data. For instance, in order to find all the letters held in a specific repository, we search for rows in the table containing the identifier for the repository in question. This computability is usually achieved by using a mathematical model: relation, in the case of databases. In this case, the logical model is a powerful formal abstraction, but it fails to represent most of the semantic information—that is, what we mean by "repository" and "creator" and "document." The conceptual model addresses this lack: it captures semantic information and offers an integral and embedded view of the data, organizing the information in such a way that the logical model can either be derived automatically or is at least very easy to derive. The distinction between the conceptual, the logical and the physical data model can be and has been applied to other areas of data modeling. We have followed this convention in our discussion of other forms of modeling, even if in most contexts it only highlights the fact that an equivalent to the conceptual model is missing.

In creating the conceptual model, an especially important aspect is abstraction. In its general meaning of identifying basic rules and features from specific examples, abstraction is a core element of all kinds of research and reflection. In computer science, it has some additional, more specific meanings. In relation to programming it refers to the principle of abstraction: the avoidance of repetition of code in two or more functions, by generalizing one function in such a way that it can be used in different contexts. In relation to data and programming, it is imperative to separate the abstract view of the data or program from the details of its implementation, and the approach to data modeling which distinguishes between the conceptual model, logical model and physical model is driven by this imperative. The separation of these layers allows us to abstract from the infinite complexity of the real world and use the conceptual model to outline the essential entities, attributes and relations, while deferring consideration of the details and constraints of the implementation. But, as with all forms of abstraction, this process is not innocent—there is no "natural" abstraction. What we deem to be essential is determined by the user requirements, but also by our world view, including our prejudices and our blind spots. And the tools of conceptual modeling have their share, as we all know, in forming the model, by making it easier to include one type of information and harder, if not impossible, to include another.

The goal of the modeling process, to fulfil the *user requirements*, also determines the relationship between the object and the data model. To understand this better, let us once again come back to our example of the letter. The text rendered at the beginning of this chapter is already a specific view of this object: a view that includes some kinds of information and disregards others. If we imagine sitting in an archive looking at the letter, we can perceive much more than just the characters on paper. We might note the size of the paper—perhaps it seems to be some standard size—and the stains on the paper which are visible at about the same place on both sides of both pages. The smell of the paper, its color, the way it has been folded and many other aspects could be part of our experience of the letter in an archive. In deciding what to preserve and what to disregard, we act on an understanding of the requirements of those who will use the modeled instances. If, for example, we are interested in creating a network visualization that will reveal the exchange of letters in a specific area at a specific time—for example, letters in Europe during the Enlightenment—then we will need some metadata about the author and recipient (such as their names and place of residence), and some metadata on the letter (when it was sent and received). If we are interested in a linguistic analysis of the language used in the letters, we will need the text of the letter itself and possibly also some linguistic annotation of components like tokens, sentences or part-of-speech information; if we are serving those who study the documents as material objects, we will need to capture information about the size, folding, and physical composition of the artifact itself. So, the intended usage of a digital entity like the transcription of a letter is the single most important factor to determine the selection, the amount and depth of the annotations and, more generally, the complexity and richness of the data model. Thus, a clear analysis of the requirements of the digital entities in question is an important step in data modeling. This is even true if the data being modeled will be only used by a single researcher interested in answering a specific research question, but it is critically important if the data will be used by a larger community of researchers or users in general.

In many ways, the process of creating a new data model or adapting an existing one is always unique, determined by the specific user requirements and the objects that are modeled. However, there are also some typical problem constellations and well-established solutions or design strategies that become familiar as one gains experience with data modeling. For example, we've already observed that by creating a distinct grouping of information *about* a data object (its metadata) we can facilitate retrieval of individual objects and management of groups of objects. Another basic modeling practice is the concept of *identifiers*: strings of alphanumeric characters that can be associated with data objects and used to locate and distinguish them uniquely. One further strategy in particular bears brief discussion here, because it enables us to create highly economical data structures: the concept of *indirection*. Imagine first our earlier example of the letter, which contains words that we know to be a name: "Mr Walt Whitman." Researchers often find names significant, so it would be of interest to add an annotation that makes explicit the fact that this is a name—for instance, thus:

```
<persName>
    <foreName>Walt</forename><surname>Whitman</surname>
<persName>
```

This simple encoding enables us to identify and extract all names from our text, but it does not tell us anything about the person named: their gender, birth and death date, and so forth, which is often crucial to the study of documents of this kind. We could expand our encoding of names to include this information:

```
<persName birth="1819-05-31" death="1892-03-26"
    gender="male">
    <foreName>Walt</forename><surname>Whitman</surname>
    <persName>
```

However, if this name appears several times in the course of the document, it will be cumbersome and inelegant (and error-prone) to repeat all of this contextual information with each reference. Instead, we can introduce an element of indirection and create a data structure elsewhere that contains this information, assign each entry a unique identifier, and then use that identifier to associate the name in the text with the biographical entry we have created.

Within the text:

```
<persName ref="#WW01">Walt<persName>
```

Somewhere else:

```
<person  xml:id="WW01"
    birth="1819-05-31"
    death="1892-03-2"
    gender="male">
    <persName><forename>Walt</forename>
        <surname>Whitman<surname>
    </persName>
</person>
```

This mechanism is directly analogous to the creation of separate tables for distinct categories of information in a relational database, using an identifier to "join" the tables. And in our networked world this reference can also be a pointer to an external authority file which provides unique identifiers for entities like persons collected by experts somewhere else—for example, VIAF:

```
<persName ref="http://viaf.org/viaf/2478331">Walt
    </persName>
```

Indirection is an important design strategy for digital information, because it improves the cleanliness of data and its usability.

The spectrum of possible usages of a digital artifact is large and it is impossible to cater to all needs in equal detail. So how in practice do we choose the requirements on which a model is based? One can observe that there are mainly two approaches arising from different digitization communities. On one hand, when digitization is undertaken by archives, libraries, and publishers, the data model is typically understood as an interchange format aimed at serving the needs of a diverse (and largely unforeseeable) user population. We might characterize this as a *curation-driven* approach to modeling, which emphasizes the open-ended usefulness of the data rather than a specific research goal. On the other hand, in cases where data is being created to support the creator's own research needs, the data model functions to express specific research ideas; this approach is more common among individual scholars and projects, and we might characterize it as *research-driven modeling*. Curation-driven modelers must make assumptions about what features of digital objects are of interest for most users and in most use cases, while research-driven modelers typically concentrate more (though not exclusively) on the needs of their own project. Curation-driven modelers in particular should keep one point in mind: the empirical study of digital resources shows that data models based on needs expressed by future users tend to be overly complex; users do not always judge realistically how they actually use digital resources. In practice, most users tend to perform only very simple keyword searches, even if the search interface offers more complex options based on specific aspects of a data model (Connaway and Dickey, 2010). So a requirement analysis in larger projects should consider basing its model on empirical studies of user behavior.

Thus, we have in practice two different approaches to the task of modeling. One seeks to anticipate and synthesize very different views on digital objects in order to establish standards, and this involves very specific processes for deciding on these user needs and connecting these new models with existing traditions of modeling—for example, those arising in library science. The other is interested mainly in expressing as exactly as possible the theoretical assumptions and research interests of one or more scholars. Curation-driven modelers often use a data model which represents a small selection of generic features that will be important to most users, and that will also enable the objects to be rendered and published in a way that will satisfy many users. Research-driven modelers, on the other hand, tend to model with greater semantic specificity and complexity, making more precise distinctions between concepts and using a larger descriptive vocabulary, enabling more specific research activities.

Thus far, we have looked at data modeling as if from the perspective of someone creating the very first data model for a given domain, but in fact that will rarely be the case. After many decades of data modeling in computer science, information science and digital humanities, most domains have one or more established modeling systems for their central research objects. Approaching the question of how to model our own data, then, may be as much a matter of appropriation and adaptation as of creation. Sometimes we find a model that exactly fits our use case. More often, we find a model that we can adapt, or which is even designed to be adapted and supports this by an explicit mechanism. Increasingly nowadays we can even find a *reference model*. Reference models are "generic conceptual models that formalize state-of-the-art or best-practice knowledge of a certain domain" (Becker et al. 2007, p. 2). They are often the results of many person-years of work and represent the knowledge of many practitioners in the domain. Thus, they often exhibit a complexity that can be daunting to a newcomer, who may wonder whether it is worthwhile to master the details of the reference model or better to simply design a model from scratch. However, it is worth thinking twice before building a completely new model. Most of the time the complexity of the models reflects the complexities of the data. What may look easy or even trivial in the beginning will become much less so if one had a closer look at the data with all its special cases and exceptions. The same is true for uses of the data, some of which become evident only further along in the design process. A well-designed reference model embodies detailed knowledge of how data in the wild can vary, and of how it is likely to be used. Those coming from outside the humanities fields may sometimes underestimate the complexity of historical and literary data, and prefer to start from scratch even if there is a reference model. Often, this approach seems to be justified by fast advances in developing an initial model, but as edge cases and less common examples come into view, the process reveals the challenges and difficulties that necessitated the complexity of the reference model. Before long, one finds oneself reinventing a system like TEI or CIDOC-CRM, but without the years of prior research and broad community input, and reworking the initial data that had seemed adequate at the outset. There are certainly cases where creating a new model is the right thing to do: for instance, in cases where a new theoretical approach is being proposed, or where the existing models suffer from known limitations. But in these cases, the responsible path to developing the new model is likely to carry the same responsibilities and degree of challenge: the need to involve domain experts, to reconcile diverse usage scenarios, and to consider the wild heterogeneity of real-world data.

There are two closely interconnected reasons why anyone doing data modeling should know about reference models: they serve as both the social and the technical aspects of formal information exchange. Reference models are not simply disembodied technical specifications: usually, there is also a community of experts working with them, developing them, exchanging ideas and spreading knowledge about them. Tapping into this font of expertise can be very useful for anyone interested in data modeling. Corresponding to this social dimension is a technical dimension: the possibility of *interoperability*. Basing a model on an existing reference model helps ensure that the resulting data can be connected as easily as possible to other data from the same domain—that is, it makes sure that the features the model has in common with the community's understanding are explicitly aligned with that understanding, via the reference model (which serves as a kind of hub). Adaptation of a reference model in this way is a common procedure in data modeling, and there are also other ways of reusing and referencing existing models. There is a useful literature that covers different approaches in detail (see, for instance, Becker et al., 2007).

6 Evaluation

There are many contexts where we need to evaluate data models. As part of their developmental workflow, digital projects have to decide on which data models to use, and if they adapt an existing model or develop their own, they need to evaluate its effectiveness. In a pedagogical context—for instance, in seminars on specific data modeling techniques like XML or relational databases, students will propose different modeling solutions, and teachers need to show the strengths and flaws in these approaches. Professional organizations seeking to recommend good practice to their members—for instance, the MLA's Committee on Scholarly Editions—need to assess available models not only in relation to their practical fitness, but also in relation to their long-term viability for the specific community.

Any evaluation of data models will take two different kinds of factors into account. First, there are internal factors that concern the properties of the data model itself—for example, whether it is consistent and free of contradictions, whether it covers the topic domain fully, whether it is scalable to different levels of use (including both simple and advanced applications), and whether it is complete and stable, or still under development and likely to change. In cases where there is a choice of data models, these considerations would inform that choice, but even in cases where there are really no alternatives, the assessment process may reveal areas where a weakness in the model can be compensated for, through adaptation or additional documentation. Along with these practical considerations, there are also some that have more to do with usability and aesthetics: Is the model succinct and economically designed? Is its architecture easy to understand and learn? These are probably not factors that would dissuade us from using a model that was the right choice in all other respects, but in identifying such weaknesses we can protect our work from their ill effects.

Second, there are external factors to consider. How does the model fit the user requirements in our specific situation? How well is the model supported with existing software? What are the costs of its application, in training, documentation, tool development, and maintenance? How is it situated in relation to other data models? Does it make use of existing standards whenever possible, or does it duplicate those standards? Does it support the creation of linked open data? Is it well supported by a strong user community? If the model is part of an ongoing research effort (and hence likely to change over time), are there open mechanisms for participation in that work?

Evaluating data models is from one perspective a highly practical matter. In this view, data models have to serve functions specified by the user requirements, and the key issue for their evaluation is how well they serve these functions. Success or failure in this case will be closely linked with the effectiveness of communication between a data modeler and the domain specialists who are supposed to work with the model at the end. However, with "curation-driven" or "archival" data models (which are developed with deliberate deferral or generalization of specific user requirements), we face a more complex situation: the dilemma between standardization and expressiveness, or, put another way, the fact that the better a model suits one specific case the worse it will fare in the general case, and vice versa. Given the prevalence of these more "archival" data modeling efforts in the digital humanities, we need to consider how to evaluate such data models in other less practically driven ways.

Data models become more robust the greater the diversity of user requirements being considered in their design; in these cases, data models will cover more use cases and will be applicable to more situations. But making provisions for a broad range of specific user needs usually increases either the complexity of the model (the TEI Guidelines offer a striking illustration) or the level of generality at which the model operates (as in the case of a standard like Dublin Core). Though a more complex model will be more likely to cover more of the user requirements of any given project in its domain, there is still a theoretical limit to that likelihood; no model can cover all conceivable needs simply through added complexity. However, resorting to generalization carries its own risks. The more general a model is in the way it represents the world—that is, the more it relies on broadly defined concepts like "creator" rather than narrowly defined concepts like "translator" or "editor"—the greater the risk that users will find it lacking in the semantic specificity needed for meaningful communication. With very generally framed models such as Dublin Core, the model fails to express differences that are considered essential to specific research domains. Interestingly, neither over-complexity nor over-generality prevents users from working with an ill-fitting model. Instead, they will try to find workarounds: by appropriating categories manifestly meant for a different purpose ("tag abuse") or by compensating for overly general semantics through local usage conventions and documentation. These behaviors can themselves be used as a kind of evaluative index to assess the fitness of a model.

The distinction between what we called above "curation-driven" and "research-driven" modeling provides an important framework for evaluation, since these two modeling approaches entail different kinds of user requirements and overall goals for relationship between the model and the data. In the case of curation-driven modeling, long-term harmonization of the model with existing reference models is a high priority, and a looser fit between data and model is usually tolerated in the interests of achieving uniformity of workflow and consistency across the data sets being curated. With research-driven modeling, it is much more important to achieve a close fit between the data and the model (such that the model needs to be more complex and less general), and the tolerance for idiosyncrasy and even experimentalism is much greater; research-driven models may be based on (or may later be harmonized with) reference models, but the motives for doing so are curatorial. Similarly, the two approaches also entail different mechanisms for revising their models based on evaluation: an individual researcher might adjust a personal research schema incrementally based on new observations about a document set or the results of a test analysis, whereas a library digitization group or standards body would typically have a formal procedure for identifying changes, assessing backwards compatibility and long-term impact, requesting public comment, documenting the changes made, and disseminating the results.

While fulfilling user requirements seems to be the most important evaluative criterion, there is also another criterion that we would call tentatively the issue of "truthfulness" or "adequacy" of a model. The consensus in the digital humanities is that data modeling makes an interpretation of an object explicit—see for example, the TEI P5 chapter, "A Gentle Introduction to XML." Modeling does not simply mirror an external reality, but is an active process that depends on the social construction of a segment of the world. If we imagine a continuum with a radical subjectivist position at one end and a radical objectivist position at the other, digital humanities data modeling activities generally occupy a position in the middle that focuses on the role of social consensus and context-dependent negotiation of meaning. It is important to emphasize that this middle ground is as importantly distinct from radical subjectivism as it is from radical objectivism: it is incorrect to imagine that if we abandon the latter we are necessarily adopting the former. The role that social consensus plays in establishing our models is precisely to move them out of the grounds of purely private meaning into a space where meaning must be negotiated and must be intelligible and plausible to others in order to be useful.

For research-driven modeling, the argumentative emphasis is on the role of interpretation as a way of demonstrating the close ties between data modeling and other activities of scholarship, and evaluation of this kind of modeling will rest on whether the modeling reveals something unexpected or novel in the source materials. On the other hand, in curation-driven data modeling there is a stronger motive to emphasize shared modeling expectations, since the goal is to create data that will serve a broad and future constituency. The CIDOC-CRM, for example, describes its goal as being "to promote a shared understanding of cultural heritage information" (CIDOC-CRM, 2016). In these cases, the modeling of an object thus has to conform to the social construction of this object, and often a fruitful way to access this social construction is a closer look into older codifications of descriptions, such as standards of book cataloguing. In this perspective, we evaluate the model not by its truth-value, but with respect to how well it captures a shared understanding of some aspect of the world, independent of more ambitious theories of truth.

A third important dimension of evaluation for data models is their robustness—their ability to perform well and retain their expressiveness across different usage environments and applications. As we have already noted, good design practice attempts as much as possible to produce data models independent from specific processing contexts, although in practice it can be difficult to avoid some dependencies or anticipation of those contexts. This might be because there is currently only one context in which we can imagine the data being used, or because the usage requirements for the model revolve around a specific application (for reasons which may be social or institutional) in ways that exercise an overriding pressure on the design process. Bearing these pitfalls in mind, we need to be especially careful to distinguish information that is needed to support a specific workflow from information that will operate more generally regardless of the context of usage. The former can be represented as part of a processing model (of which there might eventually be more than one to accommodate different processing contexts) while the latter is more properly part of the core data model that we expect to operate more universally. To evaluate the robustness of a model in a context where only one processing context currently exists, we may need to construct hypothetical scenarios: for instance, imagining future possible processing tools, adoption of our data model by different communities of users, or aggregation of our data within contexts that we do not control (such as institutional repositories). A final dimension of robustness which our evaluation should take into account is the ability to survive the rapid evolutions and revolutions of the field within which our models must operate, including changes to operating systems, software applications, data standards, and metamodels. In order to assess the robustness of our models in this respect, it may be helpful to look at historical examples and case studies to understand the vulnerabilities of specific modeling approaches.

On the first glance, choosing a data model may look like a primarily technical problem, but it soon becomes evident that it is embedded in social practices and relations. By using the framework of some larger standard like TEI or CIDOC-CRM, or the metadata scheme embedded in a tool like Omeka, one chooses a specific way of looking at digital objects, a way to discuss and even to evaluate strategies, and also a community of practice for those activities, even if one is not immediately aware of the full implications of that choice. And the reverse is also true: the decision to develop a project-specific modeling approach is also a decision concerning one's relationship to standards, and carries with it certain practical and social consequences concerning data longevity, shareability, and so forth.

There are also organizational factors that often play a decisive role in the choice of a data model—for example, the expertise of the people involved in a project. The best choice, considered abstractly, might nonetheless be a poor solution if the people who are supposed to perform the modeling lack the expertise to use it. In this last point, there may be a more complex cost-benefit analysis to be done: for a short-term project with few documents, the effort of familiarizing a scholarly team with a complex standard like the TEI might not be justified, but for a longer term project where data longevity is an important outcome, the cost of training is probably outweighed by other considerations such as sustainability and interchange.

7 Perspectives and challenges

Data modeling is not yet fully understood as a unified field with common underlying principles and concepts. Such a view would help us in the digital humanities to better apply and compare data models from different subject domains: for instance, to adapt a modeling approach (such as critical apparatus) from one domain for use in another, or to perform a comparative analysis of modeling approaches. But it would also yield a more deeply theorized understanding of our models that would translate directly into a stronger understanding of the distinct research value of our work. This book is a step towards such an understanding, but a significant amount of intellectual work has yet to be done to achieve a full theory that brings all aspects of data modeling into this integrated view.

An important resource for this fuller understanding lies in ongoing research outside the immediate domain of digital humanities. There is ongoing research in specific fields—for example, on how to improve certain aspects of relational databases, XML or graphs, so as to extend the presentational effectiveness of the models, or the ability to translate between the models. Some of this research is taking place in standards bodies that are seeking to establish new guidelines or extensions to existing standards to solve problems that have become visible through usage. The W3C is an important venue for research and development in XML-related standards, and the working groups of the TEI regularly produce new additions to the TEI Guidelines which have broad significance for data modeling as well as immediate practical import for text encoding. Computer science, with all of its applied forms, is another important source of research impetus and produces general modeling approaches in advance of specific applications. It provides a stock from which others can choose solutions.

And there is also a steady stream of new problems for data modeling created by new perspectives on our research objects, which raise the question of whether new standards may be necessary. As cultural heritage institutions expand their mission briefs to curate an ever-wider range of challenging cultural objects—for example computer games and records of game play—new data models have to be devised to support this work. And current research on innovative forms of resource and content description using text mining will produce new metadata schemas integrating these new forms of information.

These three perspectives—the research on an integrated view on data modeling, the theoretically driven research on new options in data modeling, and the research driven by new needs in handling digital objects—will create new insights into the field of data modeling. This process has been going on for some decades now and has produced many of the concepts discussed in this chapter and this book in general. But recently there have also been shifts in the pragmatics of data modeling which may change the field profoundly—at least in parts. For a long time data modeling was done by humans who formalized expert knowledge. But with huge amounts of data available, and more and more sophisticated methods of mining them for structures by using machine learning techniques, algorithmic approaches to modeling offer better and cheaper results and scale more efficiently. However, although some of these models solve specific tasks very reliably, the kinds of data on which they operate are quite difficult to align with our human understanding of the data. For instance, in word embeddings, vectors in n-dimensional space represent words, and their proximity to one another expresses similarity, but it is not clear what the vectors themselves "mean," apart from the purely comparative analysis they yield. Furthermore, the resulting modeled data doesn't yield a higher-level understanding of the data (for instance, at the documentary level) that can be applied to the analysis of other problems. These approaches thus withdraw the data model from human analysis in a way that poses a challenge to data modeling as an intellectual (as opposed to computational) field.

The trend to data-driven data modeling has been mirrored by a similar shift in the specification of user requirements. Traditionally, user requirements were defined by domain experts, who were assumed to know best how information resources would be used. But as mentioned earlier, empirical research on the usage of digital resources showed a significant trend: the real use is most often much simpler than the usage anticipated and described by domain experts. In other words, domain experts have difficulties in predicting how much work their colleagues (both experts and novices) are ready to invest in learning interfaces and query languages. This insight has led to a shift to a data-driven analysis of the requirements in curation-driven data modeling.

Last but not least, we expect new impulses from data-driven data modeling for an old discussion: the semantics of a data model. Traditionally, the semantics of a data model are conveyed by the column headers of a table, the names of an entity in an entity relationship model, the name of an XML element, its description in a handbook and its content model in the schema, or the use of an element of an ontology in an RDF triple. Even if there is a formal ontology it doesn't really describe the semantics but aligns different objects (the set of alignments can be understood as a semantic representation on its own). This approach relies at some point on humans understanding the meaning of a concept as expressed in human language in these descriptive contexts. Some argue (as Stephen Ramsay does later in this volume) that the semantics of an element in a data model are constituted by the processes attached to this element. But only few would say that the semantics, let us say, of the concept of a "name" are really described by the ability to search for it in the contacts list in our phone and then press "dial." Processes using data models foreground the functions of individual data elements, but functions are not full descriptions of the use of a term, let alone its full range of possible use. Large data collections now provide new possibilities to describe semantics using ideas from the field of distributional semantics by describing words as vectors based on the analysis of many co-occurrences. Although these approaches have yet to solve some problems like the handling of word disambiguation, they do allow for a deeper understanding of concept relations—but they have the severe drawback that the data representation is still meaningless to humans. So one of the main cornerstones of data modeling from its very beginning would be threatened by these developments: until very recently, data modeling was understood as a matter of course to be an activity which produces formal descriptions usable by machines and humans. But now we start to see models which are more efficient for machines and incomprehensible to humans. How we handle this challenge will be the basis for most work done in the realm of data modeling in the future.

Notes

1   Cited after Folsom/Price: Walt Whitman Archive. Available at: www.whitmanarchive.org/biography/correspondence/tei/loc.01920.html Line breaks and other whitespace added using the reproduction of the letter. Available at: www.whitmanarchive.org/biography/correspondence/figures/loc.01920.001.jpg.

2   "Model" in: *Longman Dictionary of Contemporary English*. Available at: www.ldoce online.com/dictionary/model_1

3   Available at: https://modelpractice.wordpress.com/2012/07/04/model-stachowiak/

4   If we choose instead to identify entities such as place names algorithmically, we are essentially relocating the modeling into the detection algorithm, which represents our understanding of what a "place name" is and how to recognize one.

5   Usually capital letters are used for the name of a set, while small letters are used for members of a set. Curly braces are used to enclose the members of the set.

6   The result of "a modulo b" is the remainder of the division of a by b—for example, 8 modulo 3 = 2. If x modulo 2 = 0, then x is an even number. Strictly speaking, the expression "x modulo 2 = 0" makes "$x \in \mathbb{N}$" superfluous.

7   See the Glossary for more information.

8   An example of this kind of approach to data modeling is the linguistic data model Text Corpus Format, which enables multi-layered annotations of text, where each layer is in XML. See https://weblicht.sfs.uni-tuebingen.de/weblichtwiki/index.php/The_TCF_ Format.

9   There is also the term "tree" in graph theory which refers to an undirected graph without loops where each vertex is connected to any other by one path. Obviously, this is more generic than the term "tree" used in XML contexts.

10   Available at: www.foaf-project.org/

11   Available at: http://schema.org/

12   Available at: www.w3.org/2004/02/skos/

13   Available at: www.w3.org/TR/sparql11-overview/

14   Available at: http://wiki.dbpedia.org/

15   In the US, see for instance the Linked Data Service at the Library of Congress at: http://id.loc.gov; in Europe, see, for example, http://labs.europeana.eu/api/linked-open-data-introduction or the Bavarian State library, one of the largest libraries in Germany at: http://lod.b3kat.de/doc/download/

16   Available at: www.w3.org/TR/rdf11-primer/

References

Becker, J., Knackstedt, R., Pfeiffer, D., and Janiesch, C., 2007. Configurative Method Engineering—On the Applicability of Reference Modeling Mechanisms in Method Engineering. In: *AMCIS (Americas Conference on Information Systems) 2007 Proceedings*. Paper 56. Available at: http://aisel.aisnet.org/amcis2007/56 (accessed August 20, 2016).

Chen, P., 1976. The Entity-Relationship Model—Toward a Unified View of Data. *ACM Transactions on Database Systems*, 1(1), pp. 9–36.

CIDOC (International Committee for Documentation), 2016. *The CIDOC Conceptual Reference Model (CIDOC CRM)*. Available at: www.cidoc-crm.org/.

Ciula, A., and Eide, Ø., 2007. Modeling in Digital Humanities: Signs in Context. *Digital Scholarship in the Humanities*, 32(suppl_1), i33–i46.

Codd, E.F., 1970. A Relational Model of Data for Large Shared Data Banks. *Communications of the ACM*. Available at: www.seas.upenn.edu/~zives/03f/cis550/codd.pdf.

Connaway, L.S., Dickey, T.J., 2010. *The Digital Information Seeker: Report of the Findings from Selected OCLC, RIN, and JISC User Behaviour Projects*. OCLC Research. Available at: www.jisc.ac.uk/media/documents/publications/reports/2010/digitalinformationseeker report.pdf.

Date, C.J., 2012. *SQL and Relational Theory. How to Write Accurate SQL Code* (2nd ed.). Sebastopol: O'Reilly.

DeRose, S.J., Durand, D., Mylonas, E., and Renear, A.H., 1990. What is Text Really? *Journal of Computing in Higher Education*, 1(2), pp. 3–26.

Edgington, D., 2008. Conditionals. In: E.N. Zalta (Ed.) 2008. *The Stanford Encyclopedia of Philosophy*. Stanford, CA: Stanford University. Available at: http://plato.stanford.edu/archives/win2008/entries/conditionals/ (accessed August 20, 2016).

Freeman, L.C., 2004. *The Development of Social Network Analysis: A Study in the Sociology of Science*. Vancouver, BC: Empirical Press.

Gruber, T., 2009. Ontology. In: L. Liu and M.T. Özsu (Eds.) 2009. *Encyclopedia of Database Systems*. Berlin: Springer-Verlag.

Halmos, P., 1960. *Naive Set Theory*. Reprint 2015. Oxford: Benediction Classics.

Harold, E.R. and Means, W.S., 2004. *XML in a Nutshell* (3rd ed.) Sebastopol: O'Reilly.

Hofweber, T., 2014. Logic and Ontology. In: E.N. Zalta (Ed.) 2014. *The Stanford Encyclopedia of Philosophy*. Stanford, CA: Stanford University. Available at: http://plato.stanford.edu/archives/fall2014/entries/logic-ontology/.

Hopcroft, J.E., Motwani, R., and Ullman, J.D., 2013. *Introduction to Automata Theory, Languages, and Computation* (3rd ed.) Edinburgh Gate: Pearson.

Kastens, U. and Kleine Büning, H., 2014. *Modellierung. Grundlagen und formale Methoden*. Munich: Carl Hanser Verlag.

Makinson, D., 2008. *Sets, Logic and Maths for Computing*. London: Springer.

Newman, M.E.J., 2010. *Networks: An Introduction*. Oxford: Oxford University Press.

Partee, B.H., ter Meulen, A., and Wall, R.E., 1990. *Mathematical Methods in Linguistics*. Dordrecht: Kluwer.

Pollard, S., 2015. *Philosophical Introduction to Set Theory*. First printed 1990. Mineola, NY: Dover.

Renear, A., 2005. Text from Several Different Perspectives: The Role of Context in Markup Semantics. In: Nicolas, C. and Moneglia, M. (Eds.) *Proceedings of the 2003 Conference on Computers, Literature, and Philology*. Florence: University of Florence, pp. 25–33. Available at: http://ebooks.mpdl.mpg.de/ebooks/Record/EB000323452.

Rosen, K.H., 2013. *Discrete Mathematics and its Applications*. New York: McGraw-Hill.

Tal, E., 2015. Measurement in Science. In: E.N. Zalta (Ed.) *The Stanford Encyclopedia of Philosophy*. Stanford, CA: Stanford University. Available at: http://plato.stanford.edu/archives/sum2015/entries/measurement-science/.

Text Encoding Initiative (TEI), 2016. *P5: Guidelines for Electronic Text Encoding and Interchange*. Text Encoding Initiative. Available at: www.tei-c.org/release/doc/tei-p5-doc/en/html/.

Part II

Topics in digital humanities data modeling

3 How modeling standards evolve

The case of the TEI

Lou Burnard

1 Standards . . .

There is a very old joke about standards which says: "The nice thing about standards is that you have so many to choose from." It is attributed by Wikiquotes to Andrew Tanenbaum (1981, p. 168) and has also recently been given a new lease of life by a popular xkcd cartoon. Like many old jokes, it plays on an internal contradiction (a structuralist might say "opposition"). On one hand, the world is a complicated place in which we value diversity and complexity; on the other, we value standards as a means of controlling that diversity. Standards may be considered to be instruments of control, managed or even imposed by a centralizing authority, or randomly spread out for our delight as if on a buffet. This contradiction is particularly noticeable when the process of standardization has been protracted, whether because the technologies concerned are only gradually establishing themselves, or because of disagreements amongst the decision-making parties, but is a tension inherent to the process. In the world of consumer electronics, for example, there is a financial market-driven imperative to establish standards as rapidly as possible so that new products may be developed more cheaply and efficiently, and at the same time an equally strong market-driven imperative not to standardize at all, so long as one's own product has significant market share in comparison with those of the would-be standardizers. Above all, successful standardization requires the existence of a shared perception, or model of how a product should look or behave, before any consensus can emerge. For this reason, it seems useful to consider how the concept of information modeling has emerged, and has itself been the subject of standardization.

In the academic research community, similar tensions underlie the gradual evolution of individual ways of thought into communities of practice, and the gradual consensus-based emergence from these of de facto and (eventually) "real" standards. Scientific research communities are tribal both by temperament and in their practice for a variety of reasons, both good and bad. Tribes define themselves by shared perceptions and priorities, by shared models of reality, and by the specific tools or methods that support their activities. (The opposition often made between methodology and discipline is thus at best debatable—as witnessed by the fact that polemical articles entitled "What is digital humanities?" generally debate it). The adoption of a particular set of assumptions about what objects and methods are fruitful and pertinent can become deeply entwined with a research community's sense of its own identity, jealously guarded, aggressively promoted, and coercively imposed on the agnostic. At the same time, if such assumptions are to be adopted by the wider community, their proponents must seek to establish a consensus. If their model is to achieve recognition, it will not be by fiat from any central body or establishment, though such entities may well play a role in facilitating a context in which consensus and (perhaps) standardization can be achieved—for example, by specific research funding policies.

Standardization has a frivolous younger sibling called fashion, whose role in determining the ways in which particular modes of thought become institutional-ized (or standardized) should not be neglected. Fashion reflects and (occasionally) affects broader socio-technological changes in ways that are hard to determine. Is the uptake of Twitter within the research community cause, effect, or symptom of shifts in the way we perceive the humanities' central role of explaining ourselves and our surroundings to ourselves? If we agree with, for example, Jones (2014) that the eversion of the digital world into the "real world" has been entirely transformative, does it make any sense to insist on a continuity in the models we apply, and the discourse derived from their application? And contrariwise, if we think that nothing fundamental has changed, and hence that the nature of the devices we use for communication is largely a matter of fashion, are we comfortable with the implication that there is a clear continuity between (say) clay tablet and mobile phone, such that the model we apply to describe messages on one will also be useful to describe the other? The higher one advances up the mountain, the easier it becomes to see the world as simply brown, blue, or green, but the harder it becomes to see the nuances in the shadows.

A good definition of modeling is that it is the process by which we construct meaning from observed data. The classic scientific procedure is to form a hypothesis and then search for observed data, either to support or to contradict it. Living now in an over-instrumented world of data-excess, we tend to do the reverse: that is, we look at the data and try to construct a hypothesis to support it, using the best tools at hand, or the tools that seem to give results consistent with our own internal model. The currently fashionable technique of topic-modeling is a case in point. Yet we do well to remember that the only reason we are now in a world awash with comparable data is precisely because standards for the representation of that data have now become reasonably pervasive and effective.

2 Data versus text

Our focus in this chapter is the evolution of standardized data models in the humanities and social sciences, and we therefore take a historical perspective. Nevertheless, much of what we discuss seems applicable more widely, both across other scientific disciplines, and even perhaps within a synchronic frame-work. One does not have to be a historian to suspect that the kinds of story we tell now about what our predecessors thought are likely to have been determined as a consequence of that body of tradition as much as they are by autonomous reflection.

2.1 Data modeling in the real world

The word "modeling" as used throughout this book is naturally inseparable from any kind of semiotic process, but in the domain of informatics began to be applied in a self-conscious and conscientious way in the 1960s and 1970s. This was the first period of massive expansion of digital technologies into the "real world" of business, public service, the research community, and, of course, the military.

This was the age of the mainframe computer, those massive power-hungry, water-cooled assemblies of transistors and storage systems based on huge magnetized ferric surfaces, on glass or metal disk, or spools of plastic tape. For our present purposes, the salient feature of those now superseded machines was not so much that they needed to be maintained in special air-conditioned environments or attended to by serious people in white coats—the same, after all, is true of the server farms deployed by Amazon or Google which have replaced them in today's world—but rather that they came in so many radically different forms. In many respects, of course, an IBM 370 and an ICL 1906, a CDC 6400, or a Univac 1100 machine all did much the same thing, relying on essentially the same set of mathematical and physical principles: a central processing unit, data storage, a set of predefined instructions for manipulating discrete pieces of data, input and output peripherals, and so on. But wherever there was scope for divergence—in the number of bits used to represent a single unit of storage, in the assembly code used to generate sequences of instructions, in the software libraries and operating systems built on top of all these things—they diverged. For this reason, as much as because of the significant amount of effort needed to keep these monolithic machines functioning at all, software developers and users alike rapidly began to focus on questions of interoperability of data and (to a lesser extent) software, and hence to participate in a variety of industry-led forums, user groups, standardization bodies, and so on. Typical also of the period was the tension between standardized programming languages such as COBOL or ALGOL, developed as a result of discussion amongst representatives of a number of interested but competitive parties, and imposed standards such as FORTRAN developed by a dominant manufacturer (in those days, IBM) or user group (in those days, the hard sciences). This applied even to such an arbitrary matter as the internal representation of character sets: IBM continued to support only EBCDIC, its own multi-flavored 8 bit code, for thirty years after the US government had mandated use of the industry-developed 7 bit ASCII code, the ancestor of today's Unicode. Again, this kind of tension does not seem entirely alien to contemporary experience.

A key driver in the impetus towards more and more standardization (and hence the focus on modeling techniques) across the data-processing departments of corporations and administrations worldwide was the rise of the corporate database.

As both commercial and government organizations surveyed their information-processing activities, the need to integrate previously discrete systems (many of them not yet digital) became more and more evident. Evangelists for data analysis, such as John Sowa (Sowa, 1984), argued that integrated database systems would offer an escape from existing preconceptions and from the design constraints inherent in pre-electronic systems. Existing manual methods were not designed to facilitate either the sharing of data or multiple ways of accessing subsets of it. When converting manual systems to electronic form, therefore, it was correspondingly important that these constraints should not be perpetuated in a new and more insidious form by requiring of the user, for example, a detailed knowledge of the minutiae of a particular computer's filing system before permitting access to the information it contained. Neither should the computerized system simply mimic the manual system it was designed to replace. The manual system had been a means to an end, not an end in itself. To achieve these objectives, deep ontological questions about the goal of an enterprise and the information it processed had to be confronted and resolved. Hence, we find database designers confidently asserting that their task was to abstract away from the mundane world of order forms, invoices, and customer address lists, in order to create a structure representing the information of which those documents were the physical trace, by which they meant the formal identification of real world entities and relationships among them. Sowa dignified this process with the name of conceptual analysis: "the work of philosophers, lawyers, lexicographers, systems analysts and database administrators" (Sowa, 1984, p. 294; see also http://ontolog.cim3.net/forum/ontolog-forum/2009-10/msg00165.html), but it would not have been an entirely strange concept for any medieval philosopher familiar with Plato.

By the early 1980s, several competing "standard methodologies" (note the plural) were being marketed for the process of defining reality in a business context—that is, those portions of reality that mattered to an enterprise, along with a wide range of complex (and expensive) software tools to simplify both that task, and the semi-automatic generation and implementation of actual data systems corresponding with the model so painstakingly arrived at. These systems naturally implemented a range of different data models. IBM, still a player at this time, had invested too much in its hierarchic system IMS not to see this as the only natural way of working; the business community, on the other hand, had worked hard in its CODASYL committee to develop what was called a network model; while in the rapidly expanding computer science research community, the relational model developed by ex-IBM staff Codd and Date was clearly the way of the future. Whether you regarded your data as hierarchically organized nodes, as a network of nodes, or as normalized relations, there was software to support you, and a community of practice to talk up the differences amongst these orthodoxies and their implications for data representation rather than their similarities.

A book called *Data and Reality* (Kent, 1978), first published in 1978, comes from that heroic age of database design and development, when such giants as Astrahan, Chen, Chamberlin, Codd, Date, Nijssen, Senko, Tschritzis, and others were slugging it out over the relative merits of the relational, network, and binary database models and the abstractions they supposedly modeled. Kent's quietly subversive message was that this was a struggle predominantly over terminology. He noted that almost all of these passionately advocated models were fundamentally very similar, differing only in their names, and in the specific compromises they chose when confronted by the messiness of reality. Whether you call them relations or objects or records, the globs of storage handled by every database system were still combinations of fields containing binary representations of perceptions of reality, chosen and combined, for their utility in a specific context. The claim that such systems modeled reality in any complete sense is easy to explode; it is remarkable, though, that we still need to be reminded, again and again, that such systems model only what it is (or has been) useful for their creators to believe. Kent is sanguine about this epistemological lacuna: "I can buy food from the grocer, and ask a policeman to chase a burglar, without sharing these people's view of truth and beauty" (Kent, 1978, p. 202), but for us, living in an age of massively interconnected knowledge repositories, which has developed almost accidentally from the world of more or less well-regulated corporate database systems, close attention to their differing underlying assumptions should be a major concern. This applies to the differently constructed communities of practice and knowledge which we call "academic disciplines," just as much as it does to the mechanical information systems those communities use in support of their activities.

In its time, Kent's book was also remarkable for introducing the idea that data representations and the processes carried out with them might be represented in a unified way. At a period when the processes carried out by computer programs were thought of as belonging to an entirely different conceptual domain from the data on which they operated, the notion that it might be convenient to consider as a single entity both a piece of data and the processes that might be associated with it was distinctly innovative. Kent's work is thus an important precursor of what we now call object-oriented processing, which is characterized by this unified approach. An object-oriented programmer defines objects that combine data structures with the methods appropriate to them, rather than defining data structures and data processes independently, as the dominant programming styles of the 1970s required. Kent's work also reminds us of some fundamental ambiguities and assumptions often swept under the carpet during conceptual analysis of any period. Are objects really uniquely identifiable? "What does 'catching the same plane every Friday' really mean? It may or may not be the same physical airplane. But if a mechanic is scheduled to service the same plane every Friday, it had better be the same physical airplane" (Kent, 1978, p. 7). The way an object is used is not just part of its definition. It may also determine its existence as a distinct object.

Kent's understanding of the way language works is clearly based on the Sapir-Whorf hypothesis of linguistic relativity: indeed, he quotes Whorf approvingly: "Language has an enormous influence on our perception of reality. Not only does it affect how and what we think about, but also how we perceive things in the first place" (Kent, 1978, p. 200). There is an odd overlap between his reminders about the mocking dance that words and their meanings perform together and contemporaneous debates within the emerging field now known as GOFAI, or "Good Old Fashioned Artificial Intelligence."[1] And we can also see echoes of similar concerns within what was in the 1970s regarded as a new and different scientific discipline called Information Retrieval, concerned with the extraction of facts from documents. Although Kent explicitly rules text out of discussion ("We are not attempting to understand natural language, analyze documents, or retrieve information from documents," Kent, 1978, p. vi) his argument throughout the book reminds us that data is really a special kind of text, subject to all the hermeneutical issues we tend mistakenly to consider relevant only in the textual domain.

This is particularly true at the meta-level, of how we talk about our data models, and the systems we use to manipulate them. Because they were designed for the specific rather the general, and because they were largely developed in commercially competitive contexts, the database systems of the 1970s and 1980s proliferated terms and distinctions amongst many different kinds of entity, to an extent that Kent (like Occam before him) argues goes well beyond necessity. This applies to such comparatively arcane distinctions as those between entity, attribute, and relationship, or between type and domain, all of which terms have subtly different connotations in different contexts, though all are reducible to a more precise set of simple primitives. It applies also to the distinction between data and metadata. Many of the database systems of the 1980s and 1990s insisted that you should abstract away all the metadata for your systems into a special kind of database variously called a data dictionary, catalogue, or schema, using entirely different tools and techniques from those used to manipulate the data itself. This is a needless obfuscation once you realize that you cannot do much with your data without also processing its metadata. In more recent times, one of the more striking improvements that XML (Extensible Markup Language: the W3C-defined de facto standard for representing information on the web) made to SGML (Standard Generalized Markup Language: the ISO standard for markup languages from which XML was derived) was the ability to express both a schema and the objects it describes using the same language. The representations of real world objects manipulated by an information system are themselves objects in the real world, and should therefore be modeled in the same way. How best to document the intended meaning of those representations—what is usually called the semantics of an XML schema—remains a matter that only a few current XML systems (notably the TEI) explicitly consider.

2.2 Data modeling in the humanities

According to the foundational myth of the digital humanities, it all began in 1950 or thereabouts when a Jesuit father called Roberto Busa conceived the idea of using a machine to tabulate every occurrence of every word, and the lemmas associated with the words, and the senses of those lemmas, in the works of St Thomas Aquinas. His vision was realized (some years later), with the aid of Thomas Watson of IBM, and you can see it still working today at: www. corpusthomisticum.org/it/index.age.

Of course, as Busa himself points out in a characteristically self-deprecating article published in 1980, he was far from having been the first person to have considered using mechanical or statistical methods in the investigation of an author's writing: for example, in the nineteenth century, the British statistician August De Morgan, and in particular a student of his, an American scientist called T.C. Mendenhall had speculated that the frequency of occurrence of certain words might be used to distinguish the writing of one person from that of another (Mendenhall, 1887). Clearly, human beings do write differently from one another, and certainly human readers claim to be able to distinguish one writing style from another. Since all they have to go on when processing writing is the words on the page, it seems not entirely implausible that the calculation of an author's "characteristic curve of composition" (as Mendenhall called it) might serve in cases of disputed authorship.

With the advent of automatic computing systems, and in particular of more sophisticated statistical models of how words are distributed across a text, it became possible to test this hypothesis on a larger scale than Mendenhall had done (he relied on the services of a large number of female assistants to do the counting drudgery), and a number of research papers began to appear on such vexed topics as the authorship of the Pauline epistles, the disputed works of the Russian novelist Sholokhov, or the Federalist Papers (a set of anonymously published pamphlets of the American Revolutionary War period). At the same time, many research groups began to contemplate a more ambitious project that might develop a new form of stylistic studies, based on empirical evidence rather than impressionistic belief or dogma. Stylometry, as this was called, and authorship studies dominated this first heroic period of the digital humanities, and continue to fascinate many researchers.[2]

At the same time, but in another part of the forest, a new tribe of linguists was emerging, re-energizing an empirical tradition going back to J.R. Firth[3] with the aid of massive quantities of machine-readable text. The emergence of the Brown Corpus in 1960 and its successors[4] represents an important moment in the evolution of the digital humanities for several reasons. The "corpus linguists," as they called themselves, were probably the first humanities researchers of whom it might plausibly be said that their research was simply not feasible without the use of digital technologies. The model of language praxis and linguistic patterning that emerged from their research was also fundamentally innovative, not to say controversial with regard to the prevailing Chomskyan orthodoxy of the time. The insights gained from their approach have radically changed the way in which such traditional activities as dictionary-making or language-teaching and learn-ing are now carried out. And, with hindsight, we can detect in their methods a distinctive approach to the modeling and analysis of textual data.

As with the stylisticians and the authorship hackers, however, the corpus linguists' shared model of text was neither formally defined nor structurally ambitious. Its focus was something called the word, variously defined as an orthographic unit, or a lexical one, even though the process of lemmatization—the grouping of individual tokens under a single lexical form—remained problematic; as the title of an article by Brunet memorably reminds us: *Qui lemmatise dilemmes attise* . . . (Brunet, 2000). Corpus linguists studied ngrams—recurrent sequences of words or tokens—but were less interested in indications of macro-textual organization or structure, except where these could be derived from an analysis of the constituent words. Individual tokens in a text were often annotated by codes indicative of their word-class (noun, preposition, and so on) but the annotation of multi-word sequences, for example, to indicate syntactic function, was more problematic and hence less standardized.

Nevertheless, the development of corpus linguistics as a defined area of research (a discipline even) owes much to the clear consensus among its practitioners concerning both core principles, methods, and objects that define the discipline, and those concerning which multiple points of view were recognized. For example, the Brown corpus instantiated a surprisingly long-lived model for the construction of language corpora that was based on fixed-size synchronic sampling of language production according to explicit selection criteria. In developing the Cobuild corpus (Sinclair, 1987) by contrast, Sinclair was one of the first to propose a model of continuous sampling from an ever-expanding and diachronic base of reference materials, and may be thought of as having initiated the perspective memorably phrased by more than one American linguist as "there's no data like more data,"[5] anticipating today's gigaword corpora, and the "web as corpus" concept. The theoretical model underlying both these projects and the many others that followed them was, however, just the same: the function of linguistic research was to identify regularities in the way language is used, and to construct a view of how language functions solely in terms of that empirically derived data, rather than from a priori theorizing about postulated linguistic systems.

If stylometrics and corpus linguistics alike thrived in the digital environment, it was perhaps because their objects of study, the raw material of text, seemed easy to model, because a consensus as to its significant particularities had long been established. The same could hardly be said of other areas of the humanities, in which the primary object of interest was not the text but the subject matter of the text, not its form but its intention, not the medium but the message. And yet it was obvious (as Manfred Thaller, Jean-Philippe Genet and others argued persuasively in the 1980s) that there was much to gain if only consensus could be achieved as to the best way of transferring the written records that constitute the primary sources for historical research into a digital form. Running through the proceedings of, for example, the annual conference of the Association for History and Computing, is a constant argument between text analysis and text representation. For those whose methods were entirely contingent on the use of particular pieces of software (statistical packages, logic programming systems, relational database systems, etc.) the source existed only to be pillaged, annotated, or reduced to some more computationally tractable form. For those with a broader perspective, wishing to produce resources that might be both adequate to the immediate needs of one research project and generic enough to facilitate its reuse and integration with other resources, the absence (or multiplicity) of standard models for their representation seemed insurmountable. In the nineteenth century, historical scholars had frequently labored (and gained recognition for their labor) to codify, transcribe, and standardize collections of medieval and early modern records from many sources in print form. How should that effort be replicated and continued into the digital age?

We can see also in those conference proceedings,[6] and in the journals of the period, a tendency for researchers in history to adopt whatever computational solutions the market was throwing up, without much effort to truly appropriate it to their perspective. Social historians in particular often embraced uncritically the methods of sociology, which required the reduction of historical data to vectors of scores in a predefined matrix, easily analyzable by tools such as SPSS or SIR, popular statistical packages that had been developed originally to aid in the analysis of survey data, rather than archival records. Many others accepted uncritically the database orthodoxy proposed by their local computing center (in those distant days, many universities provided computing services and support for them centrally) which, in practice, meant adjusting their data to the hierarchic, network, or relational model, as the case might be. Others, perhaps more surprisingly, attempted to apply the methods of logic programming, reducing historical data to sets of assertions in predicate logic: the pioneering work of the French archaeologist Jean-Claude Gardin (Gardin, 1980) was often cited in support of this idea. In the UK, there was even a short-lived vogue for recommending logic programming in secondary school teaching (see, e.g., Nichol et al., 1987). For the most part, however, few historians thought to follow their literary or linguistic colleagues in preferring to develop their own tools of analysis which might reflect models closer to their discipline's view of its data.

With a few notable exceptions, it seems that most historical researchers were content simply to adopt technical standards established by the wider data-processing community (relational databases, information retrieval systems, and so on) despite the reductionist view of the complexities of historical sources that such systems required. Amongst the exceptions we should, however, note pioneering experiments such as those of Macfarlane, 1977, or King, 1981, as well as more mature and influential systems such as Thaller's κλειο (Thaller, 1987), which demonstrated that it was possible to use the new technology to combine faithfulness to the source with faithfulness to the historian's understanding, in a kind of re-evaluation of the German tradition of Quellenkritik or "source criticism" pioneered by historians such as Leopold Ranke and Berthold Niebuhr.[7] That re-evaluation, by focusing on ways of modeling in an integrated way, both the text itself and the historian's reading of it, showed the way forward for subsequent digitally assisted humanities research in many disciplines, just as Quellenkritik originally benefited from the insights of traditional philology.

3 The apotheosis of textual modeling

What happens when a non-digital text is transformed to a digital form? If the goal is no more than to re-present that source, it is very likely that the job will be considered accomplished by a reasonable quality digital image, perhaps accompanied by a transcription of (most of) the words on the page, in a form that will facilitate a reasonably close simulation of the original to be displayed when the digital version is presented on screen or paper. Self-evidently, this approach prioritizes the visual aspects of the source at the expense of its semantics, except in so far as those are intrinsically tied to its visual aspects. It requires but does not impose the addition of metadata to contextualize and describe a source, which may or may not be stored along with the digital surrogate itself.

Nevertheless, presumably for largely practical and economic reasons, page-imaging, or facsimile production remains the common denominator of the majority of current digitization initiatives, as it has done for the past few decades. For today's digital library, in fact, we may say that the predominant model is one in which digital surrogates approximate as closely as possible a subset of the visual characteristics of a source. Note that this remains a subset: Prescott, 2008 among others has pointed out how even the most fastidiously prepared and executed digital imaging of an ancient manuscript can fail to capture all of its properties of interest. Digitization is an inherently reductive process and nothing is likely to change that. As in database design, therefore, it is essential to define precisely the limitations of the model to which one is reducing the source.

In explicitly rejecting that model of textual essence, the Text Encoding Initiative (TEI) attempted something rather more ambitious. From the start, its intention was to create an explicit model of the objects and structures that intelligent readers claim to perceive when reading a text; the explicit claim was that by modeling those readings, and assigning a secondary role to the rendition of actual source documents, the goals of integration and preservation of digital surrogates would be greatly simplified; perhaps implicitly there was also an attempt to redirect the energies of scholarly discourse away from the accidental trivia of word processing in favor of a more profound consideration of the meaning and purpose of written texts. This opposition is most clearly stated in Coombs, Renear and DeRose's foundational text on the future of scholarly communication (Coombs et al., 1987) and it is also explicit in the original design goals of the TEI as enumerated in the so-called Poughkeepsie Principles: "Descriptive markup will be preferred to procedural markup. The tags should typically describe structural or other fundamental textual features, independently of their representation on the page" (TEI, 1988).

A reading of the TEI's original design documents[8] shows clearly the influence of contemporary database design orthodoxies. For example, a working paper from 1989 called "Notes on Features and Tags"[9] defines a conceptual model in which entities such as tags are considered independently from both the abstract features they denote and the textual data strings to which they are attached, before proceeding to define a data structure to hold all the features of a given mark-up tag. This latter definition is labeled as "Design for a TAGS Database," and a mapping to a simple RDBMS provided for it. The assumption behind the model described here is that the well-attested variation in the many ways texts were converted for use by computer might be overcome by treating those variations as accidental quirks of the software in use. Essentially, this model says, there is a determinable collection of textual features of interest on which scholars agree, many of which are differently expressed by different pieces of software, but which could all be potentially be mapped to a single interchange format. The TEI was conceived of originally as an interchange or pivotal format; not necessarily as something to replace existing systems of markup, but as something to enable them to communicate, by appealing to a higher level abstract model of the common set of textual features that individual markup systems were deemed to denote.

This same working paper includes a suggested SGML DTD which might be used to organize the components of that higher level abstract model, and which is in many ways the ancestor of the schema currently used to define TEI components. The fundamental concepts of this model, for which the TEI editors coined the name ODD (One Document Does it all), have clear antecedents both in the work of Donald Knuth and in contemporary SGML documentation systems, such as that developed for a major European publishing initiative called Majour, and have not fundamentally changed since. The model is well documented elsewhere;[10] we highlight here a few of its salient characteristics, in particular those that qualify it for consideration as a meta-model, a tool for the construction of models.

There has long been a perception that the TEI is a prescriptive model, as indeed in some respects it is: it prescribes a number of very specific constraints for documents claiming to be TEI conformant, for example. However, the prescriptive part of the TEI is concerned only with how the TEI definitions are to be deployed; very few prescriptions are provided as to which of the many hundreds of TEI-defined concepts should be selected in a given context, although, of course, each choice of component has implications for subsequent choices. In this respect, the TEI system resembles a somewhat disorganized collection of independent components rather than a single construct.

Each of these components is, however, defined in a standardized way, using essentially the same set of properties: a name or canonical identifier; a description of its intended meaning (supplied in one or several natural languages); where possible, an indication of equivalent objects in other systems; its classification within the TEI's conceptual model;[11] a formal model of its possible constituent components and attributes, usage notes and illustrative examples. None of this documentation is inextricably linked to any particular enabling technology: although the first version of the TEI was expressed using SGML, later versions have used XML, and several experiments have shown the feasibly of remapping its definitions to other currently fashionable technologies such as JSON or OWL. This also is in line with (though not identical to) the original goals of the project.

As noted above, those original project goals make clear that the TEI was not originally conceived of as a standards-making exercise, but rather as a way of defining a convenient interchange format, which might perhaps be generalized to serve as an encoding format in its own right.[12] To define its interchange format, however, the TEI necessarily had to define an interlingua in which existing models of textual structure might be re-expressed without loss of information, and thus found itself inevitably working towards the definition of a meta-standard: a framework for the definition of standards. The disorganized constellation of textual features or objects found in the TEI Guidelines corresponds with the set of "significant particularities" originally identified by the members of the TEI working groups, which has been refined and revised over a period of several decades, during which new objects have been added and existing ones revised for consistency and clarity. As noted elsewhere (Burnard, 2013), the TEI system as a whole is thus not a fixed entity, but one that has evolved and developed in response to the changing needs and priorities of its user community. In this respect, it has been created in a very different way from most standards.

This shape-shifting is a continuation and intensification of a principle adopted very early on and manifest in the conspicuously consultative manner by which the TEI Guidelines were originally constructed. They do not represent the views of a small technical self-appointed elite, but rather the distillation of a consensus formulated by combining input from specialists from many academic disciplines, having in common only an interest in the application of digital technologies within those disciplines. As an internationally funded research project, the TEI project also conscientiously strove to pay equal attention to the needs of researchers separated by language and geography. Although the TEI pre-dates the World Wide Web, it was born into a world in which virtual internet-based communities were already emerging and remains, perhaps, one of the first and most successful user-focused internet-mediated projects to have been created, even without benefit of today's "social media."

The interdisciplinary nature of the TEI model is also reflected in the way the Guidelines themselves are organized and in the way that its formal definitions are intended to be used. Inevitably, most of the individual chapters of the reference manual known as TEI P3 (TEI, 1994), which constituted the first public release of the TEI Guidelines in 1994, contained much material unlikely to be of interest to every user. At the same time, every chapter contains material of importance to some user. The material combined rigorous prose definition and exemplification with formal specifications, initially expressed as a "tagset": a set of declarations expressed in the DTD language used by the SGML standard. The expectation was that the skilled user would (having read and understood the documentation) select one of a small set of "base" tagsets (prose, verse, drama, dictionaries, speech, and so on), together with a set of elements common to all kinds of text (the "core") and the metadata associated with them (the "header"). This combination could then be enriched further by the addition of any number of "additional" tagsets providing more specialized components, each reflecting a particular style of analysis (linguistic, hypertextual, text-critical, and so on). Finally, a user might elect to suppress some of the components provided, modify some of their properties, or even to add new components not provided by the TEI model at all.

This model, humorously referred to as the "pizza model" by analogy with the way that Chicago's favorite dish is typically constructed, also seems in retrospect to reflect something of the deeply balkanized intellectual and social milieu of its time. For all its good intentions and practicality, the tidiness of the pizza model seems at odds with the gradual blurring of the well-fenced frontiers between linguistics and literature, history and sociology, science and the humanities, which characterizes our current intellectual landscape, in which humanities research ranges far and wide across old disciplinary frontiers, grabbing methods from evolutionary biology to explore textual traditions, or deploying complex mathematical models to trace the evolution of literary style.

As first instantiated, the construction of a personalized model from the huge (and occasionally overlapping) range of possibilities defined by the TEI Guidelines was a relatively complicated task, requiring fairly detailed technical knowledge about SGML, as well as a good grasp of the way in which the TEI tagsets were organized. Unsurprisingly, many early adopters preferred to use a generic predefined model such as TEI Lite (TEI, 1990) or to rely on one provided by their own research community, such as the Corpus Encoding Standard (Ide and Priest-Dorman, 2000), or, more recently, the Epidoc Guidelines (Elliott et al., 2007–14). Yet the existence of many such customizations, even those that were not always entirely TEI conformant as the term was understood at the time, clearly vindicated the basic design of the project, which was to construct not a single standard model for the encoding of all texts for all time, but rather an architecture within which such models could be developed in an interoperable or at least interchangeable way, a kind of agreed lexicon from which individual dialects could be derived. The same mechanism (the ODD system mentioned above) is used to define both the TEI itself and customizations of appropriate to a given project; it is thus easy to determine the correspondence between a project-specific model and the whole of the TEI from which it was derived by specifying the TEI tagsets used, selectively choosing parts of each tagset and (where judged necessary) adding new declarations to complement or replace those provided by the TEI.

The transition from TEI P3 to TEI P4 carried out in 1999 was a largely automatic process of re-expressing the same objects in XML rather than SGML, with little of significance being changed. However, the development of TEI P5[13] was a more ambitious process. Necessarily, it involved the addition of much new material and the updating of some no longer relevant recommendations such as those concerning character encoding, but it also included changes introduced specifically to simplify and render more accessible the hitherto rather arcane customization mechanism. Firstly, the overall architecture was simplified by abolishing the distinction amongst types of tagset: in TEI P5, each P3 tagset becomes a simple collection of specifications known as a module, and any combination of modules is feasible. It is even possible (within limits) to select elements for inclusion in a model without specifying the module in which they are defined. Secondly, the class mechanism used to group elements together by their semantics, their structural role, or their shared attributes (independently of their module) was made both more pervasive and more apparent; indeed, any customization of TEI P5 beyond simply creating a subset now requires some understanding of the class system. Thirdly, simple subsetting was made very much easier, and a simple web interface called Roma was provided to achieve it.

This short review of the TEI's technical evolution suggests that the project, which was initially intended to define a basic interchange format into which any other kind of textual markup might be transformed, has instead become a framework for the definition of such markup systems. What began as a simple exercise in string processing has of necessity developed into a higher-level system, using more sophisticated and more general-purpose methods and processors. Today's TEI user is less interested in defining their own markup syntax than in finding a standard way of expressing their own textual model. We suggest that by abstracting away from the specifics of any particular markup syntax to focus on the conceptual model underlying it, the TEI designers paved the way for this change.

4 Explicitness and coercion

Perhaps there is a long-running tension within all standardization efforts between generality and customization. The more generally applicable a standard, the harder it may be to use productively in a given context; the more tailored it is to a given context, the less useful it is likely to be elsewhere. Yet surely one of the main drivers behind the urge to go digital has always been the ability not just to have one's cake and eat it, but also to produce many different kinds of cake from the same messy dough. For this to work, there is a need for standards that do not limit choice, but rather facilitate an accurate presentation of the choices made. Such an approach is also essential for a modeling standard that hopes to be effective in a domain where the objects of discourse, the components of the model, are constantly shifting and being remade, and consequently remain controversial.

Consider, for example, the common requirement to annotate a stretch of text believed to indicate a temporal expression with some normalized representation of it. This has obvious utility if we believe the expression represents the date of some event, and we wish to perform automatic analyses comparing many such— for example, to determine the chronological sequence of a collection of documents. One document says simply "Wednesday," another says "Saint Martin's day," yet another says "the 12th Sunday after Lammas Tide." Some kind of normalization is clearly essential if these are to be compared, but the norms for temporal reference vary considerably both across cultures (dates in the Islamic, Aztec, Roman, Chinese, or Jewish calendars are not all easily interconvertible), across time (the Gregorian versus the Julian calendar, for example) and even across international standards (a W3C date is not the same thing as an ISO date). Simplifying somewhat, a TEI document may choose to normalize dates using the international standard for representation of temporal expressions (ISO 3601), or the profile (subset) of that standard recommended by the W3C, or it may choose to use some other user-defined calendar system entirely. The price of this liberty is that all three options must somehow be provided for within the TEI architecture, even though in any given case it is likely that only one normalization method will be used. Leaving aside the technical detail, the TEI class system provides exactly such a mechanism: although attributes appropriate to each normalization method are defined, in any given customization only a subset will be made available. Hence, while the developer of a generic TEI processor needs to be aware that all three options are feasible, in a given case they can reliably infer which has actually been deployed by processing the ODD specification associated with the documents in question.

Ever since its first publication, the TEI has been criticized for providing too much choice, giving rise to too many different ways of doing more or less the same thing. At the same time (and even occasionally by the same people), it has been criticized for limiting the encoder's freedom to represent all the concepts of their model in just the way they please. Neither criticism is without foundation, of course: despite the best efforts of the original TEI editors, Occam's razor has not been applied as vigorously throughout the Guidelines as it might have been, and as a result life is complicated for both the would-be software developer and the conscientious digital author. Darrell Raymond remarked in a very early critique of SGML that "descriptive markup rescues authors from the frying pan of typography only to hurl them headlong into the hellfire of ontology" (Raymond et al., 1996). Standardized modeling tools such as ODD cannot entirely remove those ontological anxieties, but at least they facilitate ways of coming to terms with them, by providing a neutral space in which the system designer can make explicit their views, in particular a vehicle for them to express the degree and nature of any dissent between their model and that elaborated by the TEI. The TEI provides no tags for the description of unicorns, nor even (as yet) for botanical names, but it does provide a standardized way of defining such tags, and relating their definitions to concepts already existing in the TEI model.

At the same time, the very success of particular TEI customizations increases the risk that the TEI may eventually begin to compromise on its design principles—for example, by downgrading support for the generic solution in favor of the one that interfaces most neatly with the latest most fashionable tool set. This risk of fragmentation needs to be confronted: do we want to see a world in which various different "TEI-inspired" models for editors of manuscripts, cataloguers, linguists, lexicographers, epigraphers, or users of digital libraries of early print separate themselves from the generic TEI framework and begin to drift apart, reinstating the babel of encoding formats that inspired the creation of the TEI in the first place?

A balance must be maintained between "do it like this" and "describe it like this" schools of standardization; while the former matters most to those charged with delivering real results in the short term, the latter is our only hope of preserving the inner logic of our models in the long term. For that reason, the importance of the TEI is not only that it has formalized and rendered explicit so many parts of the digital landscape, but also that it has done so in a consistent and expandable way. Its value as a meta-model is essential to its usefulness as a modeling tool.

All spheres of standardization activity, we suggested initially, demonstrate a tension between a centralized dirigiste urge and a decentralized desire for consensus. Attempts to provide standardized conceptual models are no exception to this generalization, but the most effective and long-lived such standards seem to require a powerful meta-modeling component. This enables the modeling standard to evolve in response to changing perceptions, priorities, and technologies without losing its identity. Standards may fail for a variety of reasons, but the most common is that no genuine consensus can be established among practitioners or theoreticians of the domain concerned; a standard that facilitates diversity of theory by reserving its constraints to the meta-model level is less likely to fall foul of this problem. A standardized meta-model enables diverse models to co-exist fruitfully, by providing a channel for mutual interchange and mutual comprehension.

Notes

1 The acronym first appears in Haugeland, 1985.
2 Holmes, 1994, provides a good bibliography of earlier work; Juola, 2006, reviews more recent thinking on the topic.
3 For a persuasive historical analysis of this tradition and its development, see Léon, 2008.
4 For links to documentation of this influential corpus and its imitations, including an impressive bibliography of research derived from it, see http://clu.uni.no/icame/ manuals/
5 The phrase is often credited to Robert Mercer: see www.lrec-conf.org/lrec2004/doc/ jelinek.pdf (Jelinek, 2004).
6 See, for example, Denley and Hopkin, 1987, or Denley et al., 1989.
7 See Greenstein, 1991, for a collection of essays on the problems of modeling historical textual data sources.
8 Many of the TEI's original working documents are preserved in its online archive; some of them have also been published, notably in Ide and Véronis, 1995.
9 A lightly revised version is available from: www.tei-c.org/Vault/ED/edw05.htm
10 The current system is fully described in Chapter 22 of the TEI Guidelines; for an early article outlining its architecture, see Burnard and Rahtz, 2004; for recent technical developments, see Burnard and Rahtz, 2013.
11 The TEI architecture combines a notion of hierarchically organized element classes, similar to that found in many formal systems, with a loosely defined semantic model: the interested reader is referred to Chapter 2 of the Guidelines for further information.
12 The first of the Poughkeepsie Principles mentioned above is "The guidelines are intended to provide a standard format for data interchange in humanities research"; the second is "The guidelines are also intended to suggest principles for the encoding of texts in the same format."
13 Technical details of the transition from P3 to P5 are provided in Burnard, 2006, *inter alia*.

References

Brunet, E., 2000. *Qui lemmatise dilemmes attise. Lexicometrica.* Available at: http://lexicom etrica.univ-paris3.fr/article/numero2/brunet2000.html (accessed January 24, 2016).
Burnard, L., 2006. New Tricks from an Old Dog: An Overview of TEI P5. In: Burnard, L., Dobreva, M., Fuhr, N., and Lüdeling, A. (Eds.). *Digital Historical Corpora – Architecture, Annotation, and Retrieval.* Dagstuhl, Deutschland 3–12 December 2006. Dagstuhl: IBFI.

Burnard, L., 2013. The Evolution of the Text Encoding Initiative: From Research Project to Research Infrastructure. *Journal of the Text Encoding Initiative Issue*, 5. Available at: http://jtei.revues.org/811.

Burnard, L. and Rahtz, S., 2004. *RelaxNG with Son of ODD*. Available at: Proceedings of Extreme Markup Languages: http://conferences.idealliance.org/extreme/html/2004/Burnard01/EML2004Burnard01.html.

Burnard, L. and Rahtz, S. 2013. Reviewing the TEI ODD System. In: *Proceedings of the 2013 ACM Symposium on Document Engineering*. New York: ACM, pp. 193–196.

Busa, R., SJ, 1980. The Annals of Humanities Computing: The Index Thomisticus. *Computers and the Humanities*, xiv, pp. 83–90.

Coombs J.H., Renear, A.H., and DeRose, S.J., 1987. Markup Systems and the Future of Scholarly Text Processing. *Communications of the ACM*, 30(11), pp. 933–47.

Denley, P. and Hopkin, D. (Eds.) 1987. *History and Computing*. Manchester: Manchester University Press.

Denley, P., Fogelvik, S., and Harvey, C. (Eds.) 1989. *History and Computing II*. Manchester: Manchester University Press.

Elliott, T., Bodard, G., Mylonas, E. and Stoyanova, S., 2007–14. EpiDoc Guidelines: Ancient Documents in TEI XML (Version 8). Available at: www.stoa.org/epidoc/gl/latest/.

Gardin, J.-C., 1980. *Archaeological Constructs*. Cambridge: Cambridge University Press.

Greenstein, D., 1991. Modelling Historical Data: Towards a Standard for Encoding and Exchanging Machine-Readable Texts. In: Thaller, M. (Ed.) 1991: *Halbgraue Reihe zur Historischen Fachinformatik*, A(11). St Katherinen: Scripta Mercaturae Verlag.

Haugeland, J., 1985. *Artificial Intelligence: The Very Idea*. Cambridge, MA: MIT Press.

Holmes, D. I., 1994. Authorship Attribution. *Computers and the Humanities*, 28(2). Pp. 87–106.

Ide, N. and Véronis, J., 1995. *The Text Encoding Initiative: Background and Context*. Dordrecht/Boston, MA: Kluwer Academic Publisher.

Ide, N. and Priest-Dorman, G., 2000. Corpus Encoding Standard. Available at: www.cs.vassar.edu/CES/CES1.html.

Jelinek, F., 2004. Some of My Best Friends are Linguists. Paper presented at LREC 2004, Johns Hopkins University.

Jones, S.E., 2014. *The Emergence of the Digital Humanities*. London: Routledge.

Juola, P., 2006. Authorship Attribution. In: *Foundations and Trends in Information Retrieval*, 1(3), pp. 233–4.

Kent, W., 1978. *Data and Reality: Basic Assumptions in Data Processing Reconsidered*. Amsterdam: North-Holland Publishing.

King, T.J., 1981. The Use of Computers for Storing Records in Historical Research. *Historical Methods*, 14, pp. 59–64.

Léon, J., 2008. *Aux sources de la "Corpus Linguistics": Firth et la London School*. Langages, 3(171). Available at: www.cairn.info/revue-langages-2008-3-page-12.htm.

Macfarlane, A., 1977. *Reconstructing Historical Communities*. Cambridge: Cambridge University Press.

Mendenhall, T. C., 1887. The Characteristic Curves of Composition. In: *Science* – supplement, IX(214). Available at: https://archive.org/details/jstor-1764604.

Nichol, J., Dean, J., and Briggs, J., 1987. Logic Programming and Historical Research. In: Denley, P. and Hopkin, D. (Eds.) *History and Computing*. Manchester: Manchester University Press, pp. 198–205.

Prescott, A., 2008. The imaging of historical documents. In: Greengrass, M. and Hughes, L. (Eds.) *The Virtual Representation of the Past*. Aldershot: Ashgate, pp. 7–22.

Raymond, D., Tompa, F., and Wood, D., 1996. From Data Representation to Data Model: Meta-Semantic Issues in the Evolution of SGML. *Computer Standards & Interfaces*, 18, pp. 25–36.

Sinclair, J.M., 1987. Looking Up: An Account of the COBUILD Project in Lexical Computing and the Development of the Collins COBUILD English Language Dictionary. *Computers and Translation*, 3(3/4), pp. 263–6.

Sowa, J.F., 1984. *Conceptual Structures*. Reading, MA: Addison-Wesley.

Tanenbaum, A.S., 1981. *Computer Networks*. Englewood Cliffs, New Jersey: Prentice-Hall.

Text Encoding Initiative (TEI), 1988, revised 1990. *Design Principles for Text Encoding Guidelines* Working Paper ED P1. Available at: www.tei-c.org/Vault/ED/edp01.htm.

Text Encoding Initiative (TEI), 1990. *TEI Lite: Encoding for Interchange: An Introduction to the TEI*. Available at: www.tei-c.org/Guidelines/Customization/Lite/.

Text Encoding Initiative (TEI), 1994. *Guidelines for the Encoding and Interchange of Machine-Readable Texts: Draft P3*. Chicago, Oxford: Text Encoding Initiative.

Thaller, M., 1987. κλειο: *A Data Base System for Historical Research*. Göttingen: Max-Planck-Institut für Geschichte.

4 How subjective is your model?

Elena Pierazzo

1 The (digital) humanities and the two cultures

Modeling can be considered one of the—if not "the"—digital humanities (DH) primitives, and in fact the activity of analyzing and modeling some humanities domain or domains with the purpose of making them processable by a computer represents one of their defining characteristics. Indeed, to start this chapter by explaining what modeling is and its significance within the DH may seem unnecessary for a contribution to a book that is itself about data modeling in the digital humanities. However, just as a new point of view requires a new model (as we will see), so a new point of view also requires a new definition. This chapter will then analyze some fundamental characteristics of models and the process of building models, or modeling, with the aim of establishing the role of the subjectivity and its counterpart, objectivity, in modeling within the digital humanities. To do this, it will be necessary to reconsider the fundamental characteristics of models and the processes in building them, in order to understand in which way the inevitable subjectivity that this operation entails can be taken into account, and whether this weakens some opportunities for digital analysis. Given the particular competence and skillset of this author, most examples will be drawn from editing and transcribing manuscripts and old documents, but the principles and arguments hold much more widely than this.

For centuries, one of the main hermeneutical divides between hard sciences and the humanities has allegedly been the reliance of the former on quantitative methodologies, characterized by objectivity, and of the latter on qualitative ones, characterized by subjectivity. The discussion about the methodological divide usually goes under the name of the "Two Cultures" from the title of a book by C.P. Snow from 1960 and the consequent response by F.R. Levis in 1962. Despite widespread critique in recent decades, influenced among other things by poststructuralism, the underlying sense that science and the humanities differ on precisely this point remains deeply felt even among those who do not believe in the cruder and starker divide as Snow presents it (Porsdam, 2013). This divide has been felt differently by different scholars and disciplines: some have praised it, some have regretted it. A champion of the former attitude is Bernhard Bischoff who in his seminal work *Latin Palaeography: Antiquity and the Middle Age* (Bischoff 1979; Bischoff 1990) lamented that, thanks to "technological advances," palaeography is changing form an "art of seeing and intuiting" to an "art of measurement;" the use of the word "art" (*Kunst*) instead of "science" (*Wissenschaft*) is very important here, as underlined by Pratesi (1995, p. 346).[1] As a matter of fact, paleography is going through a transformational phase,[2] led by the perceived need to provide quantitative supportive evidence to what has been defined by Derolez an "authoritarian" discipline depending on "authority" and "faith" (Derolez, 2003, p. 9).[3] Also championing the adoption of quantitative methods is Tanselle, who declared that the quest for an authentic scientific method is the defining characteristic of the evolution of textual criticism: "[t]he search for properly 'scientific' method has been perhaps the dominant thread running through the history of textual criticism" (1995, pp. 18–19); in his analysis of the history of textual criticism he highlights, in fact, how the development of each new editorial "method" aimed at subtracting the editorial process from the subjective intuition of the editor—the so-called *divinatio* or *emendatio ope ingenii*—in favor of a "scientific" method; this aspiration is perhaps best represented by the fact that in several languages a scholarly edition is called a "scientific edition."[4]

The advent of computers, and in particular their introduction in the humanities, has been seen historically as a way of finally removing the humanities from the realm of subjectivity and qualitative methodologies: since the computer is a machine, based on deterministic quantification, therefore its elaboration can only be objective, by definition. Susan Hockey seemed to share the same view when she declared how "humanities computing has had to embrace '*the two cultures*,' to bring the rigor and systematic unambiguous procedural methodologies characteristic of the sciences to address problems within the humanities that had hitherto been most often treated in a serendipitous fashion" (2004, p. 19). This assessment is indeed worth pondering: while it can be considered perhaps as the point of view of the first generation of digital humanists, its position as the first chapter of the *Companion to Digital Humanities* (Schreibman et al., 2004), a publication that had a foundational role in the definition of the digital humanities as a field, makes it hard to consider it lightly. The chapter by Hockey (*The History of Humanities Computing*) not only has a prominence through its position at the start of the book, but is also presented as an introduction to the field, and the passage quoted occupies a good part of its very first page. What is striking here are the quick and simplistic dismissal of the humanities methods as "serendipitous" and the seemingly uncontroversial qualification of the method of DH as rigorous and systematic. The same "optimistic" opinion is reported by Rieder and Röhle, 2012, p. 72: "Digital Humanities [. . .] would seem to bridge the gap between the 'two cultures' (Snow, 1959), between the quantitative orientation of the natural sciences and the critical cultural discourses in the humanities." Such bridging, however, seems to be only monodirectional: from the humanities to Science, from qualitative to quantitative, and from subjectivity to objectivity, and this is perceived as a direct consequence of the introduction of computers. This seems to be a recurrent pattern: Daston and Gallison (2007) have demonstrated how the rise of objectivity as an epistemic virtue in science is connected with the progressive introduction of instruments and machines into the natural sciences (Rieder and Röhle, 2012, p. 72). Yet this opposition between objectivity and subjectivity does not need to be so binary, nor is it true that science is based on objectivity. In fact, the recognition of the social component in the building of consensus and ultimately of what we can consider to fulfil scientific expectations, seems to offer a more interesting approach in the evaluation of digital methodology. This approach goes under the name of intersubjectivity, as we will see.

If the digital humanities, with their interdisciplinary positioning between humanities and (computer) science seems to be invested with task of leading the humanities into science, one may ask how this works in practice, and where this quantitative method is to be found in the digital humanities. In fact, we can call the digital humanities a discipline, but they are effectively characterized by varied and ever changing sets of methods and approaches; it is therefore necessary to look for a common defining ground which is able, on one hand, to define the core of the discipline and, on the other hand, to fulfil the requirement of "bringing the rigor and systematic unambiguous procedural methodologies characteristic of the sciences" (Hockey, 2004, p. 19). For the digital humanities this common ground can be found in the use of a computer to achieve a scholarly purpose: this is what lies at the base of each activity that we will classify as being part of the field. However, this is not enough: to use a word processor to write an article does not suffice. In fact, it is the modeling of a given domain so that this domain becomes computable that constitutes the lowest common denominator of all the methods and heuristics that compose the varied landscape of the digital humanities. The essential preliminary activity that must be deployed in order to use a computer within the humanities, or indeed any other discipline, is that of modeling: only by building an explicit model of a given object can that object become computable. This view has been maintained by McCarty, for instance, who has asserted the "fundamental dependence of any computing system on an explicit, delimited conception of the world or 'model' of it" (McCarty, 2005, p. 21). Consequently, if the use of computers is to bridge the gap between the two cultures and bring a "scientific" method to the humanities and if we need to model in order to compute, it is then legitimate to ask what is the role we attribute to models in this shift from one culture to the other—that is to say, from qualitative to quantitative, and from subjectivity to objectivity.

2 Modeling the humanities: the fuzziness and the precision

Analysis and modeling are rightly considered to be at the heart of digital humanities, but, as a matter of fact, modeling is at the core of any critical and epistemological activity, as these all require the selection of particular facts (out of all observable ones) relative to a particular object or set of objects for them to be analyzed and understood. In the humanities we are not used to the words "model" and "modeling" employed in this particular sense, but nevertheless the elaboration of a particular model of an object of study is the preliminary, implicit activity that lies at the basis of most analytical endeavors. Indeed, modeling is a particularly central activity for some disciplines within the humanities. This is the case for linguistics, for instance, where seminal models established by De Saussure (1916) and Jakobson (1960) paved the way toward an extensive use of models. It is not perhaps a coincidence, then, that linguistics was one of the first disciplines in the humanities to adopt computers, and this happened with such deep consequences for the hermeneutics of the discipline that it led to the establishment of a new discipline altogether: computational linguistics (Spärck Jones, 2007). Nevertheless, the case of linguistics is not isolated: literary studies have known the production of many different models, such as the one established by Vladimir Propp describing fairy tales (1968), for example. Textual criticism also relies heavily on models: what are the graphical genealogical representations called *stemma codicum* if not models of textual transmission? The examples could indeed be multiplied.

Every analytical activity is based on a model and produces a model. This is even more the case if such analytical activity is to be pursued with the support of a computer: to compute, we need to model, and we need to do it formally, explicitly and accurately, as sloppiness or fuzziness strongly limits the potentials of the kind of processes operated by machines. However, once we attempt to model a domain in the humanities this requirement of formalization and precision can prove to be more challenging than first envisaged. An example of this can be seen by considering the dating of an event in antiquity such as, for instance, the writing of a particular document. As for most old documents, the chances that we can attribute it to a precise date are quite small: in most cases we can at most say that a document or codex may have been written between, say, the end of the tenth century and the beginning of the eleventh. This is clear enough to a human reader that understands fuzziness and its inevitability; but how does it translate into a computer-based database of manuscripts, for instance? What does the "end of the tenth century" mean? Perhaps any moment between January 1, 990 and the end of the year 1000? Or between 995 and 1000? And what happens if one of the users of this hypothetical database thinks that "end" actually means "the last fifteen years" of a century, instead of the last ten or when we try to link our open data with data produced by someone else with a different understanding of what the "end of the tenth century" means? Similar questions could be asked for the meaning of "beginning" of a century; and while the same problems are faced by someone trying to sort dating manually, it is by building large datasets that can be queried automatically that these problems are magnified and can lead to misleading if not blatantly wrong results.[5] The answer to all these questions is that such an event has occurred some time toward the end of the century and the beginning of the following one, which is a statement that describes the state of knowledge around that particular event in a more accurate way than saying that it occurred between a minute after midnight of January 1, 990 and a minute before midnight of December 31, 1000: somehow, by spelling out the range, we provide a stronger statement, a deterministic certainty that was absent in the fuzzy date. Tukey declared "Far better an approximate answer to the *right* question, which is often vague, than an *exact* answer to the wrong question, which can always be made precise" (Tukey, 1962, p. 14, cited by Rieder and Röhle, p. 73).

This example of fuzzy dates in the humanities and what modeling may entice is representative of the general paradox that lies at the base of the digital humanities: to treat a humanities domain within a digital environment, it is necessary to model it in an unambiguous way, but this cannot be done in full because ambiguity and fuzziness is an inherent characteristic of the data. What will normally happen in these and similar cases is that the person or people preparing the model will have to make choices and compromises. As we will see, the act of choosing is not only a defining characteristic of modeling, but also a crucial one for the topic of this chapter. Choosing, in fact, is an inherently subjective activity: no matter how many pros and cons one wants to consider, and how many evidences and facts there are to support a particular choice, if there is a choice to be made (i.e. a selection between two or more plausible options), it means there is a certain level of arbitrariness. In textual scholarship—for example, most of the alleged "scientificity" of the Lachmannian method is given by the fact that the choices formerly operated by *divinatio* (that is, based on the editor's best guess), in certain circumstance become "mechanical choices," which are then not real choices anymore, but statistically supported mandatory selections of readings. However, as demonstrated by Bédier (1928), the belief that any choice can be really mechanical and therefore scientific is fallacious. But if choosing is inevitably biased by subjectivity, and if choosing is at the base of modeling, which in turn is required for any form of computing, it seems evident that subjectivity is an unavoidable component of the scientific method, as much as it is for the humanities. This consideration might seem paradoxical and could even lead the current chapter to an early conclusion, ending it with the phrase "subjectivity is part of modeling: deal with it." However, a deeper analysis of models and their characteristics could bring us to a better understanding of what subjectivity is, how we can deal with it, how models can be both subjective and scholarly at the same time, and what lies at the base of the scientific method, really.

3 The defining characteristics of models (1): selection and simplification

A model is the result of an analytical activity which we call modeling. This activity consists first in the attentive analysis of a particular domain or a particular issue—for example, we could consider the case of transcribing the text from an analogue support such as a manuscript into a digital format. This analysis leads to the selection of some of the features connected with the object or domain which are considered relevant by the researcher (or modeler). The selection may also include the relationship among the features and some particular behavior connected with them; furthermore, selection is specific to a particular domain and a particular point of view. In the case of transcribing, for instance, we may consider the transcriber, the document to be transcribed, and the document to be produced as some of the relevant features to be considered, while we might consider the environment where such a transcription takes place as irrelevant: the fact that a transcriber transcribes in an office or in a library or in a bedroom may not be relevant for the model. However, if we are trying to model the transcription as a historical act that took place in the Middle Ages, then we may consider the environment in which it occurred as extremely relevant since research being conducted shows the existence of substantial differences in transcriptional techniques of monastic scriptoria compared to chanceries connected to civil establishments (Ceccherini and De Robertis, 2013).

Selection is rarely performed randomly and can be considered a scholarly activity. Unsworth (2000) lists "sampling" among his "scholarly primitives;"[6] sampling is in turn defined as "the result of selection according to a criterion." Selection as a scholarly activity is the result of an analytical process that conforms to a particular understanding, or follows a specific purpose or, in Unsworth's terms, a criterion.

The act of selecting is also an act of simplifying: by selecting some of the features of the object to be modeled and discarding others, we make such an object simpler and thereby tractable. Simplification is an essential characteristic of a model: a model must be smaller and simpler than the objects it models, as argued by the originators of the modeling theory:

> Let the model approach asymptotically the complexity of the original situation. It will tend to become identical with that original system. As a limit it will become that system itself. [. . .] Lewis Carroll fully expressed this notion in an episode in *Sylvie and Bruno*, when he showed that the only completely satisfactory map to scale of a given country was that country itself.
>
> (Rosenblueth and Wiener, 1945, p. 320)

However, the process of simplifying the objects of study has been felt by some scholars as an unbearable loss of the complexity of the object of study. This is the case, for instance, for Paul Eggert who judged skeptically the attempt of Peter Shillingsburg (1991) to classify the different levels of the text (of modeling it, shall we say). Eggert complained that in so classifying (or modeling), scholars abstract themselves from "the messy processes" that characterize book production: "when we nominalize, we are erecting our own methodologies for productive ends rather than pointing to an actual ontology of texts" (Eggert, 2009, p. 236). In his opinion, then, these models only have a limited value, because the "messy processes" that are at the core of the creation of texts, works, and documents—the domain modeled by Shillingsburg—cannot but be studied as such, in all their messiness. Eggert is right in pointing out the risk of losing something by analyzing and simplifying it. However, one could also argue that only by analyzing, clas-sifying, and simplifying, messiness makes it possible to study it analytically: by approaching messiness without a classifying and analytic eye, one risks missing the general picture, the relationship between parts and, in general, everything that the messiness hides; McCarty points out how the incompleteness of the model, its "crudeness," is "dangerous to us only if we miss the lesson of modeling and mistake the artificial for the real" (McCarty, 2008, p. 400). Indeed, Eggert himself recognizes that these simplifications may embody our editorial methodologies employed "for productive ends."

4 The defining characteristics of models (2): point of view and purpose

The criterion of sampling evoked by Unsworth is directed by a particular point of view or by a purpose of research. For instance, the FRBR model has been created with the purpose of describing the bibliographic holdings of a library. This model singles out four different entities: Work, Expression, Manifestation and Item (IFLA, 1998). Peter Shillingsburg (1991) has considered a similar domain—namely, texts, documents, and works, but with the purpose of describing the complex bibliographic reality of a writer's work; it should therefore come as no surprise that his set of entities is different and includes, among others, Material Text, Linguistic Text, Conceptual Text, and Version. Both models try to make sense of the fact that there are different conceptual objects that we call, for instance, *Jane Eyre*, including the text that Charlotte Brontë wrote and published, the abstract text contained in a given edition, the copy sitting on my shelf at home, and so on. Some of these are material and some are not, and while they all are in a sense *Jane Eyre*, they are all different and have individual characteristics. Yet the two models are very different since their point of view and purpose are different: the FRBR model aims to facilitate the retrieval of a specific bibliographic item, while Shillingsburg's model adopts an editorial point of view and aims to help in the organization of the tradition of a specific work.

Scholarly interpretation is always a central motivation in selecting documentary features to be transcribed. A model is thus always built from a certain point of view, trying to respond to a specific research need or epistemological enquiry. The impulse for the building of a scholarly model is normally that of the researcher—namely, the scholar who asks the questions, establishes the point of view and the perspective. Such an impulse is directed and casts an imprint on the entire process. Let us consider the example of a scholar who would like to analyze how a medieval text has been transmitted from its original version as conceived by its author to us; to do so this scholar (whom we would call an "editor") can choose among a few existing editorial models. First, the editor might consider to use the so-called cladistics or phylogenetic method; this method applies the same algorithm that has been developed by biologists to understand and predict genetic mutation in cells in order to describe scribal innovations and errors and, after automatically collating various versions, typically produces an unrooted tree— that is to say, the resulting model of transmission (the tree) does not stem from one lost original (the root) (Howe et al., 2012). However, if the final purpose of said editor is to actually reconstruct a lost original, a tree that organizes the witnesses in a strictly hierarchical and genealogical perspective will be more appropriate, but this must be achieved with a manual approach or by adopting a different algorithm.[7] The two models may have some level of similarity, but they will probably have an even greater level of differences. Each of them, however, will respond in different way to the needs and expectation of the scholar adopting it.

5 The defining characteristics of models (3): function

A model can also be defined by its function. In his seminal work, McCarty distinguishes two main types of models: *models-of* and *models-for*—that is to say, we can model a given domain with the purpose of knowing it better (model-of) or we can model something that does not exist yet, with the purpose of building it (model-for). This is stated in his very first and now famous definition of model: "A 'model' I take to be either a representation of something for purposes of study [model-of], or a design for realizing something new [model-for]" (McCarty, 2005, p. 24; 2008, pp. 393–6). Most research activities require both types of models to be built at different stages of the research: to build, say, new software able to support editorial activities, this activity needs first to be analyzed and modeled (model-of), and only after this stage a model of the new tool can be built (model-for). A more concrete example of a model-of is the so-called Huitfeildt-Sperberg-McQueen-Marcoux model,[8] an on-going research in modeling the activity of transcription. In particular, the authors are interested in the relationship between a document and the transcription of that document, and what it means "[w]hen we say [. . .] that a particular resource is a transcription of a particular work." They state that the purpose of making a transcription T of an exemplar E is to make a "representation that is easier to use than E. For example, T may be easier to read, or easier to duplicate" (Huitfeldt and McQueen, 2008, p. 296); when they declare that T is "easier to read" than E, and that T is a representation of E, they then imply that T is a model of E. The point for our purposes is not so much the details of the model, but rather that it does not yet have any practical outcome: the purpose is to understand how transcription works, not to build, say, a new word processor that can assist the work of a transcriber. In the same way, we could consider Jakobson's theory of the function of languages a model-of: Jakobson's elaboration of six functions of languages (referential, emotive, conative, poetic, phatic, and metalingual) was aimed at providing a better understanding of the way human beings communicate rather than being a tool for the analysis of texts, even if it can indeed be used—and has been used—for this purpose as well.

Examples of models-for can be found very easily: the drawings produced by an architect to support and guide the construction of a new building could be considered one specimen in this category, as well as the schematic representation of the tables of a relational database or the so-called wireframe of a website. A model that is at the same time a model-of and a model-for is the *stemma codicum*, the graphic representation of the genealogical relationship between the various copies (or witnesses) of a given work. This representation on the one hand shows the existing relationships among the witnesses that the editor has been able to locate (model-of), but it also constitutes the guiding principle that enables the editor to choose one variant reading over another, so it is intended to be a tool (a model-for) as well as a representation.

6 Subjectivity and the definition of models

All the defining characteristics of models (selection and simplification, purpose, and function) are the result of inherently subjective activities. But if a model has to be helpful for deepening the knowledge of a specific domain or for building something new, how can one be sure that the model itself is indeed useful beyond the author of the model itself? How can subjectivity be incorporated into modeling; how can it be compensated and accounted for?

First, it is worth reconsidering the claim that a "proper" scientific method is based on quantitative analysis and that its aim is to be as objective as possible; in order to do so, it is worth trying to distinguish concepts such as objectivity, scientific method and quantitative analysis. In a sense, these are related concepts: so-called objectivity is often based on quantitative analysis, and the fact that something is countable and measurable and therefore can be reproduced in similar circumstances is often used to suggest that it may be used to build scientific arguments. Yet not everything that is countable is objective or scientific. Let us consider, for instance, the counting of the pages of a manuscript; pages are physical entities, they are facts, and one may assume that counting them could be conducted in a fairly objective way; however, things are rarely straightforward and simple when it comes to human artifacts. In this case, for instance, one could include or exclude flyleaves, pastedowns, missing pages, inserted pages, and so on. It is clear that counting pages corresponds with a particular interpretation of what a manuscript is and what it is made of; facts are critical assertions, not abstract entities. And if pages cannot be counted without making a subjective statement, it should not then be surprising that modeling, which is result of deep analytic activity, cannot either. However, one could object that analysis can also be conducted by computers, which, we may assume, can avoid the subjective bias that characterizes human analysis. For instance, let us consider again the cladistics method for editing texts. Since the computer conducts the whole process of collating and building the tree of the surviving and conjectured witnesses, we may be induced to think that the resulting model of textual transmission is indeed less subjective than a *stemma codicum* built by editors using human-produced collation; but again, things are more complex than this. Sculley and Pasanek (2008) offer a very strong warning against the positivistic assumption that computers cannot lie, and in particular the belief that if the computer says that a given number of a particular linguistic feature can be found in a text, then these features are indeed there and in the exact quantity asserted by the computer. While it is the case that the features are there in some sense—the machine is deterministic and must presumably be counting something—it is also true that computer-generated results can be radically altered by the humans that give the instructions on how to count: the software, the algorithm used, the logical process, and the assumptions that underpin these all have deep and often underestimated consequences in the quality of the results. So, while it is certainly true that a computer cannot lie, it is also true that the implicit assumptions at the base of the computer process can distort the result to the point that computers can produce lies. The same call to caution and warning against the misunderstanding or undervaluation of the implicit assumptions behind computational processes comes from Howe et al. (2012) who respond to criticism of the phylogenetic method by remarking that some of this "is not a criticism of the phylogenetic methods *per se*, but of using them without understanding their assumptions" (p. 60). Computers, in fact, apply models, and any computational activity operated by them assumes a model, which not only is biased by subjectivity, as we have seen, but is also controlled and directed in a subjective way. According to Sculley and Pasanek, one of the more important issues with using computers within the humanities is given by the fact that scholars project their expectations onto the computer process, where the tendency is that if the end results do not correspond to initial expectations, then scholars will be tempted to believe that there were some mistakes in the programming or in the input data. In these cases, another process could be attempted or the input data could be "fixed," until the end result is considered plausible or satisfactory by scholars—that is to say, matching their expectations. Indeed, this is the standard method for computational approaches: to take a "ground truth" of "known" input data and test the algorithm against this, adjusting the results until they match initial expectations. Any assumptions or biases in the validity of the "ground truth" are therefore built into the digital system as well. The system must then also be extended to new cases where the same problem of validation arises, as does that of interpretation of results: "The model itself must be interpreted, and the critic brings his prior readings to bear on the abstract representation in just the same way he would bring them to bear on the text itself. The critic reads varieties of confirmation into the results or dismisses them" (Sculley and Pasanek, p. 410). Significantly, their article starts with a quotation from Hans-Georg Gadamer's *Truth and Method*:

> A person who is trying to understand a text is always projecting. He projects a meaning for the text as a whole as some initial meaning emerges in the text. Again, the initial meaning only emerges because he is reading the text with particular expectations in regard to a certain meaning. Working out this fore-projection, which is constantly revised in terms of what emerges as he penetrates into the meaning, is understanding what is there.
>
> (Gadamer, 2000, p. 279)

But there is more. In the digital humanities we build models to apply them to data by the means of a computational process. Such data has to be collected, by sampling (selecting) the relevant specimens, and prepared—that is to say, at the very least produced in the format expected by the computer, if not normalized and regularized in some fashion. If we return to the example of an edition built with the help of computational processing, there may be very significant differences in the ways that different scholars transcribe their texts before feeding them into the automatic collation system. A transcription is a model of the original document from which the transcription is derived (Sperberg-McQueen, 2009; Pierazzo, 2011); therefore, two transcriptions are never equal: in all but the simplest cases, two people will transcribe the same text in very different ways and the same person would transcribe the same text differently in different moments. When transcribing, editors make decisions about what is important and what is not; they select features and simplify the original documents. Howe et al., 2012 (pp. 59–60) point out that scholars manipulate their texts in order to distinguish between the real variants and the "noise," concluding that the less the data is manipulated the better; yet some level of manipulation and selection in transcription is inevitable. For instance, we know that until very recently writing systems tended not to distinguish clearly between "u" and "v"; in this case, the preservation of the original distribution of the two glyphs is rarely informative and as such is silently regularized in most cases; indeed, preserving them may lead to a proliferation of variants with little or no meaning for the transmission of the text. Yet one can certainly think of cases in which scholars have decided to preserve them.[9] The difference between preserving these or not could in turn lead to very different results in a computational context, depending once again on the algorithms used and the assumptions that underlie them. The case study described by Sculley and Pasanek (2008) tells a similar story: the way texts are "prepared" in order to be processed by the data-mining program changes the quantity and quality of the results one can hope to obtain from it. A text, each text, is a model, either of a specific document or of a work (for this distinction, see Tanselle, 1989), and therefore it is already biased by the point of view of the person that produces it. In the humanities (but arguably not only in the humanities) there is not such a thing as "raw data," since the data we feed our algorithms is unavoidably already biased by the scholarly point of view and the sampling and simplification process. Data is already models and is made so by the scholars that consider it.

This analysis has led us to conclude that the act of modeling is subjective, the way the model is used is subjective, and also the data that is used is subjectively smoothed and put together. From this assessment one may be tempted to conclude that the statement offered by Hockey, according to which the digital humanities use methodology that takes the humanities toward science is based on a delusion, and that the scientific method is nothing else than a misrepresented subjective (qualitative?) method. In reality, there is more than quantification to the scientific method and subjectivity does not mean arbitrary manipulation of evidence. Daston and Galison (2010) in their tale of the history of objectivity in sciences observe how from the beginning of the 1900 aspiration to "mechanical objectivity" is gradually substituted by a new idea, the one of "trained judgement"—namely, the interpretation of evidence by experts. Such allowance for human interpretation does not undermine the rigor of the scientific method, while the expectation that "operated by machines" equals "objective" and therefore "better" is based rather on a "misconception," that stems from the historical notion of mechanical objectivity—namely, "the impression that machine processing endorses results with higher epistemological status" (Rieder and Röhle, 2012, p. 72). However, this enduring fallacy not only has no real scholarly foundation, but with its reliance on the alleged superior trustworthiness of machine-led scholarship, it may result in a simplistic representation of the research method, a phenomenon that Rieder and Röhle call "black-boxing" (2012, pp. 75–7): the computer says it is true, so it is true, without the need of further or deeper explanations. This lack of proper accounting can be due to different factors: lack of access to the source code of the software and a low level of computer literacy on behalf of the researcher (or the reader) being the most important ones. Accountability (and not objectivity) is, however, the defining characteristic of the scientific method: it is only by providing to the community of peers the tools and the data to understand and verify our work that we can build new knowledge.

Knowledge is a social construction, and not the result of a solipsistic act. It may be worth remembering here that, in fact, when Kant introduced the word "objectivity" into Western vocabulary, he did not think of an objectivity generated by lack of human interpretation, but as a form of social agreement: "If the judgement is valid for everyone, provided only he is in possession of reason, its ground is objectively sufficient" (Kant, 1965, p. 645). This type of social agreement is central to recent theories of knowledge formation; Michael Ford (2008), in fact, shows very clearly how the building of new knowledge in any given (scientific) discipline is socially constructed, principally, but not exclusively, through the mechanism of peer review: "The process by which [. . .] authority is achieved involves a dialectic between the individual scientist who works to construct a case for a new knowledge claim and the community that critiques the case" (p. 406). He then discusses the way that scientists' claims are made accountable: "in science, claims are accountable to the way nature actually behaves. Nature is what it is, despite our ideas about it" (p. 407). However, to rely simply on nature would be a "naïve empiricism" since "nature does not simply show up 'at the table' of debate" and this is "because the ways scientists frame, measure, and represent nature are directly related to the theoretical notions they are asserting" (p. 408). In order to build what Ford calls the disciplinary authority, a lot of effort is deployed "in making nature's behavior apparent for peers to support arguments about theory" and

> thus although authority for deciding upon knowledge claims in science lies in the community, decisions are not arbitrary, but depend on how successful scientists are in demonstrating a clear conformity between the knowledge claim and the behavior of nature, within the accepted rhetorical form.
>
> (Ford, 2008)

The mechanism through which such acceptance is demonstrated is mainly peer review, to which one has to add all the other venues where scholarly critique is deployed (conferences, reviews, and social networks, among others).

In this way, Ford illustrates how science does not deny subjectivity in knowledge building; on the contrary, it is the recognition of its inevitability that has led to the development of the solid scholarly infrastructure we know and use nowadays. His use of "nature" as a benchmark for the verification of scientists' claims can be generalized (and therefore applied to the humanities) by incorporating into "nature" all objects in a spatio-temporal world, and therefore including cultural artifacts. The models we build to study and analyze them become acceptable to the community of peers when we are able to make these models and their implication evident to the community of peers with which we share a body of pre-existing knowledge. To do so, we will have to use an adequate "rhetorical form"—that is to say, to comply with the expectations of our own community of reference.

The fact that we build knowledge by mutual agreement is also a well-known anthropological phenomenon that goes by the name "intersubjectivity" (a theory traditionally attributed to Edmund Husserl);[10] according to this theory, humans mutually share knowledge about objects in the spatio-temporal world in spite of accessing them from their own subjective perception. The concept of inter-subjectivity was deeply influential in the development of modern epistemology, sociology and psychology, as well as linguistics, while in the digital humanities it seems that we are still lingering on a misconception of which epistemic virtues are at the basis of the scientific method.

The digital humanities have been seen as bridging the gaps between the "Two Cultures," yet it seems clear that, so far, our ideas of the two cultures and of where the gap really lies is perhaps not as clearly defined as we thought. The gap to be bridged (because there is one) is not just between qualitative and quantitative, but is on the methodological reflection as well. Sciences have developed a much deeper self-awareness in the description and specification of their own heuristics as well as the need of making them public that we have done in the humanities: and this is why a book on modeling is certainly contributing toward that bridging.

Notes

1 The translation of Bischoff's quote from the German is mine and is significantly different from the one provided by Dáibhí Ó Cróinín and David Ganz (Bischoff, 1990). The original reads "eine Kunst des Sehens und der Einfühlung" (1979, p. 17), translated in the English version by Cróinín and Ganz as "art of seeing and comprehending" (1990, p. 3), but, as argued by Gumbert (p. 397), "Einfühlung" is more "intuition" than "comprehension"; the Italian translation (Bischoff, 1992) in fact reads "arte dell'osservare e dell'intuire." Both the contributions by Gumbert and Pratesi mentioned above are part of a series of responses to a question launched in 1994 by the journal *Scrittura e Civiltà*, that invited its readers to submit their responses to that particular sentence. Such comments were published between 1995 and 1998.
2 In a forthcoming article, Stokes argues, however, that such a phase started much earlier: "The advent of photolithography in the nineteenth century, for example, coincided with the foundation of the Palaeographical Society in the United Kingdom, which sought (among other things) to produce reproductions of manuscripts on a scale

larger than that seen before in an attempt to bring objective evidence to what they saw as the science of palaeography" (Stokes, forthcoming).

3   Such a development in palaeography is witnessed by the three volumes by Rehbein et al., 2009, Fisher et al., 2010, and Duntze et al., 2015, as well as by the *DigiPal* project (Stokes et al., 2014).

4   This is the case, for instance, for French (*édition scientifique*) and Italian (*edizione scientifica*).

5   This is no fictional example: all digital projects dealing with historical artifacts have to face this issue, as demonstrated by a series of blog posts by Peter Stokes recounting the difficulties and the theoretical reflections triggered by the need to catalogue several hundred eleventh-century manuscripts (Stokes, 2012a, 2012b, and 2015).

6   Unsworth defines scholarly primitives as "basic functions common to scholarly activity across disciplines, over time, and independent of theoretical orientation."

7   For a survey of several phylogenetic methods, see Howe et al., 2012, and Andrews and Macé, 2013.

8   The first contribution to this debate was produced by Claus Huitfeldt and Michael Sperberg-McQueen in 2008.

9   This is the case, for instance, of the edition of Giacomo da Lentini (1979).

10 Duranti (2010), however, argues for a more complex consideration of Husserls's theories.

References

Andrews, T.L. and Macé, C., 2013. Beyond the Tree of Texts: Building an Empirical Model of Scribal Variation through Graph Analysis of Texts and Stemmata. *Literary and Linguistic Computing*, 28(4), pp. 504–21.

Bédier, J., 1928. La tradition manuscrite du Lai de l'ombre. Réflexions sur l'art d'éditer les anciens textes. *Romania*, 54, pp. 161–196, 321–356.

Bischoff, B., 1979. *Paläographie des römischen Altertums und des abendländischen Mittelalters*. Berlin: Erich Schmidt Verlag.

Bischoff, B., 1990. *Latin Palaeography: Antiquity and the Middle Ages*. Translated by D.Ó. Cróinín and D. Ganz. Cambridge: Cambridge University Press.

Bischoff, B. 1992. *Paleografia latina. Antichità e Medioevo*. Translated by G.P. Mantovani and S. Zamponi. Padova: Antenore.

Ceccherini, I. and De Robertis, T., 2013. *Scriptoria e cancellerie nella Firenze del XIII e XIV secolo*. In: CILP (Comité International de Paléographie Latine) *XVIIIe Colloque International de Paléographie Latine* (online) St-Gall, Switzerland, 11–14 September 2013. Available at: www.palaeographia.org/cipl/stGall/abstracts2013a.htm#ceccherini.

Daston, L. and Galison, P., 2010. *Objectivity*. New York: Zone Books.

Derolez, A., 2003. *The Palaeography of Gothic Manuscript Books: From the Twelfth to the Early Sixteenth Century*. Cambridge: Cambridge University Press.

De Saussure, F., 1916. *Cours de Linguistique Générale*. Edited by C. Bally and A. Sechehaye, with A. Riedlinger. Paris: Payot.

Duntze, O., Shassan T., and Vogeler, G. (Eds.) 2015. *Kodikologie und Paläographie im Digitalen Zeitalter 3—Codicology and Palaeography in the Digital Age 3*. Norderstedt: Books on Demand.

Duranti, A., 2010. Husserl, Intersubjectivity and Anthropology. *Anthropology Theory*, 10(1), pp. 1–20.

Eggert P., 2009. *Securing the Past: Conservation in Art, Architecture and Literature*. Cambridge: Cambridge University Press.

Fischer, F., Fritze, C., and Vogeler, G. (Eds.) 2010. *Kodikologie und Paläographie im Digitalen Zeitalter 2—Codicology and Palaeography in the Digital Age 2.* Norderstedt: Books on Demand.

Ford, M., 2008. Disciplinary Authority and Accountability in Scientific Practice and Learning. *Science Education*, 93(3), pp. 404–23.

Gadamer, H.-G., 2013. *Truth and Method.* London: Bloomsbury Academy.

Gumbert, J.P., 1998. Commentare "Commentare Bischoff." *Scrittura e Civiltà*, 22, pp. 397–404.

Hockey, S., 2004. The History of Humanities Computing. In: S. Schreibman, R. Siemens, and J. Unsworth (Eds.) 2004. *A Companion to Digital Humanities.* Oxford: Blackwell, pp. 3–19.

Howe, C.J., Connolly R., and Windram H.F., 2012. Responding to Criticisms of Phylogenetic Methods in Stemmatology. *Studies in English Literature 1500–1900*, 52(1), pp. 51–67.

Huitfeldt, C. and Sperberg-McQueen, C.M., 2008. What is Transcription? *Literary and Linguistic Computing*, 23(3), pp. 295–310.

Kant, I., 1965. *Critique of Pure Reason.* Translated by N. Kemp. New York: St. Martin's Press.

Jakobson, R., 1960. Closing Statement: Linguistics and Poetics. In: T. Sebeok (Ed.). *Style in language.* Cambridge, MA: MIT Press, pp. 350–77.

IFLA (International Federation of Library Associations and Institutions), 1998. *Functional Requirement for Bibliographic Records* (FRBR). Available at: www.ifla.org/publications/functional-requirements-for-bibliographic-records.

Lentini, G. da, 1979. *Poesie.* Edited for print by R. Antonelli. Rome: Bulzoni.

McCarty, W., 2005. *Humanities Computing.* Basingstoke: Palgrave Macmillan.

McCarty, W., 2008. Knowing . . .: Modeling in Literary Studies. In: R. Siemens and S. Schreibman (Eds.) 2008. *A Companion to Digital Literary Studies.* Oxford: Blackwell, Ch. 21.

Pierazzo, E., 2011. A Rationale of Digital Documentary Editions. *Literary and Linguistic Computing*, 26(4), pp. 463–77.

Porsdam, H., 2013. Digital Humanities: On Finding the Proper Balance Between Qualitative and Quantitative Ways of Doing Research in the Humanities. *Digital Humanities Quarterly*, 7(3). Available at: www.digitalhumanities.org/dhq/vol/7/3/000167/000167.html.

Pratesi, A., 1995. Commentare Bischoff. *Scrittura e Civiltà*, 19, pp. 243–348.

Propp, V., 1968. *Morphology of the Folk Tale.* Austin, TX: University of Texas Press.

Rehbein M., Sahle, P., and Schassan, T. (Eds.) 2009. *Kodikologie und Paläographie im Digitalen Zeitalter—Codicology and Palaeography in the Digital Age.* Norderstedt: Books on Demand.

Rieder B. and Röhle T., 2012. Digital Methods: Five Challenges. In: D.M. Berry (Ed.) 2012. *Understanding Digital Humanities.* Basingstoke: Palgrave Macmillan.

Rosenblueth, A. and Wiener, R., 1945. The Role of Models in Science. *Philosophy of Science*, 12, pp. 316–22.

Schreibman, S., Siemens, R., and Unsworth, J. (Eds.) 2004. A Companion to Digital Humanities. Oxford: Blackwell.

Sculley, D. and Pasanek, B.M., 2008. Meaning and Mining: The Impact of Implicit Assumptions in Data Mining for the Humanities. *Literary and Linguistic Computing*, 23(4), pp. 409–24.

Shillingsburg, P.L., 1991. Text as Matter, Concept, and Action. *Studies in Bibliography*, 44, pp. 31–83.

Snow, C.P., 1960. The Two Cultures. The Rede Lecture, 1959. In: C.P. Snow, 1998. *The Two Cultures*. Cambridge: Cambridge University Press.

Spärck Jones, K., 2007. Computational Linguistics: What About the Linguistics? *Computational Linguistics*, 33(3), pp. 437–41.

Sperberg-McQueen, C.M., 2009. How to Teach Your Edition How to Swim. *Literary and Linguistic Computing*, 24(1), pp. 27–52.

Stokes, P.A., 2012a. The Problem of Digital Dating, Part I. *DigiPal Blog* (blog) November 20, 2012. Available at: www.digipal.eu/blog/the-problem-of-digital-dating-part-i/.

Stokes, P.A., 2012b. The Problem of Digital Dating, Part II: Some Further Principles. *DigiPal Blog* (blog) December 17, 2012. Available at: www.digipal.eu/blog/the-problem-of-digital-dating-part-ii-some-further-principles/.

Stokes, P.A., Brookes, S.J., Noël, G., Buomprisco, G., Watson, M., de Matos, D.M., Caballero, B., Caton, P., Hügel, S., Jakeman, N., and Vieira, J.M. (Eds.), 2011–14. *DigiPal: Digital Resource and Database of Palaeography, Manuscripts and Diplomatic.* Available at: http://digipal.eu/.

Stokes, P.A., 2015. The Problem of Digital Dating: A Model for Uncertainty in Medieval Documents. In: ADHO (Alliance of Digital Humanities Organisations). *Digital Humanities 2015. Book of Abstracts*. Sydney, Australia, June 30–July 3, 2015. Available at: http://dh2015.org/abstracts/.

Stokes, P.A. (in press) Computing and Palaeography in Theory: Putting the Palaeographer in Charge. In: S. Brookes, M. Rehbein, and P.A. Stokes (eds.) *Digital Palaeography*. Aldershot: Ashgate.

Tanselle, G.T., 1989. *A Rationale of Textual Criticism*. Philadelphia, PA: Pennsylvania University Press.

Tanselle, G.T., 1995. The Varieties of Scholarly Editing. In: D.C. Greetham (Ed.) 1995. *Scholarly Editing: A Guide to Research*. New York: Modern Language Association of America, pp. 9–32.

Tukey, J.W., 1962. The Future of Data Analysis. *The Annuals of Mathematical Statistics*, 33, pp. 11–67.

Unsworth, J., 2000. Scholarly Primitives: What Methods do Humanities Researchers Have in Common, and How Might our Tools Reflect This? In: King's College London, *Humanities Computing: Formal Methods, Experimental Practice*. London, May 13, 2000. Available at: www.people.virginia.edu/~jmu2m/Kings.5-00/primitives.html.

5 Modeling space in historical texts

Ian Gregory, Christopher Donaldson,
Andrew Hardie, and Paul Rayson

The texts used as sources in the humanities tend to be rich in information about place and space. Much of the information about place in such sources comes directly from the place-names mentioned in them. However, some come indirectly through more ambiguous, descriptive geographical references, as in the phrases "near the hills" or "beyond the town." In either case, the spatial information can be difficult for a human reader to conceptualize effectively. Even when a reader is familiar with the area described, identifying the location of the places to which that source refers and conceptualizing how those places relate to one another can be difficult; when the reader is unfamiliar with the area it is all but impossible. Beyond this, gaining an in-depth understanding of the way that different places are represented with a text often requires the places to be represented or modeled in non-textual form. One solution to this problem is to map the places to which the source refers. The effectiveness of this approach has been explored elsewhere (see, for example, Moretti, 1998). However, manually mapping textual information is time-consuming and the resulting maps are inflexible and, therefore, have only limited analytical potential.

Digital technologies present new opportunities for modeling, analyzing and interpreting the geographical information contained within texts. This chapter will explore some of these opportunities, focusing particularly on the modeling, analysis and interpretation of geographical information in texts, and on the difficulties of integrating space in textual analysis. Although texts are a particularly rich source of geographical information, extracting this information from them is challenging. The approaches documented here describe how place-names and the themes associated with them can be identified, visualized and analyzed. Although these are applied to a specific corpus, they are inherently transferable, and can be readily adapted and applied to other sources.

The corpus utilized in this chapter is a digitized collection of historical texts about the English Lake District, a canonical literary and cultural landscape in the north-west of England. The corpus contains 80 individual works, which range in date from 1622 to 1900 and together comprise over one and a half million words. It includes both famous and highly influential accounts of the Lake District, such as Thomas West's *Guide to the Lakes* (1778) and William Wordsworth's *Guide through the District of the Lakes* (Wordsworth, 5th ed., 1835), as well as a number of lesser known, but significant works, such as *Black's Shilling Guide to the English Lakes*, which appeared in no fewer than 22 editions between 1853 and 1900 (Black, 1853; Baddley ed., 1900). It also includes a selection of famous literary texts, such as the 1622 edition of Michael Drayton's *Poly-Olbion* (Drayton, 1622), and personal testimonials, such as the letters composed by the poet John Keats during his walking tour through the Lake District in 1818. Drawing on this corpus, in what follows, we will demonstrate how space and the themes associated with it can be modeled and analyzed—using a combination of geographic information systems (GIS) and other technologies. In the process, we will explain the procedures involved in translating textual data into a GIS format and evaluate the analytic opportunities that this affords.

1 Modeling features and their locations using GIS

Geographical information is conventionally represented digitally using a geographical information system (GIS). Effectively, GIS software takes conventional database functionality that allows data in tabular form to be stored, manipulated and queried, and combines this with a mapping system that, as well as mapping, also provides a range of other functionality for manipulating and querying information about location. To implement this, a GIS requires two types of data: first, there are the tables of text or numbers that are typically thought of as "data" and are familiar to users of database management systems such as Microsoft Access, MySQL or even Microsoft Excel. In GIS parlance, these are referred to as *attribute data*. The mapping system requires that each row of data be given a location representing the feature's location on the Earth's surface. These are referred to as *spatial data* and are based on co-ordinates. Simple features can be modeled using a single co-ordinate representing a point that models—for example, a village or a mountain top. Lines use a string of co-ordinates to represent, for example, roads or rivers. Areas, such as lakes or parishes, are represented using polygons, which are areas completely enclosed by one or more lines. Spatial data may also take the form of a *raster surface* in which the study area is broken down into a matrix of small regular pixels. Raster surfaces are often used to represent height. Taken together, the spatial data represent *where* features are located, while the attribute data provide information about *what* the features are (see, for example, Chrisman, 2002; Heywood, Cornelius, and Carver, 2002; Gregory and Ell, 2007).

This data model is well suited to representing, visualizing, and analyzing data from the Earth, and environmental sciences and the social sciences. Figure 5.1a illustrates the use of a GIS *layer* (as the combination of spatial and attribute data is called) to display historical census data representing population in and around the English Lake District in 1851. The attribute data are contained within the table, a fragment of which is shown in Figure 5.1b. In this case, the attribute data include information about the name of the parish and which district and county it is in, as well as statistical information on the total population in 1841 and 1851. The spatial data are the polygons that represent the historical parishes of the region.

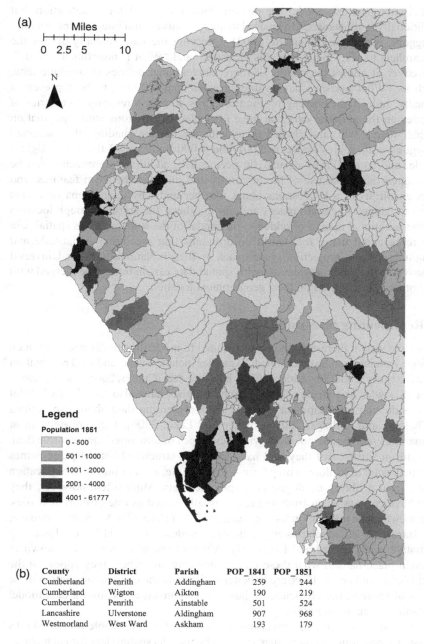

(b)	County	District	Parish	POP_1841	POP_1851
	Cumberland	Penrith	Addingham	259	244
	Cumberland	Wigton	Aikton	190	219
	Cumberland	Penrith	Ainstable	501	524
	Lancashire	Ulverstone	Aldingham	907	968
	Westmorland	West Ward	Askham	193	179

Figure 5.1 A conventional GIS data model of 1851 census data. (a) The spatial data are the polygons whose boundaries are shown and whose areas are shaded using values taken from the attribute data; (b) a fragment of attribute data.

This two-part data model has obvious merits as a tool for visualization, but additionally it allows space to be used to query, analyze, and integrate information (Gregory, Kemp, and Mostern, 2003). Querying the data spatially allows the researchers to ask, "What is at this location?" and "What is near this location?". Moreover, it allows the results of more conventional queries of attribute data, such as "What parishes have values greater than 4,000?", to be represented visually. Indeed, the shading on Figure 5.1a is, in fact, a response to a series of queries on the attribute data that have first selected polygons with a population greater than 4,000, and shaded them with the darkest shading, then selected polygons with values between 2,001 and 4,000 and shaded them in a lighter shade, and so on. From an analytic perspective, additional approaches can be developed that make use of the proximity and distances between features, and thus enable us to ask questions about whether and why phenomena or events seem to happen in certain places and not in others. Integration through location allows additional data to be added to the model of the study area. As spatial data are represented using real-world co-ordinates that are either in latitude and longitude, or in a projection system such as British National Grid or Universal Transverse Mercator, any dataset with spatial data can, in theory, be merged with any other dataset based on their geographical location.

2 Representing texts using GIS

GIS have shown themselves to be well suited to modeling tabular data for which precise locations can be determined. Examples include census and vital registration data (Gregory, 2008; Beveridge, 2014), land-use data (Cunfer, 2005) and economic data (Knowles and Healey, 2006). Archaeologists have also found GIS helpful for conducting landscape surveys and for representing data about excavations (Wheatley and Gillings, 2002; Conolly and Lake, 2006). Unfortunately, most humanities scholars do not work with these types of structured, quantitative data. Instead, in some cases they will have relatively structured lists of place-names that they want to explore in map form—for example, a list of places of publication taken from a library catalogue or corpus metadata. More often, however, they will have corpora of unstructured texts, usually stored as one or more text files, that may include mark-up in formats such as XML (eXtensible Mark-up Language; see Hardie, 2014) which possibly follows a standard such as TEI (Text Encoding Initiative; see Barnard and Ide, 1997). Although these texts may be known to contain place-names, what these place-names are and where they appear in the text is often unknown. If we are to better understand the geographies within these types of sources, the challenge is thus how to convert a text into a data model suitable for inclusion in GIS.

The major challenge in converting a text into a format suitable for use in GIS is usually providing a co-ordinate that can be used as spatial data for each place-name. When a researcher already has a list of place-names, such as places of publication, converting this to GIS format is relatively straightforward. The easiest way to do this is to use a place-name gazetteer such as Geonames.[1] A gazetteer

Input table		
Text ID	**Date**	**Place-name**
1	1769	London
2	1771	Kendal
3	1773	Keswick
4	1784	Ulverstone
5	1790	London

Gazetteer		
Place-name	**Longitude**	**Latitude**
London	51.5	-0.1
Kendal	54.3	-2.8
Keswick	54.6	-3.1
Ulverston	54.2	-3.1
Carlisle	54.9	-2.9
Whitehaven	54.6	-3.6

Output table				
Text ID	**Date**	**Place-name**	**Longitude**	**Latitude**
1	1769	London	51.5	-0.1
2	1771	Kendal	54.3	-2.8
3	1773	Keswick	54.6	-3.1
4	1784	Ulverstone		
5	1790	London	51.5	-0.1

Figure 5.2 A simplified example of adding co-ordinates to an input table using a gazetteer.

is effectively a database table that includes place-names and their co-ordinates (Southall, Mostern, and Berman, 2011). A relational join can be used to attempt to automatically match all the place-names from the researcher's list to the gazetteer. This will create a new table that adds the co-ordinates and any other relevant information from the gazetteer to the researcher's original data. The researcher needs to check the results, as relational joins often fail to match due to minor spelling variations. There may also be additional problems such as place-names that do not occur in the gazetteer, or ambiguous place-names that can refer to more than one entry in the gazetteer. These will need some manual intervention from the researcher. Figure 5.2 shows an example of this process: an input table that contains a hypothetical list of place-names associated with a text is joined with a gazetteer to add co-ordinates. In one case, Ulverstone, the match has failed because of different spellings between the two tables; this would need to be rectified manually. It is also important to note that the gazetteer is likely to have many more place-names than the input table, but those which do not match any of the input data are not copied over to the output table.

Once we have a table where co-ordinates have been added to a list of place-names, importing this into GIS software should be a simple task. Any GIS software package should be able to take such a table of data and use the co-ordinates to *geo-reference* it, as providing real-world co-ordinates is called. The result is a point layer that can be displayed as a dot map.

Where a user has an unstructured text containing place-names, an additional level of complexity is added. Converting this into GIS format now becomes a two-stage process, where first the place-names have to be identified and then they have to have co-ordinates allocated to them. Given a relatively small corpus, this can be done by reading through the whole text and manually identifying the place-names (Gregory and Cooper, 2009; Cooper and Gregory, 2011). They can either be copied and pasted into a table which can then be geo-referenced as described above, or they can be tagged using XML (as described below) to allow them to be extracted at a later stage. Manual identification of place-names gives high levels of accuracy, but is too labor-intensive to be practical for all but small corpora.

Identifying place-names and allocating them to co-ordinates can be done automatically on larger corpora using a process called *geo-parsing* (Grover et al., 2010). The first stage in this involves using techniques from natural language processing (NLP; see Jurafsky and Martin, 2009; Manning and Schütze, 1999, for introductions) to attempt to identify all of the place-names within the text or corpus in question. This takes advantage of the fact that place-names are proper nouns, or named entities, which can be identified and tagged using advanced NLP techniques. Geo-parsing techniques can also exploit contextual information to suggest whether the proper nouns are place-names as opposed to personal names or the names of organizations. This provides a list of "candidate" words that are suspected of being place-names. The list of candidates is then matched to a gazetteer in the way described above. In the case of geo-parsed candidate place-names, the very fact of whether or not the candidate can be matched in the gazetteer is one factor that can help us decide whether that candidate is really a place-name. When a text is geo-parsed, information from the gazetteer is usually encoded back into the text using XML tags. The output from this process is thus the original text with added XML elements that identify place-names, with their co-ordinates and potentially other information as attributes.

Figure 5.3 shows an example of the output produced by the automated geo-parsing of West's (1778) *Guide to the Lakes* using the Edinburgh Geo-parser (Grover et al., 2010). This particular geo-parsing software identifies all candidate place-names using an "enamex" tag.[2] Where these refer to place-names a range of additional information is stored as attributes, including the word number of the place-name within the text ("sw") and its longitude and latitude ("long" and "lat"). Other information derived from the gazetteer includes: the type of place that it is, its gazetteer ID, and a standardized version of its spelling ("type," "gazref," and "name" respectively). A confidence score, calculated by

To render the tour more agreeable, the company should be provided with a telescope, for viewing the fronts and summits of the inaccessible rocks, and the distant country, from the tops of the high mountains *<enamex sw="w14842" long="-3.123" lat="54.655" type="mtn" gazref="unlock:11284755" name="Skiddaw" conf="2.4">*Skiddaw*</enamex>* and *<enamex sw="w14854" long="-3.012" lat="54.530" type="mtn" gazref="unlock:11169753" name="Helvellyn" conf="2.4">*Helvellyn*</enamex>*.

Figure 5.3 An example of output from the Edinburgh Geo-Parser.

the geo-parser to help disambiguate places with the same name ("conf"), is also included. Thus, in Figure 5.3 we can see that the two identified place-names—Skiddaw and Helvellyn—are mountains (type="mtn"), have standardized spellings that are the same as their spelling within the text, and have been assigned latitudes and longitudes.

Although tools such as the Edinburgh Geo-parser enable us to geo-parse large corpora automatically, manual intervention will ensure a higher degree of accuracy. Place-name identification is a complex and subjective process, and there are multiple sources of geo-parsing errors. Common examples include: failing to identify a proper noun and thus missing a place-name; wrongly identifying a personal name or other word as a place-name; giving the wrong co-ordinate to a place-name; spelling variations between the source text the gazetteer (including those caused by digitization errors); and so on. As an example, take the following sentence: "Travelling over the Raise, the Bishop of Carlisle paused to admire the view of Windermere before continuing on to Langdale."[3] Carlisle is a city near the Lake District but, as "Bishop of Carlisle" is a title, in most cases, but perhaps not all, we would not want to include this as a place-name. Windermere is both a lake and town. Whereas a human reader is likely to infer that the reference here must be to the lake, a computer is unlikely to be so subtle. In the center of the Lake District there is a valley called Great Langdale, which runs parallel to a smaller valley called Little Langdale. Colloquially, the name "Langdale" is used to refer to Great Langdale; however, there is an entirely separate but comparatively unknown valley called Langdale in North Yorkshire, east of the Lake District. A computer comparing candidate place-names from the text with names from a gazetteer is most likely to match Langdale to the last of these, whereas a human is likely to assume that it refers to Great Langdale. Finally, is "the Raise" a place-name at all? It is likely to refer to "Dunmail Raise," a pass that connects Grasmere and Thirlmere, but it is highly unlikely that a geo-parser would identify it as this. Moreover, one might argue that because the word "raise" is a generic, regional term for a pass, "the Raise" should not be identified as a place-name at all. A counter-argument would be that, because it is spelt with a capital "R," "Raise" is being used as a proper noun and should thus be considered a place-name. In the context of a non-modern corpus, this argument is further complicated by the fact that, as we go back in time, English *common* nouns are more likely to receive the capitalization that more modern English applies only to proper nouns. All this goes to show that the decision of what is and is not a place-name can be highly subjective and a researcher's definition may evolve as the research proceeds.

Errors such as these meant that, in their own assessment of the accuracy of the Edinburgh Geo-parser, Tobin et al. (2010) found that 75 percent of place-names were correctly located when using a 13-million word corpus of official reports from the nineteenth and early twentieth centuries. Although this represents a good start, clearly this contains a lot of error; moreover, the extent to which this will bias results and cause problems with an analysis is unclear. Additionally, when a different corpus is geo-parsed, it is not clear whether the results will be better or worse than this. One way to address this is through the use of *concordance geo-parsing* (Rupp et al., 2014). This is based on the idea that geo-parsing the entire corpus in one go is both unnecessary and difficult to correct. Instead, only the text that occurs near to a search-term of interest is geo-parsed. As an example, if we are interested in the term "sublime" (which is a recurrent term in historical writing about the Lake District), we would first identify and extract all the instances of this word from the text along with their *concordance lines* (the text that occurs either side of them). In this case, we extract concordance lines containing 50 words to the left and 50 words to the right of the search-term to provide co-text for the geo-parser to work with. Extracting this is relatively simple using corpus analysis software such as AntConc or CQPweb (see Anthony, 2013, and Hardie, 2012, respectively). These concordance lines are geo-parsed using the Edinburgh Geo-parser. The results can then be examined for errors both by mapping and reading the concordance lines. Because there are far fewer words to explore than in the entire corpus, it is far easier to check these results. Any corrections that need to be made are then written to an updates file so that, when another search-term is used, these updates will be automatically applied as part of the geo-parsing process. In this way, the researcher can check and correct material manually, ideally starting with a search-term that is relatively rare in the corpus—in order to ensure that the amount of checking remains manageable—and working up to more common terms as the updates file develops. While this semi-automated process takes time, it greatly improves accuracy as the researcher is now in control of the process. Additionally, it encourages the researcher to become familiar with the ways that place-names are used in the corpus and, therefore, to become aware of issues such as "Raise" and "Bishop of Carlisle" and to make their own decision about whether these are place-names that should be assigned co-ordinates and, if so, to which location each particular instance of this term should refer. For large corpora, there is an additional advantage, since, when billions of words are involved, the processing time of geo-parsing the entire corpus may be too long to be practical; thus, it makes more sense only to geo-parse as required.

The output from the geo-parsing process is a text with additional XML mark-up that identifies place-names and gives their co-ordinates. The last stage is to convert this text into a GIS layer. This involves using a program that extracts information about every occurrence of a place-name from the XML and writes it to a table. At a minimum, this table needs to have the place-name and its associated co-ordinates. To make it more usable, however, a range of other fields are also likely to be needed. One obvious source of information that is likely to be required is the other data about the place-name which, in Figure 5.3, would be additional information from the attributes of the "enamex" tag. Some additional textual information is also likely to be required. A word number to give the location of the place-name within the text might also be helpful. If concordance geo-parsing is used, the search-term should also be used as well as the text of the concordance line itself, so that both place-name and search-term can be viewed in context. This presents some problems as in most databases, including those that underlie popular GIS software, text fields can only be a maximum of 255 characters long. Additional metadata that shows the source of the information may also be included.

Figure 5.4 shows one example of the columns of the table based on a concordance geo-parsing around the word "sublime" in our Lake District corpus. The first four records, down to "title," are derived from the corpus metadata and give information about the text in which the place-name was found. The next five, down to the standardized place-name, are taken from the geo-parser output (other fields such as "type" and "conf" from Figure 5.3 could also have been included). The last six items are from the text itself, giving the place-name as it appears in the text, the search-term, and the co-text found to the left and right of both of these. In this example, co-text fields have been restricted to ten word tokens.[4]

Field	Explanation	Example Value
FileId	Unique ID for the text the place-name came from	34
Author	...of this text	Anon.-T. Ostell (pub.)
Year	...the text was published	1804
Title	...of the text	Observations, Chiefly Lithological, Made in a Five Weeks' Tour
WordNo	Location within the text where the place-name occurs	w25383
Latitude		54.545899
Longitude		-3.275492
GazRef	Identifies the gazetteer record used to geo-parse this place-name	unlock:11094751
StName	Standardised spelling of the place-name	Buttermere
LPlCotext	The co-text to the left of the place-name	, the sign of the Salmon . The scenery about
PlName	The place-name as it occurs in the text	Buttermere
RPlCotext	The co-text to the right of the place-name	is truly sublime and august . On a promontory to
LSTCotext	The co-text to the left of the search-term	of the Salmon . The scenery about Buttermere is truly
SearchTerm		sublime
RSTCotext	The co-text to the right of the search-term	and august . On a promontory to the east of

Figure 5.4 Example fields used to convert a geo-parsed text file to a table suitable for GIS and a sample record.

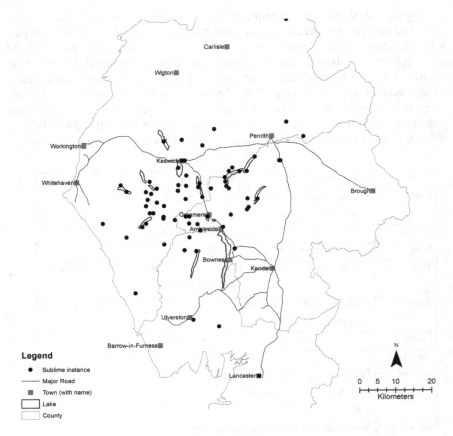

Figure 5.5 Instances of "sublime" in the Lake District corpus.

Geo-parsing allows the geographies associated with themes within a particular text to be explored. Themes are identified using one or more keywords and their geography is established based on which place-names collocate with these keywords. Obviously, concordance geo-parsing is well suited to this. Figure 5.5 shows an example of modeling the geography of the word "sublime" in the Lake District corpus using a point map of the type that can quickly be created once a text has been geo-referenced. The points on the map represent place-names that occur within ten words of the word "sublime." This map is clearly only a first stage in understanding the geography of this theme: while we have managed to locate the place-names that collocate with our search-term, the map itself tells us little about the geographical collocation pattern, what is creating it, or how it changes over time or between different genres. Understanding the pattern thus requires further modeling and analysis.

3 Analytic modeling of space

Figure 5.6 moves towards a more analytic modeling of a point pattern to enable us to understand the geographical distribution of place-name instances. It is based on the data from Figure 5.5, showing the geography of "sublime"; however, rather than use points, the pattern has been smoothed to indicate which places have the highest number of points nearby. This is a process known as *density smoothing* (Lloyd, 2007, Ch.7). Technically, in GIS terminology, what is happening here is that we are converting from a point layer to a raster surface made up of small pixels. The values for the pixels are calculated from the distance from each pixel to its surrounding points, with nearer points given a higher weighting. The density-smoothed map shows us a much clearer pattern than the points in Figure 5.5. It is easily seen that there are some clear clusters of places

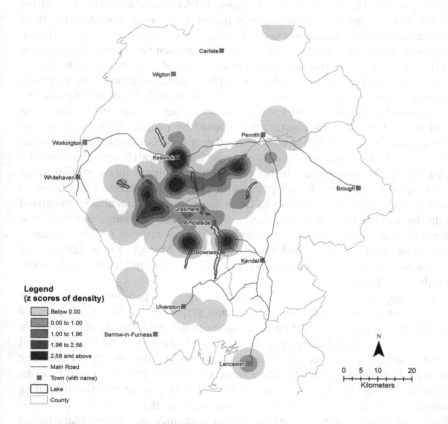

Figure 5.6 Density smoothed map of "sublime" instances. Class intervals are based
          on critical values of z-scores of positive density values so 0.00 is the mean,
          1.00 is one standard deviation over the mean, 1.96 is the 5 percent
          threshold (two-tailed) and 2.58 is the 1 percent threshold.

that tended to be described as sublime. Working roughly clockwise, these include Keswick, Borrowdale (south of Keswick), Ullswater, Windermere, Coniston, and the western fells from Sca Fell to the Pillar. Some caution must be used in interpreting this map. Geo-parsing represents all locations using points including the large lakes such as Ullswater, Windermere and Coniston. The Ullswater point lies in the crook of the lake, approximately half-way along its length. Windermere and Coniston are both the names of villages as well as lakes, and the points representing them lie in the locations of the villages, on the east side of Windermere and the north-west of Coniston. All of these clusters may, therefore, refer to larger areas than they appear to on the map so the maps must be interpreted accordingly.

Figures 5.5 and 5.6 illustrate the basics of modeling how a theme varies over space. They are, however, only crude abstractions that provide basic descriptions of the patterns. Geographical Text Analysis (GTA) (Murrieta-Flores et al., 2014) is a set of techniques that allows us to go further. It allows us to identify locations where place-name instances cluster together, and find what words collocate with the place-names in this cluster. Clusters can then be compared to see how different places vary. The spatial pattern of a particular search-term can also be compared with the overall distribution of place-name instances in the corpus to see where the search-term occurs more or less than would be expected given this background population. This enables the researcher to evaluate the extent to which a pattern such as Figure 5.6 is caused by people visiting and writing about places such as Keswick more than other places. Geographical patterns can also be compared—for example, to see whether two search-terms have similar geographies; to investigate whether two authors or genres follow similar geographies; or to compare the geographies of place-name instances that occur in writing from different time periods. Other sources of data can also be integrated into the analysis to explore the relationship between place-name instances and, for example, heights, population density, roads or railway stations. Gregory and Donaldson (2016), Donaldson, Gregory and Murrieta-Flores (2015), and Donaldson, Gregory and Taylor (2017) provide some examples of this for work on the Lake District.

GTA approaches are types of "macro-reading" in which we move from the bare text to abstract summaries such as maps, graphs or statistics. These are used to identify patterns, and we then re-engage with the text in an attempt to explain the patterns found. (The preservation of concordance text in the GIS table is of great practical use in helping us get back to reading the underlying language of the text or corpus.) An alternative approach is to use Place-Centered Reading (Hastings, Gregory, and Atkinson, 2015). This is a more traditional reading approach, but rather than reading in a linear manner, the researcher's reading is based around place-names. The first stage is to identify one or more place-names of interest and search the corpus for these. The text around the place-names is then studied closely and other relevant place-names are identified. The researcher then builds up a qualitative understanding of everything that has been written about a particular area.

4 Conclusions

This chapter has explored some of the basic challenges of how space can be modeled from digital texts. The major challenge in doing this lies with how to identify place-names within a large corpus and allocate them to a co-ordinate. Geo-parsing presents a solution to this issue, and our refinement of concordance geo-parsing offers further advantages in terms of accuracy and checking. Geo-parsing will not always be necessary. With smaller texts, perhaps up to a few tens of thousands of words, it may be possible, or even desirable, to simply identify place-names manually by reading through the whole text. Alternatively, a researcher may not need to identify all place-names within the text, but may instead only be interested in locations that are associated with a text as a whole—for example, place of publication. Whatever the nature of the source, the text is abstracted to a table that contains place-names, their co-ordinates, and other information about the place derived from the text or the gazetteer. The co-ordinates are then used to create a GIS point layer. More sophisticated analysis can then be used to describe, visualize and understand the patterns further.

One major limitation with these approaches is that computers require representations of geography that are very precise and unambiguous. Humanities sources that consist of human language-in-use—that is, a discourse which, for us as humans, is inseparable from the social and cultural context in which it is situated—are rarely precise and unambiguous, and this causes a range of issues. For example, gazetteers tend to provide a point location for place-names. While this is suitable for features such as towns or mountains, it is far less suitable for others such as lakes, valleys or rivers. Lakes or rivers could be georeferenced using polygons or lines respectively, but it is in fact not entirely clear that these represent an improvement. If a text talks about "walking along the banks of Ullswater" or "we crossed the River Greta," it is not referring to the entire lake or river; therefore, is representing the entire feature really an improvement on using a single point? If we do use lines and polygons, a second issue is how we can compare these with the points that represent other features. There is also the issue that we mentioned above, of place-names such as "Windermere," which can refer to different features depending on context.

A second limitation is that rather than modeling space, the approaches described above actually model place-names and are less effective with less precise representations. One example of this is if a writer says, for example, "the road from Keswick to Ambleside is scenic," an automated technique will wrongly identify that it is the two towns that are scenic, rather than the road between them. More intractable problems arise when place-names are not used or are only implied. When a writer uses phrases such as "a magnificent view of the hills" or "we arrived into town," it may, or may not, be obvious to a reader what time or place they are talking about; however, a computer is not able to work out the reference of such phrases reliably, and it is unlikely that technical developments will enable them to do so in the foreseeable future. Geography may also be taken as a more generic concept—for example, how writers represent upland areas, valleys or forests may be of interest, rather than the specifics of named places. Some of the ideas outlined above might help in understanding this—for example, by identifying which words collocate with terms such as "mountain" or "forest," but these would require different forms of visualization than mapping.

Identifying and extracting the geographical information in a text or corpus is only the first stage in modeling its spatial characteristics, but is frequently the hardest and most time-consuming. Once this information has been extracted, further modeling allows it to be analyzed in more depth. This can involve using techniques from GIS, spatial analysis, time-series analysis, corpus linguistics (Adolphs, 2006; McEnery and Hardie, 2012) or combinations of these. These approaches provide macro-reading summaries of the text, and the spatial and potentially temporal patterns associated with particular themes. It can also involve using spatial references to allow the texts to be read in a non-linear way, such that a reader can read everything the corpus says about a particular place or area, perhaps at a specific time or in relation to a particular theme. Crucially, however, at all stages of the research process, the researcher needs to be wary and critical of what the map or other visualization is showing. The types of maps produced by GIS provide an excellent way of crudely summarizing spatial patterns; however, for the researcher to understand the patterns that emerge, and the reasons why they exist, requires significant further work in exploring the parts of the text from which the points on the maps were derived. In some cases, this will lead to the map or graph being refined. Thus, a map in a GIS is very different from a map created by manual cartography. In manual cartography, the map is in many ways the end product. In GIS, a "map" in the form of a layer of geo-referenced data is produced early in the research process, and it is explored, corrected, queried and enhanced throughout the research process. The final output is not simply a static map or maps in a publication; the actual intellectual product we are working towards is the analysis or argument that the map helps to illustrate—an analysis or argument that was, in turn, derived from the process of creating and refining the map.

Acknowledgements

The research leading to these results has received funding from the European Research Council (ERC) under the European Union's Seventh Framework Programme (FP7/2007–2013)/ERC grant "Spatial Humanities: Texts, GIS, places" (agreement number 283850). We are also grateful to Dr. Claire Grover (University of Edinburgh) for her assistance in providing us with the Edinburgh Geo-parser and to Dr. David Cooper (Manchester Metropolitan University) for his work on creating the Lake District corpus.

Notes

1   See www.geonames.org. Other gazetteers are available, including Getty Thesaurus of Geographic Names (www.getty.edu/research/tools/vocabularies/tgn) and the Ordnance

Survey 1:50,000 Scale Gazetteer (www.ordnancesurvey.co.uk/business-and-government/products/50k-gazetteer.html).

2　In XML, tags are enclosed by "<" and ">" symbols and the information to which each tag refers concludes with an end-tag ("</. . .>").

3　This is an artificial sentence designed to illustrate the issues, not an actual quotation.

4　Corpus linguists refer to individual instances of words in a text as "[word] tokens." In most corpus software, a punctuation symbol is counted as a separate token; thus "red, white and blue" is five tokens (four words and a comma).

References

Adolphs, S., 2006. *Introducing Electronic Text Analysis*. London: Routledge.

Anthony, L., 2013. Developing AntConc for a New Generation of Corpus Linguists. In: UCREL (University Centre for Comupter Corpus Research on Language), *Proceedings of the Corpus Linguistics Conference (CL 2013)*. Lancaster, UK, July 22–26 2013. Available at: http://ucrel.lancs.ac.uk/cl2013/ (accessed September 11, 2015).

Baddley, M.J.B. (ed.), 1900. *Black's Shilling Guide to the English Lakes*. London: Adam and Charles Black, 1900.

Baines, E., 1829. *A Companion to the Lakes of Cumberland, Westmoreland, and Lancashire: In a descriptive account of a family tour and excursions on horseback and on foot*. London: Simpkin & Marshall.

Barber, S., 1892. *Beneath Helvellyn's Shade: Notes and Sketches in the Valley of Wythburn*. London: E. Stock.

Barnard, D.T. and Ide, N.M., 1997. The Text Encoding Initiative: Flexible and Extensible Document Encoding. *Journal of the Association for Information Science and Technology*, 48, pp. 622–8.

Beveridge, A.A., 2014. The Development, Persistence, and Change of Racial Segregation in U.S. Urban Areas, 1880–2010. In: I.N. Gregory and A. Geddes (Eds.) 2014. *Towards Spatial Humanities: Historical GIS and Spatial History*. Bloomington, IN: Indiana University Press, pp. 35–61.

Black's Shilling Guide to the English Lakes, 1853. Edinburgh: Adam and Charles Black, 1853.

Conolly, J. and Lake, M., 2006. *Geographical Information Systems in Archaeology*. Cambridge: Cambridge University Press.

Cooke, C., 1827. *The Tourist's and Traveller's Companion to the Lakes*. London: Sherwood, Jones & Co.

Cooper, D. and Gregory, I.N., 2011. Mapping the English Lake District: A literary GIS. *Transactions of the Institute of British Geographers*, 36, pp. 89–108.

Cunfer, G., 2005. *On the Great Plains: Agriculture and Environment*. College Station, TX: Texas A&M University Press.

Chrisman, N., 2002. *Exploring Geographic Information Systems* (2nd ed.) New York: John Wiley & Sons.

Dalton, J., 1755. *A Descriptive Poem, Addressed to Two Ladies, at their Return from Viewing the Mines near Whitehaven*. London: J.J. Rivington.

Donaldson, C., Gregory, I., and Murrieta-Flores, P., 2015. Mapping 'Wordsworthshire': A GIS Study of Literary Tourism in Victorian England. *Journal of Victorian Culture*, 20, pp. 287–307.

Donaldson, C., Gregory, I.N., and Taylor, J.E., 2017. Locating the Beautiful, Picturesque, Sublime and Majestic: Spatially Analysing the Application of Aesthetics Terminology in Descriptions of the English Lake District. *Journal of Historical Geography,* 56, pp. 43–60.

Drayton, M., 1622. *Poly-Olbion, or A Chorographical Description of Tracts, Rivers, Mountaines, Forests, and other Parts of this renowned Isle of Great Britaine.* London: M. Lownes et al.

Gilpin, W., 1786. *Observations, Relative Chiefly to Picturesque Beauty.* London: R. Blamire.

Gregory, I.N., 2008. Different Places, Different Stories: Infant Mortality Decline in England & Wales, 1851–1911. Annals of the Association of American Geographers, 98, pp. 773–94.

Gregory, I.N. and Cooper, D., 2009. Thomas Gray, Samuel Taylor Coleridge and Geographical Information Systems: A Literary GIS of Two Lake District Tours. *International Journal of Humanities and Arts Computing,* 3, pp. 61–84.

Gregory, I.N. and Donaldson, C., 2016. Geographical Text Analysis: Digital Cartographies of Lake District Literature. In D. Cooper, C. Donaldson, and P. Murrieta-Flores P. (Eds.) *Literary Mapping in the Digital Age,* pp. 67–87. Abingdon: Routledge.

Gregory, I.N. and Ell, P.S., 2007. *Historical GIS: Techniques, Methodologies and Scholarship.* Cambridge: Cambridge University Press.

Gregory, I.N., Kemp, K., and Mostern, R., 2003. Geographical Information and Historical Research: Current Progress and Future Directions. *History and Computing,* 13, pp. 7–21.

Gregory, I., Cooper, D., Hardie, A., and Rayson, P., 2015. Spatializing and Analysing Digital Texts: Corpora, GIS and Places. In D.J. Bodenhamer, J. Corrigan and T.M. Harris (Eds.) 2015. *Deep Maps and Spatial Narratives.* Bloomington: IN, Indiana University Press, pp. 150–78.

Grover, C., Tobin, R., Byrne, K., Woollard, M., Reid, J., Dunn, S., and Ball, J., 2010. Use of the Edinburgh Geoparser for Georeferencing Digitized Historical Collections. *Philosophical Transactions of the Royal Society A,* 368, pp. 3875–89.

Hardie, A., 2012. CQPweb – Combining Power, Flexibility and Usability in a Corpus Analysis Tool. *International Journal of Corpus Linguistics,* 17, pp. 380–409.

Hardie, A., 2014. Modest XML for corpora: Not a standard but a suggestion. *ICAME Journal,* 38, pp. 73–103.

Hastings, S., Gregory, I.N., and Atkinson, P., 2015. Explaining Geographical Variations in English Rural Infant Mortality Decline Using Place-Centred Reading. *Historical Methods,* 48, pp. 128–40.

Heywood, I., Cornelius, S., and Carver S., 2002. *An Introduction to Geographical Information Systems* (2nd ed.) Harlow, Essex: Prentice Hall.

Jurafsky, D. and Martin, J.H., 2009. *Speech and Language Processing: An Introduction to Natural Language Processing, Speech Recognition, and Computational Linguistics* (2nd ed.). Harlow, Essex: Prentice Hall.

Knowles, A.K. and Healey, R.G., 2006. Geography, Timing, and Technology: A GIS-Based Analysis of Pennsylvania's Iron Industry, 1825–1875. *Journal of Economic History,* 66, pp. 608–34.

Lloyd, C.D., 2007. *Local Models for Spatial Analysis.* Boca Raton, FL: CRC Press.

Manning, C. and Schütze, H., 1999. *Foundations of Statistical Natural Language Processing.* Cambridge, MA: MIT Press.

McEnery, A.M. and Hardie, A., 2012. *Corpus Linguistics: Method, Theory and Practice.* Cambridge: Cambridge University Press.

Moretti, F., 1998. *Atlas of the European Novel 1800–1900.* London: Verso.

Murrieta-Flores, P., Baron, A., Gregory, I., Hardie, A., and Rayson, P., 2014. Automatically Analyzing Large Texts in a GIS Environment: The Registrar General's Reports and Cholera in the 19th Century. *Transactions in GIS*, 19 (2), pp. 296–320.

Radcliffe, A., 1796. *A Journey Made in the Summer of 1794*. London: G.G. and J. Robinson.

Rupp, C.J., Rayson, P., Gregory, I., Hardie, A., Joulain, A., and Hartmann, D., 2014. Dealing with Heterogeneous Big Data when Geoparsing Historical Corpora. In: IEEE (Institute of Electronical and Electronics Engineers), IEEE Conference on Big Data. Bethesda, MD, October 27, 2014. Available at: http://ieeexplore.ieee.org/xpl/article Details.jsp?reload=true&arnumber=7004457.

Southall, H., Mostern, R., and Berman, M.L., 2011. On Historical Gazetteers. *International Journal of Humanities and Arts Computing*, 5, pp. 127–45.

Tobin, R., Grover, C., Byrne, K., Reid, J., and Walsh, J., 2010. Evaluation of Georeferencing. Proceedings of the 6th Workshop on Geographic Information Retrieval. Zurich, Switzerland, January 28–9, 2010. New York: ACM.

West, T., 1778. *A Guide to the Lakes: Dedicated to the Lovers of Landscape Studies*. London: Richardson & Urquhart.

Wheatley, D. and Gillings, M., 2002. *Spatial Technology and Archaeology: The Archaeological Applications of GIS*. London: Taylor & Francis.

Wilkinson, T., 1824. *Tours to the British Mountains, with the Descriptive Poems of Lowther*. London: Taylor & Hessey.

Wordsworth, W., 1822. *A Description of the Scenery of the Lakes in the North of England*. London: Longman & Co.

Wordsworth, W., 1835. *A Guide Through the District of the Lakes in the North of England* (5th ed.). Kendal: Hudson and Nicholson.

Young, A., 1770. *Six Months' Tour through the North of England*. London: W. Strahan.

6 Modeling time

Benjamin Schmidt

Time is deceptively simple to model. The basic units—months, days, years—are perhaps more venerable than any of the other fundamentals that humanists encode or enumerate. Most facets of experience present difficulties of categorization that are obvious (for instance, genre) or hard-earned difficulties in representation (e.g., gender or nationality). The basic categories of time, on the other hand, seem paradoxically the most eternal.

There is a rich history of deep thinking on time in the humanities; questions of temporality and experience were essential to the foundational works of what is now called "critical theory" in the early twentieth century (Husserl, 1991; Heidegger, 1962; Benjamin, 1940). Those insights are more elusive, however, than the most recent critical discourse on social structures like race, which centrally involves an awareness of power as yielded in the social world. The deepest critical insights into social structures lie within living memory, and their insights continue to power vast areas of the humanities to the present day (West, 2001; Butler, 2011; etc.). The implications for scholarship—let alone data modeling—of the early twentieth century theories of time is much less clear.

More than for almost any other category, that is to say, we have a standard model of time: as linear, regular, and fundamentally understandable by all human beings. The challenges and opportunities in modeling time lie in two directions. First, fully understanding the complexities and implications of the standard linear model of time, and making use of its resilience to exploit the remarkable properties of a linear and intersubjective understanding of time; and second, pushing at the limits to see where and how the standard model falls apart, in order to avoid mistakes and find ways to model and identify uniquely difficult or uniquely interesting cases.

There is, quite literally, a "standard model" of time. The International Standards Organization, the non-governmental organization that promotes standardization for "intellectual, scientific, technological and economic activity" has been codifying various formats for time since its formation in 1947. The ISO first unified its various temporal modeling categories in 1988 into ISO 8601: the latest revision, from 2004, offers a singularly well-thought-out distillation of centuries of temporal modeling practices.[1] While the goal is to create an unambiguous format for interchange that will be both machine-readable and legible across linguistic barriers, for humanities data modeling it carries particular interest as the result of an international and pan-disciplinary attempt to codify the ways people need to describe time. It describes a set of practices for representing times and periods in a standard way that attempts to supervene problems of language and locality. While not all its shortcomings are problems with the wider cultural understanding of time, they do represent the most important single attempt to reconcile standard practice with the widest variety of cases. Before moving into the complications, anyone wishing to model time should understand its basics and a few of its intricacies.

The ISO 8601 standard presents time as a hierarchy of discrete elements that can be refined to describe any arbitrarily small period. As precision increases, more terms are tacked on to the end. Valid ISO dates can be rounded at any level. This matches the differing specificities required for historical dates: for example, the communist bloc disintegrated in 1989, French revolutionaries stormed the Bastille on 1789-07-14, and the first tower of the World Trade Center collapsed at 2001-09-11T08:46. In this last example, 2001-09-11 gives the day, date, and year, and T08:46 gives the time to the minute in local time. To specify it universally, the date could be concluded T12:46Z-04:00 to indicate that the event took place in a local time context four hours behind Greenwich mean time.

It is worth noting that the ISO standard is a textual one, not a numerical one. Although it is easy to think of time as linear and therefore quantitative, fully numeric models of time tend to be stopgaps rather than useful standardizations. Despite (and because of) its self-evident modelability, misrepresentations of time have greater potential to cause catastrophe than almost any other form. The world's popular media awaited the millennium in fear that the Y2K bug—caused by the frequent shortcut in Fortran programming of representing a year as two integers rather than four—might cause the engines of economic life to grind to a halt as the switch from year "99" to year "00" produced a profusion of retirees with negative ages, power plants believing they had not been maintained in decades, or credit card balances suddenly accumulating a century's worth of interest. Debate remains on whether the immense investment in updating code averted a true disaster, or if the whole affair was simply a moral panic driven by a public uneasy with the role that computers played in society and hungry for any properly millenarian tale of hubris bringing destructive cleaning. Some adherents of the former view, though, and a few more besides, still warn that the real danger lay not in Fortran's customary practices, but in the more explicit data model of the only slightly less venerable Posix system's explicit representations of time, which converts text to numbers by counting in seconds from January 1, 1970. The 32-bit integer holding "POSIX time" will reach its maximum value on January 19, 2038, potentially bringing not just C programs, but those in whole families of languages built on it over the last forty years to a standstill.

These lessons can be taken to suggest a simple solution, and one that most projects would do well to accept as a practical matter: the ISO standard is the *only* acceptable way to render dates. In an international, multilingual world where later intelligibility and reuse should be a core value of every archival project, this is sound advice. In particular, it should be counterposed against the temptation to leave dates entirely in their original form. Natural language month formats are difficult to parse. The ambiguous date formats in common use, such as 7/5/2014, can mean either May 7th or July 5th, depending on national context. And peculiar calendrical regimes, like dates under the French Revolutionary calendar, are generally susceptible to translation of some sort.

The parade of temporal modeling disasters hanging from supposedly straight-forward temporal regimes indicates a tension at work more substantial than simple carelessness. A textual representation like the ISO is relatively difficult to misrepresent; but it is also extremely limiting. It exists more as an interchange format than as a useful model in its own right. Our *understandings* of time are only occasionally textually grounded. For computers to model time effectively, they must usually translate it into a number. And although human beings possess a much richer set of interpretive frameworks than computers, we, too, must transform time in order to understand it, whether into numbers, some other kind of text, or something else entirely.

Alongside the question of *standardization*, this question of *representation* is the primary one facing the humanist modeling time. For those whose primary goal is the ability to interface with other document sources, following the ISO is the only acceptable choice because it promotes machine-readability and international exchange. But when the human interpretability of temporal objects matters, standard forms may require non-standard representations. Time can be visualized, narrated, or framed in sound. Each of these representations may imply or embody a model of time on its own; some are compatible with the standard model, but others may not be.

Temporal representation is so important that it has played a role in cementing the standard, linear model of time. To appreciate just how much cognitive work went into the creation of linear time, it is worth reflecting on the representations that made it possible. The timeline, linear time in its classical form, is a creature of the enlightenment (Rosenberg and Grafton, 2010; Friendly, 2009). The first modern timeline was produced by Jacques Barbeu-Dubourg, as a 54-foot long scroll mounted in a box; Barbeu-Dubourg's timeline was exhibited through Europe and an object of fascination for decades. Even more widely circulated was the chart of biography produced by the English polymath Joseph Priestley in 1764. Priestley knew his readers would require enormous help in being led to accept time as a line in space. In addition to his chart of men, he spent pages describing just what a timeline would be:

> the abstract idea of TIME, though it be not the object of any of our senses, and no image can properly be made of it, yet because it has real quantity, and we can say a greater or less space of time, it admits of a natural and easy representation in our minds by the idea of a measurable space, and particularly that of a line; which, like time, may be extended in length, without giving any idea of breadth or thickness. And thus a longer or a shorter space of time

may most commodiously and advantageously be represented by a longer or a shorter line.

(Priestley, 1764, p. 5)

In many ways, Priestley's text presents a more fascinating artifact for today's humanists than his chart. Priestley knew his innovation was not the particular findings of who lived and when. (Indeed, the spectacularly successful chart presented nothing to its viewers that was not clearly stated in standard biographies.) Instead, Priestley presents the model of time *itself* as the innovation, and one he hopes the audience will understand as natural only after reflecting on their existing vocabulary and imagination of time. Priestley's exhaustiveness suggests the complexities hidden in an understanding of linear time, and raises the question of what understandings it might replace.

The rest of this chapter deals with some of these models. The challenges of modeling and representing time lie in making it possible to apply the best possible model, and in representing time in formats that can be easily understood and easily transformed for representations. For both of these, the textual representation of the ISO and the visual representation of the timeline are justifiably the standard. While neither Priestley's timeline nor the ISO standard are the standard model of time, they are both successful because they represent it so well in visual and textual form, respectively. The timeline captures the linearity at the heart of the contemporary notion of time; the ISO standard faithfully folds in a variety of practices from disparate fields into contemporary practice. By regularly referring back to both through this chapter, I hope it will be easier to imagine successfully extending our models of time without reproducing problems that the current conceptions successfully solve.

1 Models of time

1.1 Cyclical times

At the heart of many problems with temporal representation is that most units of time are not, as the timeline representation would have it, linear at all. Years and days are both experienced by human beings as cycles (of shortening and lengthening days for the former, and sunlight and nighttime for the latter). Calendars and timekeeping devices have added to those two astronomical cycles a number of others; months, days of the week, hours, and minutes are all temporal measurements that are better expressed as a circle than a line.

This cyclical understanding is built into the ISO standard. A fully linear representation of time as years would use a decimal representation of years; the midpoint of 2001 would be 2001.5, July 4th would be at about 2001.5041, and with any further resolution specifiable through the use of real numbers. POSIX time, by measuring duration in seconds from a fixed origin, in fact adopts such a strictly linear understanding; so does TAI, the international atomic standard kept since 1955. For most uses, though, such linear measures are inappropriate.

Instead, the ISO standard explicitly represents time as a series of cycles with only the final element, the year, operating as a truly linear variable. Smaller divisions are added in turn that form, in essence, epicycles upon the larger whole. That is to say, a date like 2000-01-01 is represented as a set of positions that can be thought of as a point on a line, but also a set of different positions in a cyclical space: there are various ways in which January 1 of that particular year more closely resembles January 1 of 1995 than it does June 1 of 2000. (The weather, the fact of it being a major holiday in Russia, the nearness to the beginning of an academic year).

For extremely precise modeling purposes in the sciences, these conventional definitions are too inexact to be useful; neither the Earth's orbit around the sun nor its axis is a useful measurement. The "base unit of measurement of time" is now not the year or the day, but the second, now defined according to the international system of units in terms of the emission of radiation from a cesium atom. This violates the etymology of the word; minutes and seconds were both originally subdivisions of hours just as they are of degrees, with the second taking its name as the "second" of the two smaller divisions of the hour.[2]

1.1.1 Cyclicality beyond the calendar

Cyclicality is so heavily ingrained in the calendar that it should be no surprise that cyclical representations of time are widespread outside of it. The most venerable, perhaps, are the theories of history or calendars that hold that time itself must be cyclical on the year level as well as all lower levels. This supposition may be taken literally, as in the widely known example of the Mayan calendar whose turnover in 2012 was supposed to bring with it the end of the world.

Western histories, as well, have drawn from cyclical models as frequently as they have drawn from linear ones. The historian Frank Manuel, a half-century ago, described two co-existing models of time in the Western tradition. One, from the Christian tradition, moves forward in a line towards an ultimate goal; the other, from the Greek tradition and adopted by figures like Vico and Spengler, sees cycles of recurrence (Manuel, 1965). Historical representations of cyclicality will most naturally lend themselves to representations not as uniform times, but relative to the baselines of a cycle. Many objects of study easily lend themselves to being thought of as recurrent cycles. In modeling economic phenomena, it is common practice to display trend lines where the x-axis is not year, but rather months or quarters from a number of different starts. The economics blogger Bill McBride, for example, regularly updates a chart showing employment relative to peak employment for each of the recessions since World War II: such a chart quickly and efficiently shows both the remarkable depth and extent of job losses after the recession in 2008 (McBride, 2014).

To call events like recessions or the rise and fall of empires "cyclical" meets common usage; but a more precise definition might insist that events be not just cyclical but *regularly periodic*. Both legally and in the natural world, a number of such institutions exist. The summer Olympic Games occur every four years; cicada swarms emerge from the ground at intervals of 13 or 17 years. When this periodicity is exact, a number of mathematical processes allow significantly more efficient analysis. Techniques such as the Fourier transform can make it possible to represent sinusoidal waves over time as a single point in what is called the "frequency domain." For pure cycles, such approaches can be intensely useful, but in many cases they are only useful when the periodicity is absolute. In other cases, the use of assumptions from purely cyclical theories of time can lead to unlikely results or confusion.

1.2 Discontinuous time and periodization

Discontinuous models of time assume that time entities have ontological realities that are sharply divided rather than yielding gradually to each other. The idea of the timeline assumes that temporal events are continuous and infinitely sub-dividable: discontinuous models of time instead posit them as discrete events that transition instantly from one state to another. Years, as described by the ISO vocabulary, are absolute even if they contain smaller units. In popular memory, each decade and century has a fixed character. Virginia Woolf played with the idea of fixed discontinuities in *Orlando* by placing her protagonist on the night of January 31, 1799:

> Now—she leant out of her window—all was light, order, and serenity. There was the faint rattle of a coach on the cobbles. She heard the far-away cry of the night watchman—'Just twelve o'clock on a frosty morning'. No sooner had the words left his lips than the first stroke of midnight sounded. Orlando then for the first time noticed a small cloud gathered behind the dome of St Paul's. As the strokes sounded, the cloud increased, and she saw it darken and spread with extraordinary speed. [. . .] As the ninth, tenth, and eleventh strokes struck, a huge blackness sprawled over the whole of London. With the twelfth stroke of midnight, the darkness was complete. A turbulent welter of cloud covered the city. All was darkness; all was doubt; all was confusion. The Eighteenth century was over; the Nineteenth century had begun.
>
> (Woolf, 1928, p. 216)

The joke, for Woolf, is that reality would never actually oblige to match the boundaries of stereotypes of historical time. The challenge in data modeling is that in many cultural domains, these stereotypes are more important than the precise dates that an event happened. Certain temporal categories are so fundamental that they must be marked off. In economics, each recession is a singular event that shapes the perception of all other trendlines. In the standard visualization representations of economic phenomena, for example, the Federal Reserve Bank of St. Louis wisely chooses to present economic data not simply as a timeline, but as one with periods of recession shaded to highlight their extraordinary status.[3]

In some cases, these makeshift periods are the best evidence that we have. An excellent example from the humanities are the precise period vocabularies for the ancient world generated by the Pleiades Project. Time periods in the ancient world tend to be represented around ruling empires, and the extensive geographic and temporal scope of the Pleiades project mean that almost all "temporal" markers also have a geographic scope. The Pleiades vocabulary for periods contains at once, for example, the terms "Parthian Middle East (140BC–AD226)," "Roman Middle East (140BC–AD640)," and "Roman-Early Byzantine Middle East (140BC–AD850)." While the time periods and geographies dealt with in the Pleiades project are among the largest that humanistic projects typically encounter, they serve as a reminder that periods as constituted are not simply temporal entities themselves, but instead represent the intersection of time with geography, domain, and a variety of other subjects.

The practice of placing within a period is in this way a critical act. Just as an event out of time can be a jarring anachronism, an event out of place can constitute an anatopism (from *topus*, place). Sometimes the framing itself may be a useful provocation: simply the term "the Victorian United States" at once highlights and questions the degree to which traditionally British stereotypes of period might be fruitfully applied outside the political domain of their origin. (This practice is standardized in the description of architectural styles in the United States, where "Second Empire" and "Victorian" can denote two buildings from the same year but owing elements of their construction to France and Britain, respectively. The normal American term for the period, the "Gilded Age," has no major architectural style of its own.)

The notion of "revolutions" plays a particularly interesting role in computational attempts to model discontinuous times. In the classical sense, a revolution is a cyclical phenomenon; a moment when the wheel of time rotates and a different group returns to its period atop the hierarchy. In the modern period, however, a revolution has come to mean a sharp break or discontinuity. In the Marxist tradition, these revolutions can represent moments of possibility outside the constraints of power structures in a way that evokes older religious eschatologies (Benjamin, 1940). But the search for "revolutions" is also particularly amenable to modern quantitative methods, which can ascribe any major change in patterns as reflecting a substantive shift at a particular moment in time (Mauch et al., 2015).

1.2.1 Events as discontinuous times

While periods are often designed as useful abstractions to contextualize time, "events"—a related, and also frequently discontinuous category—are frequently the object of study in themselves. The University of Virginia Temporal Modeling Project, directed by Johanna Drucker and Bethany Nowviskie in the mid-2000s, created a particularly thoughtful framework for the modeling of events. It defined an ontology of events for different forms of modeling events including things like reference frames, narrative events, and speech acts. The project shows one of the primary uses of a standard vocabulary for events: that a visual or exploratory vocabulary useful for one set of problems (say, describing the plot of one particular novel) might be easily transformed as a framework for the analysis of other events. An ontology that distinguishes between moments, frames, and reflections on time scales outside the present frames might offer a useful vocabulary for interchange. The difficulty lies primarily in the lack of a standard reference frame for events.

A related model that might be particularly useful would complement a typology of events with a vocabulary of interconnection. Relations of succession, causation, superseding, and mutual exclusion are fundamental to the connections among events and periods. A standard vocabulary, or even a standard meta-vocabulary, is unlikely to encompass all of the various models of temporal relation in common and academic use. But some subset of them might offer a particularly useful alternative to the timeline that would show events as contingent and related to past events, rather than the implicitly unidirectional, unbounded approach of purely linear time.

1.2.2 Discontinuous time in the ISO

The need for discontinuous models of time in standard representations is indicated by how much they proliferate in the ISO model. The representation of periods is relative easy; standard forms of separation allow a period of any length to be straightforwardly represented. (World War II at a monthly resolution could be cast as 1939-08/1945-05). Periods can also be represented in terms of time *after* a particular date, or expressed as recurrences. (This is primarily useful in calendrical representations for formally describing expressions such as "Every other Thursday for 10 meetings.") The representation of years and centuries in ISO format is more ambiguous, but the simple date 19 can refer to the entirety of the twentieth century. (It is not, on the other hand, permissible to terminate an ISO date after three digits to abbreviate a decade).

Standard representations of time become more complicated because of the cultural assumptions built into calendars. Arithmetic on time quickly becomes hazardous because calendars have been designed to line up with astronomical cycles, which requires a number of stopgap solutions that quickly render standard calendars problematic. Linear times like atomic time, kept since 1961, or POSIX time, fall out of phase with Universal Standard Time because universal time adds "leap seconds" to keep itself in line with astronomical midnight. These seconds are added irregularly to the calendar with only a few months of notice; both of the last two additions (in 2015 and 2012) caused much software, including popular websites such as Twitter or Reddit, to break or function unpredictably (Knapton, 2015). The better known problem of leap years (which by analogy to leap seconds would better be called "leap days") further complicates arithmetic. But more complicated temporal arithmetic fully breaks down before the adoption of the Gregorian calendar, when 10 days were dropped at once. By its own terms, the ISO standard is inapplicable except "by agreement of the partners" before the adoption of the new calendar in Western Europe in October 1582.

Yet more vexing is the problem of the year zero. The enumeration of years according to the birth of Christ was made before the use of zero and negative numbers was standardized in Europe. December 31, 1BCE is immediately followed by January 1, 1CE; depending on convention, the year 0CE either does not exist at all or is entirely coincident with the year 1CE. In the infinite representation of sequential years suggested by the ISO (and implemented in common languages like Javascript), however, the year 0 corresponds to "1BCE" in standard notation. This can create problems in research and representation, since a year such as "–10CE" is easily mistaken for "10BCE," but actually corresponds to "11BCE."

As a practical matter, these discontinuities create problems both for the encoding and the analysis of temporal data that span any of the time breaks. Temporal formatting that extends over the introduction of the Gregorian calendar or the year 1 must be explicit about its method of encoding; analysis that uses numbers must be careful to use appropriately designed tools.

1.3 Distended times

Even when time is not depicted as containing abrupt breaks or loops, it may still be *distended*—that is to say, for many purposes a data model that depicts any two time periods of a given length as equivalent may greatly depart from human experience of time. One can agree with Joseph Priestley that time is linear without accepting that it creeps on at exactly the same petty pace from day to day; the idea that time might "fly" or "slow to a crawl" is as common in popular parlance as the idea that it has duration. The chief challenge of modeling distended times is finding a way to make these fits and starts meaningful, interpretable, and constant.

In describing certain works of fiction, this distension can be mapped quite directly. Thomas Mann's *The Magic Mountain*, for example, emulates the experience of accommodating to a new setting by playing narrative position against the linear time of history, so that large parts of the reader's experience of Hans Castorp's years in a sanatorium take place inside the first few months, while the later period speeds away quickly. Any serious attempt to model the time inside that novel would need to properly represent both the calendar time and the subjective time as Mann depicts it. For works of fiction, that can be easy enough; page numbers offer an alternate accounting that corresponds roughly to the distinction of *fabula* and *syuzhet* in Russian formalism. There is some case to be made, however, that similarly phenomenological approaches would be usefully applied to human experience. Johanna Drucker has suggested that timelines might better describe reality if they allowed themselves to be compressed, distorted, or looped (2011). The chief question for data modeling is whether these attempts to map subjective time are closer to acts of scholarly criticism or artistic license.

Certain patterns of distension remove the potential for capriciousness. Just as periods can be irregular or mathematically regular and therefore easily describable, so can distensions. If the Fourier transform is the most fundamental representation of cyclic time, many other methods offer better methods for the detection or modeling of regular events whose periodicity may wax and wane.[4]

Logarithmic models of time have become particularly common in recent years. Thanks in large part to the personal interest of Bill Gates, "Big History" has become a common organizational scheme for teaching (Sorkin, 2014). In its initial incarnations, it was an irregular set of "thresholds"; in more recent iterations, it has become more strictly *logarithmic*, so that the most recent ten years occupy the same space as the previous hundred, the thousand before that, and so on.

In this usage, the log scale is among the most natural ways to view time in one of science's most frequently used alternatives to standard time representations, which uses not "years before the common era" but instead "years ago" as the basic measurement of time. On geologic and astronomical time scales, there is often no functional difference between the present and the year 1CE.

While the logarithmic approach breaks down past a point (few find the most recent hour as interesting as the previous two years, for instance), it offers a useful form of representation for timeframes in which linear assumptions do not apply. One of the most interesting opportunities, from a user interface perspective, lies in constructing better timelines. Consider, for example, the construction of an interface for browsing a hundred years of a single newspaper. A typical use case will demand exact control over navigation over the surrounding single days, but will also benefit from the ability to jump back or ahead decades at a time.

One useful option might be to allow some sort of cyclical controls; viewers might want to move to the same issue from a week later, or a month, or a year. Another is the approach typically taken by search results, which allow the user to advance a page at a time, or else jump straight to the end. A logarithmic time scale centered on the present with a fixed maximum resolution offers an easy form of interface that shows a variety of time distances at once in a coherent fashion from a particular perspective.

1.4 Multiple frames of reference

Time is relative. The ISO/timeline model represents one particularly useful framework for situating events relative to each other; but historical time is not the only chronology in common use. The ISO is, in part, one *frame of reference*; modelers must frequently choose to describe events along multiple different frames. Frames of reference present particularly interesting challenges for temporal modeling because they immediately lay bare one basic assumption of the timeline: that only one single dimension of time is relevant or worth modeling. For fiction, in particular, this is often obviously incorrect; the language we use to narrate time frequently describes a wide variety of time horizons at once. The distinction of *syuzhet* and *fabula* is useful for the temporal modeler in part because it reduces a work of fiction to the singular temporal dimension of the *reader's* experience; but the timeframes described inside a work may be much more complicated.

Some frames of reference are explicitly encoded in a work and subject to complex but unambiguous exposition. Some of this is explored in Inerjeet Mani's recent work on temporal modeling. Mani's work lays forward a visual practice for multiple embedded timelines to describe passages like the opening of Proust's

In Search of Lost Time, which consists of complexities such as a narrator's present in relation to an ambiguously delimited period in the past ("For a long time, I used to go to bed early") and repeated actions within that frame ("half an hour later the thought that it was time to go to sleep would awaken me"). Mani ventures the possibility that automatic extraction in computational linguistics might automatically extract timelines for vast corpora of narratives and "launch (or revive) an empirical discipline of literary studies of time"; in any case, it is a task that relies on effectively marking up sample corpora with standardized measures of time (Mani, 2010, pp. 49, 76).

Other markers of narrative time may require greater interpretive effort. For example, out-of-order timelines are a frequent feature of narrative. An edition of a work like Toni Morrison's *Beloved* could choose to annotate each of the chapters by adding information about the order in which its chronologically scattered chapters appear; it could even disentangle and identify some of the several independent timelines that *do* appear in chronological order in the novel, with dates estimated. The time periods for these events may be relative; the ISO provides a mechanism for designating periods of various standard lengths, but there may be cases where only relative ordering can be derived from the source. Implicit chronological ordering is particulary common in media like film and television, where events are presented without a narrative voice and techniques of montage frequently imply simultaneity of action. In these cases, some custom descriptions of ordering relative to a specific narrative may be necessary if markup or modeling is necessary; in most cases, a simple linear ordering will suffice, although other forms of conventional time (for example, time of day) may still apply.

The simplest case of multiple frames of references involves cases in which multiple actions have to be juxtaposed in some way on a single timeline. The implication of a second dimension to time carries on a long and complicated history in timeline representations. Many of the early timelines that followed in the wake of Priestley and Barbeu-Dubourg carried an implicit geographical arrangement that tried to represent the expansion and contraction of empires on the y-axis so that the alluvial flow of Rome was greatest at its period of dominance. Drucker and Nowviskie's model allows for alternate horizontal lines to emerge out of the timeline reflecting an actor's reflection on the course of time.

In many cases, it is useful to consider *both* the y- and x-axes as representing time. In this case, any point in a field represents not a moment, but the *interaction* of two frames of reference with each other. Each point can represent, for example, the similarity along some metric of two times to each other. Such an approach has been used similarly as a form of data exploration in musicological exploration of structural elements, where the timeframes are several minutes of a recorded song. Points represent similarities between any two periods of time (using some measure of similarity in the digital audio signal). Large-scale homologies in the song–the repetition of a refrain, or similarities in two verses—thus emerge in the two-dimensional field as lines and shapes that quickly encode dense patterns of interference for further analysis (e.g., Cooper and Foote, 2003). The purest case of a verse-chorus song might satisfy certain elements of periodic time if all bars were of regular length. But the advantage of a dual timeline visualization is that unlike modeling approaches from physics, they make no overall assumptions about regularity. Cooper and Foote's work explores songs by the Beatles that frequently end in long codas; the method is also highly adaptable to musical forms like the rondo where certain elements are repeated more frequently or at different intervals than others.

2 Futures of time

2.1 Standardization

One set of challenges revolves around furthering standardization so that it works more effectively for the sorts of sources that humanists encounter. This may mean periodization; projects like PeriodO are working to extend standard vocabularies of periodization to cover more historical cases than a domain-specific project like Pleiades and with greater flexibility to attribution than standard authority files like the periods in the Library of Congress subject headings.[5] In specific domains, it could also mean widespread standardization of best practices for temporal references in areas not covered by the ISO standard. A number of these have been mentioned in passing above, but they include the Julian calendar, calendrical regimes from Asia and the Americas, and better computational support for modeling time periods before 1BCE.

One place where standardization may be particularly useful revolves around the computational study of narrative, as suggested in the work by Mani described above. Large-scale comparisons of narrative structures have recently been attempted by many in the digital humanities, but they tend to rely on crude measures for segmenting works by time (Jockers, 2015; Piper, 2015; Schmidt, 2015). More sophisticated forms of markup might help to model more sophisticated notions of narrative, including the interplay of *fabula* and *syuzhet*.

2.2 Uncertainty

Humanistic projects find themselves struggling with modeling temporal uncertainty, a condition that arises with incredible frequency in working with data of historical or literary origin. While distension, discontinuity, and periodicity all carry fairly straightforward implications for visual representation and mathematical modeling, uncertainty does not. The problem is a basic one: Priestley's chart of biography dealt with the issue of uncertain birth and death dates for classical figures by using dashed lines for periods when an individual might not be alive.

Two particularly ambitious projects for modeling time, the Virginia Temporal modeling project discussed above and the proposed Topotime standard developed by Karl Grossner and Elijah Meeks (2013) at Stanford, have highlighted problems of uncertainty as central to temporal modeling. Topotime's organizing principle is that homologies between practices of geography and of temporal modeling can fruitfully inform the creation of a new standard. Topotime's basic unit is not a line (as for Priestley), but a *polygon*; time flows from left to right, but also varies up and down in probability. If a person is known to be born between 1900 and 1910 and to have died in 1963, their life occupies a shape on the timeline that slopes up from zero to one hundred over the first ten years of the decade, and abruptly drops from 100 to 0 in 1963.

One of the greatest challenges of uncertainty in temporal modeling is that there are many different dimensions of uncertainty itself. Among the most significant challenges lies in the distinction between ambiguity and uncertainty. Straightforward uncertainty is often easily quantifiable through rules of statistical distribution. Quantitative models of time, whether timelines or something else, are easily adapted to problems where the distribution of time maps to instrumental imprecision. Radiocarbon dating produces estimates of when an event happened based on radioactive decay that are easily translated into a space of uncertainty. But quantitative models fail much more easily on cases of ambiguity around subjective categories.

There can be uncertainty about *whether* an event happened or not. A timeline of the reign of King Herod the Great might include the massacre of children in Bethlehem described in Matthew 2, but would likely also want to note that many scholars find the Gospel's account unlikely. There can also be uncertainty about the timing of a date: *Hamlet*'s first performance took several hours in either 1600 or 1601, but the precise timing is unclear. A known period might have unknown edges; we know that the Roman biographer Suetonius was alive at least between 80 and 130CE, but the outer boundaries of his lifespan are uncertain. But while these markers are uncertain, they can be presumed to exist. The uncertainty about the boundaries of the "Silver Age" of Latin literature which Suetonius inhabited is quite different; whether literature from the reign of Marcus Aurelius should be counted inside the Silver Age is subject to debate on the front of what the Silver Age itself is. Different authorities constitute the Silver Age around different years; moreover, any individual might hold the belief that a period is transitional, or partly in one period and partly in another.

Natural language descriptions of time assume a great deal of information and convention in their descriptions of uncertainty. Take, for example, the usage of the word "circa." "Circa January 15, 1945," "circa 1789," and "circa 1500" each express considerably different degrees of certainty. A reasonable reader might take the first to be accurate with a week or so, the second within a few years, and the third within only a few decades. In historical sources, the silent use of rounding can create unusual problems for modelers; bibliographic records, for example, tend to have large numbers of works assigned to years ending in "00" that were actually written later in the century. Census records so regularly over-represent even numbers that the phenomenon has had a name for decades (the "Whipple effect") and can be used to estimate education levels in historical populations (A'Hearn, Baten, and Crayen, 2016). Formal representations of time, or translations of existing metadata into them, will have an extremely difficult time taking these various ambiguities into account. In many cases, purely linguistic representations of uncertainty and precision (as described in the TEI Guidelines) may be best.

These uncertainties can be expressed in natural language perfectly well, but are not particularly susceptible to modeling. Projects intended to model temporal uncertainty often adopt the accommodation of making certainties themselves quantitative. This is a necessary concession to visual representation, but also a problematic one, because it usually involves encoding uncertainty as a probability. One interpretation of this process is as expressing the chances of an event happening in multiple different outcomes of the same process. But outside of the most literal frameworks of cyclical time, there is very little meaning that can be attached to something like the statement "140BCE is 40 percent of the Silver Age."

These difficulties conspire to make uncertainty in temporal modeling nearly at cross-purposes with standardization. Schemata that accurately represent the uncertainty in a particular dataset may have great difficulty interchanging with any other source.

2.3 Innovations in representation

Some of the most exciting innovations in temporal modeling for readers of humanistic scholarship may come in new ways of *representing* time. The linear timeline is just one possible way of situating events temporally; by building on advances in standardization or descriptions of uncertainty, we should be able to present clearer pictures of how time operates.

Some of these may involve trading on representations of time from the computational sciences, particularly in domains like signal processing, and the increasingly sophisticated tools from computational linguistics for activities such as event extraction and narrative alignment (for example, Miller et al., 2015). These are opportunities for large-scale comparisons; computational methods are potentially of use for discovery (e.g., finding novels with unusual narrative structures) and comparison (describing changes over time in the temporal scope of historiography).

For smaller corpora, new ways of thinking about time may be particularly interesting because of new affordances for using time in interface design. Automatic timeline generations have already become relatively common. More striking is the much greater possibility of using time *itself* as a dimension in visual representations. Priestley's innovation of time as a phenomenon on the x-axis was a constraint dictated by the need to disseminate results on paper; contemporary data visualizations, however, regularly are able to make use of animation that can make time itself into an element of graphic representation. This presents tremendous opportunities for clearer visualization of temporal phenomena. This is particularly true, for instance, in mapping: showing change over time cartographically is considerably easier done using animations than any other method.

In combination, these methods can all help to further unlock time itself as a useful category of study. The invisibility of time and the dominance of the standard model are grounded to some extent in the ways that temporal organizations exist everywhere and nowhere. But changing subjective relationships to time are also constitutive of the experience of modernity (most famously in Thompson, 1967; more recently in reference to weeks by David Henkin, 2015). The experience of time becomes much more tractable as an object of study itself as it becomes possible to arrange or search by the various expressions of time that past actors have used.[6] The promise of temporal modeling in these cases may sometimes be the excitement of further clarifying our understanding of how our own experience of time itself might work.

Notes

1   ISO 8601:1988; ISO 8601:2004. For the process of actual temporal standardization before the ISO, see Ogle (2015).
2   Weeks offer a different cyclical format; instead of specifying a date by month and day, week and day is also a permissible form in the ISO system. The third week of 1988 is represented as 1988-W03.
3   Federal Reserve Bank of St. Louis, 2016. In other cases, periodic phenomena ascend to a peculiar legal status: Mary Dudziak has described how popular and legal assumptions about the limited extent of "war time" becoming regularized have allowed extraordinary legal practices to persist, often indefinitely (Dudziak, 2012).
4   For example, wavelets (Percival and Walden, 2006).
5   perio.do/. See also Shaw and Rabinowitz (2015).
6   Scholars of computational culture have particular advantages here, because in digital timestamps they have records of human activity at a level of temporal specificity unimaginable a few decades ago.

References

A'Hearn, B., Baten, J., and Crayen, D., 2016. Quantifying Quantitative Literacy: Age Heaping and the History of Human Capital. *The Journal of Economic History*, 69(3), pp. 783–808.
Benjamin, W., 1940. On the Concept of History. In: M.W. Jennings (Ed.) 2003 *Selected Writings: 1938–1940*. Cambridge, MA: Harvard University Press, pp. 389–400.
Butler, J., 2011. *Gender Trouble: Feminism and the Subversion of Identity*. London: Routledge.
Cooper, M. and Foote, J., 2003. Summarizing Popular Music via Structural Similarity Analysis. In: *Applications of Signal Processing to Audio and Acoustics, 2003 IEEE Workshop on*. IEEE, pp. 127–30.
Drucker, J., 2011. Humanities Approaches to Graphical Display. *Digital Humanities Quarterly*, 5(1). Available at: www.digitalhumanities.org/dhq/vol/5/1/000091/000091.html.
Dudziak, M.L., 2012. *War Time: An Idea, Its History, Its Consequences*. Oxford: Oxford University Press.
Federal Reserve Bank of St. Louis, 2016. *Civilian Unemployment Rate*. Available at: https://fred.stlouisfed.org/series/UNRATE.

Friendly, M., 2009. *Milestones in the History of Thematic Cartography, Statistical Graphics, and Data Visualization*. Available at: www.math.yorku.ca/SCS/Gallery/milestone/milestone.pdf.

Grossner, K. and Meeks, E., 2013. *Topotime v0.1 gallery & sandbox*. Available at: http://dh.stanford.edu/topotime/.

Heidegger, M., 1962. *Being and Time*. San Francisco. CA: HarperSanFrancisco.

Henkin, D., 2015. Hebdomadal Form. *Representations*, 131(1), pp. 52–67.

Husserl, E., 1991. *On the Phenomenology of the Consciousness of Internal Time (1893–1917)*. Translated from German by J.B. Brough. Dordrecht: Kluwer Academic Publishers.

Jockers, M., 2015. Revealing Sentiment and Plot Arcs with the Syuzhet Package. *Matthew L. Jockers* (blog), February 2. Available at: www.matthewjockers.net/2015/02/02/syuzhet/.

Knapton, S., 2015. Leap Second Confuses Twitter and Android. *The Telegraph*, July 1. Available at: www.telegraph.co.uk/news/science/science-news/11710148/Leap-Second-confuses-Twitter-and-Android.html (accessed April 18, 2016).

Mani, I., 2010. *The Imagined Moment: Time, Narrative, and Computation (Frontiers of Narrative)*. Lincoln, NE: University of Nebraska Press.

Manuel, F.E., 1965. *Shapes of Philosophical History (The Harry Camp Lectures)*. Stanford, CA: Stanford University Press.

Mauch, M., MacCallum, R.M., Levy, M., and Leroi, A.M., 2015. The Evolution of Popular Music: USA 1960–2010. *Royal Society Open Science*, 2(5). Available at: http://rsos.royalsocietypublishing.org/content/2/5/150081.

McBride, B., 2014. May Employment Report: 217,000 Jobs, 6.3% Unemployment Rate. *Calculated Risk* (blog) June 6. Available at: www.calculatedriskblog.com/2014/06/may-employment-report-217000-jobs-63.html (accessed August 20, 2015).

Miller, B., Olive, J., Gopavaram, S., Zhao, Y., Shrestha, A., and Berger, C., 2015. A Method for Cross-Document Narrative Alignment of a Two-Hundred-Sixty-Million Word Corpus. In: *Big Data (Big Data), 2015 IEEE International Conference on*. IEEE, pp. 1673–7.

Ogle, V., 2015. *The Global Transformation of Time: 1870–1950*. Cambridge, MA: Harvard University Press.

Percival, D.B. and Walden, A.T., 2006. *Wavelet Methods for Time Series Analysis*. Cambridge: Cambridge University Press.

Piper, A., 2015. Novel Devotions: Conversional Reading, Computational Modeling, and the Modern Novel. *New Literary History*, 46(1), pp. 63–98.

Priestley, J., 1764. *A Description of a Chart of Biography: By Joseph Priestley*. Warrington: Printed at Warrington. Available at: https://archive.org/details/adescriptionach00priegoog (accessed August 20, 2015).

Rosenberg, D. and Grafton, A., 2010. *Cartographies of Time: A History of the Timeline*. New York: Princeton Architectural Press.

Schmidt, B.M., 2015. Plot Arceology: A Vector-Space Model of Narrative Structure. In: *2015 IEEE International Conference on Big Data (Big Data)*. IEEE, pp. 1667–1672.

Shaw, R. and Rabinowitz, A., 2015. A Sharing-Oriented Design Strategy for Networked Knowledge Organization Systems. *International Journal on Digital Libraries*, 17(1), pp. 49–61.

Sorkin, A.R., 2014. So Bill Gates Has This Idea for a History Class . . . *The New York Times*, September 5. Available at: www.nytimes.com/2014/09/07/magazine/so-bill-gates-has-this-idea-for-a-history-class.html?_r=0.

Thompson, E.P., 1967. Time, Work-Discipline, and Industrial Capitalism. *Past & Present*, 38, pp. 56–97.
West, C., 2001. *Race Matters*. Boston, MA: Beacon Press.
Woolf, V., 1928. *Orlando: A Biography*. Oxford: Oxford University Press.

7 Visualizing information

Isabel Meirelles

1 Introduction

In 1765, Joseph Priestley (1733–1804), British theologian, scientist, and philosopher, published the *Chart of Biography*, an innovative visual method for representing historical events over time. Considered a landmark in the history of visualization, the chart was originally devised for use in his "Lecture upon the Study of History," and later published as a pedagogical device aimed at students as well as the general public. Rosenberg and Grafton describe the *Chart of Biography* as the most influential timeline of the eighteenth century (2012, p. 118). With this chart, Priestley introduced many graphic conventions still in use in contemporary timelines, such as the use of a timescale, time and line indicators, and thematic sections, to mention a few.

While timelines are effective at providing a unifying chronological narrative of events, they tend to impose a linear structure, sometimes even implying causation among events. This fact, however, has not precluded researchers from using timelines to understand certain temporal aspects of history or phenomena (e.g., Rosenberg and Grafton, 2012; Meirelles, 2013). Similar to other visualization methods, timelines entail compromises and cannot represent all dimensions of the data. If we were not to compromise, we would need to reconstruct the world we live in and devise one-to-one scale representations, which is impractical to say the least. How do we go about making informed compromises? What types of visualizations are effective for specific enquiries? How do visual representations manifest the deeper intellectual models and data models that shape these enquiries? The chapter addresses these questions by offering a framework for understanding how visualizations represent data models and ultimately contribute to humanistic enquiry, especially at early stages of the research process. The proposed framework is organized around the strengths and limitations of information structures vis-à-vis research questions. By providing design, cognitive, and perceptual principles as they relate to the structures under discussion, the goal is to enhance critical awareness of the role that visualizations might have in modeling assumptions.

This chapter analyzes the ways in which visual representations—diagrams, visualizations, maps, and so on—work in association with traditional humanistic methods of enquiry to help model humanistic research. It shows how visualizations work to concretize and interrogate our underlying models throughout the research process and not only as an end tool for communicating humanistic findings. By spatializing content (data) as well as argument, visualizations can act as generative humanistic tools that will, ultimately, help foster insight and new modes of interpreting and reasoning.

2 Why use visualizations in interpretative research processes?

Literature in cognition explains that we use both internal and external representations of knowledge to complement and strengthen our mental abilities, whether knowledge is propositional, analog or procedural (e.g., Tversky, 2001; MacEachren, 2004; Ware, 2012). It is often the case that mental activity is externalized in some form so as to minimize cognitive load and enhance cognitive abilities. External representations have a long history and can take different forms (i.e., maps, graphs, notation systems, etc.) as well as serve different purposes (i.e. for recording, for instructing, for analyzing, and so on).

Broadly, visual representations, such as diagrams and information visualizations, use graphical space to represent data and/or ideas to support both analytical and interpretative activities. Our visual systems and visual perceptual abilities are incredibly powerful and we can use them to help gain new insights. For example, visual representations might highlight outliers and other relevant features not easily known if it were not for spatializing data—making them visible. As Shneiderman explains:

> Evolutionary needs have made the human visual system extremely well adapted to recognizing patterns, extracting features and detecting unexpected items. Humans can rapidly process enormous amounts of visual information and take action rapidly. The human perceptual apparatus integrates interpretation so that people can rapidly identify familiar faces or recognize threats.
>
> (2001, p. 470)

Information visualizations can serve two distinct, although sometimes related, purposes: for exploration of data and for communication of findings. The first relates to visualizations that are frequently generated at early stages of the research process, for purposes such as helping with discovery of patterns and hypothesis generation; whereas the second aims mostly at communicating information to specific audiences, whether informing experts (e.g., in journals or proceedings) or communicating findings to general audiences (e.g., in blogs or news media). There are two main directions used during data exploration: knowledge discovery that involves mining the data for extraction of useful information and patterns of interest, and question-driven data scrutiny that aims at revealing specific perspectives of the dataset.

Independent of the method, exploratory visualizations help to reveal underlying structures and features—both known and unknown—that will guide the next steps in the research process, such as further data inspection, and even further data collection. Devised as direct mappings of the data, early stage visualizations frequently depict basic questions at the intersection of columns and rows. These questions are non-speculative but descriptive in nature, such as who, what, where, and when. It is by means of these initial questions that we can gain insight and develop arguments that will involve more complex questions and arguments. The result could be considered as descriptive representations, in that they mostly summarize the data by making explicit their dimensions, which would not be available otherwise if it were not for using our visual systems to extract relevant features.

3 From descriptive to argumentative visualizations

Descriptive representations are essential to the research process due to being fertile platforms for interpretation and insight, which will, ultimately, lead to argumentative representations and generation of new knowledge. Take, for example, exploratory questions such as "where events happened" or "when they happened" that would result in a geographical representation and a timeline respectively. It is the interpretation of these visualizations that might lead to further questions, such as the reasons behind the patterns revealed at this initial stage.

While descriptive visualizations offer opportunities for new perceptions about the content under scrutiny, care should be taken so as not to consider them as definite proofs or deterministic models. In general, visualizations are unstable artifacts, in the sense that there are several possible visual outputs that can be produced from the same system (dataset). Not only can we generate different outputs based on different facets (perspective) of the dataset, but for each selected facet we might generate a set of different representations. This is especially evident when we look at relational graphs that are automatically generated. At each iteration, the visualization algorithm will output a different representation, affecting once again our perceptions and inferential abilities (Foucault Welles & Meirelles, 2015).

This is not to say that visualizations are not accurate representations of the content they depict, which for the most part, they are.[1] Analogous to music notation that can receive diverse interpretations across time and performances, a dataset affords several possible visualizations, each offering a soundboard for new insight. Moreover, different types of structures will afford visual analysis of different underlying features, such that when we structure data into a timeline we might uncover temporal patterns that would not be known if we were only spatially representing data in a map, for example. Though both map and timeline can be considered *accurate* representations of the same dataset, they will provide diverse access to the content under scrutiny.

On the other hand, and similar to other types of knowledge representations, visualizations entail compromise and are not devoid of bias. For example, when querying a dataset we are imposing constraints that will affect the visual outputs we generate. Furthermore, like other visual representations, visualizations involve visual rhetoric content whether or not intentionally included (e.g., Barthes, 1977; Buchanan, 1985; Joost and Scheuermann, 2007). Certain visual/graphical elements lead to persuasive as well as argumentative frames and responses that we need to be aware of when displaying data especially for communicative purposes. Buchanan contends, "Design is an art of thought directed to practical action through the persuasiveness of objects and, therefore, design involves the vivid expression of competing ideas about social life" (1985, p. 7). I find it useful to propose the concept of "argumentative visualization" to describe the ways in which certain kinds of visualizations offer this kind of strongly argumentative framing.

The distinction between descriptive and argumentative visualizations is subtle, since at some level all visualizations make a visual argument concerning the data being represented. We can situate them on a continuum: while descriptive visualizations are more direct and unambiguous, argumentative visualizations tend more towards the speculative. The generative potential offered by descriptive representations enables us to arrive at new propositions and meanings, such as argumentative visualizations. The latter facilitate new knowledge formations, possibly through informational connections that are selective or conjectural. An early example of argumentative representation is Aby Warburg's unfinished *Mnemosine Atlas* (1924–29), in which panels visually articulate his research on the migration of symbols and the iconic continuities linking Antiquity with the Renaissance.[2]

4 Graphical space produces meaning

By using graphical space to represent information, visualizations provide spatial models and concrete ways for understanding concepts. Due to our limited perceptual and cognitive systems, visual representations of information involve several spatial manipulations, from schematic miniaturization or enlargement, to simplification and distortion. In addition, the process involves distillation and omission of information. The opposite scenario is offered by Borges in the short story *Funes, His Memory* where he describes a man who was unable to generalize given his inability to forget. The narrator in the story concludes, "I suspect, nevertheless, that he was not very good at thinking. To think is to ignore (or forget) differences, to generalize, to abstract. In the teeming world of Ireneo Funes there was nothing but particulars—and they were virtually immediate particulars" (1998, p. 137).

World maps are examples of schematic miniaturization and distortion due to serving specific purposes. We tend to take for granted that all map projections— which are mathematical transformations of the curved three-dimensional surface of the globe onto a flat, two-dimensional plane—result in distortions of one or more of the geometric properties of angles, areas, shapes, distances and directions. In 1569, when the Flemish cartographer Gerardus Mercator introduced the projection that carries his name, he provided early explorers with an effective tool for navigation, as straight lines in the map resulted in lines of constant bearing. However, every time that we use a Mercator projection as the geographic base for depicting thematic information, we are imposing on our viewers a perception of the world that largely distorts areas and shapes according to latitude, reaching extreme distortions in the polar regions. As Robinson and colleagues warn, "There is no such thing as a bad projection—there are only good and poor choices" (1995, p. 70).

Although the humanistic research process is not a problem-solving one, but is rather centered in experiential and interpretative methods, it is relevant to point to the article "Why A Diagram is (Sometimes) Worth Ten Thousand Words" by Larkin and Simon (1987), as it relates to the topic of this chapter—that is, the construction and use of visual representations of information as devices to amplify cognition. Their study examined how well engineer students solved problems when using either sentential or diagrammatic propositions. The two representations differ fundamentally in how data structure is indexed: in a verbal description by position in a sequence, and in a diagrammatic representation by location in the plane. Their result indicated that diagrammatic representations facilitated information-processing and were effective in: 1) preserving explicitly the inform-ation needed for inference (usually implicit in the sentential representation); 2) supporting perceptual inferences; 3) facilitating recognition of relevant inform-ation due to perceptual cues; 4) facilitating search due to spatial grouping of information needed to be located together for inference (as opposed to sentential, where search was linear and information was not necessarily adjacent).

Literature in cognition corroborates with their findings, and shows that visualizations support several cognitive principles, such as conveying meaning, facilitating search and discovery, supporting perceptual inference, enhancing detection and recognition, providing models of actual and theoretical worlds, and enabling manipulation of data (e.g., Tversky, 2001, Hegarty, 2011; Ware, 2012).

On the other hand, Larkin and Simon warn that the use of a diagram does not insure efficiency in problem solving—that will depend on how well the diagram takes advantage of cognitive features (listed above); hence the term *sometimes* in the title of their seminal article. They suggest that not only is it crucial to understand the extent to which diagrammatic representations support efficient operations of search, recognition, and inference, but, more importantly, that the knowledge to construct the most useful representation with which to solve a problem is itself central to problem solving. I would argue that the same is true for humanistic research.

5 The use of space and meaning making

Visualizations convey meaning by the way in which data structure is indexed in graphical space, where graphical attributes and structure stand for elements and relations in the source domain. Efficiency in conveying meaning will depend on whether the correspondences between graphical representation and source domain are well defined, reliable, readily recognizable, and easy to learn (Pinker, 1990).

The use of space in visualizations is always schematic, whether elements are depicted directly or metaphorically. In representations of physical data (e.g., spatial phenomena), graphical proximity represents proximity in physical space. The distance between two cities in a geographic map corresponds (in a given scale) to the physical distance between these places in real space. In representations of abstract domains (e.g., non-spatial phenomena like relational or temporal data), graphical proximity corresponds to conceptual proximity, such as a shared property. For example, in a graph depicting the relationships among characters in a particular novel, distance in graphical space represents distance in that social fabric, such that pairs of characters with little or no interactions are positioned far away from each other. Graphical space is mapping the source domain of social interactions and not the physical space between characters, such as their home addresses, for example.

In the case of abstract domains, which lack spatio-visual information and are not inherently visible, defining an effective graphical structure and encoding system is a crucial stage and, often times, not a trivial one. Theories on metaphor and categorization can assist us in finding the most fitting schema for structuring abstract domains, as they help to provide natural correspondences, such as physical analogs and spatial metaphors based on our experience of the world. In the seminal book *Metaphors We Live By*, Lakoff and Johnson (2003) describe how basic-level and image-schematic concepts structure our experience of space and are used metaphorically to structure other concepts. Metaphors, they contend, are part of our conceptualizing processes in that they help us understand one domain of experience in terms of another, mostly due to preserving the cognitive topology of the source domain. In other words, to grasp concepts that are abstract or not clearly delineated in experience, we use other concepts that are clear to us such as spatial orientations, physical experiences, known objects, and so on. Lakoff sums it up, "Image schemas thus play two roles: They are concepts that have directly-understood structures of their own, and they are used metaphorically to structure other complex concepts" (1987, p. 283).

If we take a look at genealogies, we will see that over time the most common graphical depictions are trees and wheels (Klapisch-Zuber, 2003; Lima, 2014). The two image-schemas are both familiar and consistent with the inherent nature of the source domain that is hierarchical relationships between generations. The schemas are meaningful because they provide a concrete way—through direct and bodily experience—to structure the abstract domain of genealogy. Furthermore, part-whole image-schemas are well suited for hierarchical structures (Lakoff and Johnson, 2003). The structural elements of a part-whole schema are a whole, parts, and a configuration. Because the parts can exist without constituting a whole, it is the configuration that makes it an image-schema. For example, we experience our bodies as wholes with parts that we well understand in terms of limbs with specific connections between them. Lakoff explains: "We have general capacities for dealing with part-whole structure in real world objects via gestalt perception, motor movement, and the formation of rich mental images. These impose a preconceptual structure on our experience" (1987, p. 270).

6 Encoding data

Visual representations are dependent on visual perception for both their creation (encoding) and their understanding and use (decoding). Visual encoding is the process of matching the information, which is provided by the dataset (data type and attributes), to the most suitable representation (graphical elements and visual properties). The process requires knowledge of the constraints imposed by our visual systems—perceptual and cognitive, as well as the operations afforded by the data types—nominal, ordinal or quantitative.

Objects, names, and concepts are examples of nominal data. We distinguish nominal datum on the basis of quality: A is different from B. The questions we can ask about nominal data are who, what and where. Nominal data have no implicit quantitative relationship or inherent ordering, and require external forms of organization, such as ordering data alphabetically or ranking them according to a quantitative variable. For example, we could rank countries according to the number of Nobel Prizes awarded for each discipline. Nominal data can share characteristics that might distinguish it from others and, more importantly, allow grouping. Because categorization plays a major role in manipulating nominal data, it is often called categorical data.

Ordinal data can be arranged in a given order or rank, such that we can say which comes first or second, which is smaller or larger, and so on. Ordinal data provides the order, but not the degree of differences between the elements. In other words, intervals are not measurable, only the attributes are ordered. For example, we might know which country ranks first in the scale of Nobel prizes for literature, but not know by how much more in relation to the second place, unless we explicitly state the information.

Quantitative data can be measured, and as such, data can be numerically manipulated, such as with any arithmetic or statistical methods. Quantitative data have magnitudes and require that we ask questions of how much or how many. Quantitative data can be discrete or continuous. Discrete data are composed of individual items (integers) that are countable, whereas continuous data can take infinite values within a range (real or float numbers). Sometimes, discrete data, such as population, is transformed into continuous data by mathematical computations, as in the population density of an administrative unit.[3]

7 Systems for encoding

The French cartographer Jacques Bertin is considered to be the first to have proposed a theory of graphical representation of data for use in maps, diagrams, and networks, published in his seminal book *Semiology of Graphics* in 1967 in France, with the first English edition in 1983. His theory is based on semiology and associates the basic graphic elements with visual variables and types of phenomena. Bertin's system has been widely adopted and expanded to include other variables not considered initially, including, for example, tactual properties for visually impaired users and dynamic variables for representations changing over time.

Encoding systems, such as the one proposed by Bertin, offer effective guidance for matching source domain to variables based on our perceptual system, which involves fast and automatic thought processes. However, as Kahneman's and Tversky's research on cognitive bias has shown, both intuitive and deliberate thought processes affect our judgments (Kahneman, 2011). All in all, visual representations can serve as an effective interface between perception and cognition.

The system reproduced in the figure presents an expanded version of Bertin's original proposal. In it, visual marks correspond to the basic elements of geometry. Because data can have zero, one, two, or three dimensions, they can be represented by the elements of point, line, plane, and volume, respectively. For example, a point data such as a person (nominal) or an aggregated value of population (quantitative) in a city (nominal) can be symbolized by point marks. Area phenomena, such as the population density (quantitative) of a county (nominal), can be represented by area marks.

Visual marks are described according to visual variables, which correspond to visual channels and the way features are extracted in our brains. The system organizes the variables into two groups: positional—in space (where) and in

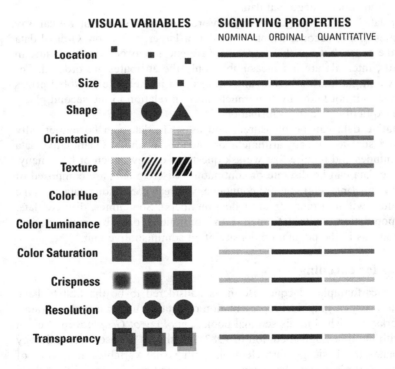

Figure 7.1 An extension of Bertin's original system by MacEachren. The appropriateness of each variable for encoding nominal, ordinal and quantitative data is shown as good (dark grey), marginally effective (middle grey) and poor (light grey). See MacEachren, 2004, p. 279.

time (when)—and visual properties of the entity (what). Originally, Bertin named them planar and retinal respectively. Literature in visual perception explains that spatial properties (position and size) and object properties (e.g., shape, color, texture) are processed separately by the brain (Cleveland, 1994; Kosslyn, 1994). Furthermore, position in space and time has a dominant role in perceptual organization, as well as in memory (Card et al., 1999; MacEachren, 2004). Known examples are mnemonic systems, which throughout history have relied on spatial information to augment long-term memory (Yates, 1966).

The final dimension of the system corresponds to data types. The correlation between all three dimensions—visual marks, visual variables, and data types—provides guidance on visual encoding according to levels of appropriateness. For example, in cases involving ordered data, visual order should be perceived in the corresponding visual encoding. If that is not the case, then the visual encoding is unsuitable and could be misleading. The visual variables of color hue and shape are unsuitable for encoding rankings, as we cannot say that yellow comes before blue or that triangles precede squares. On the other hand, color luminance and size would be more effective visual variables to depict ordered data. As Ware explains, "Good design optimizes the visual thinking process. The choice of patterns and symbols is important so that visual queries can be efficiently processed by the intended viewer. This means choosing words and patterns each to their best advantage" (2008, pp. 174–5).

There are limits, however, to how much information we are able to superimpose in a visual representation without loss of legibility. Multiple representations are often used to solve this problem, such as in the construction of several maps, each depicting data for a different time stamp, for example. Interactive visualizations provide yet another powerful way to solve this problem, with the advantage that one can further experiment with different encodings and structures, in addition to filtering data.

8 Concluding remarks

As this chapter has shown, we can visually represent underlying data models in at least two ways. Descriptive representations are mostly beneficial at the early stages of the research process as they provide a visual means to further understand the data by graphically revealing both known and unknown features. While such visualizations may be designed to reveal specific features of the data and their modeling, they may also inadvertently uncover aspects of the modeling of which we were not aware: for instance, discrepancies in levels of precision or local differences in nomenclature. When used for communication, descriptive representations might lack informational value due to being the result of direct mappings of the dataset, or, to put it in another way, the translation of data into graphical form aimed at synoptically (re)presenting content. Ultimately, descriptive visualizations will point to new research directions and to the creation of what I have called argumentative representations. Removed from the factual determinism of descriptive visualizations, argumentative representations help create new knowledge, such as advancing new and alternative conceptual models.

I would like to end with a word of caution: it should not be concluded from all the benefits highlighted above that visual representations will always act as fertile ground for generative thinking. The design process of creating visualizations does not insure that the outputs will necessarily be effective or productive. We all have experienced visualizations that lack informational value, or, in a worse scenario, misrepresent the modeling of the data. Similar to other research methods, visualizations are tools for reasoning and arguing, and, if used appropriately, will provide effective visual means for exploring data, synthesizing information, as well as articulating novel perspectives and assumptions.

Notes

1   For a discussion on accuracy and truthfulness of representations of information, I recommend Floridi's texts listed under References.
2   Visit the website *Mnemosyne: Meanderings Through Aby Warburg's Atlas* to examine ten of its panels at: http://warburg.library.cornell.edu/
3   Discrete and continuous data can be easily exemplified, and many times confused, by the use of bar versus line graphs.

References

Barthes, R., 1977. *Image, Music, Text*. Translated by S. Heath. New York: Hill & Wang.
Bertin, J., 1983. *Semiology of Graphics: Diagrams, Networks, Maps*. Translated by W.J. Berg. Madison, WI: University of Wisconsin Press.
Borges, J.L., 1998. *Collected Fictions*. Translated by A. Hurley. New York: Penguin Books.
Buchanan, R., 1985. Declaration by Design: Rhetoric, Argument, and Demonstration in Design Practice. *Design Issues*, 2(1), Spring, pp. 4–22.
Card, S.K., Mackinlay, J., and Shneiderman, B. (Eds.) 1999. *Information Visualization: Using Vision to Think*. San Francisco, CA: Morgan Kaufmann.
Chen, M. and Floridi, L., 2013. An Analysis of Information Visualisation. *Synthese*, 190(16), pp. 3421–38.
Cleveland, W.S., 1994. *The Elements of Graphing Data*. Murray Hill, NJ: AT&T Bell Laboratories.
Floridi, L., 2010. *Information: A Very Short Introduction*. New York: Oxford University Press.
Floridi, L., 2011. *The Philosophy of Information*. New York: Oxford University Press.
Foucault Welles, B., and Meirelles, I., 2015. Visualizing Computational Social Science: The Multiple Lives of a Complex Image. *Science Communication*, 37(1), pp. 34–58.
Hegarty, M., 2011. The Cognitive Science of Visual-Spatial Displays: Implications for Design. *Topics in Cognitive Science*, 3, pp. 446–74.
Joost, G. and Scheuermann, A., 2007. *Design as Rhetoric, Basic Principles for Design Research*. Zurich: Symposium of Swiss Design Network.
Kahneman, D., 2011. *Thinking, Fast and Slow*. New York: Farrar, Straus & Giroux.
Klapisch-Zuber, C., 2003. *L'Arbre des Familles*. Paris: Éditions de La Martinière.
Kosslyn, S.M., 1994. *Elements of Graph Design*. New York: W.H. Freeman.
Lakoff, G., 1987. *Women, Fire, and Dangerous Things: What Categories Reveal about the Mind*. Chicago: University of Chicago Press.

Lakoff, G. and Johnson, M., 2003. *Metaphors We Live By*. Chicago: University of Chicago Press.

Larkin, J.H. and Simon, H.A., 1987. Why a Diagram is (Sometimes) Worth Ten Thousand Words. *Cognitive Science*, 11(1), pp. 65–99.

Lima, M., 2014. *The Book of Trees: Visualizing Branches of Knowledge*. Princeton, NJ: Princeton Architectural Press.

MacEachren, A.M., 2004. *How Maps Work: Representation, Visualization, and Design*. New York: The Guilford Press.

Meirelles, I., 2013. *Design for Information: An Introduction to the Histories, Theories, and Best Practices Behind Effective Information Visualizations*. Beverly, MA: Rockport Publishers.

Pinker, S., 1990. A Theory of Graph Comprehension. In: R. Freedle (Ed.) *Artificial Intelligence and the Future of Testing*. Hillsdale, NJ: Lawrence, pp. 73–126.

Robinson, A.H., Morrison, J.L., Muehrcke, P.C., and Kimerling, A.J., 1995. *Elements of Cartography* (6th ed.). New York: John Wiley & Sons.

Rosenberg, D. and Grafton, A., 2012. *Cartographies of Time: A History of the Timeline*. Princeton, NJ: Princeton Architectural Press.

Shneiderman, B., 2001. Supporting Creativity with Advanced Information—Abundant User Interfaces. *Human-Centred Computing, Online Communities, and Virtual Environments*. London: Springer-Verlag, pp. 469–80.

Tversky, B., 2001. Spatial Schemas in Depictions. In: Meredith Gattis (Ed.) 2001. *Spatial Schemas and Abstract Thought*. Cambridge, MA: MIT Press, pp. 79–112.

Ware, C., 2008. *Visual Thinking for Design*. Burlington, MA: Morgan Kaufmann.

Ware, C., 2012. *Information Visualization, Perception for Design* (3rd ed.). San Francisco, CA: Morgan Kaufmann.

Yates, F., 1966. *The Art of Memory*. Chicago: University of Chicago Press.

8 Ontologies and data modeling

*Øyvind Eide and Christian-Emil
Smith Ore*

In this chapter we will give an introduction to ontologies as they are currently used in digital humanities, with some notes on possible future use. Simply speaking, ontologies are formalized shared conceptualizations. While the current use of the word ontologies is different from traditional use in philosophy, there are also some links between the disciplines we will mention briefly in the following.

This is not a general introduction to ontologies; see, for example, Staab and Studer (2009) and Hofweber (2011) for that. The aim of this chapter is to introduce ontologies in a digital humanities setting, with an emphasis on the links to cultural heritage documentation. We will also explore the relationship between data models and ontologies. We will present the underlying thinking behind ontologies rather than giving a presentation of specific ontologies important for the digital humanities. The examples will mostly be drawn from CIDOC-CRM[1] and FRBRoo,[2] with a link to data models that strictly speaking are not ontologies, such as TEI (Ore and Eide, 2009; Eide, 2015).[3] No previous knowledge of these models is assumed.

1 Models and ontological analysis

To better understand an object of study, it can be useful to construct a model of it. The model can, for instance, be on paper, in a computer, or realized in some physical material. The process of constructing such a model will usually require a deep and detailed study of the original. Even the design of a gingerbread model of a medieval stave church (Figure 8.1) has given one of the authors a deeper understanding of the principles of the structure of a stave church of the basilica type. The resulting model can then be used to show some features of the original besides being eaten.

The archives of the Hanseatic League in the North German city of Lübeck are important sources of information about the trading activities and thus political issues in the region in late medieval times. The information in the archives is or was organized according to the local practice of their time—that is, according to an implicit data model. The rationale behind the model does not have to have any direct connection to what the information is about. An archive can be ordered according to the physical nature of the items—for example, the size of the objects.

Figure 8.1 (a) Borgund Stave Church (photo L. Buskoven, CC-BY 4.0) and (b) a model
(photo C.E. Ore, CC-BY 4.0).

The tables found in a relational database will often be a result of a trade-off
between fast data recovery and ease of maintenance. What we may call engineering
considerations are important factors for the organization of information in physical
archives as well as in computerized databases.

The design of a model as in the case of the gingerbread church can have the
purpose of describing important aspects of the real world—for example, the basic
structure of the church. Such models are often implicit. In the more scholarly

example of the medieval archives of the Hanseatic League, it is evident that one needs a good understanding of the North European medieval societies to be able to interpret the documents in a meaningful way.

A historian working on a macro history of late medieval and early modern Northern Europe will be interested in trade information from a number of different organizations, including the Hanseatic League. Information of this kind is now available in digitized archival collections and databases that draw on them. However, each archive and database may have its own way of describing and organizing the material, which makes it difficult for our historian to search and compare information across collections. A more ideal solution would be to develop a formal conceptualization of how accounting works in this historical context, and then have all of these resources express their data using this shared conceptualization.

Such a shared formal conceptualization is what would be called an ontology for historical accounting. The scope can vary from more specialized schemes covering a single region or time period to more generalized schemes covering, for example, all Western accounting up to today. One should, however, keep in mind that a very wide coverage may result in a too general and thus less useful conceptual model. Whatever scope is selected, it is important that the user understands the underlying assumptions about the real world and the way the ontology is organized in order to understand the kind of questions it can provide answers to. In a similar way, an ontology of church architecture can provide a framework enabling comparison between different church reconstruction projects, be they in 3D computer-based tools or in edible form.

These observations are not new. They are mentioned here in order to pinpoint possible differences between data models and ontologies. The real world knowledge in the above examples represents ontological knowledge or ontological assumptions. The literal meaning of the term "ontology" is "the study of being" and is borrowed from philosophy where it denotes a philosophical subdiscipline with close connections to metaphysics. Mental models are important in the development of any system, but what we call ontologies in the context of this book are mediated explicit models. This means that a concept in the model is related to other concepts in a formalized and consistent way, and also that the concepts have clear semantics—that is, their meanings are clearly expressed and well defined. In a well-designed ontology there will be both an anchoring to human understanding through textual scope notes with examples and connections to other concepts through hierarchical links and other relationships as described below.

In the software industry, a data model is usually a formalized description of how to organize data in an information system. In the development of data models, the developers will focus on how to organize the data to fulfil the customers' specification of the functionality of the system. The focus will be on data consistency, ease of maintenance, use of storage and performance. A good information system should also be in line with the users' mental model of the task to be solved. The developers must try to understand this mental model and use it at least as a starting point in the development of the technical data model used in the implementation of the system. Ideally, the technical data model should be a formalization of the mental model expressed in some software specification language—for example, UML.[4]

The border between technical data models and formalized conceptualization of parts of the real world is not clear-cut. There is a long tradition in computer science of using terms from psychology, linguistics and philosophy metaphorically. This adds to this fuzziness and blurs the distinctions between the real world, models of the real world and implementations of these models. This is especially visible in artificial intelligence, knowledge engineering and semantic technologies, the most innovative but also the most speculative fields of computer science.

In this chapter we will focus on the relationship between models and the objects being modeled rather than on technical issues connected to modeling. We will explain some major trends and building blocks used in the types of formalizations we find in models and ontologies. Many of the examples in this chapter are taken form the CIDOC-CRM, the most important conceptual model in the cultural heritage sector.

2 Ontology and ontologies

For many in the humanities, "ontology" first and foremost denotes a philosophical discipline, a part of metaphysics studying the nature of being. This field has a history of at least 2500 years. "Ontology" is also used in philosophy as a countable word, denoting a possible conceptualization of a part of the world. It has been much debated whether it is possible to express such conceptualizations in formal languages. That is one of the questions we will discuss in this chapter.

Some decades ago, the word "ontology" was introduced in the areas of artificial intelligence and knowledge engineering based on the use in philosophy, but not connected to existential questions. It is used rather to denote models of a part of the world to be used by computer systems: "An ontology is an explicit specification of a conceptualization. The term is borrowed from philosophy, where an ontology is a systematic account of Existence. For AI systems, what 'exists' is that which can be represented" (Gruber, 1993, p. 1).

The term "ontology" has more recently been taken up by other areas of computer science and eventually also in digital humanities. In computer science and also in digital humanities, the term is often used as a near synonym to "data model," "thesaurus," and even to "closed vocabulary." This extended use is particularly unfortunate in digital humanities because the term "ontology" is still mostly associated with philosophy in the humanities at large. Using "ontology" in the sense of any data model may cause confusion and also create an impression of being less serious. This does not mean that the word "ontology" should not be used, but we should use it in a precise way and limit the use to denote formally expressed conceptualizations with clear semantics and inheritance structures rather than just any database diagram or any structured collection of subject headings. That said, we have to remember that term "data model" was used long before

Gruber introduced the term "ontology" in AI. From this perspective, ontologies can be considered a special kind of data model dealing with formalized conceptualizations rather than implementation issues.

As defined above, an ontology is a formalized specification of a conceptualization. Such a specification can be expressed in many ways. It is commonly done in the form of a set of classes and properties representing the concepts and their relationships. The concepts are usually organized in hierarchies. Such hierarchies express generality versus specialization. Each class except for the most general ones is a subclass of one or more classes at a higher level. This is called an is-a relationship. If class A includes for its members all attributes and properties that class B includes for its members, and if class A in addition has something that class B has not, then each member of class A is-a member of class B. The use of such hierarchies has a long tradition in Western sciences. Examples include the biological classification introduced by Linnaeus in 1735, the Dewey Decimal System used in libraries (introduced in 1876), and the modern Getty Arts and Architecture Thesaurus (AAT) used in museums. The domain of an ontology does not have to exist in a physical sense; we also have, for instance, ontologies of literary characters.

An example of an is-a hierarchy is domestic cats, which belong to the species *Felis catus*, genus *Felis*, family Felidae, order Mammalia. Lions belong to the species *Panthera leo*, genus *Panthera*, family Felidae. All cats and lions are members of Felidae and hence they are all mammals. The nodes in the hierarchy represent universals—that is, sets or classes of individuals and not single individuals, which are usually called particulars. A class may belong to several hierarchies in a so-called multi-hierarchy. This is often called multiple inheritance. Thus, for example, domestic cats also belong to the class of domestic animals: *Felis catus* is-a Domestic animal.

Such hierarchical classification systems are usually called thesauri. To the extent they imply ontological commitments—that is, claims about the real world, thesauri can be called ontologies following the definition in Gruber (1993). It is not possible to make a clear-cut distinction between thesauri and ontologies. If the intended use is classification and cataloguing, one should use the term "thesaurus." The term "ontology" can be used when we are not only interested in the classification aspect, but also in modeling how the entities (the particulars belonging to the classes) interact.

As we saw, a class can be a subclass of more than one superclass in multi-hierarchies. This also applies to persons. We usually consider a person to be a physical object, especially when walking on a crowded sidewalk. Another important property of a person is the ability to act. So a person also belongs to a class of actors. In that class we can also include groups, companies, governments and legal bodies. Thus, the class of persons is in an is-a relationship to two super classes. This is another example of a multi-hierarchy. The way in which we model a person brings us to the question of completeness. It is clearly more to a human being than being a biological object and being able to act. Our model is

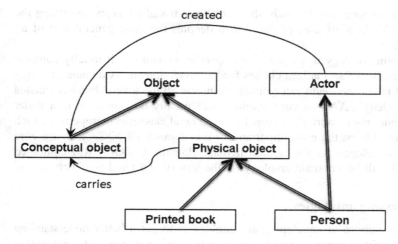

Figure 8.2 A simple event-oriented ontology with multiple inheritance.

a simplification, as all models are. For example, in most models in theoretical economy, a human is assumed always to act rationally. Such considerations are examples of ontological commitments—that is, what assumptions we make about the domain we model.

When we conceptualize entities we relate them to each other in various ways. In addition to the is-a relationship described above, we also have other types of relationships between entities of the various classes, expressed as properties or relationships between the classes. In Figure 8.2 the double arrows represent is-a relationships and the curved lines properties.

While properties link entities of the various classes to each other, they are generalized at the class level and are expressed between the classes, as shown in Figure 8.2. Any physical object can carry information so there is a property "carries" that links the class of physical objects to the class of conceptual objects. Similarly, any actor may create a conceptual object, not only a single person, so the property "created by" goes from actor to conceptual object. In this formalism a subclass inherits the properties of all its super classes. It is therefore implicit in Figure 8.2 that the intellectual content of a book (a conceptual object) can be created by a person and that a book can carry the content.

In the literature about ontologies, one will frequently meet the terms upper- or top-level ontology, domain ontology and core ontology. As for many other terms concerning conceptual modeling and ontologies the meanings of these terms are somewhat fuzzy.

By upper ontology one usually means an ontology with generalized concepts covering a wide range of domains. Other ontologies can then be "plugged into" such upper ontologies. Some upper ontologies attempt at covering all domains; however, it is often claimed that this is either impossible or meaningless since there is no general way to establish a set of non-trivial concepts describing the entire world. In most uses of the term it denotes the most general part of an ontology.

A domain ontology is a model for a specific domain and it usually contains a large number of specialized classes for the given domain. A domain ontology for an art history museum can typically comprise all the several hundred classes found in Getty's AAT. A core ontology will usually be connected to a wider domain, but only comprise a minimal set of general classes and properties which are supposed to be the most important for this domain. CIDOC-CRM is a core ontology developed for the cultural heritage domain. CIDOC-CRM combined with AAT will be a domain ontology for the history of art and architecture.

3 Expressing ontologies

The main purpose of developing an ontology is to get a better understanding of the domain in question and to create a tool for analyzing data concerning the domain. One example of such data is the archives of the Hanseatic League, another is systematic biology, and a third is a museum collection of arts and cultural history. The development of a data model is usually based on an explicit or implicit ontological analysis of the field in question. Our experience shows that a good ontological analysis has to be performed in order to develop a well-functioning data model. The data model can, for instance, be a specification for implementing a database compatible with the given ontology. More formally, the data model is a concrete model for the ontology resulting from the conceptualization of the domain.

An important purpose of ontologies is to share an understanding of a domain. Thus, we need to express them in some suitable formalism. In most cases the best solution is to structure the ontology in an object-oriented way in which the entities found in the domain in question are organized as classes. These classes are ordered in a hierarchy similar to what we find in traditional thesauri. Between the classes there are properties or relationships, as the simple book and poem example in Figure 8.2 illustrates. A class hierarchy and a network of properties can be expressed in many formal languages. First-order logic is the most prominent one and perhaps the most stringent. A much more widespread and easily implemented choice is the RDF family of standards developed by the World Wide Web Consortium.[5]

RDF stands for Resource Description Framework and was introduced 15 years ago as a tool for the Semantic Web. It has later become central also to linked data, a way of publishing data in a structure based on RDF. The basic idea is that all resources accessible on the web are identified by a unique and persistent identifier, in the form of a web address called a Uniform Resource Identifier (URI). Two resources on the web can be linked via a directed link, creating a three-part data structure called a "triple." The three elements of a triple are called the subject, predicate and object respectively and each element is identified by a persistent identifier, a URI. The subject is in a relationship with the object that is expressed by the predicate. RDF triples can be stored in triple stores which can be accessed with the query language SPARQL. All the three elements can have a type identified by another URI. A set of triples may be linked to form a directed graph of linked data resources on the web—hence, the term "linked data." In order to provide for data integration it is vital that unique identifiers are minted to provide a basis for the addressability of entities. In a museum context, for instance, this should be done by each museum for their artifacts, as the museum holding an object is the only one that can assert its identity with confidence.[6] In other contexts, this can be difficult because not all things have clear identities—the identity criteria for a concept such as "compassion" is much more complex than for "the painting by Leonardo known as Mona Lisa." Still, it is a goal to have such identifiers whenever it is possible and makes sense.

RDF is not designed to deal with the data types of the nodes in a graph—that is, metadata for the nodes (subject, object) and properties (predicate) of the triples. The extension RDFS, RDF schema, is written in RDF and enables the expression of a data model for the nodes and relationships. The language/ formalism OWL, Web Ontology Language, is built on top of RDFS. OWL can be used to express data models and ontologies for a set of triples. So-called Descriptive Logic (DL), a weakened first-order logic, can be expressed in OWL. Advanced triple-stores with so-called DL reasoners enable logical queries on RDF triples with an OWL-metadata model. Basically, this is an improved and computable version of the

E21 Person

Subclass of: E20 Biological Object, E39 Actor

Scope note: This class comprises real persons who live or are assumed to have lived. Legendary figures that may have existed, such as Ulysses and King Arthur, fall into this class if the documentation refers to them as historical figures. In cases where doubt exists as to whether several persons are in fact identical, multiple instances can be created and linked to indicate their relationship. The CRM does not propose a specific form to support reasoning about possible identity.

Examples:
- Tut-Ankh-Amun
- Nelson Mandela

Properties: P152 has parent (is parent of): E21 Person

P152 has parent (is parent of)

Domain: E21 Person
Range: E21 Person
Subproperty of:
Quantification: (2,n:0:n)

Scope note: This property associates an instance of E21 Person with another instance of E21 Person who plays the role of the first instance's parent, regardless of whether the relationship is biological parenthood, assumed or pretended biological parenthood or an equivalent legal status of rights and obligations obtained by a social or legal act. This property is, among others, a shortcut of the fully developed paths from 'E21Person' through 'P98i was born', 'E67 Birth', 'P96 by mother' to 'E21 Person', and from 'E21Person' through 'P98i was born', 'E67 Birth', 'P97 from father' to 'E21 Person'.

Figure 8.3 The definitions of the class E21 Person and the property P152 "has parent" (is parent of) in CIDOC-CRM (Le Boeuf et al., 2015, pp. 13, 97).

```
<rdfs:Class rdf:about="E21_Person">
        <rdfs:label xml:lang="de">Person</rdfs:label>
        <rdfs:label xml:lang="fr">Personne</rdfs:label>
        <rdfs:label xml:lang="en">Person</rdfs:label>
        <rdfs:label xml:lang="ru">Лицо</rdfs:label>
        <rdfs:label xml:lang="el">Πρόσωπο</rdfs:label>
        <rdfs:label xml:lang="pt">Pessoa</rdfs:label>
        <rdfs:label xml:lang="zh">人物</rdfs:label>
        <rdfs:comment xml:lang="en">
                This class comprises […] possible identity.
        </rdfs:comment>
        <rdfs:comment xml:lang="de">
                Diese Klasse umfasst […] Identität zu unterstützen
        </rdfs:comment>
        <rdfs:subClassOf rdf:resource="E20_Biological_Object"/>
        <rdfs:subClassOf rdf:resource="E39_Actor"/>
</rdfs:Class>


<rdf:Property rdf:about="P152_has_parent">
        <rdfs:label xml:lang="en">has parent</rdfs:label>
        <rdfs:comment xml_alng="en">This property […] to 'E21 Person'. </rdfs:comment>
        <rdfs:domain rdf:resource="E21_Person"/>
        <rdfs:range rdf:resource="E21_Person"/>
</rdf:Property>


<rdf:Property rdf:about="P152i_is_parent_of">
        <rdfs:label xml:lang="en">is parent of</rdfs:label>
        <rdfs:domain rdf:resource="E21_Person"/>
        <rdfs:range rdf:resource="E21_Person"/>
</rdf:Property>
```

Figure 8.4 The class E21 Person and the property P152 "has parent" (is parent of)
              expressed in RDF(S) linearized in XML. Only some examples of available
              versions in different languages are shown.

PROLOG databases from the 1980s. In the literature this is called semantic reasoning. We see a tendency to call any data model expressed in OWL-RDF an ontology. This is dangerous because the concept "ontology" risks being emptied. The somewhat sloppy use of the term also hides the difference in the level of abstraction between data, data models and ontologies.

The risks notwithstanding, RDF, RDFS, OWL, and the corresponding machinery are still very useful tools. They are especially well suited to combine data from different databases and they have enabled us to link data and create distributed search systems into many web-based datasets. Used wisely, the tools are real openers of data silos.

As pointed out in the short introduction to RDF-based formalisms above, both data models and ontologies can be expressed in RDF/OWL. This is handy since in a triple store the models are stored together with the data and both can be queried using the same tools. We also mentioned above that the formalisms can only express the formal structure of an ontology—that is, the class hierarchy and properties (relationships) between the classes. When using an ontology we also need

```
<?xml version="1.0"?>

<rdf:RDF xmlns:rdf="http://www.w3.org/1999/02/22-rdf-syntax-ns#"
        xmlns:crm="http://www.cidoc-crm.org/cidoc/">
    <crm:E21_Person rdf:about=" http://viaf.org/viaf/97119817">
        <crm:P131_is_identified_by>
            <crm:E82_Actor_Appellation
                rdf:about="http://www.example.com/persname/ALingren01">
                <rdf:value>Lindgren, Astrid</rdf:value>
            </crm:E82_Actor_Appellation>
        </crm:P131_is_identified_by>
        <crm:P152i_is_parent_of>
            <crm:E21_Person rdf:about="http://viaf.org/viaf/309337853"/>
        </crm:P152i_is_parent_of>
    </crm:E21_Person>

    <crm:E21_Person rdf:about="http://viaf.org/viaf/309337853">
        <crm:P131_is_identified_by>
            <crm:E82_Actor_Appellation
                rdf:about="http://www.example.com/persname/KarinNyman_01">
                <rdf:value>Nyman, Kari</rdf:value>
            </crm:E82_Actor_Appellation>
        </crm:P131_is_identified_by>
    </crm:E21_Person>

</rdf:RDF>
```

Figure 8.5 RDF linearized in XML for two instances of E21 Person, the Swedish author
Astrid Lindgren and her daughter Karin Nyman linked with an instance of
P152i "is parent of." P152i is the inverse of P152, which means that P152
"has parent" can be computed-based on P152i "is parent of."

a shared understanding of how the formal structures should be interpreted. The
absolute best tool for expressing the rules for such interpretations is natural
language. Scope notes and examples must be an integrated part of the definition of
an ontology. A short label is rarely enough to convey the intended scope of a class.
Especially in digital humanities, it is usually better to use plain prose combined
with a formal or semiformal framework, as we saw in the examples above. This
will make an implementation easier also when it is delayed to a later stage.

Figure 8.3 shows the complete definition of the class E21 Person with
scope note in CIDOC-CRM. Figure 8.4 shows how the class and property from
Figure 8.3 can be expressed in RDF/OWL. Figure 8.5 shows an example of how
to use the system for real data.

4 The role of ontologies

The fundamental idea of RDF and linked data is that anybody can say anything
about anything ("cats are mammals"; "the Mona Lisa is located at the Louvre"),
and these statements can be interrelated and adjudicated to form a network of
knowledge. It is the policy of letting a thousand flowers bloom. Ontologies and
data models have the purpose of bringing order and reducing the entropy in the

study of a domain. On one hand, a common and widespread formalism is good since it is easy to use the data and data models made by others. It is easy to compare your model with another, and it is easy to adjust and extend existing models and ontologies that can be found on the web. On the other hand, shopping bits and pieces from available ontologies on the web and putting them together into one whole without really understanding the intended use of the classes and properties may give a false impression of order. To include some classes and properties from an existing ontology and reuse them with a (slightly) different meaning is often called "ontology hijacking." Good documentation of a model in natural language is necessary in order to reduce the risk of such hijacking.

Does an ontology need to be consistent and what does it mean that an ontology is consistent? An ontology is usually formulated as a formal definition of classes and properties supplied with scope notes describing the intended meaning of the classes and the properties. It is common to define the formal part in OWL (Web Ontology Language) and Descriptive Logic—that is, it is possible to prove a statement and its negation. Inconsistency at this level is simply inconsistency in the sense of formal logic. If an ontology is intended to be used in a formal deduction system, it has to be consistent in this formal sense.

This formal requirement is not the most central seen from a digital humanities point of view. It is the text of the scope notes that tell us how the designers of the ontology try to model the domain in question. For example, in an ontology for historical persons, there will usually be classes for birthdate, places, persons and timespan. According to a common conceptualization of the world, a physical person can only be born once and not at two different places. Since we can formulate a formally consistent ontology allowing for multiple birth events and places for a given person, the restriction is based on our conceptualization and is not a necessary formal restriction.

From historical sources, it is not always possible to deduce a unique place of birth. For example, the birthplace (and time) of the Greek philosopher Diogenes of Apollonia is uncertain and is usually considered to be either Apollonia in Phrygia or in Crete. How can this information be expressed in the restricted ontology mentioned above? One solution is to weaken the restrictions and open for multiple birth events or a birth event occurring at several locations and times. This solution is close to the philosophy behind RDF, linked data, and the Semantic Web. This is not recommended if the intention is to create an information system with consistent high quality data. Instead, one should try to analyse what the reason for such apparently inconsistent information is, as, for example, found in the case of the birthplace of Diogenes of Apollonia. In this case, there are at least two different claims about the correct place, but no claims about a multiple birth. A simple solution is to add so-called reification—that is, who said what. A better solution is to extend the ontology with a model of claims and inferences. This is, for example, done in an extension of the CIDIC-CRM called CRMInf. This extension describes how chains of inferences found in or based on source material can be modeled.

A formal ontology aims at expressing someone's conceptualization of a part of the world. For a conceptual model to be an ontology, the ontological commitments and simplifications involved should be made explicit. The group behind the CIDOC-CRM took as a starting point the documentation practices observed in museums and tried to make a common conceptualization of the world view expressed in the documentation practice. For example, in practical museum documentation, the salient characteristics of human beings have to do with their ability to serve as agents (as creators, subjects, and so forth). Their other properties—however important in other contexts—are irrelevant and can be ignored. Thus, in CIDOC-CRM the class of persons is simply a subclass of the classes of biological objects and actors. The model is a result of an analysis of the domain aimed at a particular goal, and not an attempt to give a complete description of the world.

CIDOC-CRM is a formal ontology intended to facilitate the integration, mediation, and interchange of heterogeneous cultural heritage information. It has a strict division between endurants (objects) and perdurants (events). It is a core ontology where the classes represent universals. There are no classes for all particulars, unlike, for instance, the Getty's Art and Architecture Thesaurus (AAT), which includes thousands of concepts. The original scope was the integration of museum documentation, but it has later been proven suitable for a much wider domain. CIDOC-CRM is not an upper ontology in the most common sense of the expression, as it makes no claim to cover the entire world. However, if we see upper ontologies as ontologies where the scope is general rather than domain specific, CIDOC-CRM includes upper-level parts.

In the library sector, IFLA's working group on FRBR designed a data model expressed in the Entity Relationship (ER)[7] formalism supplied by detailed prose descriptions. The main ontological commitment was the acceptance of the four levels: Work—Expression—Manifestation—Item. FRBR has since been reformulated as the conceptual model FRBRoo, and harmonized with the CIDOC-CRM model. The development of FRBRoo included an ontological analysis of the implied world view expressed in FRBR. On the basis of this analysis, FRBRoo was expressed in the same formal framework as CIDOC-CRM, based on the same type of ontological commitments. FRBRoo models the understanding of the world as we find it in the FRBR family of standards for library documentation.

Single data models and search interfaces can work well for one set of data or for data within a specific domain. However, if approaching several diverse collections, a user will at best spend a considerable amount of time searching different interfaces based on different data models, at worst getting lost or giving up. Standardization is necessary in order to facilitate better services. As we will see below, evidence from the development of standards for information systems in a cultural heritage context strongly indicates that the ontological approach is a good approach to such standardization.

But what can be gained by using ontologies for standardization? The idea of this approach as it has been implemented in the CIDOC-CRM is to create one common ontology that can express information from a large number of different databases. This ontology is evidence-based in the sense that it is a condensed expression of shared knowledge developed over centuries of museum documentation and decades of computer-based information systems. If one sets out to integrate data from ten different information systems one could in principle map each of them to each other. That would lead to 99 mappings and no clear centre of gravity to be used for searching. If one maps each of the information systems to CIDOC-CRM, one only has to make ten mappings. The data can then be exported using these mappings to a common system facilitating searches across the collections.

This common system can facilitate searching beyond what is possible in the source information systems. One reason for this is the well-defined hierarchical is-a system. In CIDOC-CRM, there is a set of classes including E12 Production, E65 Creation, and E66 Formation that are all subclasses of E63 Beginning of Existence. Each of these three classes is-a E63 Beginning of Existence. If source database A has a number of E12s, E65s, and E66s, and source database B has only E63s, the inheritance system means that information from these four classes can be integrated as if they all belonged to the same class E63, facilitating better information integration.

5 Ontological analysis and data modeling

Proper and detailed analysis of information is crucial in digital humanities, as it is in any other field using computer-based methods. The modeling of data may be more challenging in the humanities than in other fields, since the specifications tend to be less rigorously defined, and the relationships we find in our data are more complex than in most other application areas.

The development of a data model will often be an integral part of the ongoing development of a field of study. An example is the development of encoding in the case of the Menota XML schema.[8] The schema itself was developed by scholars in the field and reflects their understanding of manuscripts, of the way scribes work, and on how the text is represented on the parchment. This specific analysis is limited to Old Norse, but is similar to other traditions. Thus, the Menota schema is a specialization of the more general TEI Guidelines. The TEI Guidelines also rely on a series of ontological commitments, but these are less specific than for Menota. They include the existence of books, manuscripts, traceable writing styles, persons, places, and so forth.

Another example can be found in archaeology. An archaeological excavation is a non-repeatable process in which the object of study is destroyed. For this reason, the documentation has to be as good as possible. There exists, however, no objective, theory-independent way to do this documentation. Still, an excavation database should be in accordance with the selected theory. For example, in current British archaeology, a widespread method is to analyze the site as a chronological sequence of deposited layers, each of which constitutes a so-called context. These layers are confined by surfaces. A post hole from a destroyed wooden building is represented by the surface of the original pit, the remains of the burned or rotten pole, and the infill around the pole in the pit. These surfaces can be given a relative chronology and an event can be associated to each surface, as described by Harris (1989). An excavation database has to be based on a data model reflecting the world view underlying this theory in order for it to be suited for analytic work in the Harris tradition.

Both examples show how encoding schemata and data models are based on scholarly traditions conceptualizing a given part of the real world. In the text encoding example, this is assumed human intention, whereas in the archaeology example, it is physical phenomena such as the decay of a building in the real world. Other models in the humanities include conceptualizations of fictional worlds representing characters in fiction or in mythology, as in the development of the OntoMedia ontology,[9] which is used to describe the semantic content of media expressions. Conceptualizations can be extended to cover the variety of research found in the humanities.

How did this approach come to be so central to cultural heritage information? Data modeling has been used in digital humanities for decades. All data systems developed since the early days of computer applications in the humanities were based on data models, if not explicitly then at least on implicit ones. In the development of community standards such as TEI a significant part of the work was in data modeling.

From the 1990s, some areas faced problems in the then commonly used data modeling paradigms, leading to a need for other solutions which were found in ontologies. We will here present the history behind the development of CIDOC-CRM as an early example of how ontologies solved problems found to be impossible to solve with any other method. The growing use of CIDOC-CRM in digital humanities during the last ten years shows how this approach is important also beyond museum informatics and cultural heritage information management.

CIDOC-CRM is based on previous attempts to develop general data models for museum information. In 1994, CIDOC finalized a large data model expressed as an Entity-Relationship (ER) model called CIDOC-ER (Reed, 1995). The aim was to create a common data model for museum databases in order to facilitate data integration and interchange. The model was based on practical museum documentation and not only on the existing database systems at the time. In order to understand how ontologies can anchor meaning in clearer and more useful ways than other models it is important to spend some time on the historical development leading from CIDOC-ER to CIDOC-CRM.

The CIDOC-ER model introduced five basic entities representing what can be documented: people, places, things, events, and concepts. It was claimed that "These five entities and the relationships among them can document anything in the entire spectrum of human (or inhuman) experience" (Reed, 1995). This is a strong statement, but it is in line with what has more recently been claimed by the Semantic Web community.

Expressed as an entity-relationship model, CIDOC-ER turned out to collapse under its own weight, but the statement cited above was very much to the point: it simply needed a different type of formalism to work in practice. While there is nothing in the definition of "ontology" quoted above that prevents one from defining an ontology as an ER model, it is closely tied to relational databases and turned out to be a cumbersome approach for the development of conceptual models. The object-oriented approach with its class hierarchy and inheritance mechanism is much more flexible and leads to more compact models.

The first step in the development of the CIDOC-CRM consisted of reformulating the original ER model as an object-oriented model with a compact definition using abstraction and generalization through the inheritance mechanisms of is-a hierarchies. Reformulating CIDOC-ER into CIDOC-CRM also made the philosophical aspects more explicit, by enabling the basic properties of the model to be documented clearly. The ideas behind the original statement were brought forward in a formalization where the event formed the core with the other four basic concepts connected to it. CIDOC-CRM is thus event-centric: the event concept forms a natural center of gravity as it enables us to relate a museum object to its historical context—that is, model the intangible part of cultural heritage. The conceptual objects can then be connected to events—for example, creation—which makes it easy to represent works and abstract motifs in visual art. This means that the events form the basic units of analysis, connecting other concepts to them. The central idea is that the notion of historical context can be abstracted as things, people and ideas meeting in space-time. In addition, the model contains identification of real world items by real world names (appellations), a generalized classification mechanism (types), part-decomposition of immaterial and physical things, temporal entities, groups of people (actors), places and time (time span), location of temporal entities in space-time and physical things in space, reference of information objects to any real world item (aboutness), and intellectual influence of things and events on human activities.

As an illustration of how events can be modeled in CRM, we included a model of a traditional English wedding in Figure 8.6. The event is at the core of the

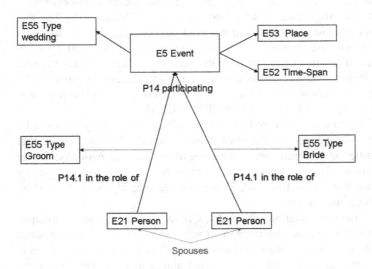

Figure 8.6 A CRM diagram for a traditional English wedding.

model, both conceptually and visually. The event occurred at a specific location, and the persons, including the groom, the bride, and the groom's best man, are connected to it. Their roles and the event itself are classified by types, which can be selected from a thesaurus. In an information system the formal relation between the spouses has to be deduced by checking whether the two have participated in the same wedding event in the role of bride and groom. Alternatively, one may introduce the short-cut relationship "spouses" indicated in grey at the bottom.

While a significant part of the work in digital humanities is text-based, other sources for information about the current and past culture and history have always been important. Scholars in disciplines such as art history, musicology, archaeology, and media studies base a significant part of their work on non-textual sources. An ontological analysis of the domain in question can establish a conceptual model and a corresponding vocabulary of how physical and abstract objects are related.

In the humanities, a traditional medium for discussion and information integration has been the creation of textual descriptions of non-textual sources. Analysis and interlinking have then been based on the descriptions. A typical example is archaeology where written sources are available together with the results of archaeological excavations. Links back to non-textual sources in the form of inventory numbers and shelf marks are commonly found in footnotes, catalogues, and type collections. These links have been difficult to follow in practice, as one had to go to the specific locations where the artifacts were kept.

Non-textual sources have always been (re)mediated. In recent years, remediation and publication have become significantly cheaper due to the development of digital media and the internet. An image of a painting is a remediation. The ontology lets us make a representation of the artifact itself with a set of reconstructed links to other artifacts, persons, places, dates, and events. This enables us to create a Semantic Web of cultural heritage information based on many different types of material organized in a way which is different from narrative texts. This has the potential of opening up human culture to new kinds of humanities research, giving access to different types of contexts for historical sources compared to what has previously been feasible to present.

6 The Semantic Web and the future of ontologies

Whichever ontologies we may use in digital humanities, from the few described here to countless others, many of them local to specific projects, there are important things to remember when it comes to long-term preservation and integration with other material. From the development of linked data we have seen the importance of giving "things" unique identifiers. For digital humanities and culture heritage applications these identifiers should, as far as possible, be locations on the Semantic Web that are organized according to an agreed upon model. Today, the best language in which to express the meanings and contexts of these identifiers is RDF. While this is not tied to ontologies in the strict sense, or to the use of standards such as the ones described in this chapter, it will be necessary for a truly functional Semantic Web for the humanities that the linked data are based on well-defined and agreed upon ontologies so that the entities and the relationships between them have well-defined meanings.

These additions to the basic linked data approach are vital to our domains. Expressing meaning in the humanities is based on the fact that information is generated through exclusion based on meaningful distinctions. Conceptual models or ontologies can be used to express such distinctions. Data organized using ontologies can be expressed as RDF triples. Consequentially, linked data can function as a medium for generating meaningful statements about data—that is, linked data can enable us to share meaningful information. Not using consistent models creates problems that are similar in effect to storing texts in different languages in a common text database, where a free text search for words from one language may match unrelated words in one of the others.

No common system for meaningful distinctions exists for all of the humanities and cultural heritage. Accordingly, we cannot expect all-encompassing standards —we must operate within domains. In order for a domain ontology to work well for data integration, it must be agreed upon by at least a significant part of actors in the domain. A meaningful global Semantic Web for everything will require a common upper ontology—that is, a conceptual model comprising everything. For this to work, a significant part of the world has to agree, which is inconceivable for many reasons including cultural, political, and economic ones. There are many examples of comparable historical attempts that turned out to be futile. It may be a relevant point in this respect that the so-called "ontological argument" in Western philosophy is the field of constructing a proof for the existence of God. The question of standard upper ontologies has been both researched and debated for a long time, and it is indeed an argument against the viability of such ontologies that no general agreement has been made. "The initial project of building one single ontology, even one single top-level ontology, which would be at the same time nontrivial and also readily adopted by a broad population of different information-systems communities, has however largely been abandoned" (Smith, 2004).

It may be too strong to claim that it is impossible that anything along the line of widely accepted and widely used general upper-level ontologies will be made in the future. But as such things are not foreseeable in the near future, current implementations cannot be based on their existence. We should still work towards common models for given domains, and we should harmonize models.

The future development of ontologies is closely connected to the Semantic Web and linked data. While both of these areas have significant potential, they are also buzzwords and there are risks involved in the way in which they are currently developed. Good digital humanities practice in this area must be closely connected to cultural heritage, including digital libraries. Developing a functional Semantic Web for the humanities is impossible without such connections, both in methods and for the data. We must share data, but we must also agree how to formalize them. Not only the data, but also the links must be meaningful. We will never agree on one universal formalism for all the humanities, but we need common practices both at type level and at the level of particulars.

Both creating and using ontologies will necessarily involve data modeling. Further, data modeling will always involve ontological considerations. While all ontologies are data models, not all data models are ontologies. Ontologies can be developed at many different levels, from a tailor-suited system to be used for the analysis of, say, one specific poem to widely used and adopted data standards. Whether one develops ontologies just for one's own research or for a large user base, it is important to consider the future potential of integration with other ontologies. In many cases, the flexibility of a local formalism is needed, especially in research. But for long-term use of data, also research data, mappings to other formalisms are best practice and should be prioritized.

Notes

1   The International Committee for Documentation (CIDOC) of the International Council of Museums (ICOM)—Conceptual Reference Model (LeBoeuf et al., 2015). CIDOC-CRM was made and is still developed by interdisciplinary teams of experts coming from fields such as computer science, archaeology, museum documentation, art history, natural history, library science, physics, and philosophy under the auspices of CIDOC. Available at: www.cidoc-crm.org/.
2   FRBR (Functional Requirements for Bibliographic References) was developed by IFLA, the international organization for libraries. FRBR has since been reformulated as the conceptual model FRBRoo and harmonized with the CIDOC-CRM model. In 2017 IFLA introduced the Library Reference Model (LRM), a consolidation of the separately developed IFLA conceptual models: FRBR, FRAD, FRSAD (Riva et al., 2017). Like FRBR, LRM is expressed in the ER formalism and harmonized with CIDIC-CRM as LRMoo. The FRBR examples in this book is also valid under LRM.
3   The TEI Consortium has created and maintains a set of guidelines for how to best encode documents. It can be used for different purposes; making printed and digital editions of texts are important examples. These guidelines are widely used in the humanities. Available at: www.tei-c.org/. For the history of TEI, see, for example, Burnard (2013).
4   Universal Modeling Language, used for object-oriented computer science modeling. See www.uml.org.
5   Available at: http://w3c.org/RDF/.
6   See, for example, ICOM-CIDOC's Statement on Linked Data identifiers for museum objects, 2012. Available at: http://network.icom.museum/fileadmin/user_upload/minisites/cidoc/PDF/StatementOnLinkedDataIdentifiersForMuseumObjects.pdf.
7   On ER models in general, see, for instance, Simsion and Witt (2005).
8   The Menota schema is a TEI-based schema for encoding Medieval Nordic manuscripts. Available at: www.menota.org/.
9   K. Faith Lawrence, Michael Jewell, and Mischa Tuffield, "The OntoMedia Model." Available at: https://web.archive.org/web/20070914095952/http://ontomedia.ecs.soton.ac.uk.

References

Burnard, L., 2013. The Evolution of the Text Encoding Initiative: From Research Project to Research Infrastructure. *Journal of the Text Encoding Initiative*. Available at https://journals.openedition.org/jtei/811.

Eide, Ø., 2015. Ontologies, Data Modeling, and TEI. *Journal of the Text Encoding Initiative*. Available at: https://journals.openedition.org/jtei/1191.

Gruber, T.R., 1993. A Translation Approach to Portable Ontology Specifications. *Knowledge Acquisition*, 5(2), pp. 199–220.

Harris, E.C., 1989. *Principles of Archaeological Stratigraphy* (2nd ed.). London: Academic Press.

Hofweber, T., 2011. Logic and Ontology. In: E.N. Zalta (Ed.) *The Stanford Encyclopedia of Philosophy*. Stanford, CA: Stanford University. Available at: http://plato.stanford.edu/entries/logic-ontology/.

Jannidis, F. and Flanders, J., 2013. A Concept of Data Modeling for the Humanities. In: *Digital Humanities 2013: Conference Abstracts*. Lincoln: Center for Digital Research in the Humanities, pp. 237–9.

Le Boeuf, P., Doerr, M., Ore, C.-E., and Stead, S. 2015. *Definition of the CIDOC Conceptual Reference Model*. Version 6.2. Available at:www.cidoc-crm.org/Version/version-6.2.

Ore, C.-E., S. and Eide, Ø., 2009. TEI and cultural heritage ontologies: Exchange of information? *Literary and Linguistic Computing*, 24, pp. 161–72.

Reed, P.A., 1995. *CIDOC Relational Data Model, A Guide*. Available at: http://database answers.org/data_models/museums_simple/cidoc_datamodel.pdf.

Riva, P., Le Bœuf, P., Žumer, M. 2017. IFLA Library Reference Model A Conceptual Model for Bibliographic Information www.ifla.org/files/assets/cataloguing/frbr-lrm/ifla-lrm-august-2017.pdf.

Simsion, G.C. and Witt, G.C., 2005. *Data Modeling Essentials*. Amsterdam: Morgan Kaufmann Publishers.

Smith, B., 2004. Ontology. In: L. Floridi (Ed.) *The Blackwell Guide to the Philosophy of Computing and Information*. Malden, MO: Blackwell, pp. 155–66.

Staab, S. and Studer, R., 2009. *Handbook on Ontologies*. Berlin: Springer.

9 Where semantics lies

Stephen Ramsay

A debate once raged—and occasionally reappears—over whether s-expressions should have been used instead of the syntax we use for XML.[1] Taken at face value, this means nothing more than a preference for this:

```
(dictionary

        (e-mail "electronic mail")

        (html "hypertext transport language")

        (xml "extensible markup language")
```

... over this:

```
    <dictionary>

        <email>electronic mail</email>

        <html>hypertext transport language</html>

        <xml>extensible markup language</xml>

    </dictionary>
```

Neither example contains any attributes, but it is easy to imagine how we might add them. If we had:

```
<dictionary>

    <e-mail acronym="false">electronic mail</email>

    <html acronym="true">hypertext transport language</html>

    <xml acronym="true">extensible markup language</xml>

</dictionary>
```

. . . we could express the same thing in s-expression syntax with something like this:

```
(dictionary

        (e-mail :acronym false "electronic mail")

        (html :acronym true "hypertext transport language")

        (xml :acronym true "extensible markup language")

)
```

Look closely, and you will see that these two representations are structurally identical, in that both provide ways of annotating hierarchical text data. From a computational standpoint, there is nothing you can do with the one that you cannot do with the other. The two representations differ mainly in terms of syntax: their choice of notational delimiters.

So you might suppose that one element of the debate involved syntax, and that is certainly true. Some people argued quite vociferously that XML is simply a needlessly verbose form of s-expression syntax. The standard reply was that "syntax matters" (Prescott, 2003)—that XML's more prolix syntax made it easier for humans to read the format—but that was not actually the center of this debate at all. The center of the debate was the charge that XML has "no semantics."

But what would it mean for something to "have a semantics?" In the computational realm, the most frequently offered answer to that question is that "semantics"—a term almost always used in reference to formal languages such as those we use for programming—refers to the *meaning* of a computational representation. Terrence Parr, the author of a popular tool for creating programming languages (and therefore someone who presumably knows what "semantics" is) says, "Loosely speaking, semantic analysis figures out what the input means (anything beyond syntax is called *the semantics*)" (Parr, 2010, p. 4). This appears in a book called *Language Implementation Patterns*, which is hardly light reading, but not a textbook on formal languages; he can surely be forgiven for speaking loosely. Even when we turn to actual textbooks on formal languages, though, we get statements that amount to the same thing: "This book is an analytic study of programming languages. Our goal is to provide a deep, working understanding of the essential concepts of programming languages . . . Most of the essentials relate to the semantics, or meaning, of program elements" (Friedman, 2008, p. xv). If these statements are in any way consistent with the critique of XML having no semantics, then the charge is not simply that XML is needlessly verbose, but that it is *just syntax*, and therefore fundamentally *meaningless*.

On one hand, that statement is obviously false; humans might differ in their interpretation of the lists offered above (though probably not widely), but no one would claim that the XML is without meaning (still less that the XML is meaningless and the s-expression meaningful). If anything, we would be inclined to say that both forms "have a semantics"—even that they have the same semantics—because they both mean something and they both mean the same thing. Whatever the one has that the other does not cannot be a function of the syntax, but of some other condition (perhaps a context or a wider framework of mutual understandings) in which that syntax appears.

This idea of meaning (or semantics) as "syntax plus something else" bears a strong resemblance to an argument made by Ludwig Wittgenstein, in the *Philosophical Investigations* on the nature of meaning. He wrote: "For a large class of cases—though not for all—in which we employ the word 'meaning' it can be defined thus: the meaning of a word is its use in the language" (Wittgenstein, 2009, p. 42). It can be difficult to see at first what is so radical about this conception. Taken superficially, it might seem to be a statement about context—about this other condition in which syntax appears. But Wittgenstein goes considerably further than this, by rejecting the entire notion that something could be, as a philosopher might put it, "analytically true" or true without reference to exterior conditions. In fact, what he really says is that there is nothing but "use in context." There is nothing to speak of beyond this complex web of relations. "What is justice?" "Justice" is the set of moments in which the term is (and can be) deployed. That does not make the question itself nonsensical or unanswerable ("What is justice?" is, after all, an instance in which the term is employed), but it does make it unlikely that we will get very far in forming a useful, all-purpose definition. And since forming useful, all-purpose definitions has often been one of the goals of philosophy, Wittgenstein's definition serves as a bold attack on certain branches philosophy itself.

What is useful about all of this for our purposes, though, is the fact that this idea of "meaning as use" gives us not only a way to talk about semantics, but also a way to describe computation itself. Following Wittgenstein, "semantics"— whether in the context of natural language or computational processing—is all about actions. We say that humans "understand" data, while computers do not, and that humans are able to derive "meaning" from data, while computers cannot. Such notions presuppose that matters such as understanding and meaning can be verified apart from a set of actions or changes of state. Suppose, for example, that I presented you with a picture of a horse. Upon what basis would I be able to determine that you had "understood" what a horse is (or what the picture "means")? The answer is that I have no basis at all without you *doing* something. You might *say*, "That is a horse," or, "Thank you, I have always been fond of equines." You could *point to* another horse, produce a similar picture, or make the sound of a horse. Whatever the case, you have to take the information (the data) that I gave to you, and give something else back that is demonstrably relevant. We do not typically describe it this way, but situations like this represent a processing regime, and like computational or information processing, it is largely about moving information from one state to another in a way that is felt to be coherent by participants and/or observers. If you have a mechanical process that can take information and produce more information, we call that process "a computation." This is what happens when you press the equals sign on a calculator, and it is what happens when you friend someone on Facebook.

Moreover, a full understanding of the precise process by which the state is changed is not required. In the former case, it is possible to "do addition," say, without understanding what addition really is (imagine a very small child, entirely ignorant of arithmetic operations, which delights merely in the fact that when four buttons are pressed in a row, a new figure appears on the screen). In the latter case, it is entirely probable that the user has no idea what was happening behind the scene when someone was "friended." This is likewise the case with natural language. Someone, looking at an XML document, might say "I understand what <pageBreak> means," and in the ordinary course of our dealings we may be fully satisfied that this person understands the semantics of the <pageBreak> tag. But suppose it were later revealed that the person did not know how to use it in a document?

Wittgenstein draws upon extreme examples in order to drive this point home, and it is worth providing a couple of examples that are in the same spirit. Consider the sentence "I understand orange." At first, it appears to be nonsense. In fact, it appears to be a kind of *grammatical* nonsense—evidence that the person speaking does not understand the rules of the English language. When it is revealed that this utterance occurred in an art class during a discussion of color theory, the sentence becomes intelligible. But suppose the teacher were to demand that the student demonstrate their ability to produce orange from a set of primary colors. In that case, it might be revealed that the student did not understand color. Wittgenstein's contention is that these two actions—an apparently abstract utterance and a concrete action—are not essentially different. Both are "actions"— specific moves in what Wittgenstein called "language games." "I understand orange" produces a state change as surely as any mixing of paint (perhaps the lecture continues without further discussion of orange).

To say that something "has a semantics" is therefore to say that we have some process for producing various kinds of actions or procedures (of which transformations are one species). This restates Wittgenstein's point quite succinctly. The information has meaning—has a semantics—because we can produce other states from it. In the absence of such productions (whether actual or potential), the information is literally "meaning-less." And while that condition might be rare, it sets a boundary condition on semantics. Computational representations "have a semantics," because we can perform computations on them. This is perhaps why Friedman and Wand (from whom I drew the quotation above about the essentials of programming languages having to do with semantics), go on a few sentences later to say, "The most interesting question about a program as object is, 'What does it do?'" (Friedman, 2008, p. 4). If meaning is use, then who can argue?

So when someone says that XML "has no semantics," they are presumably referring to the fact that *by itself*, XML has no inherent ability to produce anything at all. Any XML file, taken on its own, exists solely as an information structure whose syntax can be understood by reading the XML specification (which tells us which parts are markup and how that markup is structured). In order to do anything with this information structure—transform it, operate on it, understand the meaning of its elements—something else needs to happen. You need to outline some process by which that representation either is transformed into some other kind of representation, or otherwise results in an action. But is that any less true of s-expressions? Is not an s-expression *also* a representation in search of a means by which it can be translated into some other representation? What could possibly cause someone to say that s-expressions "have a semantics," while XML does not?

The answer to that question lies with the fact that s-expressions make up the syntax of the Lisp programming language. That itself does not automatically endow it with a semantics (XML is also used as the syntax for a programming language as well: XSLT). S-expressions can only be said to have a semantics if you also have some program that can read those expressions and produce some other action or information state, which, in practice, means having a "Lisp runtime" (a system for supporting the execution of Lisp code). The corresponding notion for XML is that XML has a semantics if—and only if—you also have a way of taking that representation and using it to produce something else, which, in practice, means having some means for transforming the XML data (either XSLT or some other programming language with its own runtime) and perhaps also a schema that allows for validation of the data (a process that also effects an information state in the form of an output declaring the document to be valid or not).

But notice the difference there. If you have s-expressions, all you need is a Lisp runtime. If you have XML, you need to have the semantics described in two places: some of it (the part of chief interest to the data modeler) in the schema, and some of it in the runtime. The difference, in other words, has less to do with angle brackets and parentheses, and much more to do with *where* the semantics lies within the overall system.

It is possible, of course, to process s-expressions without using the Lisp programming language and its runtime; any programming will do. It would also be possible to separate various constraints on an s-expression into a separate document from the entity responsible for affecting the transformation and still be "doing Lisp." The point here is not that Lisp has affordances or redundancies that XML does not, and in particular the point is not that either system would be better if it more closely resembled the other. We are not talking about some kind of new affordance offered by Lisp, some deficiency in the XML ecosystem, or the other way around. When it comes to taking things from one information state to another, either system could be designed either way. The question, rather, is this: Does it matter at all where you put the semantics? Does it matter whether we separate the semantics of usage/processing as fully as possible from the data, or whether we integrate those elements? And the answer to that is, I think, "yes"—and for more or less the same reason that "syntax matters." To decide *where* the semantics lies in a system is to decide how a set of relationships among human actors is going to be structured.

The XML ecosystem implicitly imagines a radical decoupling between the act of data modeling and the act of processing data. In fact, it breaks the act of data modeling itself into several discrete stages, which, in practical terms, translates into a decoupling of the social act of marking up texts from the social act of modeling data, and both of these from the social act of processing data. I use the term "social act" as a way of designating different potential functions—job descriptions, if you like—in the overall job of computation. In the world of XML as used in a digital humanities context, there is one job involving the development of a grammar for a set of documents: the schema designer. There is another job involving the application of that grammar to a particular set of documents: the encoder. And there is a third job involving the processing of the grammar and the document to translate their information to another state: a programmer or web developer. These roles carry quite different skills—at least partly because they map onto other roles in the ecosystem such as "the scholar/editor" or "the technical person." Conversely, you can have a system in which these various elements are closely combined. Some partition of roles is, of course, still possible, but in practice, the Lisp ecosystem more or less demands that data modeling and data processing are never far from one another. While it is possible to imagine an s-expression tagger, it is less easy to imagine that person not also being, at some level, a programmer. The issue, then, is whether the distributed, decoupled model embodied in the XML ecosystem (and in other systems like it) limits or expands our ideas about data modeling, as compared to a more centralized workflow in which data modeling is never far from data processing.

An XML schema (and here I am talking about any kind of schema whatsoever) describes a grammar. In practical terms, this, and not any encoded document, is the "data model." Typically, a schema defines a set of data types (usually, though not necessarily tied to natural language semantics) and a set of ordering constraints. But why stop there? Why not use that schema to define a set of procedures for processing data? Again, "processing" here means any kind of doing. It might describe, for example, a set of rules for how humans should express their insights when talking about the data, or it might refer to the result of having applied a stylesheet. The point is that the schema is the place where we attempt to constrain or de-constrain the processing. Like any data model—in fact, like information itself—it stands in some relationship to a processing model. I would even suggest that the question, "Are the data models we have proposed for the humanities sufficient to the task?" is equivalent to the question, "Does the semantics reside in the right place in our overall processing regime?"

This is not because shifting the semantics around gives you new processing powers, but because to the degree that any data model attempts to stay neutral with respect to future processing regimes, it must limit the practical affordances offered by that model to the data modeler. To provide such limits might be to commit an act of magnanimity; to construct a data model in the absence of any particular judgment about future processing is presumably to allow a thousand processes to flourish. But it is also to limit what can be modeled—because that is exactly where the decisions about semantics are being made. We may comfort ourselves with the thought that every step up the chain of abstraction allows more flexibility at the processing level, but a dark voice remains (and should remain): every step up the chain of abstraction also means separating further and further from the details of processing—which are, again, the very thing that gives a data model semantics in the first place. To give the processor more power is necessarily to give the data modeler less control, and not just less control over the processing, but less control over the data model itself. So we really must ask ourselves this: does having *less* control over the data model—which is not the same thing as saying "more flexibility"—make sense for our data?

There is no right answer to this question. In some cases, the right data modeling protocol is the one written on the back of an envelope—the one that forsakes all possibility of computational tractability in favor of successful communication between two people about what has been learned from a dataset. In other cases, though, the right data modeling protocol is the one so close to machine tractability that it is itself a programming language. The pun in my title is meant to suggest that we should not assume that we know the contexts that will give rise to meaning, that we should consciously consider where our semantics is being defined in our computational systems, and that we should avoid the kind of hopeless debate in which we imagine that syntax possesses some power beyond the contexts in which it is embedded.

Note

1   Evidence of this debate is abundant online. A reasonable summary may be found at:
    http://c2.com/cgi/wiki?XmlIsaPoorCopyOfEssExpressions

References

Friedman, D.P. and Wand, M., 2008. *Essentials of Programming Languages* (3rd ed.) Boston, MA: MIT.
Parr, T., 2010. *Language Implementation Patterns*. Raleigh: Pragmatic Programmers.
Prescott, P., 2003. *XML is not S-Expressions*. Available at: http://xahlee.info/comp/XML_ is_not_S-Expressions.html.
Wittgenstein, L., 2009. *Philosophical Investigations* (4th ed.) Malden: Wiley-Blackwell.

10 Constraint

Julia Flanders, Fotis Jannidis, and
Wendell Piez

1 Introduction

What is constraint, in the context of data modeling? A constraint hems us in, restricts our motion, whereas data models are abstractions, tools for thinking with. Models are representations of the properties of an informational system: a set of informational conditions that are taken to define the significant characteristics of that system. The TEI schema, for example, provides a "model" for bibliographic citations (dictionary entries, scholarly apparatus, and so forth) which identifies the features that differentiate bibliographic citations from other textual structures: its identification of author, title, publication data; its representation of the layers of the bibliographic object, and so forth. We can also have models for physical structures: when you plug in an Ethernet cable, you rely on a standard, which ensures that the RJ45 plug from the cable you bought at Heathrow Airport will fit into the socket in your hotel room in Oslo. The "model" here—which regulates the design of that plug—expresses the ideal measurements of that plug and also the tolerances governing the permitted variation from that ideal. Data models can be purely descriptive, but when they are used as standards—for instance, to enable interoperability between data and tools—and thus have the power to regulate, they constitute a set of limitations with practical impact on the world. And this "regulation" is a shorthand way of describing something complex that deserves more careful attention.

The concept of "constraint" describes the operation of data models and the ways in which we actually experience their power to govern and shape. The TEI schema proposes an idea about what is meant by a bibliographic citation, but it also offers a specific set of tests by which we can assess whether a modeled instance—a specific piece of TEI-encoded text—actually matches that idea. Constraint is a process of measurement and enforcement whose goal is to enable interaction between systems: between data and tools, between plugs and sockets, between different senders and receivers of information. We can see constraint of this kind in operation in the physical world, in the form of gauges and specifications, but the stakes are particularly high in systems that process digital information, because in those systems there is less room for approximation. They require clear and unambiguous parameters to define their operation, and that clarity—the constrained terms within which information is meaningful—is evident from the lowest level of the layered Open Systems Interconnection model up to the highest level standards for data models that enable semantically rich applications.

Constraints operate by defining conditions of significant difference. A standard specifies that a conforming entity should be *like this* and *not like that:* a plug *should be* 11.68 mm wide, and *should not be* more than 0.5 mm larger or smaller. The fundamental unit of digital information, the bit, is nothing more than the discernible distinction between two possible states, represented conventionally as on/off, true/false or 1/0. While different computer hardware may use different voltage levels to represent the 1 and the 0, the important thing is that they *differ significantly*—that is, that the system can detect and operate upon the difference as a form of information. Gregory Bateson described a bit as "a difference that makes a difference" (1972): the problem of architecture and design in computers is how to define the difference each bit will make—to formulate, follow and enforce the rules of working bits in combination and in combinations of combinations. These rules take the form of data types, protocols, functions and operations, formats, syntax, grammars, languages, APIs and data models, and they are both explicit (specified and documented) and implicit (left to builders to discover on our own), and they are implemented and enforced at every level of the digital computer, from the design of its hardware, CPU and memory through its operating system, and up into the application software we run on it and the interfaces we use to work with it.

Constraint may be expressed and enforced through formal mechanisms such as schemas, through broader social agreements such as information standards, and also through social and practical means, all of which we will discuss in more detail below. But it is useful to start by first considering some of the intellectual inheritances on which our ideas of constraint draw, to help us understand more fully why specific constraint systems are designed as they are, and how they operate.

One of the most archetypal places where constraint is experienced in the modeling of humanities data is in the use of schemas for text encoding, whether in HTML, TEI, EAD, or any of the other XML languages in common usage. In these contexts, the operation of constraint is often explained by making a comparison with literary genre. Genre represents a descriptive consensus about the features we expect to find in a given kind of texts, and text encoding seeks to identify what is "generic" about a particular entity to be represented: what structural features it must have, or may have, or may not have, as in our example of poetry above. Schema design of this kind focuses on genre and the generic because from a modeling perspective, classes of things are more interesting—and more useful—than things that are purely idiosyncratic. A document or data object in which each feature was completely unique, not named or propertied like any other, would be a document whose modeling was not meaningful except in the minimal sense of distinguishing elements from one another, saying "this one is not like any of these others." In other words, data modeling is ordinarily an exercise in classification—the establishment of groupings that enable us to see common properties—not only description. Constraint thus emerges as a way of describing and formalizing a set of generic expectations: in an XML language, the schema describes a class of documents (a "genre") which obey the same set of constraints and are free to vary in all other respects.

The term "class" is worth further scrutiny here, as it has special meaning and function where constraint is concerned. Class in this context is closely related to the mathematical concept of the "set"[1] (discussed in the introductory material to this volume). The defining properties of the set—the qualities that determine the collection of entities that make up its membership—are called its "intension," and we can understand the intension of a set as being analogous to the definition of a class. If we define a database field that represents the month of birth (e.g. of an author), and stipulate that the field must contain an integer between 1 and 12 (representing the 12 months of the year), we have created a two-part constraint whose first part is the invocation of a class—the class of integers—and whose second part adds the limitation to values between 1 and 12. (It is worth noting that in computer science, the term "constraint" is typically used for this latter limitation, not to the former.)

What does it mean, though, to define a class for the purposes of constraint, and how do we do this in contexts that are less clear-cut than mathematical definitions? This task is essential to many different fields—mathematics, linguistics, philosophy, psychology, logic—and they share an essential set of closely related terms. The mathematical term "set" is closely related to the philosophical notion of "concept": the intension of a set is directly analogous to the definition or intension of a concept, and the extension (i.e. the collection of actual entities that are members of the set) is analogous to the collection of entities to which the concept may actually refer.[2] The classical Aristotelian approach to the definition of concepts enumerates those properties that are necessary and sufficient to define it—in other words, the properties that identify all, and only, the entities that the concept refers to, and that can also predict what new entities it might describe. A well-known example is the definition of "bachelor" by the properties "man" and "unmarried": the term describes all, and only, unmarried men, and whatever the current set of such entities may be (if we could list all of the unmarried men in the world), whenever a new one comes into existence, the concept describes that one as well.

This classical approach to concept definition is very common in computer science because it can be modeled so easily. Each property here works as a constraint: it is easy to check whether the digital representation of an entity has a specific property. However, for digital humanities purposes, while clear formal definitions of properties are often desirable (and often possible, in cases where our concepts are subject to negotiation and standardization), there are also many situations where the things we want to model are human concepts, and as such are not designed to be clear. As formal modelers, we need modeling tools that let us reconstruct the innate indeterminacy—unclear boundaries, edge cases, difficulties of definition—of the objects of our study. One very interesting approach in this context is the "prototype" model, which comes from the field of psychology where it attempts to account for the ways in which humans create their most basic understanding of the world. Applied to the classification of concepts, this approach assumes that there are good instances of a concept and also less good instances, a shading rather than an absolute difference. We could think of this in probabilistic terms: "concept *C* has probabilistic structure in that something falls under *C* just in case it satisfies a sufficient number of properties encoded by *C*'s constituents" (Margolis and Laurence, 2014). This approach can handle the effects of classes that are well known to humanists: good and bad examples of a class, borderline cases, and many more. Interestingly enough, both the prototype and the classical approach leave unexplored the potentially relational features of concepts: the ways in which concepts are defined in relation to one another rather than independently. At the moment, most data models (including those commonly used in digital humanities) use constraints as in the classical model: through rigid class definitions. This limits the expressiveness and the fitness of data models to entities from the realm of the humanities, but enables access to all the operations built on these data models. Only in recent years have we seen the modeling of constraints in a way more "natural" to a prototype approach with its understanding of gradations of differences, and the exploration of these approaches and their application to the digital humanities as a field is an important area for further research.

Thinking about models in terms of classes is useful because it directs our attention to the ways in which these things are abstractions. But the prototype approach to class definition is useful precisely because it also acknowledges that classes are classes of *things*—that is, of real entities, actual instances, even if those instances are of intellectual rather than physical objects. And in the real world, the intension and extension of a set are more difficult to pin down than they are in abstraction. For one thing, in our examination of actual entities (documents, artifacts, persons) quite often we cannot actually consider all members of the set; instead, we must extrapolate from a sample. That extrapolation process is conjectural, and it depends on the representativeness of the sample. In addition, unlike in set theory, the extension of a real-world set may change over time as new documents are written or discovered, or as geographical boundaries change. Perhaps most importantly, the properties we identify as the intension of a real-world set—that is, the characteristics we take as definitional—carry an intellectual importance of their own. In set theory, it does not matter whether the set {3,5,7} has the intension "odd numbers between 2 and 8" or "prime numbers between 3 and 10". But if we are studying a collection of pamphlets and determining what other documents belong in the collection, it matters what properties constitute its definitional boundaries: date, genre, authorship, topic, geography, and so forth. Those properties serve as the basis for constraint on any future data creation, to ensure that the data set continues to express the same set of intentions (with a "t") that originally motivated it.

The principles of set theory and classification offer a particular kind of perspective on constraint: its function of enforcing a division of the world into "the things that belong" and "the things that do not belong." From this perspective, our attention is directed macroscopically at groupings of objects, taxonomies, metadata fields that enable us to organize the materials of our research universe into functional groupings. But this same work of differentiation comes into play microscopically as well as the very condition of information and signification. At the most fundamental level, constraint tells us how to differentiate the 1 from the 0 and the signal from the noise: it offers the basic conditions necessary for communication.

2 The operations of constraint

2.1 Constraint through formal mechanisms

How do we actually experience constraint? How are constraints mechanisms expressed and made known to us, and how in practice is our behavior actually influenced by these mechanisms?

First and most obviously: as we have already seen earlier in this volume, constraints on our data can be expressed explicitly through formal mechanisms like schemas, the rules of XML well-formedness, or the rules that govern the structure of a relational database. We might call these "technical" constraints, in the sense that they operate within the specific horizons of a particular tool set. When we ask an XML-conformant tool to operate on our data, that data must first be intelligible *as data of a certain kind*; in other words, its permissible forms of variation must be limited to those described by the constraint system that is XML. Similarly, our ability to query data within a database system is predicated on the data being intelligible to that system. The formal constraints in operation establish the parameters within which meaningful variation on a pattern—information— can take place.

Our experience of these formal constraints varies depending on our relationship to them, our own role in the system. For the creator of a schema, or the designer of a database, the constraint system expresses a set of intentions that attempt to map out an entire field of information. The vision these constraints encompass is perceptible in its entirety to the designer; it may be an imperfect or partial realization of that vision if the work of data analysis is not yet complete, but all of its aspects are accessible. Indeed, the term "constraint" in this context requires some inflection: the designer acts to constrain the universe of possibility, of signifying potential, for a given field of data.

From the viewpoint of someone using these constraints to create or interact with data, however, the experience may be quite different. A novice user— someone unfamiliar with the schema, or perhaps even unfamiliar with the meta-constraints of the database or of XML—discovers the very existence of the constraint system by colliding with its boundaries. A common scenario that we have all experienced is the inscrutable search interface offered by a library catalogue. When we type into the search box, knowing nothing about the structure of the data we are attempting to query, we discover that structure by trial and error: learning by the results we receive (or don't receive), whether a date needs to be in a specific format, or whether "name" means "author." Another scenario common in digital humanities projects is the novice data creator—a student or volunteer transcribing a text, or creating metadata, or entering data in a web form, and discovering the boundaries of the constraint system through error messages. The intentions (the designer's "vision") that put those boundaries in place may be entirely invisible. Lacking the knowledge to understand the full logic underlying the system, users experience a lack of power to communicate fully their understanding of the data. The phenomenon of "tag abuse" (making a choice that is technically valid but semantically inappropriate) is a natural response: without access to the animating logic of the system, only to its punishments, the user can only use the system by appeasing it.

With greater expertise, the scenario changes. A data creator who is fully aware of the constraints but is not invested in their motivations—or is actively discontented with them—may also commit tag abuse, but in a different spirit: a kind of hacker approach in which features of the system are deliberately misappropriated to achieve some other goal. For instance, an author forced to use TEI for a journal article might use the <emph> element to italicize foreign language words and book titles, simply out of a desire for expediency and a lack of interest in the more nuanced semantics available in the language. Or someone entering metadata in an overly simplistic interface that only offers "first name" and "last name" fields might deliberately put a middle name in the "first name" field, knowing it was incorrect but wanting the name to show up in the data nonetheless. The most comfortable and enabling role is that of the expert user who is privy to the design process and its rationale, and thus has an entirely different relationship to these constraints: one of being *on their side*, of being *part of the system* rather than trapped within it. Indeed, one important result of increasing expertise in data modeling among humanities scholars is to provide access to this space of empowerment and knowledge.

2.2 Constraint through standards

The formal constraints described above are themselves situated in a larger context: a set of standards and agreements that constitute a kind of social contract concerning the nature of information and the modes of its expression. These standards constrain the tools we use—for instance, most modern authoring tools (word processors, text editors, web forms, etc.) represent textual data as one of several encodings of Unicode, with each character captured as a byte sequence representing (according to the rules of the encoding) a specific Unicode code point. These tools participate in a broad agreement that we will all save our data as Unicode (and we expect data we receive from other tools to be in Unicode as well). Because the various possible encodings our tools or we might select each maps to Unicode (UTF-7, UTF-8, UTF-16, or more obscure ones), they also faithfully map (with no collapse or loss of information) to one another. Our "Unicode characters" (a set of discrete entities, defined by and as a set of constraints) will survive on different systems and systems we have never seen, even despite their differences—as long as they all use Unicode (in some form or another). When all tools operate on this assumption, the system is seamless and we never notice a problem. Other examples include specifications like the HTTP protocol, which specifies how web browsers communicate with the data resources that constitute the web, and also more fundamental agreements on concepts and their realization as information—for instance, specific data types such as integers or floating point numbers, date formats such as ISO 8601, or the language codes defined by the IETF.

These specifications are built into the tools we use in ways that are not subject to our deliberate choice (or even awareness), but those tools do themselves constrain our behaviour. By using Unicode-based tools, we humans produce Unicode data now without making any decision choice to do so (and we're not free to do otherwise). When we use a web browser, we necessarily communicate with servers worldwide using HTTP and its various commands. But even in the absence of tools to realize them, these standards would still be in force: if all text editing tools and software were eradicated from the face of the earth, the Unicode specification would still exist, and could be reimplemented in the next generation of tools. The tools may provide the initial motivation and sense of necessity for creating the standard, but once created, the standard stands apart from the tools that use it. In this sense, these standards operate most meaningfully as a set of agreements—first of all, agreements that there are mutual benefits to using a common standard, and then agreements about how that standard will be developed, and finally agreements about what it will look like and what it will regulate. And the resulting standards in turn are based on the difficult work of understanding and reconciling a very complex set of needs: mapping out the things a specific system needs to do, and formalizing them as a set of rules. In the case of Unicode, this meant taking an inventory of all of the world's writing systems and deciding what constituted meaningfully different "characters": how many different kinds of dots are there? Is an umlaut the same thing as a diaeresis? Should diacritical marks have their own separate code points or should they be combined with alphabetic characters, and, if so, with which? And this process must be continued as the political and technical circumstances evolve. For example, in the case of Unicode, emojis and other new characters have to be included, and sometimes the characterization of a given set of characters may change. The symbols on the Voynich manuscript are currently believed to be ciphers for a living language and therefore are not included in the Unicode standard, but if someone could show that they do represent a heretofore unknown natural language, they would be included. In a standard like TEI, new domains of scholarly activity gain importance and need to be accommodated, as in the case of the recent creation of markup to support genetic editing.

As we have seen in the introductory chapter to this volume, constraints operate within data modeling systems at different technological levels, from the very deep level systems like character encoding (which dictates the number of bits of information that will be devoted to the representation of each written character, and how the boundaries of those informational packages will be recognized by the system) to the high-level constraints exercised by XML schemas and data entry forms. These constraints differ importantly in the kinds of agencies responsible for their creation. Data representation standards such as Unicode are built into the information infrastructure at a very deep level and in order to succeed they must operate almost universally; as a result, their creation entails an almost diplomatic process. Establishing such standards requires cross-cultural negotiation about the representation of language and its building blocks. Metamodels like XML and RDF are typically major international standards designed by committees of experts for very broad applicability, and may have strong industry influence since the metamodels determine the behavior of tools. Specific models (XML schemas, ontologies, and the like) that regulate particular data sets are often aimed at supporting research data for a specific intellectual community and hence, like TEI or CIDOC, are often designed by domain experts who attempt to reflect the broad needs of the researchers who will be using the model. But such models may also operate more locally and may be designed by individual researchers with more personal or local aims and horizons of usage. Individual usage practices may be even more personal and may not even be formally expressed as models, but they operate as significant constraints nonetheless: a group of researchers might maintain a set of notes that guide their agreed-upon transcription practice for a digital edition. At all of these levels, constraints serve to regulate the information that circulates, according to the agreements established by the relevant agencies.

These layers of constraint systems represent different spheres of jurisdiction and definitional power, but each layer also depends informationally upon those that underpin it, and the conditions of operation within a given layer are regulated by assumptions that are established in the layer below. Thus, metamodels like XML and RDF assume the existence of underlying standards (like Unicode) which establish how characters—the basic units of meaning—are identified and defined. Specific models like TEI and FOAF assume the existence of underlying metamodels (like XML and RDF), which establish the notational conventions through which these models constitute their meaning and differentiate code from content. Encoded instances (a specific TEI-encoded document) assumes the existence of the TEI model, which establishes the conditions of meaning for specific tags and attributes. For each layer, the rules of the layer beneath constitute its laws of gravity and determine the horizons of agency for those operating within that layer. We might nuance this further by considering different ways of experiencing this agency. For each layer, there are those who design its affordances; we might term these its "programmers." For instance, within the metamodel layer, the "programmers" are those who create new metamodels: the developers of the XML specification or the relational model. There are also those who use the layer's affordances to create constraints; these we might call "designers" and within the metamodel layer, these would be the creators of specific models such as TEI or the MARC standard. And finally, for each layer there are those who operate within the constraints established by the designers, whom we might term "users". To some extent, within any layer, the constraints in play will tend to become naturalized and invisible except in cases where they are violated, but this is especially true in cases where the agents in question are unaware of the layers beneath their own. Agents at any level (and in any role) are likely to be more effective the more they understand the constraints that operate in the surrounding layers. In a digital humanities context, this awareness constitutes an important form of scholarly self-reflexivity with respect to the modeling systems we inhabit. We might take this a step further and suggest that a politics or aesthetics of the digital might gain purchase from such an awareness, experienced as frictionality, along the lines of William Morris's idea that art requires "resistance in the materials." Code poetry, critical code studies, and experiments with new or alternative data models (at any level of the stack), all provide potentially illuminating perspectives for further exploration of this idea.

2.3 Constraint through function

The formal mechanisms and standards described above constitute the most intellectually salient forms of constraint on our data models: they are the parts of the modeling universe that receive the most academic scrutiny and also the most concerted attention from the perspective of strategic planning and discipline formation. But constraint also operates through mechanisms that, while they receive much less attention, exercise very significant influence over our data and its modeling: through the working systems in which the data will be used.

To give a concrete example: imagine that we have an XML publishing system for an online journal that includes a set of stylesheets designed to format certain data elements in specific ways. These might take the document metadata and present it as a kind of "title page," generate a table of contents from the section headings, and format the content of each section in a legible manner so that headings, list items, and block quotes are distinct from ordinary paragraphs. The authors' contributions are submitted in a variety of word-processing formats, and the journal's team of encoders convert them into XML using a public conversion tool (such as OxGarage). This XML includes some elements that will be used by the publication system (for searching or to produce formatting), as well as others that result from the conversion process but are not directly required for publication. One way to constrain this resulting XML data and test whether it will work in the publication system is to develop a schema that represents the ideal state of the data expected by the system. Such a schema might require the data elements needed for the essential parts of the publication (the metadata elements for the title page, the division headings needed for the table of contents), and might also stipulate what other elements (paragraphs, block quotations, lists) are permitted within the data, based on the features the stylesheets are designed to accommodate. If designed with a very high degree of precision, such a schema would constitute a formal expression of the functional constraints operating within the publication. But another form of constraint is the publication system itself. The stylesheets' behavior is a constraint, in the sense that it provides visible evidence about the suitability of the data: if an unforeseen data element is included and the resulting output includes a glaring anomaly, that anomaly is itself a report (as much as a schema error message) on whether the data is obeying the expectations of the system.

As a practical matter (but also an interesting philosophical point), the question thus arises of where our constraints are most effectively and elegantly exercised. What are the things a schema is best positioned to test, and what can we best enforce by the functional constraints of the system itself: for instance, through diagnostics within the publication system, or through a preview function that enables the editors to check each article for anomalies? The more complex the publication system, the more difficult it will be to design and maintain a schema that accurately represents its requirements. But if the process of ingesting data into the publication system is lengthy and costly—for instance, if the publication process entails a large-scale batch upload that will take hours to complete—then being able to catch and fix errors in advance could be an enormous benefit. This benefit is compounded if the publication system is being operated by someone else, perhaps a vendor who will have to send the data back to us for fixing if the ingestion process fails, and who will charge us for the time spent. Perhaps more interestingly from a design perspective, we might be creating data for multiple publication systems with different requirements, with a whole suite of schemas to help ensure that in aligning our data with the needs of one system we are not inadvertently breaking it for another.

In this scenario, the schema is operating as an expression of, or proxy for, a functional system: the constraints it expresses are not those of discipline or research agenda, but rather those of operational efficiency. Such constraints are not as central to digital humanities research as those arising from the disciplinary community to express scholarly data models (e.g. TEI, CIDOC, EAD, etc.), but they are nonetheless significant for digital humanists because they represent important end states for our data. We may create and archive our research data in TEI, but we disseminate it as HTML, PDF, OAI, CoinS, ePub, and through tools like OJS, Omeka, WordPress, Dspace, BookWorm, the Versioning Machine, Juxta, Islandora. These systems do constrain our data—they constitute the final horizons of its usage—even though those constraints are not part of our formal intellectual economy.

3 Social dimensions of constraint

The final aspect of constraint we will examine here is the constraint that operates socially: our expectations about data and our unspoken conventions about its purpose, and the conceptual context of human knowledge within which our data operates. Even the unspecified membership of the pronoun "our" here must be acknowledged as part of this social constraint: the "we" for whom expectations and conventions can be described constitutes an all-important boundary on intelligibility, motivation, and usefulness.

One aspect of constraint at this level concerns the establishment of consensus—at varying degrees of coherence—about the relation between the formally defined components of our data and the human meaning we attach to them. For instance, the TEI Guidelines define a vast set of data elements representing features of textual structure and content that are assumed to be familiar to scholars and cultural heritage practitioners in the developed world. But the TEI assumes a much vaster shared knowledge about documents, and a shared set of expectations about what they are for and why they are important, that would be very difficult to express to anyone who did not share it. And even a gigantically detailed specification like TEI does not pin down all of the concepts that operate within it, although it does at a first approximation. For instance, the TEI <bibl> element is defined as "a bibliographic citation" but that term is not in turn defined; the documentation assumes that we already know (or can find out) what that is. A less familiar concept like "metamark" is defined in more thorough and basic terms ("contains or describes any kind of graphic or written signal within a document the function of which is to determine how it should be read rather than forming part of the actual content of the document."), but even these assume that we agree on concepts like "content" and "graphic or written signal." To some extent these are now being formalized through mechanisms like ontologies, which make it possible (to some degree) to create systems of definitions that can anchor such concepts and permit them to be reasoned with computationally. For instance, FaBiO, the FRBR-aligned Bibliographic Ontology, documents a formal set of entities and relationships for describing and reasoning with bibliographic items. But even these ontologies serve ultimately as a formal expression of a human consensus; if that consensus changes, our digital formalisms would need to change with it.

Another aspect of social constraint is the standards of good scholarly practice that emerge from specific disciplines, editorial traditions, and community history. These affect digital modeling systems inasmuch as they dictate things like transcription practices, expectations about the regularization of data, notational conventions such as those involved in critical apparatus, and the inclusion or omission of certain kinds of metadata. Because such standards are often very widely understood within a given disciplinary community, they may go unstated; practitioners learn them as part of their early professional development. Digital humanities work practices have tended to make these conventions more visible: the very fact of working in collaboration with others outside the community of expertise (library staff, graduate students, information designers) requires that unstated assumptions be expressed and documented. In addition, the data representation systems used in digital humanities—markup language, metadata vocabularies, and so forth—bring data handling practices into much greater visibility and thus prompt reconsideration and transparency. The editorial declaration in the TEI header asks the editor to describe specific choices—for instance, in the handling of hyphenation or spelling regularization; information about data handling processes that may affect scholarly interpretation can also be captured in metadata standards like PREMIS or METS. Coming from the other direction, documentation of good practice has been presented for specific disciplinary communities in works like Peter Shillingsburg's *Scholarly Editing in the Computer Age: Theory and Practice* (1996) and Mary Jo Kline's *A Guide to Documentary Editing* (2008). More recently, professional organizations like the Modern Language Association are now also establishing guidelines for best practices for scholarly editors that include recommendations for digital editions.

4 Conclusions

Because our direct experience of models is so often through our encounter with a set of constraints—a schema, a form, a tool—it is easy for digital humanists to imagine models as nothing more than constraints, and to imagine constraints as a full expression of a model. In fact, the constraints that operate on our data are a kind of reductionistic proxy for a whole model: they are like the walls that we collide with in a darkened room, or like marker buoys in a harbor telling us of the existence of reefs and deep water. A model is implemented through constraints, but (necessarily) in a very limited way, since constraints must be imposed through specific technical mechanisms that are often not a good approximation of the actual concepts we want to model. The much studied problem of XML tree structures as a way of modeling documentary data is a case in point. Furthermore, if constraints are often a poor approximation of our models, they are an even remoter approximation of the concepts those models seek to represent. In intellectual processes like document analysis or ontology development, we develop concepts and definitions that we can use to think about the aspects of the world we care about—poetry, or linguistics, or archival documents. But our modeling of those concepts in formal systems is, at the moment at least, aimed at pragmatic outcomes, rather than at reflecting a full, rich understanding of concepts in the world. The TEI's modeling of poetry is a case in point: it describes the essential structural building blocks of poetry (the line, the line group, the concepts of rhyme and meter) in a way that can permit them to be analyzed and published, but it in no way approaches a full account of the concepts that are comprised in the term "poetry." At best, the TEI might be said to offer a reduced model of some properties observable in some poetry. Within its terms (limited though they may be), it makes some kinds of analysis computationally tractable and automatable. In order to do a different kind of analysis, a different model is required.

We thus need to understand constraint as having an indirect but significant relationship with the concepts of humanities scholarship that deserves our close attention. Constraint systems are evolving slowly, primarily under impetus from practical concerns such as processability, but with consequences for the intellectual aspects of our modeling. The shift from SGML to XML was largely motivated by the new technical requirements and affordances of the web, but in producing a generalizable form of addressability (the URI) it also enabled scholars to use the concept of the network more fully in modeling documentary information. Research into non-tree-based forms of markup has spawned many proposed technical solutions,[3] but also a sustained line of research on how hierarchical structures do or do not frame our understanding of text. From the perspective of the evolution of digital humanities as a field, the crucial question is how strongly our constraint systems affect the way we think about and represent core humanistic concepts. For example, does our understanding of the concept of literary style change when we filter it through the constraints of stylometric tools, and, if so, what do we learn from that change?

Constraint is a condition of the interpretability of data; without constraint to establish the parameters of significance, there can be no communication at all. And yet we also chafe at constraint and constantly test its limits. The arbitrariness of the edges it imposes runs counter to our experience of human ideas and language, but constraint mechanisms like schemas are in fact attempting (in a vastly simpler way) the same feat that we attempt with language: to complete a circuit of meaning, to make meaning social. The definition of constraint systems is thus also a social process and one that is deeply implicated in systems of power.

Notes

1   There is a specific understanding of the term "class" in modern set theory distinguishing between "set" and "class." However, it is of no importance in the context of our discussion, for which naive set theory is fully adequate.
2   The definition of concepts has been a major focus of philosophical and in recent times also of psychological research (Margolis and Laurence, 2014).
3   See, for example, the contributions to the concept "Concurrent markup/Overlap" in the annual Balisage conference proceedings. Available at: www.balisage.net/Proceed ings/topics/Concurrent_Markup~Overlap.html.

References

Alexander, C., 1979. *The Timeless Way of Building*. New York: Oxford University Press.
Bateson, G., 1972. *Steps to an Ecology of Mind: Collected Essays in Anthropology, Psychiatry, Evolution, and Epistemology*. Reprint 2000. Chicago: University of Chicago Press (specifically "Form, Substance and Difference," pp. 454–71).
Hutchins, E., 1995. *Cognition in the Wild*. Cambridge, MA: MIT Press.
Juarrero, A., 1999. *Dynamics in Action: Intentional Behavior as a Complex System*. Cambridge, MA: MIT Press.
Kline, M.J. and Perdue. S.H., 2008. *A Guide to Documentary Editing*. 3rd edition. Charlottesville: Univ. of Virginia Press. http://gde.upress.virginia.edu/.
Margolis, E. and Laurence, S., 2014. Concepts. In: E.N. Zahlta (Ed.) 2014. *The Stanford Encyclopedia of Philosophy*. Stanford, CA: Stanford University. Available at: http://plato. stanford.edu/archives/spr2014/entries/concepts/.
Maturana, H.R. and Varela, F.J., 1998. *The Tree of Knowledge: The Biological Roots of Human Understanding*. Boston, MA: Shambhala.
McLuhan, M., 1964. *Understanding Media*. Cambridge, MA: MIT Press.
Shillingsburg, P., 1996. *Scholarly Editing in the Computing Age*. 3rd edition. Ann Arbor: Univ. of Michigan Press.
Simon, H.A., 1996. *The Sciences of the Artificial*. Cambridge, MA: MIT Press.
Wiener, N., 1961. *Cybernetics: or Control and Communication in the Animal and the Machine* (2nd ed.). Cambridge, MA: MIT Press (especially Chapter VIII, "Information, Language and Society").

11 Modeling and annotating complex data structures

Piotr Bański and Andreas Witt

1 Introduction

Although it is possible to associate an unlimited number of arbitrary, complex layers of annotations with a text, an image, or an audio/video file, the most common applications almost always follow the classical approach: additional information associated with primary data is expressed in an ordered hierarchy, using a tree structure as its underlying data model.

The present contribution offers a brief review of the more popular ways of data structuring and highlights some of the problems that each of them is meant to handle. The first part of the present chapter focuses on the most relevant issues of data modeling for researchers in the humanities and reviews the basic kinds of the relevant data models. The second part addresses ways to capture these abstract models in concrete encoding formats available to digital humanists. We focus here on approaches that use XML, but the models can also be applied more generally.

Information and communication are tightly related: communication relies on the exchange of information, but just as the individual information containers are determined by many kinds of variables, organizing these containers into higher level structures is vital for ensuring success in transmitting complete and compact messages. Finding the appropriate level of complexity for the structuring of information is one of the key problems in the field of digital humanities. Simple information packages are quick to set up, process and visualize, but as the individual fields of study develop, more and more information needs to be accommodated within a vertically tight space of electronic documents.[1] Packaging of complex information raises new theoretical questions and demands new, more efficient, technological solutions.

For the purpose of an introductory example, let us assume that the "information containers" are words, subject to the choice of the natural language but also, on the technological plane, to, for example, the selection of the character encoding, such as ISO 8859-1 (known as "Latin-1") or Unicode. These words are grouped into larger units: phrases, sentences, or utterances. The structure of these larger units, on the one hand, is dictated by the internal syntactic rules of the given language but, on the other, it is also modeled technologically by the selection of the given XML document grammar (schema). Words may also have semantic or presentational properties of interest: they can be highlighted in various ways (italicized, struck out, capitalized, etc.), or they can be linguistically distinctive—for example, Latin intrusions in an English text—and we may even want to encode the information on where they can be split if they would otherwise exceed the page margins. Longer sequences of words can be formatted as section headers or may be split into enumerated lists, grouped into paragraphs, sections, and so on.

Digital humanists are information architects nearly by definition. Apart from the language- or text-internal features mentioned above, they might decide to accommodate more information within their markup. In the example at hand, this may mean further grammatical or prosodic features of individual words or word groups, or it may be information that fleshes out the relationships between words or their roles in the discourse or in verse. Finally, the encoder may wish not to privilege a single theoretical model but to record instead the potentially *conflicting* information provided by very different theoretical approaches—after all, examination of the discrepancies among the predictions made by different theories may also be of value, both in research and in teaching.

Nowadays, the reasons for adding information can be manifold: scholarly, didactic, practical, with the eventual results typically performing more than one function. However, this has not always been the case. In the very early days of markup standards in the 1970s and 1980s, there was mainly only one reason for enriching text with additional information: to provide technical means to enhance the typesetting process. These origins have strongly influenced the structure of all formalisms used to add information to primary texts and have led to an essentially linear and sequential approach to information structuring. This linear focus arose even though it was noted early that books contained many techniques (such as cross-references) for escaping the linear structure of a text, and even though scholars had long been aware that a focus on a linear structure is neither intellectually nor technologically adequate. The literature on the so-called "OHCO thesis," which initially stated that text is an "Ordered Hierarchy of Content Objects," illustrates the gradually developing acceptance of the fact that tree-based structures can only offer handy approximations for modeling *selected views* of the text.[2]

The additional data items containing analytical information about text are typically referred to as *annotations*. In the context of the technology assumed here and centering on XML and its ilk, annotations are typically realized as *markup*—that is, special markers (tags) directly or indirectly added to the text stream.

In the remainder of the present chapter, we provide an overview of modeling approaches to annotation (section 2) and then, in section 3, we review selected ways of implementing the abstract conceptual structures, focusing mostly on techniques that make use of XML, which is still the most popular markup formalism used in digital humanities. Our examples come mostly from the linguistic domain, but they straightforwardly translate into other domains and applications.

2 Modeling complex information

Various definitions of complex documents can be offered depending on the individual bias and the research angle. Our classification of complexity is based on a range of initiatives focusing mostly on linguistic aspects of document modeling and interpretation, but not confined to these aspects alone. This is because there exists no clear division between linguistic markup and "digital humanities markup," not only because linguistic considerations at large are part of the digital humanities landscape, but also because of wide areas of overlap among the various subdisciplines of digital humanities and broadly understood linguistics, involving, for example, discourse structure or meter.

We distinguish among three major types of complexity that commonly occur in annotated data. We shall refer to these arrangements of data as "linear," "complex," and "concurrent." An additional factor that complicates the picture is the nature of what precisely gets annotated—annotations can be constructed over a single data stream or over multiple parallel streams of data—we shall refer to such construals as "single-stream" and "multi-stream," respectively. Below, we provide a brief overview of the above-mentioned data arrangements. Sections 2.1 through 2.3 assume a single-stream arrangement, while section 2.4 adds one more dimension, introducing "horizontal" alignments between data streams and/or annotations built over them.

2.1 Linear arrangement

Linear arrangement is the simplest case out of those that are of interest to us here. It concerns a single layer of objects that exhaustively or partially cover the data stream.

Such an arrangement of objects is practically unproblematic for any approach. However, the complexity that we wish to recognize in this case occurs when more than one information package is attached to a single textual object. While various formal classifications can be provided for such an arrangement, for the purpose of our discussion, we shall continue to use the term "linear" when referencing this kind of complexity.

Figure 11.2 shows the same text annotated with two kinds of information, added, for example, by two different annotation tools.[3] That this is not exotic at

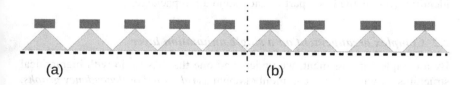

(a)　　　　　　　　　　(b)

Figure 11.1 Exhaustive (a) and non-exhaustive (b) coverage of a data stream by a linear arrangement of annotation objects. The dashed line symbolizes a sequence of characters.

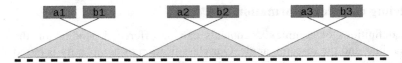

Figure 11.2 Multiple information packages attached to single elements of the document: series "a" is provided by one tool (or one human annotator), and series "b" by another.

Layer	—	Foundry	Die	Irakische	Kommunistische	Partei	IKP	wurde	im	März	1934	gegründet	und
d		xip											VMAIN	
i		cnx		Irakisch	Kommunistisch	partei	IKP	werden		märz	1934	gegründet	und
		mate		Irakisch	kommunistisch	partei	ikp	werden	in	märz	1934	gründen	und
		tt		Irakische Irakisch	Kommunistische kommunistisch	Partei	ikp	werden	im	März	1934	gründen	und
		xip		Irakisch	kommunistisch	Partei	IKP	werden	in	März	1934	gründen	und
m		cnx			Prop			IND PAST					
		mate		case:nom degree:pos gender:fem number:sg	case:nom degree:pos gender:fem number:sg	case:nom gender:fem number:sg	case:nom gender:fem number:sg	mood:ind number:sg person:3 tense:past	case:dat gender:masc number:sg	case:dat gender:masc number:sg			
ne_dewac_175m_600		corenlp		I-ORG	I-ORG	I-ORG	I-ORG						
ne_hgc_175m_600		corenlp		I-ORG	I-ORG	I-ORG	I-ORG						
p		cnx		A	N	N	N	V		NN	NUM	A	CC
		mate		ADJA	ADJA	NN	NE	VAFIN	APPRART	NN	CARD	VVPP	KON
		opennlp		ADJA	ADJA	NN	NE	VAFIN	APPRART	NN	CARD	VVPP	KON
		tt		ADJA NN	ADJA NN	NN	NE NN	VAFIN	APPRART	NN	CARD	VVPP	KON
		xip		ADJ	ADJ	NOUN	NOUN	VERB	PREP	NOUN	NUM	VERB	CONJ
syn		cnx		@PREMOD	@PREMOD	@NH	@NH	@MAIN		@NH	@PREMOD	@NH	@CC

Irakische Kommunistische Partei by Jergen; 4; published on 2005-03-28 as [IT,02914 (WPD)]

Figure 11.3 A fragment of KorAP annotations, visualized in the form of a table. Among other pieces of information, the table shows various part-of-speech tags (visible in row "p") supplied by different tools. "cnx," "mate," "opennlp," "tt," and "xip" are names of the particular foundries (that is, sets of annotation layers, cf. section 3 below).

all can be demonstrated with an example from the KorAP system (Bański et al., 2013), which organizes annotations into so-called foundries, to which we return in section 3.

At the level of conceptual modeling, we do not establish *how* the information packages are added to the text. They may end up enclosing each relevant text fragment or they may merely point at it. In the latter case, the identity of each span in a simple linear arrangement can be established by comparing the character offsets of the beginning and/or end of the span. However, it is often useful to provide a level of indirection between annotations and text, by including a unique identifier (ID) as the basic part of each annotation package.

2.2 Complex arrangement on a single annotation layer

By a complex arrangement, we understand one that has to do with hierarchical structures, or with what is commonly known as *relational* or *dependency graphs*. Consequently, in order to provide a gross taxonomy for the purpose of discussion in the present chapter, we divide complex arrangements into hierarchical (see section 2.2.1), relation-based (s. 2.2.2), and mixed (s. 2.2.3).

2.2.1 Hierarchical structures

Hierarchical structures arrange abstract nodes into trees (technically, a restricted type of directed acyclic graphs) by means of relations of dominance and precedence. In the figure below, the node labeled "S" is the root—it dominates all other nodes; the node labeled "NP" precedes the node labeled "VP" (as well as, indirectly, the terminal nodes V and N that the VP dominates). In trees, each node other than the root node must be dominated by at most a single node (in other words, while a node can have multiple children nodes, it can only have one mother node).

In Figure 11.4, the information package in each case has to minimally contain the grammatical label ("NP" for noun phrase, etc.), and the ordered reference(s) to the items that it dominates. Note that in an ID-based system, the references target IDs, and therefore an ID must be included in the information package. An alternative is to use the offsets of the beginning and the end of the fragment of base text to which the given annotation refers. In such a case, an additional mechanism is needed to properly arrange the last NP and N, because they address the same spans.

We use a syntactic tree diagram in order to illustrate this kind of arrangement, but in fact arrangements of this type are ubiquitous: HTML, TEI, and more generally, all SGML- and XML-based formats are based on this kind of tree-based hierarchy, even if in actual practice the hierarchy is enriched with additional non-hierarchical devices, to which we now turn.

2.2.2 Relational arrangements

Relational arrangements of the simplest kind typically focus on relationships among the objects identified in linear arrangements (cf. section 2.1). As an example of simple structures of that sort, we use so-called grammatical dependency relationships. Information packages in such cases typically contain the name of the relation (e.g., "subject of," etc.) and an ordered sequence of pointers at the elements of that relation.

In Figure 11.5, the middle element (most commonly a verb) points to its grammatical subject on the left, and the grammatical object on the right.

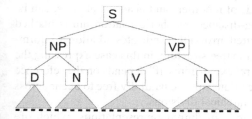

Figure 11.4 An example of a hierarchical annotation (syntactic tree).

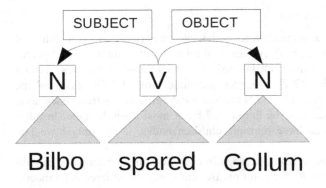

Figure 11.5 Dependency relationships among elements of the sentence (as an example, assume a three-word sentence such as "Bilbo spared Gollum").

The information encoded here identifies the source and the goal of the grammatical relation, together with its name.

Note that at the conceptual modeling stage, we do not determine how exactly the relevant information is encoded. In more concrete terms, it may be placed either together with the individual text fragments, or it may point at them remotely—this depends both on the choice of the concrete realization (e.g., XML or a set of RDF triples), and on the type of approach (in XML, it can be represented as local inline markup, or as remote standoff markup).

2.2.3 Mixed complex arrangements

It is not uncommon in syntactic trees to find long-distance relations linking terminal nodes with more or less remote non-terminal nodes. In order to build on the examples used above, we present a case where dependency information is mapped onto hierarchical structure. This example features also a more complex case: an anaphoric relationship among parts of the tree structure: a word-sized element (the reflexive pronoun "himself") referencing a constituent (the noun phrase "the boy") *across* the tree structure.[4]

In Figure 11.6, first, the two grammatical relationships from Figure 11.5 have been mapped onto the corresponding branches of the tree (other kinds of information, identifying various kinds of modifiers and heads of phrases, can be added by analogy). Second, the long-distance anaphoric relationship is marked by a so-called "secondary edge" (dotted arrow) that indicates additional inform-ation that relates constituents across the tree structure, in this case expressing the information that the reference of the reflexive "himself" depends on the reference of the noun phrase "the boy"; such relationships are naturally free to occur across sentence boundaries or any other hierarchical divisions.

The mixed arrangement is notorious in digital representations, which are typically based on hierarchical data models of HTML or XML, and use *links*

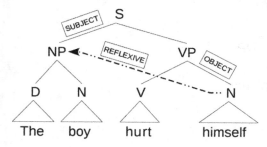

Figure 11.6 An example of a hierarchical relationship mixed with relational information of two kinds.

(or more generally, *references*), in order to cope with the constraints imposed by the tree structure. Naturally, such references are not restricted to pointing at fragments of the current document and can also point outside of it (in which cases we talk about *external links*).

2.3 Concurrent arrangement (multiple annotation layers)

Concurrent arrangement is found where two or more annotation layers are built on a single stream of data. The layers may then differ in how they order the data described (i.e., in the structures assigned to the data) or the structures may be identical but differ in the content. The former case is exemplified in Figure 11.7, where two different tokenization (segmentation) structures are assigned to the same sequence of characters.

In Figure 11.7, lexicalized expressions such as "mother-in-law" may well be tokenized as a single element. However, many linguistic tools will treat them as sequences of three (or even five) tokens that may be relinked at another stage of annotation. Multi-word idioms, numbers or names fall under this pattern as well.

The latter case is exemplified in Figure 11.8, which shows identical tree structures with different labels attached to them, corresponding to two possible and equally likely analyses.

While for ease of illustration, the example in Figure 11.8 invokes a linguistic structure of an obvious structural ambiguity ("They are making planes fly" vs. "These are planes that fly"), the principle goes beyond ambiguities: we may be

Figure 11.7 Concurrent tokenizations of a single compound noun.

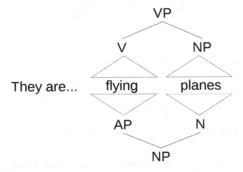

Figure 11.8 Examples of concurrent analyses of a single tokenized stream.

looking at competing syntactic analyses or even competing structural divisions of a single text.

Similarly, we can build hierarchical and dependency annotations on the same base text, thus effectively putting together structures such as those shown in Figures 11.5 and 11.6.

2.4 Multi-stream arrangement

In the data configurations reviewed above, we have been assuming that documents contain a single base data stream (for convenience, taken to be a stream of characters in a text). Multi-stream arrangements are found where the document contains more than a single base data stream. This is attested in parallel corpora (with two or more translations arranged in parallel and aligned on the sentence and word levels), transcribed speech corpora (with the transcription in a phonetic alphabet running along the orthographic transcription), but also textual variation in cultural heritage texts, where it is very often the unaligned gaps that scholars find interesting.

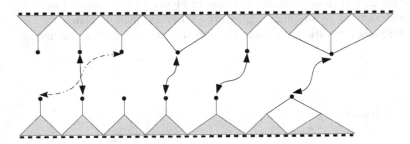

Figure 11.9 Multi-stream arrangement: this is nearly the simplest example imaginable, though with a level of indirection that is usually needed in such cases.

In Figure 11.9, we present nearly the simplest case, enhanced with a level of indirection: we may assume the dashed line to indicate characters that are grouped into tokens, which in turn are grouped into larger entities ("word forms" or phrases, cf. ISO MAF, ISO 24611:2012), and those entities are aligned with the corresponding groups built upon the other data stream. It can be seen that such a simple model already allows for expressing one-to-many and many-to-many alignments, and to identify mismatches. The above model may be used for a parallel corpus of two languages/dialects, but also for multiple versions/editions of a manuscript, in which case we can identify relationships of transposition (marked above with a dashed arrow), deletion, and insertion.

Naturally, this model can become even more complex if we decide not only to align segments (words/phrases), but also to include their annotations of various degrees of complexity. A simple example is provided below, where one stream consists of tokens annotated with glosses (literal translations), and grouped into a syntactic structure, while the other stream consists of phonetic segments (note that mismatches at this point are possible).

Finally, it is also possible to have more than two parallel data streams aligned in such a fashion—for multilingual corpora, but also for video, audio, and subtitles (in the last example, we would naturally not use characters to measure the granularity of the data stream, but rather time stamps of more or less arbitrary sampling intervals).

Note that this is a borderline category: on many approaches, multi-stream arrangement is not considered to be a representation for single documents, but rather for structures involving multiple documents (such an interpretation comes naturally when looking at parallel corpora or manuscript variation encoding).

3 Representing complex information

There are theoretically no limits to how much annotation information could be added to the text. However, from the practical point of view, things look different. The main causes of *practical* difficulties concerning the addition of multiple annotations to a single text are the various ways in which the data is "packaged" or meant to be "unpackaged."

Token	de	la	crème	glacèe
Gloss	some	the	cream	iced
Phonemics	dla		krEm	glase
Syntax	P		NP	

Figure 11.10 Multi-stream annotation structure: the original token stream (in French) is accompanied by a parallel stream of glosses (in English), and a stream of phonetic transcription. Copied from Wörner et al., 2006.

The digital switch in the humanities was much more than merely a transfer from a paper-based, largely linear medium to an electronic and potentially multidirectional one. Apart from speeding up and making more precise the calculations and operations that could otherwise take a very long time (with regard to calculating word/phrase frequencies and degrees of co-occurrence, or to querying individual words), and apart from opening the same text to potentially multiple different visualizations, the electronic medium has gradually made it possible to equip individual words with extra "vertical" space (in the sense discussed earlier), in which additional data could be placed, and then to use those extra data both as simple enrichment of the content, but also as the basis for various correspondence mechanisms.

These mechanisms (generally referred to as *linking*, as will be seen below) have made it possible to flesh out the dependencies that, in the general printed medium, were mostly (practically only with the exception of footnotes or bibliographical references) realized only by associations made and maintained in the mind of the reader. In contrast to such implicit and often subjective mechanisms, in the electronic medium, it is possible to explicitly link speeches by the same character in a drama, passages of uniform narration in works where narration or the narrator change, or to make use of anaphoric mechanisms or finally to encode grammatical dependencies among words in a single sentence.

On the packaging side, the problem lies in how to express the fact that a single information container (i.e., our example word) may be annotated with more than one information package, or in how relationships among such containers (e.g., the subject and the main verb in a sentence; two or more rhyming verses or the alliterating word fragments in a poem) can be encoded, or finally in how these individual elements can be grouped together (into paragraphs, sentences or stanzas).

In this section, we offer a bird's-eye view of the landscape of approaches both to encoding and to the general architecture of text resources that have been used in the e-humanities in order to enrich the primary text with annotations of various degrees of complexity. It has to be borne in mind that these technologies are often conditioned by extremely non-theoretical factors, such as funding schemes, their primary processing/visualization purpose (which may change over years), or even the habits and fashions of the local IT departments. Because of that, what follows cannot be taken as a definitive review or recommendation—the decision to adopt one kind of technology over another is influenced by too many variables.[5] Finally, we briefly present the advantages of a solution that we have adopted in the KorAP project, as an example of how some complex annotations are built and used in our everyday research.

For ease of description, and making use of the terminology introduced by Goecke et al. (2010), we divide text-annotation representations into *single-layer*, whereby the data is enriched along a single dimension (modulo cross-element references), and *multi-layered*, where it is a priori assumed that a single view of the data is either not achievable or not advisable.

3.1 Single-layer representations

Single-layer representations allow for simple linear and hierarchical arrangements that may be enhanced with cross-references that enrich the representations by providing means of relating elements that are not adjacent or that are not parts of the same hierarchy. Examples of such approaches may be simple TEI XML as exemplified below, or HTML.

HTML has a very impoverished representation model, so we mention it only for the sake of its popularity as a means to visualize the results, in the form that would in most cases not be suitable for further processing, because in most cases the transformation from the underlying data format into HTML is monodirectional—that is, since HTML is not able to express complex annotations, information is lost during the conversion from a more expressive format into HTML. Another outstanding problem that HTML faces is that, without some cumbersome workarounds, it cannot handle linear arrangements that have more than a single piece of additional information of the same kind attached to a single document element (see Figure 11.2 above).

Both HTML and simple TEI XML are mono-hierarchical: added information of any kind intervenes within the original text stream, which goes counter the principle of keeping the base text pristine for the sake of its sustainability and for the purpose of offering multiple and potentially conflicting views of the underlying data.

The example that follows shows two ways to accomplish the simple task of annotating line divisions and basic speaker information in the text of Euripides's *Medea*, taken from the Oxford University Text Archive (OTA, cf. http://ota.ox.ac. uk/desc/2414). What changes from one example to the next is what we refer to as the packaging of information.

```
<      THE MEDEA OF EURIPIDES      >

<P MHD.>

<S TR>

<V 0001>

EIQ' WFEL' $ARGOUV MH DIAPTASQAI SKAFOV

<V 0002>

$KOLCWN EV AIAN KUANEAV $SUMPLHGADAV,

<V 0003>

MHD' EN NAPAISI $PHLIOU PESEIN POTE
```

Figure 11.11 Euripides's *Medea*: fragment of an Ancient Greek text transliterated to English in an unknown system.[6] COCOA format, part of the OTA.[7]

```
<text>

  <body>

    <head type="author">MHD.</head>

      <speaker>TR</speaker>

        <ab>EIQ' WFEL' $ARGOUV MH DIAPTASQAI SKAFOV</ab>

        <ab>$KOLCWN EV AIAN KUANEAV $SUMPLHGADAV,</ab>

        <ab>MHD' EN NAPAISI $PHLIOU PESEIN POTE</ab>
```

Figure 11.12 The same fragment of *Medea* converted to TEI P5.

Figure 11.11 presents the text encoded in a legacy COCOA format (Russell, 1965), and Figure 11.12 shows the same fragment encoded in TEI P5 XML.

The dramatic difference between the two markup techniques is in how precise XML can be with respect to delimiting the content of the particular element or defining the hierarchical structure visible already in such a short fragment, and in how much space is provided for the various XML attributes for annotations inside element tags.

```
<sp>

    <speaker>Prospero</speaker>

    <l part="Y">I'll deliver all,</l>

    <l>And promise you calm seas, auspicious gales,</l>

    <l>Be free and fare thou well. <stage type="exit">Exit

      Ariel</stage> Please you, draw near. <stage

          type="exit">Exeunt all but Prospero</stage>

        <note place="margin">Epilogue</note>

    </l>

    <l>Now my charms are all o'erthrown,</l>

    ...

</sp>

<stage type="mix">He awaits applause, then exit.</stage>
```

Figure 11.13 Prospero's speech from Shakespeare's *The Tempest*.[8]

While a simple XML format exemplified above can help tackle the basic annotation tasks, the encoder will run into problems when facing the need to encode conflicting annotations, both at the basic level (e.g., tagging the pronoun *they* as "PPHS2" in the CLAWS7 tagset or as "PNP" in the BNC tagset[9]) and at the more complex level (e.g., the division into verses as well as the division into sentences, or where one grammatical theory constructs phrases in a different manner from another). An example of more complex markup, where a line of a play had to be split in order to make the result obey certain formal conditions, is presented below.

Apart from the aim of enriching basic data with more and more information, anyone dealing with digital data formats nowadays is aware of the principle of data sustainability (see Schmidt et al., 2006; Rehm et al., 2009). Despite the decreasing prices of storage and the increasing processing power of CPUs, there is a sure way to dramatically increase the cost of data production and curation: by locking the data within an unsustainable format and risking that in five or ten years, it will be extremely difficult and costly not only to retrieve and process the annotations added to the data, but even to retrieve the data itself, as we hinted in the discussion of Figure 11.11 and Figure 11.12. As has been argued by many by now, data should best be stored in open, well-documented and well-supported formats, and preferably kept separate from annotations. The latter guideline points at technical solutions commonly labeled as *standoff*—featuring markup of whatever sort that is not interspersed among the fragments of base data, but rather points at the data remotely. As we shall see below, this kind of approach makes it much more feasible to store multiple annotations for a single data fragment.

3.2 Multi-layered representations

The term "multi-layered representations" refers to data arrangements which it would be impossible, or highly impractical, to model on a single layer. Theoretically, such a task opens a hierarchy of choices, the first of which is whether to abandon the XML medium altogether and experiment with other data models and syntaxes, or whether to keep to the well-established technology and stretch it wide enough to allow for multiple representations to coexist, while at the same time being able to efficiently manipulate, curate, and query the data. The former path is represented by, among others, LMNL (Layered Markup and Annotation Language; e.g., Tennison and Piez, 2002; Piez, 2013), while the latter either relies on branching a single XML tree into subparts that encode the separate (and potentially conflicting) representations, linking them by internal XML devices, or on spreading the multiple layers across multiple documents, which can then be associated by various means.[10]

Much of this has been studied under the heading of "markup overlap" and resulted in research reported among others in the *Extreme Markup Languages* and later, the *Balisage* conference series (cf. Hilbert et al., 2005, for an overview). Part of these approaches involve annotating a single text stream with multiple series of tags, resulting in potentially major issues concerning the curation of such resources. A partial solution to this was offered by an approach known as *multiply annotated text* (cf. Goecke et al., 2010), whereby text with multiple and potentially conflicting annotations was exploded into more than one physical document (with in-line markup) under the crucial condition that the underlying text stream provided the common baseline to the various annotation trees. This is shown in Figure 11.14, where the three annotation layers describe three identical copies of the very same text.

Figure 11.14 shows three instances of the same text annotated in-line (ideally), one layer per document. The character stream is the sole pivot that makes it possible to combine or compare the annotations. The three example character offset positions (0, 3, 6) are provided as a means of visualizing the mismatch among the annotation spans and the resulting impossibility of building a single tree structure over them.

A theoretically descendant approach (although it dates at least as far as Durand et al., 1995 and Thompson and McKelvie, 1997) is one known as *remote* or *standoff markup*, whereby the base text stream is either only lightly annotated in-line (mostly to introduce the basic XML skeleton) or not annotated in-line at all, with all the annotations in separate documents and addressing the base text "remotely," by a mixture of structural information and string offsets (see Bański, 2010, for more terminology and illustrations). See Figure 11.15.

Goecke et al.'s multiply annotated text was proposed (originally in Witt, 2005) as a way to overcome the technical difficulties in reassociating standoff annotations with the text, and entailed a shift of focus from maintaining and curating the annotation-text relationship to synchronizing the multiple copies of text, each with different kinds of markup.

When it is necessary to maintain a rich variety of concurrent annotation layers, and consequently to cope with multiple sources of annotation data and potentially numerous files in which they are stored, an approach based on "foundries" (or distinct sets of informational components) becomes a virtual necessity. This approach, introduced in the KorAP project (Bański et al., 2013), implements a

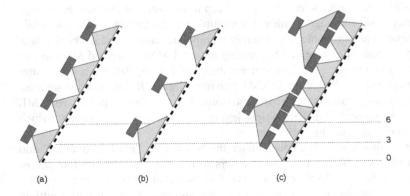

(a)   (b)   (c)

Figure 11.14 An example of multiply annotated text.

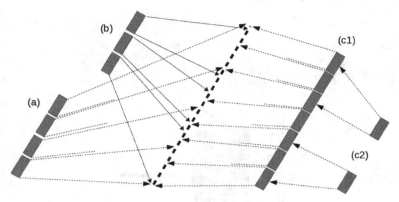

Figure 11.15 A sample of standoff annotation. Numerous annotation documents (a–c1 correspond to the annotations in the preceding figure) point at the same base text document, or at another document containing annotations (cf. c2). Some association lines have been shortened for the sake of clarity.

model in which each well-defined set of annotations forms a separate component of a corpus document, with its own metadata section describing the origin and the various properties of the individual annotation layers. This is diagrammed in Figure 11.16.

In Figure 11.16, each foundry contains a well-defined set of annotations that provide separate interpretations for the data described. Cross-foundry dependencies are possible—for example, foundries B and C may rely on segmentation

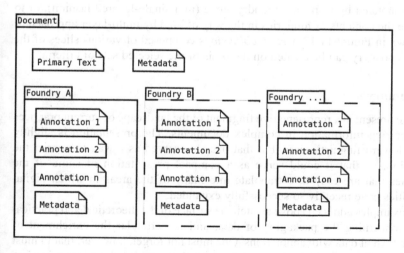

Figure 11.16 A document in the KorAP data model consists of the primary text (base data) that is kept separate from foundries.

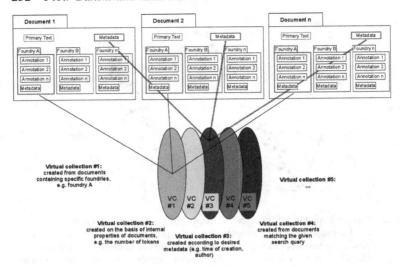

Figure 11.17 Illustration of the versatility of the KorAP document model. Virtual collections can be created on the basis of practically any subpart of the document, depending on the research needs.

information provided by foundry A, but offer their own annotation sets, based on different tagsets and according to different grammatical theories or modules.

Each document consists of the base text, document metadata (expressible, e.g., in the form of a TEI Header), and one or more foundries, which contain the annotation information. This kind of arrangement allows to view the text as if it was annotated by a specific foundry alone (in a single-layered fashion), or to compare the contents of foundries in the way offered by multi-layer approaches. As shown in Figure 11.17, *virtual collections* composed of various slices of the source repository can be created on the basis of the selected sets of criteria.

4 Summary

We have presented a representative fragment of the landscape of current practices of structuring information in complex documents. The presentation is slightly geared toward linguistic uses, but that has also served as a way to restrict the discussion, so that it could serve as a compact presentation of some of the principles that are easy to extrapolate into many of the areas in which digital humanities have recently so successfully expanded.

The examples adduced above scratch the surface of the theoretical and practical issues concerning the packaging of data, and in particular the enrichment of primary textual data with annotations. One must not forget, however, that in most cases, the packager has a further goal than merely arranging the information in a neat manner: that information should then be put to work. It should be interpretable and processable by computers—for example, it should be easy to query, and to visualize in various ways. Exploring these issues would take us beyond the scope of this chapter and into the land of standardization, data exchangeability and tool interoperability.

Notes

1 By "vertical space," we refer to the growth of information in paradigmatic terms (to be exemplified below); the "horizontal space" of linear growth can be more readily accommodated year by year, with the development of storage technologies always staying ahead of digitisation efforts.

2 A good deal of the debate took place within the lively platform of *Extreme Markup* and its descendant *Balisage* conferences. As an entry point, consider DeRose, 2004.

3 In the process of the creation of linguistic resources, tools are used to add various kinds of grammatical information automatically, often at the cost of accuracy. Because different tools introduce different errors or are based on different theoretical assumptions, it makes sense to process the same text with more than one tool.

4 Nodes in trees can only have a single mother (that is, can only be dominated by a single node). Therefore, the relationship between the antecedent noun phrase (*the boy*) and the reflexive (*herself*) cannot be encoded as part of tree structure because the reflexive is dominated by the VP node. Note that a tree structure is not a necessary condition for the presence of references of this kind; a similar effect could be created in the linear arrangement in Figure 11.1, by having, for example, the last token reference the first one, in this way circumventing the linear ordering.

5 It is worth mentioning at this point that initiatives aiming at standardization of many aspects of linguistic annotation have found their home within the ISO Technical Committee 37, Subcommittee 4, "Language resource management." While some of the solutions proposed there are very specific, many can be re-used by scholars in e-humanities in their projects, especially given that the ISO efforts have been increasingly tied to aspects of the TEI Guidelines. See Burnard (this volume) for further remarks on the role of standardization in the e-humanities.

6 The corresponding text in Ancient Greek is as follows:

Εἴθ᾽ ὤφελ᾽ Ἀργοῦς μὴ διαπτάσθαι σκάφος
Κόλχων ἐς αἶαν κυανέας Συμπληγάδας,
μηδ᾽ ἐν νάπαισι Πηλίου πεσεῖν ποτε

(cf. http://data.perseus.org/citations/urn:cts:greekLit:tlg0006.tlg003.perseus-grc1:1-48)
Note, among others, that the decision to use capital letters has forced *ad hoc* markup by means of the "$" character (as in $ARGOUV vs. Ἀργοῦς), and that most of the accentual information is missing.

7 We are grateful to Sebastian Rahtz for pointing us to this example, which also demonstrates that sustainability of digital texts is a very real issue. The conversion was facilitated by the cocoa-to-tei.xsl script by James Cummings and Sebastian Rahtz, available from https://github.com/TEIC/Stylesheets.

8 XML adapted from TEI Consortium (Eds.) "Prologues and Epilogues," Guidelines for Electronic Text Encoding and Interchange. Version 2.8.0. Available at: www.tei-c.org/release/doc/tei-p5-doc/en/html/DR.html#DRPRO.

9 Both tagsets can be found at http://ucrel.lancs.ac.uk/claws/. "Tagging" refers to the process of labeling words with, for example, part-of-speech tags, whereby the individual labels come from a closed inventory of symbols called a tagset. Various tagsets have been proposed, depending on which grammatical features of words needed to be distinguished.

234 Piotr Bański and Andreas Witt

10 The existence of supplementary specifications such as Xinclude blurs the distinction to some extent, by allowing parts of a single XML hierarchy to reside in separate documents that can be processed either as free-standing XML instances, or as part of the entire original tree.

References

Bański, P., 2010. Why TEI Stand-off Annotation Doesn't Quite Work: And Why You Might Want to Use It Nevertheless. In: *Balisage: The Markup Conference 2010.* Montreal, Canada, August 3–6, 2010. Rockville, MD: Mulberry Technologies.

Bański, P., Bingel, J., Diewald, N., Frick, E., Hanl, M., Kupietz, M., Pęzik, P., Schnober, C., and Witt, A., 2013. KorAP: The New Corpus Analysis Platform at IDS Mannheim. In: Z. Vetulani and H. Uszkoreit (Eds.) 2013. *Human Language Technologies as a Challenge for Computer Science and Linguistics: Proceedings of the 6th Language and Technology Conference.* Poznan: Fundacja Uniwersytetu im. A. Mickiewicza.

Burnard, L. How Modeling Standards Evolve: The Case of the TEI. In: J. Flanders and F. Jannidis (Eds.) 2018. *The Shape of Data in the Digital Humanities.* London: Routledge.

DeRose, S., 2004. *Markup Overlap: A Review and a Horse.* Proceedings of Extreme Markup Languages. Available at: http://conferences.idealliance.org/extreme/html/2004/DeRose01/EML2004DeRose01.html.

Durand, D., Ide, N., LeMaitre, J., and Véronis, J., 1995. Internal Standard Formats. MULTEXT Deliverable 1.3.1B. Available at: www.cs.vassar.edu/~ide/papers/MultextD1.3.1B.ps (accessed February 23, 2015).

Goecke, D., Metzing, D., Lüngen, H., Stührenberg, M., and Witt, A., 2010. Different Views on Markup. Distinguishing Levels and Layers. In: A. Witt and D. Metzing (Eds.) *Linguistic Modeling of Information and Markup Languages: Contributions to Language Technology.* Dordrecht: Springer, pp. 1–21.

Hilbert, M., Schonefeld, O., and Witt, A., 2005. *Making CONCUR Work.* In: Proceedings of Extreme Markup Languages. Available at: http://conferences.idealliance.org/extreme/html/2005/Witt01/EML2005Witt01.xml.

International Standards Office (ISO), 2012. *ISO/FDIS 24611:2012(E) Language Resource Management—Morpho-Syntactic Annotation Framework (MAF).* Geneva: ISO.

Piez, W., 2012. Luminescent: Parsing LMNL by XSLT Upconversion. In: *Balisage: The Markup Conference 2012.* Montreal, Canada, August 7–10. Rockville, MD: Mulberry Technologies.

Rehm, G., Schonefeld, O., Witt, A., Hinrichs, E., and Reis, M., 2009. Sustainability of Annotated Resources in Linguistics: A Web-Platform for Exploring, Querying, and Distributing Linguistic Corpora and Other Resources. *Literary & Linguistic Computing,* 24 (2009/2), pp. 193–210.

Russell, D.B., 1965. COCOA—A Word Count and Concordance Generator (computer program). Associates Technology Literature Applications Society.

Schmidt, T., Chiarcos, C., Lehmberg, T., Rehm, G., Witt, A., and Hinrichs, E., 2006. *Avoiding Data Graveyards: From Heterogeneous Data Collected in Multiple Research Projects to Sustainable Linguistic Resources.* EMELD (Electronic Metastructure for Endangered Language Data). Available at: http://emeld.org/workshop/2006/proceedings.html.

Shakespeare, W., 1623. *Mr. William Shakespeares Comedies, Histories, & Tragedies.* London: Jaggard and Blount.

TEI Consortium, 2015. TEI P5: Guidelines for Electronic Text Encoding and Interchange. TEI Consortium. Available at: www.tei-c.org/Guidelines/P5/.

Tennison, J. and Wendell, P., 2002. *The Layered Markup and Annotation Language (LMNL)*. In: Proceedings of Extreme Markup Languages. Available at: http://conferences. idealliance.org/extreme/html/2002/Tennison02/EML2002Tennison02.html.

Thompson, H.S. and McKelvie, D., 1997. *Hyperlink semantics for standoff markup of read-only documents*. Proceedings of SGML Europe. Available at: www.ltg.ed.ac.uk/~ht/sgmleu97.html.

Witt, A., 2005. Multiple Hierarchies: New Aspects of an Old Solution. *Interdisciplinary Studies on Information Structure (ISIS)*, 2, pp. 55–85.

Wörner, K., Witt, A., Rehm, G., and Dipper, S., 2006. *Modelling Linguistic Data Structures*. In: Proceedings of Extreme Markup Languages. Available at: http://conferences. idealliance.org/extreme/html/2006/Witt01/EML2006Witt01.html.

12 Linguistic and computational modeling in language science

Elke Teich and Peter Fankhauser

Linguistics is concerned with modeling language from the cognitive, social, and historical perspectives. When practiced as a science, linguistics is characterized by the tension between the two methodological dispositions of rationalism and empiricism. At any point in time in the history of linguistics, one is more dominant than the other. In the last two decades, we have been experiencing a new wave of empiricism in linguistic fields as diverse as psycholinguistics (e.g., Chater et al., 2015), language typology (e.g., Piantidosi and Gibson, 2014), language change (e.g., Bybee, 2010) and language variation (e.g., Bresnan and Ford, 2010). Consequently, the practices of modeling are being renegotiated in different linguistic communities, readdressing some fundamental methodological questions such as: How to cast a research question into an appropriate study design? How to obtain evidence (data) for a hypothesis (e.g., experiment vs. corpus)? How to process the data? How to evaluate a hypothesis in the light of the data obtained? This new empiricism is characterized by an interest in *language use in context* accompanied by a commitment to computational modeling, which is probably most developed in psycholinguistics, giving rise to the field of "computational psycholinguistics" (cf. Crocker, 2010), but recently getting stronger also in corpus linguistics.

The predominant domain of corpus linguistics is language variation, aiming at statements on relative differences/similarities between linguistic varieties (time periods, registers, genres). Corpus analysis is thus comparative by nature; technically, this involves comparing probability distributions of (sets of) linguistic features (e.g., the relative frequency of passive vs. active voice in narrative vs. expository genres) and assessing whether they are significantly different or not. Here, descriptive statistical techniques come into play but also language modeling and machine learning methods (e.g., clustering, latent semantic analysis, or Bayesian modeling). Similarly, corpus processing—that is, preparing text material for analysis—relies on computational models, for example, for annotation. What is important to note here is that processing and analysis are broken up into different steps, each using a different computational *micro-model* that takes care of a specific task (e.g., labeling linguistic units in annotation) and consists of a *descriptive component* (set of allowed labels) and an *analytic* or *algorithmic component* (procedure by which labels are assigned).

In this chapter, we focus on one such task—part-of-speech tagging (in linguistic terms: grammatical word classification)—and the class of computational models addressing this task. In so doing, we discuss the differences between models constructed by human observation and computational models induced from corpus data. The major points we would like to stress here are that all models (human or machine-made) (a) are approximations and will never achieve the "perfect" description, and (b) start from a set of prior assumptions about modeling. Regarding computational models, it is then up to the human user to decide whether the model assumptions are reasonable and whether the degree of descriptive accuracy achieved is good enough for a given purpose of analysis.

The remainder of the chapter is organized as follows. We briefly introduce the basic workflow adopted in corpus-based research and relate its components to the relevant types of data as well as to the kinds of theoretical sources that inform the micro-models in different stages of processing/analysis. We then introduce a standard linguistic model for parts-of-speech, including a historical perspective, and discuss in more detail the role of modeling assumptions in computational approaches to part-of-speech tagging. In the concluding section we discuss implications of the perspectives on modeling presented in this article for modeling in the language- and text-oriented humanities more widely.

1 Types of data and theoretical sources for modeling

We assume the now common technical conception of a corpus-linguistic workflow as a processing pipeline distinguishing between processing of raw and primary data and analysis of primary data for obtaining secondary data (cf. Himmelmann, 2012, from the perspective of language documentation). Raw data can be recordings of spoken language (audio/video) or written text documents. Primary data can be transcriptions of audio/video or plain text or annotated text with structural mark-up, tokenization, part-of-speech tagging, and so forth. Secondary data can be descriptive statements—for example, dictionary entries or grammatical descriptions, but also frequency distributions and their interpretations. While raw data are unique, primary and secondary data are not: there are always alternative ways of processing raw data and different kinds of primary as well as secondary data can be derived from it. Here, the difference between primary and secondary data is sometimes not clear-cut. However, primary data is typically closer to the linguistic signal than secondary data, and secondary data requires primary data as input (e.g., in order to calculate a probability distribution of the word classes in a text or corpus, it needs to be tagged first in terms of parts-of-speech).

Each data type (raw, primary, secondary) is associated with a particular processing stage and requires specific methods for processing. Procedures to get from raw data to primary data may involve full text digitization, text normalization, sentence segmentation, tokenization, lemmatization, morphological analysis, part-of-speech tagging, and syntactic parsing, but also manual annotation (e.g., annotation of semantic roles and relations). Together, these processing steps enable the derivation of primary data from raw data. Each of them has its own underlying micro-model in the sense defined above, that is, a descriptive and an algorithmic model for a specific processing task. Depending on the nature of the task, these models are theoretically informed by linguistic theory, probability theory and/or information theory. The steps in deriving secondary data (e.g., a probability distribution) again follow particular micro-models that define input and output, based on formal grammar (e.g., regular expressions for corpus query) and descriptive statistics or data mining (for assessing probability distributions). Figure 12.1 summarizes the commonly adopted processing steps in relation to data types and theoretical sources for modeling.

Importantly, the performance of each micro-model can be tested separately by measuring how well it fits a given data set and predicts the behavior of new data. Again, it is important to note that 100 percent accuracy will never be attained, but knowing about model quality, we can decide how the error rate may affect the next steps in processing or analysis.

Why would it be interesting to compare linguistic modeling as carried out by humans and computational modeling as carried out by machines? There is necessarily a gap between a model that is designed for computation and a model that is designed for human consumption. While both require determining the object of modeling, making explicit the descriptive categories to be used and providing criteria for assigning categories, the goals of modeling may be different, the task itself may need to be differently defined, and consequently the models themselves (both descriptive and analytic) will be different. A model that was

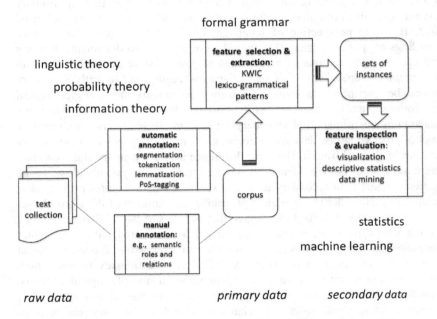

Figure 12.1 Processing pipeline, data types, and theoretical sources for modeling.

designed for/by humans can thus typically not be straightforwardly applied by a machine, and vice versa models designed for/by machines are not necessarily easy to interpret for humans.

For illustration, we look at the classification of words into parts-of-speech (PoS)—in computational terms, part-of-speech tagging. We discuss the relation of a linguistic model of parts-of-speech as we would typically find it in a standard grammar (e.g., Quirk et al., 1985 for English) and computational models for automatically assigning PoS tags to strings.

2 Grammatical classification of words

Traditionally, linguistics is concerned with classification—that is, abstracting from observations of linguistic instances to classes. The goal of classification is to come up with a descriptive model of a given object (syllable, word, clause, etc.).

A standard work for many centuries after it appeared, the *Téchnē Grammatikē*, a description of Ancient Greek, is attributed to Dionysius Thrax (*c.* 100BC). The two basic *units of description* identified were the *sentence* and the *word*. The word was defined as the smallest meaning-bearing unit that was not further decomposable (there was awareness of morphology, but no term for it yet). Observing the behavior of the word, Thrax came up with the following eight word classes (parts-of-speech): noun, verb, participle, article, pronoun, preposition, adverb and conjunction (cf. Robins, 1997, p. 41). The properties on the basis of which these classes were distinguished were mainly to do with the internal properties of words—for example, nouns (onoma) and verbs (rhema) were distinguished on the basis of case inflection (+ / −) as the sole distinctive feature. Interesting cases are the recognition of the participle as a separate class and the non-recognition of the adjective as a separate class. In Ancient Greek, the participle is both case- and tense-inflected—so it has properties of nouns and verbs; the adjective is very similar to nouns in morphology and syntax, so adjectives and nouns were subsumed under one class. Each class is described in terms of its attributes referring to grammatically relevant differences in the forms of words, essentially what we refer to today as grammatical categories (such as gender, case, tense, voice, mood, person etc.) and some syntactic criteria (e.g., preposition placed before other words, adverb modifying a verb).

Thrax's classification can be called a micro-model in that it focuses on one particular constituent of language, the word, so Thrax must have been aware of the necessity to break down a complex object (language) into manageable sub-parts. Furthermore, Thrax's classification is an instance of a descriptive model; in today's computational linguistic terminology, it is a part-of-speech tag set. We cannot be entirely sure about how Thrax arrived at this model, but he definitely proceeded in an empirical fashion. The data he used was taken from written texts by accepted authors of the time and he must have inspected this data very closely. Regarding the analytic part of his model, we do not have much evidence. Generally, Thrax will have applied Aristotelian methods of classification, but there is no explicit account of the criteria he used. As mentioned above, the criteria he will have applied are to a large degree to do with the internal properties of words and to a lesser extent syntactic and distributional.

A contemporary classification of words, which basically applies across languages, assumes eight word classes—noun, verb, adjective, pronoun, article, adverb, interjection, conjunction, and preposition—and is only slightly different from Thrax's classification (interjection has been added, participle has been removed). The differences are due to more insights into the properties of words, notably morphology, but also their syntactic behavior and distributional properties. The latter are crucial in defining criteria for grammatical disambiguation. Consider examples (1) and (2).

(1) The file has been deleted.
(2) Can you file the report?

This kind of ambiguity is particularly common in English because noun-to-verb conversion is very productive. In isolation, the word *file* is ambiguous between a noun (1) and a verb (2), but in the context of a preceding article (1) *file* can only be a noun and in the context of a preceding pronoun, it can only be a verb (2). We will come back to the importance of syntactic context in the following sections on computational modeling.

While there are clearly many languages in the world that have only been partially described (or not described at all), methodologically grammatical word classification counts as a solved task in modern linguistics: the principles of word classification and the procedures linguists use to detect word classes are course-book knowledge. They include substitution tests, syntactic tests (e.g., reordering of elements) as well as distributional information. One general insight from the experiences in linguistic modeling is that any model will be approximate: linguistic classes are typically gradient, some members being at the core of a class exhibiting all defining features, others carry only some of the defining features and are at the periphery of a class.

In summary, traditionally the goal of modeling in linguistics is to come up with a descriptive model of a linguistic object. For modeling purposes, language is broken up into manageable parts that are linguistically relevant (such as words). The task of modeling consists of detecting the classes (descriptive model) and providing criteria for distinguishing between them (analytic model).

3 Part-of-speech tagging

Part-of-speech (PoS) tagging belongs to the most commonly applied types of corpus processing. Words are a linguistically relevant unit for grammatical and semantic study; but even if we are not specifically interested in studying words, PoS are a very useful abstraction from strings that we can use—for example, in corpus search. The importance of PoS tagging was recognized quite early on in corpus-based research in the late 1960s and considerable efforts went into

```
Emma/NNP Woodhouse/NNP ,/, handsome/JJ ,/, clever/JJ ,/,
and/CC rich/JJ ,/, with/IN a/DT comfortable/JJ home/NN
and/CC happy/JJ disposition/NN ,/, seemed/VB to/TO unite/VB
some/DT of/IN the/DT best/JJS blessings/NNS of/IN
existence/NN ;/;

word classes: NNP= proper noun, JJ = adjective, CC =
coordinating conjunction, IN = preposition, DT =
determiner, NN = noun singular, VB = verb, TO = to, JJS =
adjective superlative, NNS = noun plural
```

Figure 12.2 A sample of Jane Austen's *Emma*, tagged with parts of speech.

manual tagging—for example, the work on the Brown and LOB corpora carried out by Francis and Kučera (1982). Nowadays, automatic PoS tagging achieves a very high accuracy (95–97 percent), so that its output can serve as input for further processing and analysis.

Consider a sample sentence (the first sentence from Jane Austen's *Emma*) tagged with parts-of-speech with the Stanford tagger and associated tag set (Toutanova and Manning, 2000):

> (3) Emma Woodhouse, handsome, clever, and rich, with a comfortable home and happy disposition, seemed to unite some of the best blessings of existence;

We can see here a number of differences to traditional linguistic word classification. First, not only words are being tagged, but also punctuation marks. Second, the tag set is more extensive than the commonly used set of word classes, partly because it encodes some grammatical categories (e.g., number in nouns) as well as semantic categories (e.g., proper vs. common nouns).

In contrast to traditional linguistic word classification, the overall goal of part-of-speech tagging is to assign tags to *all tokens* in a text rather than just to words; also, if it is easy to cover grammatical categories in tagging, they are encoded in tags (in linguistic classification, grammatical classes and categories are strictly kept separate). Therefore, the descriptive models of word classification and PoS tagging differ.

The analytic part of a PoS tagger can either be rule-based (e.g., Brill, 1992) or statistically based (e.g., Schmid, 1994; Toutanova and Manning, 2000). In statistical approaches, modeling is based on conditional probabilities and can follow a supervised or an unsupervised approach.

3.1 Supervised part-of-speech tagging

Conditional probabilities are widely used in statistical *language modeling* (Rosenfeld, 2002). Based on word n-grams they calculate the probability of an upcoming word *w* based on the context of the previous words (typically one, two, or three words)—that is,

$$P(w_n \mid w_{n-i} \ldots w_{n-1})$$

In contrast to plain word n-gram based approaches, part-of-speech tagging includes an abstraction step in that it calculates the probability $P(w_n \mid c_n)$ of a word w_n, given its class c_n, which in turn is conditioned on the sequence of preceding classes: $P(c_n \mid c_{n-i} \ldots c_{n-1})$. The task of part-of-speech tagging is thus to predict the class of a given word based on the sequence of preceding classes, and possibly also its following classes, which can be derived from the above probabilities on the basis of Bayes's rule:[1]

$$P(c_n \mid w_n, \ldots) \propto P(w_n \mid c_n) * P(c_n \mid c_{n-i} \ldots c_{n-1}) \qquad \text{(Equation 1)}$$

The underlying modeling assumption is that a given linguistic event (e.g., a word) in a sequence of linguistic events is dependent on previous (and following) events in the sequence. More specifically, words are assumed to be generated by the following two-stage stochastic process:

For every word w_n

(1) choose a class c_n from the class-sequence distribution

$$P(c_n \mid c_{n-i} \ldots c_{n-1})$$

(2) choose the word from the class-word distribution

$$P(w_n \mid c_n)$$

In supervised part-of-speech tagging, these probabilities can be directly estimated from a training corpus. Of course, this simplified model does not really capture all aspects of what constitutes a word class. In the simplest approach, $P(w_n \mid c_n)$ just memorizes the frequencies of observed words in a class, and does not take into account, for example, morphological characteristics of words, which presumably served as a basis for Thrax's classification. Moreover, $P(c_n \mid c_{n-i} \ldots c_{n-1})$ is only characterized in terms of rather coarse syntactic categories, and only considers a context of fixed length, thereby disregarding long-range syntactic dependencies. In fact, state-of-art part-of-speech taggers use more elaborate features that do take into account morphology and other characteristics of words in context.

Still, this type of model constitutes the conceptual foundation for algorithmic part-of-speech tagging (see Hidden Markov Models (HMMs) as described, for example, in Manning and Schütze (1999: Chapters 9 and 10)). The original idea goes back to Markov (1913) who applied it to the initial 20,000 characters of Pushkin's *Evgeni Onegin* in order to predict vowel-consonant sequences—a task very similar to part-of-speech tagging.

3.2 Unsupervised part-of-speech tagging

Hidden Markov models can also be deployed in an unsupervised fashion. Rather than estimating the class-word distributions $P(w_n \mid c_n)$ and the class sequence n-grams $P(c_n \mid c_{n-i} \ldots c_{n-1})$ from labeled training examples, Equation 1 is used to estimate latent classes. Thus, the modeling assumption is fully reduced to the generative stochastic process described above, there exists no descriptive model in form of a given set of word classes; only the number of classes and the length of context (order of the HMM) is given.

One of the first approaches to this end was introduced by Brown et al. (1992). In the analysis below, we use the Bayesian approach introduced by Goldwater and Griffiths (2007), which uses annealed Gibbs sampling based on Equation 1 to approximate the class-word and class-sequence distributions. It is instructive to compare this to the Gibbs sampling equation used for topic modeling (Steyvers and Griffiths, 2007, cf. Underwood, this volume):

$$P(z \mid w, \ldots) \propto P(w \mid z) * P(z \mid d) \qquad \text{(Equation 2)}$$

where $P(w/z)$ is the topic-word distribution, and $P(z/d)$ is the document-topic distribution. The underlying generative process is very similar:

For every word w

(1) choose a topic z from the document-topic distribution $P(z/d)$}
(2) choose the word from the topic-word distribution $P(w/z)$.

Thus, the essential difference between topic models and unsupervised Hidden Markov models is that the document-topic distribution considers the bag of topics of an entire document as context, whereas the class-sequence distribution $P(c_n \mid c_{n-i} \ldots c_{n-1})$ considers only the local, ordered class context. Griffiths et al. (2004) describe an approach that combines these two latent modeling approaches.

For illustration, we have applied this approach to the Brown/LOB family of corpora (Francis and Kučera, 1982), comprising about 4.7 million tokens of British and American English. Table 12.1 lists the PoS classes using a HMM of order 2 (two preceding classes) and assuming 25 classes. All classes except *sentence marker* are latent classes, their grouping, description, and labeling with tags from the Penn tagset (Marcus et al., 1993) are derived by qualitative analysis of the class-word distributions and most frequent class sequences. The column labeled "Ent." gives the entropy of the class-word distributions measured in bits, with low values indicating a closed class consisting of only few different words, and high values indicating an open class. The resulting class-word distributions illustrate the strengths but also the limitations of the underlying modeling assumptions: Some major syntactic categories (*nouns, verbs, adjectives, prepositions, conjunctions, personal pronouns*) are identified quite well. *Nouns* are differentiated into two noun singular classes, noun plural, proper nouns (titles), and countables. *Personal pronouns* are roughly differentiated by their grammatical

Table 12.1 Latent PoS-Classes with a HMM of order 2

%	Ent.	Tags	Description	Top 5 Words				
4.9	0.6	SENT	sentence marker	.	?	:	!	"
5.3	0.9	PUNC	punctuation	,	;	;	than*	'
7.2	11.3	NN	noun singular (1)	time	man	way	year	day
3.3	10.8	NN	noun singular (2)	part	number	sense	end	kind
5.1	9.5	NNS	noun plural	people	men	women	children	things
2.2	11.6	NP	title, first name	mr	john	mrs	sir	miss
2.3	9.5	NN/CD	countable	years	2	1	per	3
4.6	5.4	PP	personal pron. (1)	he	i	it	she	they
2.5	10.5	PP	personal pron. (2)	it	him	them	me	her
2.0	10.9	JJ*	adjective (1)	good	important	true	possible	better
3.3	10.3	JJ*	adjective (2)	first	new	own	same	old
10.3	2.7	DT/JJ/PP$	before noun	the	a	his	an	this
4.4	10.7	DT/JJ/PP$	bef. Noun plur.	These	their	other	two	new
8.0	4.4	IN	preposition (1)	in	to	for	with	on
3.1	0.8	IN	preposition (2)	of	between	that*	is*	called*
3.9	8.0	VV(D)	verb lexical	is	was	said	are	had
2.6	9.0	VB/VD/VV	verb infinitive	be	do	make	see	get
3.7	10.4	V*G/V*N	verb participle	made	used	going	taken	given
4.4	4.3	V*/MD	verb auxiliary	'*	is	was	had	are
1.6	1.2	TO/MD	before verb inf.	To	will	would	can	may
3.4	5.8	RB/VB/VH	before verb	s	be	not	been	have
2.9	7.5	RP/PP	after verb	t	it	out	up	him
2.9	4.8	CC	conjunction (1)	''	but	if	then	however
3.3	2.0	CC	conjunction (2)	and	or	but	as	so
2.7	5.8	W*/CC	rel. clause/conj.	That	which	as	if	when

case, *verbs* by four major grammatical categories, and *conjunctions* by their position in sentence: (1) in sentence initial position, and (2) within a sentence. Punctuations are also clearly recognized as an individual class.

Some other classes are less well separated: *Determiners* get mixed up with other classes that may occur before a noun, such as demonstrative articles and adjectives. *Auxiliary verbs* contain almost 25 percent of apostrophes arising from either possessive "s" or verb contractions ("don't")—these get separated into individual classes, when working with a larger number of classes. Most prominently, *adverbs* are not separated well at all, but get mixed up with other classes that may occur before or after a verb. Here, neglecting morphological characteristics in estimating the class-word distributions seems to strike particularly hard. Regular adverbs in English are signaled by the suffix "ly," which may be due to the difficulty of recognizing adverbs by their syntactic context alone.

The class *before verb infinitive* is particularly interesting: 87 percent of its probability mass is accounted for by "to"+infinitive, and the next most frequent words are modal verbs typically followed by an infinitive. However, as the examples in Table 12.2 show, "to"+infinitive (right) is well distinguished from "to" as a preposition (left). The latent syntactic context—prepositions cannot be followed by an infinitive—serves well to disambiguate between the two uses of "to."

In a similar vein, Table 12.3 gives examples of the disambiguation between "be/have/do" as lexical verbs (left) and as auxiliary verbs. Also in these examples, the right context of the verb (determiner vs. verb or verb participle) enables the disambiguation. The two examples "it is possible" and "it is difficult" constitute interesting borderline cases. Strictly speaking "is" followed by an adjective is to be classified as a lexical verb, but apparently the model cannot pick up the subtle difference between "is" followed by a participle (e.g., "she is educated") vs. followed by an adjective. Note that supervised part-of-speech taggers using the Penn tagset classify all occurrences of "be/have/do" as "VB/VH/VD"—that is, the distinction between lexical and auxiliary verbs is not regarded at all.

In summary, unsupervised approaches to part-of-speech tagging are a natural generalization of supervised approaches. This does not only hold for part-of-speech tagging; also other generative models, such as topic models, can span the continuum between fully supervised and fully unsupervised modes of operation

Table 12.2 Disambiguation of "to" into preposition vs. "to"+infinitive

Occ.	RP/PP	PP	DT	Occ.	VV(D)	TO	VB/VD/VV
232	back	to	the	94	seems	to	be
201	up	to	the	90	seemed	to	be
149	on	to	the	58	was	to	be
142	away	from	the	57	had	to	do
133	up	in	the	53	appears	to	be

Table 12.3 Disambiguation of lexical vs. auxiliary verbs

Occ.	PP/EX	VV(D)	DT	Occ.	PP	VB/VD/VH/MD	V*G/V*N/VV
602	there	was	a	67	it	is	possible*
585	there	is	a	62	he	was	going
575	it	was	a	61	we	have	seen
422	it	is	a	59	i	would	like
352	it	was	the	58	it	is	difficult*

(Ramage et al., 2011). However, because part-of-speech tagging, at least for well-resourced languages such as English, is so well understood, it allows to understand the limitations of overly simplistic generative models by means of qualitative and quantitative analysis, as exemplified above by the apparent importance of the morphological regularity of adverbs in English for their classification. When applied to less-resourced languages or more specialized language varieties, the weak modeling assumptions can also serve for discovering specific patterns and classes that cannot be captured with a fixed class vocabulary.

4 Conclusion and envoi

We have discussed selected aspects of modeling language from the linguistic and the computational perspectives. Ultimately, linguistics is interested in generalizations about language as a cognitive and a social system. Modeling linguistic data–that is, describing it and generalizing from it—is a means to this end. Analysis is broken down into manageable subparts, for which descriptive and analytic micro-models are devised that are increasingly computationally supported. We currently experience a push towards empirical approaches, even in areas that have hitherto been committed to a rationalist perspective (cf. section 12.1). With this development comes the need to reflect more on analytic processes and to model these processes. Providing such models on the part of computational linguistics/computer science and getting accustomed to working with them on the part of linguistics paves the ground for a new linguistic empiricism that is computationally informed.

What can be learned from these experiences for the humanities more widely? At a first glance, the computationally informed empirical turn in linguistics seems to widen the gap between it and the humanities. However, this would be adopting a rather traditionalistic perspective (cf. Bod, 2013, for related discussions). In fact, with the recent developments in digital humanities, it may even turn out to be the contrary. First, linguistic data are humanistic data—that is, they are contextualized in time and space. (Computational) linguists realize more and more that extra-linguistic context is extremely important in the analysis of language and the interpretation of linguistic acts (cf. Halevy et al., 2009). But how exactly context can be modeled beyond the immediate context of words remains an open question (cf. also Church, 2011, for a discussion in computational linguistics).

In the digital humanities, in turn, recent advances in computational processing show that there may be more information in the linguistic signal than humanists may have hitherto assumed. This is shown in studies of text using machine learning in fields as diverse as history (e.g., Hinrichs et al., 2014, uncovering historical facts in nineteenth-century global economy) and literary theory (see e.g., Chambers and Jurafsky, 2009 or Mimno et al., 2014, for approaches automatically detecting narrative structure). What characterizes this direction of research is, first, the awareness of the need to stick closely to the linguistic signal in order to capture patterns that can subsequently be interpreted at more abstract levels and, second, the readiness to apply methods and techniques from machine learning to detect patterns that would otherwise remain hidden.

What should also be kept in mind is that computational language models are linguistically informed—that is, they take (some of) their model assumptions from linguistics. Grammatical word classification is a very well-understood task in linguistics and computational models are thus fairly well linguistically informed. Discussing a concrete model of unsupervised part-of-speech tagging using distributional criteria alone, we have seen that fairly good analysis results may be achieved on this basis, but if additional linguistic criteria were taken into consideration (e.g., morphology), such a model would clearly perform better. Moreover, while part-of-speech tagging is a very well-understood task, there are many other kinds of phenomena that are much less well understood, such as the encoding of writer/speaker attitude in text, principles of text structuring, or genre classification. In such areas, computational models perform much worse, simply because we do not have very good criteria yet that we can use for informing them.

In summary, the opportunities that arise from engaging in computational modeling for humanists are both practical and conceptual. From the practical perspective, we can use computational models as tools to get a particular analytic task done (e.g., part-of-speech tagging) that may be a prerequisite for getting on to other, more complex kinds of analysis (e.g., analysis of genre-specific syntactic patterns). From the conceptual perspective, computational modeling can assist us in devising better models in areas we do not yet understand very well (cf. Underwood, this volume). And finally, using computational models will provoke reflection on some of our long-standing assumptions about language, pushing us to revise or revive them. In linguistics, cases in point are Chomsky's assumptions about language learning which have repeatedly been called into question (cf. Lappin and Shieber, 2007, on insights from machine learning) or the revival of the Firthian assumption of the context-dependent nature of meaning ("You shall know a word by the company it keeps," Firth, 1957, p. 11), now so popular in linguistic semantics.

Note

1   $\propto$ stands for *proportional to*; the actual probability can be derived by normalizing with the sum of the right-hand-side over all classes. For notational convenience, we conflate random variables with their values.

References

Bod, R., 2013. *A New History of Humanities. The Search for Principles and Patterns from Antiquity to the Present*. Oxford: Oxford University Press.

Bresnan, J. and Ford, M., 2010. Predicting Syntax: Processing Dative Constructions in American and Australian Varieties of English. *Language*, 86(1), pp. 186–213.

Brill, E., 1992. A Simple Rule-Based Part of Speech Tagger. In: Association for Computational Linguistics, *Proceedings of the Third Conference on Applied Natural Language Processing (ANLC '92)*. Trento, Italy, March 31–April 3, 1992. Stroudsburg, PA: Association for Computational Linguistics.

Brown, P.F., deSouza, P.V., Mercer, R.L., Della Pietra, V.J., and Lai, J.C., 1992. Class-Based n-gram Models of Natural Language. *Computational Linguistics*, 18(4), pp. 467–79.

Bybee, J., 2010. *Language, Usage, and Cognition*. Cambridge, UK: Cambridge University Press.

Chambers, N. and Jurafsky, D., 2009. Unsupervised Learning of Narrative Schemas and their Participants. In: ACL and AFNLP (Association for Computational Linguistics and Asian Federation of Natural Language Processing), *Proceedings of the 47th Annual Meeting of the ACL and the 4th International Joint Conference on Natural Language Processing of the AFNLP*. Singapore, August 2–7, 2009. Stroudsburg, PA: Association for Computational Linguistics.

Chater, N., Clark, A., Goldsmith, J., and Perfors, A., 2015. *Empiricism and Language Learnability*. Oxford: Oxford University Press.

Church, K., 2011. A Pendulum Swung Too Far. *Linguistic Issues in Language Technology (LiLT)*, 6(5), pp. 1–27.

Crocker, M.W., 2010. Computational Psycholinguistics. In: Clark, A., Fox, C., and Lappin, S. (Eds.) 2010. *The Handbook of Computational Linguistics and Natural Language Processing*. Oxford, UK: Wiley-Blackwell. Pp. 482–513.

Firth, J.R., 1957. *Papers in Linguistics 1934–1951*. London: Oxford University Press.

Francis, W.N. and Kučera, H., 1982. *Frequency Analysis of English Usage: Lexicon and Grammar*. Boston, MA: Houghton Mifflin.

Goldwater, S. and Griffiths, T., 2007. A Fully Bayesian Approach to Unsupervised Part-of-Speech Tagging. In: ACL (Association for Computational Linguistics), *Proceedings of the 45th Annual Meeting of the Association for Computational Linguistics*. Prague, Czech Republic, June 23–30. Stroudsburg, PA: Association for Computational Linguistics.

Griffiths, T., Steyvers, M., Blei, D.M., and Tenenbaum, J., 2004. Integrating Topics and Syntax. In: Bottou, L., Saul, L.K., and Weiss, Y. (Eds.) 2005. *Advances in Neural Information Processing Systems 17*. Cambridge, MA: MIT Press, pp. 537–44.

Halevy, A., Norvig, P., and Pereira, F., 2009. The Unreasonable Effectiveness of Data, *IEEE Intelligent Systems*, 24(2), pp. 8–12.

Himmelmann, N., 2012. Linguistic Data Types and the Interface between Language Documentation and Description. *Language Documentation & Conservation*, 6, pp. 187–207.

Hinrichs, U., Alex, B., Clifford, J., and Quigley, A., 2014. Trading Consequences: A Case Study of Combining Text Mining & Visualisation to Facilitate Document Exploration. In: ADHO (Alliance of Digital Humanities Organizations), *Proceedings of DH 2014*. Lausanne, Switzerland, July 7–12, 2014. Available at: http://dharchive.org/paper/DH2014/Paper-373.xml.

Lappin, S. and Shieber, S.M., 2007. Machine Learning Theory and Practice as a Source of Insight into Universal Grammar. *Journal of Linguistics*, 43, pp. 1–34.

Manning, C.D. and Schütze, H., 1999. *Foundations of Statistical Natural Language Processing*. Cambridge, MA: MIT Press.

Marcus, M., Santorini, B., and Marcinkiewicz, M.A., 1993. Building a Large Annotated Corpus of English: The Penn Treebank. *Computational Linguistics*, 19(2), pp. 313–30.

Markov, A.A., 1913. An Example of Statistical Investigation of the Text *Eugene Onegin* Concerning the Connection of Samples in Chains. *Proceedings of the Academy of Sciences (St. Petersburg)*, 7, pp. 153–62.

Mimno, D., Broadwell, P.M., and Tangherlini, T.R., 2014. The Telltale Hat: LDA and Classification Problems in a Large Folklore Corpus. In: ADHO (Alliance of Digital Humanities Organizations), *Proceedings of DH 2014*, Lausanne, Switzerland, July 7–12. Available at: http://dharchive.org/paper/DH2014/Paper-163.xml.

Piantadosi, S.T. and Gibson, E., 2014. Quantitative Standards for Absolute Linguistic Universals. *Cognitive Science*, 38(4), pp. 736–56.

Quirk, R., Greenbaum, S., Leech G., and Svartvik, J., 1985. *A Comprehensive Grammar of the English Language*. London: Longman.

Ramage, D., Manning, C.D., Dumais, S., 2011. Partially Labeled Topic Models for Interpretable Text Mining. In: ACM (Association for Computing Machinery), *Proceedings of the 17th ACM SIGKDD International Conference on Knowledge Discovery and Data Mining*. San Diego, CA, August 21–24. New York: Association for Computing Machinery.

Robins, R.H., 1997. *A Short History of Linguistics*. London: Longman.

Rosenfeld, R., 2002. Two Decades of Statistical Language Modeling: Where Do We Go from Here? *Proceedings of the IEEE*, 88(8), pp. 1270–8.

Schmid, H., 1994. Probabilistic Part-of-Speech Tagging Using Decision Trees. In: *Proceedings of International Conference on New Methods in Language Processing*, Manchester, UK: UMIST. Pp. 44–9.

Steyvers, M. and Griffiths, T., 2007. Probabilistic Topic Models. In: Landauer, T., McNamara, D., Dennis, D., and Kintsch, W. (Eds.) 2007. *Latent Semantic Analysis: A Road to Meaning*. Mahwah, NJ: Laurence Erlbaum. Available at: http://psiexp.ss.uci. edu/research/papers/SteyversGriffithsLSABookFormatted.pdf.

Toutanova, K. and Manning, C.D., 2000. Enriching the Knowledge Sources Used in a Maximum Entropy Part-of-Speech Tagger. In: ACL (Association for Computational Linguistics), *Proceedings of the Joint SIGDAT Conference on Empirical Methods in Natural Language Processing and Very Large Corpora (EMNLP/VLC-2000)*. Hong Kong, China, October 7–8. Stroudsburg, PA: Association for Computational Linguistics.

13 Algorithmic modeling

Or, modeling data we do not yet understand

Ted Underwood

When humanists talk about "models," we are often thinking of data models, and perhaps especially of templates that inform representation. But for social scientists, the typical shape of a model is an equation, expected to predict or explain the relations between variables. For instance, the probability that a bill will become law may be partly explained by the level of support it receives from the wealthiest ten percent of voters (Gilens and Page, 2014). So a political scientist might express the relationship between those quantities as an equation. The probability of a bill's passage is equal to some base probability, α, plus its level of support from wealthy voters multiplied by a coefficient β. Given evidence, we can estimate α and β. Because social scientists are usually talking about probabilities rather than deterministic processes, their equations are often called "statistical" models.

Of course, social scientists also do data modeling, because quantitative methods have to start from some underlying representation of the evidence. And lately it is also true, conversely, that humanists are interested in statistics. Humanists are attending to large social phenomena more often than we used to, and we are finding statistical models a useful part of that project. New techniques like topic modeling have spread rapidly, and are now being used in roughly similar ways by political scientists and historians, linguists and literary critics (Blei and Jordan, 2003; Mohr and Bogdanov, 2013).

But although these modeling traditions now overlap, the relationship between them is still far from clear to practitioners. For researchers who are used to statistical modeling, complex data models can seem rife with arbitrary choices. On the other hand, researchers from a data modeling tradition often wonder whether statistical models have obscured their own implicit choices about representation.

My goal in this chapter is to interpret these two traditions to each other, and especially to explain the assumptions about data modeling that underlie certain quantitative methods now being introduced to the humanities—methods that are not just statistical, but algorithmic. The topic is difficult partly because humanists are being introduced to statistical modeling at a moment when that tradition is itself undergoing rapid change. Interdisciplinary conversation would be simpler if we were only meeting models of the classic kind that posit an algebraic relation between two or three variables. But much recent discussion focuses on statistical models where hundreds of parameters are estimated at once.

The challenges created by these new techniques are commonly framed as a question about humanists' assimilation of methods from other disciplines—or even as a question about a subfield called "digital humanities." But it may be helpful to begin with a wider view of the problem, because humanists are actually joining a debate that has continued for several decades, and that has stretched scientists as much as it now stretches humanists.

A useful starting point may be Leo Breiman's article "Statistical Modeling: The Two Cultures." Breiman described a conflict of cultures that already involved multiple disciplines in 2001, and whose ramifications have since continued to spread. I will summarize his article loosely here, with an eye not just on its original social context but on subsequent implications.

Breiman begins by observing that all statistical models are ways of understanding a relationship between some inputs (or predictor variables) and outputs (or response variables). He then outlines two different ways of making that connection. In what Breiman calls "the data modeling culture," researchers attempt to design a model that directly explains the mechanism relating variables in nature. For instance, if we are trying to understand voting behavior, we might hypothesize that age, personality type, and social class are the causal factors, and fit a regression model to infer their relative weights.

Breiman's quantitative "data modeling culture" may not include everything called data modeling in this volume, but it is loosely congruent, inasmuch as it involves a conscious effort to discern latent categories that make sense of data. Against this approach, Breiman contrasts a smaller "algorithmic modeling culture" that he associates with a subfield of computer science called machine learning—still fairly young in 2001. The algorithmic approach to modeling supposes that the actual causal or conceptual relations being modeled are "complex and unknown" (Breiman, 2001, p. 199). So instead of trying to directly model the real relations between variables in nature, researchers try to find an algorithm that will be functionally equivalent to them, in the sense that the algorithm can reliably *predict* the response variables given some set of predictors. This more modest goal makes it unnecessary to begin from a hypothesis about high-level organizing concepts like "personality type" or "social class." Instead, researchers can take a relatively disorganized mass of observed data (credit card balances, tax returns, or, for that matter, the name of your pet), and feed it all into a learning algorithm—an algorithm that generalizes from evidence to construct a model. We count on the algorithm to give each dimension of the evidence as much or as little weight as necessary to achieve predictive accuracy. (The name of your pet will probably be ignored, unless pet names turn out to predict voting behavior—which is, after all, possible.)

Because learning algorithms aim directly at the goal of prediction, they come with a built-in evaluative logic: we can tell whether models are precise enough, or general enough, simply by asking whether they make reliable predictions about previously unseen examples. A "prediction" in this context is a statement about evidence that was not used to form the model—not necessarily a statement about the future. Commonly, an existing dataset is divided into two parts. One part, a "training set," is used to form a model, which is then tested on the second part, the "test set." Since the model has not been shaped by evidence in the test set, its predictions about those cases will reveal whether it has learned a generalizable pattern or just (so to speak) "memorized" a particular set of examples.

I began by observing that statistical models always rest on some underlying model of the data. Texts, images, or human behavior all have to be formalized as sets of variables before we can draw inferences from them mathematically. But the quantitative methods now making waves in the humanities often have surprisingly little to say about the specific data models they expect as evidence. Discussion of a learning algorithm may start only after texts or images have already been reduced to lists of "features" (or predictor variables). I have taken us back to 2001 in order to explain this curious indifference to details of representation.

As Breiman explains, a central advantage of algorithmic modeling is that it allows us to grapple with problems where we have not yet identified the best way to represent our data. Instead of attempting to identify key variables in advance, we can begin with a relatively arbitrary, unsophisticated, and omnivorous data model. A typical approach is to treat every form of information as a distinct variable. If some of the evidence is qualitative, all the possible values of that qualitative category can be enumerated and treated as separate numeric variables. Researchers may represent a collection of texts, for instance, by treating each dictionary word as a variable and counting its occurrences in each text. This data model ignores word order (reducing texts to "bags of words"), but for many problems it turns out to be good enough, because even in isolation, words are significant little things (O'Connor, 2012).

But learning algorithms are not necessarily bound to any particular data model. If we need to model word order, we can count transitions between words or phrases (Rabiner and Juang, 1986). We can count red pixels, for that matter, or measure page shapes and inkblots, if there is any chance they will be useful for a given problem. If a feature turns out not to increase predictive accuracy, we can discard it. In text mining, we may, for instance, discard a list of common "stopwords" if we are less interested in style than in conceptual distinctions that depend on uncommon words. But these choices are not finally governed by any philosophical principle or linguistic rule; they grow simply from the observation that some models of the data produce better accuracy than others.

When defining a feature set requires human ingenuity targeted at the particular categories to be recognized, the process tends to be called "feature engineering." Taken to an extreme, this would move us back in the direction of Breiman's data modeling culture: models would be based on a small number of carefully crafted variables. But more commonly, researchers who are applying machine learning start with a very large set of possible features (say, all the words in a corpus), and construct a data model simply by selecting a subset. This process is called "feature selection," and although it can be refined in various ways, straightforward approaches often suffice. For instance, we might start with a list of all the words in a dataset, and eliminate the less common words progressively until predictive accuracy reaches a maximum (Manning, Raghavan and Schütze, 2009, pp. 271–79).

I am dwelling on the plasticity and simplicity of the data models used by learning algorithms because this has been a major source of misunderstanding when humanists encounter algorithmic methods. Since humanists think of modeling as a representative process, our first instinct is to inquire about the adequacy and completeness of the initial representation. The discipline of machine learning has had little to say about those concerns, and even seems to prefer perversely simple representative strategies, like counting words. This preference for large numbers of simple variables is not enforced by quantification itself. It is perfectly possible to include a complex concept like "personality" in a statistical model, if we are confident that we understand personality (Digman, 1990). But if we understand a problem well enough to characterize it with high-level variables like "personality," we probably do not need to use an algorithm to model it. Since learning algorithms can handle thousands of variables, they excel when we are not yet confident that we know how to define key concepts or organize the problem space. They excel, in other words, at modeling concepts we do not yet understand.

1 Supervised learning

Concepts we do not fully understand are common in the humanities: our generalizations about periods and genres, or about elite and mass culture, are rarely more than provisional. Moreover, where social scientists may have a small number of well-defined variables like "yearly income," we have unstructured data (texts, images, sounds). Conventional statistical models are hard to apply to unstructured material, since it is hard to identify a small number of key variables in advance. But Leo Breiman's algorithmic modeling culture might be very much at home here, if we can learn to apply it effectively.

To begin with the most obvious problem: how can we even begin to model concepts that we cannot define? The answer may depend on how deep our ignorance runs. If we can at least name a concept to be modeled and recognize examples of it, we may be able to "supervise" a learning algorithm that models it in more detail. If our ignorance is closer to total, we might instead use "unsupervised" methods to reveal patterns that we proceed to study in more depth.

In supervised learning, a researcher creates a set of examples (a "training set") that the algorithm takes as ground truth in its effort to model a pattern. The simplest and most familiar models are designed to divide instances into two classes–say, by characterizing a document as poetry or prose. A researcher might be able to provide examples of those categories, without necessarily possessing a clear definition of the difference. The algorithm generalizes from examples to infer a "decision boundary" between the classes (Hastie, Tibshirani and Friedman, 2009, pp. 9–14). If documents were characterized by only two variables, we might envision each document as a point in two-dimensional space. Then we could model the difference between categories by drawing a line likely to separate examples we encounter in the future. In Figure 13.1, for instance, we have used logistic regression to infer a decision boundary between hypothetical pages of prose and poetry. In reality, since models tend to involve hundreds of variables, and each variable can be understood as a different dimension of the space being modeled, one needs to imagine a decision boundary in multidimensional space—which is, alas, hard to draw.

The geometry of a decision boundary can vary from algorithm to algorithm. Linear classifiers construct a boundary that is essentially a hyperplane (a plane in, perhaps, 1000-dimensional space). Other algorithms, such as support vector machines and decision trees, can model surfaces with an indefinite degree of complexity. Although geometrical flexibility might appear to be an advantage, this is not always the case. In Figure 13.1, for instance, it would have been possible to draw a complicated curve that would put absolutely all the examples of prose on the same side of the line. But while that alteration would improve performance on the particular instances in this training set, there is a good chance that it might weaken performance on other possible samples—a mistake known as "overfitting" the data. To avoid overfitting, an algorithm is typically trained on one subset of examples, and tested on another ("cross-validated").

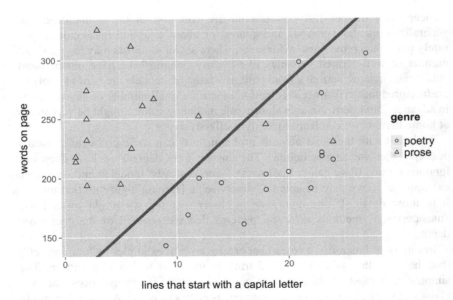

Figure 13.1 A decision boundary between pages of poetry and pages of prose.

2 Prediction and interpretation

Although we can test a model by examining its predictions about individual cases, humanists and social scientists are typically more interested in interpreting underlying patterns. When a model contains a small number of variables, this is easy: we can examine each predictor variable in the model and describe its influence on the result. For instance, researchers have modeled the American legislative process using the opinions of different classes as predictor variables. It turns out that the opinions of Americans near the 90 percent income percentile predict the success of a legislative proposal much more strongly than the opinions of Americans near median income (Gilens and Page, 2014). It might be hasty to express this as a causal connection, if we do not yet know whether laws directly reflect the opinions of the wealthy or just coincide with them for structural reasons. But even expressed as a correlation, this pattern certainly aids interpretation of American laws.

When models contain hundreds or thousands of variables, interpretation becomes more challenging. Partly, this is a rhetorical effect: complex patterns are simply harder to summarize. But there are also mathematical sources of murkiness at this scale. To handle thousands of variables, learning algorithms rely on strategies that optimize predictive accuracy at the expense of transparency (Shmuéli, 2010). This effect varies from algorithm to algorithm: neural networks are notoriously opaque, while logistic regression provides a measure of the effect of each variable. But there can be complexities even in a regression model: as variables proliferate, they may interact with each other in ways that make it hard to precisely estimate the significance of any single variable.

On the other hand, the opacity of machine learning could be overstated. Precise estimates may be elusive, but it is still possible to identify important variables in an algorithmic model (Breiman, 2001). The more urgent question for humanists is whether the patterns revealed by this sort of model are patterns with disciplinary meaning. In literary studies, for instance, it has been clear for several years that poetry can be distinguished from prose, and Gothic novels from sensation fiction, using only evidence about word frequency (Allison et al., 2011; Jockers, 2013; Underwood, 2014). But it is not yet clear whether we should understand these predictive successes as contributing anything meaningful to a critical account of genre.

In the case of poetry, we inherit a long critical tradition that describes rhythm as an essential attribute of poetic language, while disparaging "poetic diction" as an ephemeral convention, or at best a side-effect of poetic intensity (Wordsworth, 1800). If we trust this tradition, we might conclude that modeling poetry through word choice is a strategy that, in principle, will be incapable of revealing the genre's underlying logic. And that could be true, even though models based on diction make very accurate (> 90 percent) predictions: it is possible for a model to achieve predictive accuracy by relying on epiphenomena of some deeper, unobserved cause.

But it is also possible that the success of a predictive model will lead us to reconsider our definitional assumptions. If poetry can be distinguished from other genres purely on the evidence of diction—not just in the eighteenth century (where poetic diction is notoriously stylized) but also in the nineteenth and twentieth—then perhaps we do not understand the differences between genres quite as well as we thought. At a minimum, we might need to revisit claims about the declining significance of poetic diction in the nineteenth century. Specialized diction may turn out to be more durably central to poetry than William Wordsworth claimed. If, on the other hand, models based on rhythmic evidence turn out to recognize poetry more accurately than models based on diction, that evidence might go in the other pan of the scales (Algee-Hewitt et al., 2014).

In short, it is true that a predictive model of a category is not the same thing as a definition or a causal explanation—and also true that the complex models produced by learning algorithms can be challenging to interpret. But there are, nevertheless, many ways to use these models as evidence. The classic social-scientific approach that interprets a model by focusing on a subset of significant variables may not be the only way to proceed here. Sometimes the mere fact that a model can achieve predictive accuracy is the most important evidence it provides. And sometimes, as I will suggest in the next section, a model's interpretive significance may, after all, reside in its specific predictions about individual cases.

3 Using supervised learning to reveal shades of gray

When humanists hear that researchers are using algorithms to categorize texts and images, their first concern is typically that the process will impose a rigid and simplistic classification scheme. What about works that belong to four genres at once, or works that are located midway between two genres? Will those nuances be flattened by a data model simplified for computers?

The truth is closer to the reverse: one of the main reasons to model boundaries computationally is that it becomes easier to reason about shades of gray. I began by describing prose/poetry as a binary opposition, but only for expository convenience. The discipline of machine learning has spent a great deal of time reasoning about "multiclass" models, where each model has to decide between multiple categories, as well as "multilabel" classification, where each instance can belong simultaneously to more than one category (Witten, Frank and Hall, pp. 40, 164). These approaches allow categories to overlap in a wide range of ways ("this is poetry, but not necessarily verse"). There are also algorithms designed to think about temporal or spatial relationships. Natural language processing, for instance, depends heavily on models that learn to segment sequences of words. These approaches can be combined to make the data models produced by algorithms as complex as we like.

In particular, algorithmic models excel at questions of degree. When large numbers of images or documents have to be sorted manually, binary choices may be a necessary simplification for human coders: either we assign a given tag, or we do not. But most classification algorithms can express their predictions as a probabilistic gradient (Witten, Frank and Hall, pp. 343–46). These degrees of confidence can be used to select particularly clear examples of a category, or alternatively, to highlight ambiguous edge cases.

For this reason, the predictions you get out of a supervised model are often more nuanced and more informative than the labeled examples you originally used to train it. Jordan Sellers and I recently trained a model to distinguish nineteenth-century poetry reviewed in prestigious magazines from volumes of poetry selected at random from a digital library (which are often more obscure). The labels we provided the model were binary: either we had found a volume reviewed in a prominent periodical, or we had not. But the model's predictions revealed literary prestige as a continuous gradient, ranging from authors who aligned very strongly with the literary standards implicit in the whole dataset (like Alfred Tennyson), through a wide range of intermediate cases, to volumes that typified the kind of poetry reviewers were certain to ignore (Underwood and Sellers, 2015).

Taking this approach one step further, comparisons between multiple models can be used to map degrees of blurriness or instability in a dataset. For instance, in studying literary reviewing, we wanted to know not only what standards had governed the reception of nineteenth-century poetry, but how rapidly those standards had changed. To find out, we trained models on four different quarters of a century, and then asked each model to make predictions about the other three periods. If a model trained on evidence from the period 1850–74 can predict reviewing practices in the last quarter of the century almost as accurately as a model trained directly on evidence from the end of the century, we can infer that

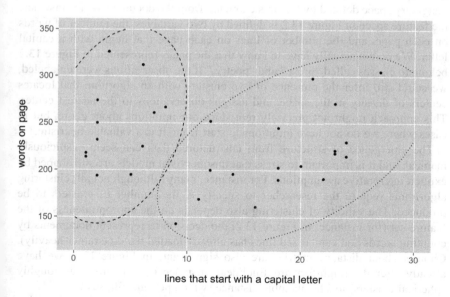

lines that start with a capital letter

Figure 13.2 Unsupervised inference of clusters in the data from Figure 13.1, with genre labels removed.

the standards governing reception changed relatively slowly. On the other hand, if a model's accuracy does decline when it projects into its "future," we might frame questions about literary change by asking where and why it goes astray (Underwood and Sellers, 2015).

In short, supervised algorithms do not simply reproduce the categories used to train them; they can provide new leverage on a wide variety of questions— turning binary oppositions into probabilistic continua, and revealing that some boundaries are blurrier or more unstable than others. But researchers who need an even more open-ended method, less dependent on assumptions about the categories to be mapped, can turn to unsupervised learning.

4 Unsupervised learning

Instead of beginning with a set of target categories, unsupervised learning algorithms are designed to infer structure latent in the data itself (Ghahramani, 2004). This is obviously a task of great relevance to the humanities; in a sense, it is the basic interpretive problem that has always confronted researchers who encounter an unfamiliar period or cultural form. Ideally, one would like to elicit categories latent in the material, rather than imposing one's own preconceptions. The discipline of machine learning has approached this hermeneutic task with its own kind of theoretical rigor, but neither humans nor machines are capable of beginning interpretation from a completely blank slate.

The simplest example of unsupervised learning might be a clustering algorithm that organizes documents into groups using some metric of distance in an imaginary space defined by features extracted from the documents—for instance, the feature space in Figure 13.2 is defined by two variables: the number of words on each page, and the number of lines on each page that begin with a capital letter. We do not actually have to know that the pages represented in Figure 13.2 belong to classes called "prose" and "poetry." If the observations were unlabeled, we could still infer the presence of two clusters with an algorithm that locates centers of density in the space, and assigns observations to the nearest center. This approach might not precisely reproduce our intuitions about genre, but in cases where we do not have intuitions to start from, it is a valuable heuristic.

The emergence of structure from unstructured data can seem suspiciously magical, and it is important to stress that unsupervised models are still shaped by explicit interpretive assumptions. For instance, many (although not all) clustering algorithms require the researcher to specify k, the number of clusters to be produced. The validity of clustering also depends on the appropriateness of the feature set (for instance, in Figure 13.2, the decision to represent documents by counting words and capitalized lines has already loaded the dice rather heavily). Choices about distance metrics are also significant. In Figure 13.2, we have already altered straightforward Euclidean distance (which produces roughly spherical clusters) to Mahalanobis distance (which permits ellipses).

Although clustering is a simple example of unsupervised learning, clustering strategies that rely simply on the "distance" of observations from each other are rarely used in the humanities. Part of the problem is that ordinary measures of distance do not work well in high-dimensional spaces, where our intuitions about nearness and similarity are troubled by a set of paradoxes known picturesquely as the "curse of dimensionality" (Parsons, Haque and Liu, 2004). For instance, as the number of dimensions increases, it becomes more and more likely that every pair of points in a space will be roughly the same distance from each other. Applying a simple clustering algorithm (like k-means clustering) to a high-dimensional problem (say, a collection of texts where every word is a distinct variable) tends to produce a few giant unintelligible clusters, and a few outliers.

Partly for this reason, many clustering strategies are designed to reduce the dimensional complexity of a problem either before, or during the clustering process. There are a number of ad hoc ways to do this. For instance, principal component analysis can be applied to a dataset in order to compress a large number of correlated features into a smaller number of variables that retain roughly the same discriminating power (Underhill et al., 2007).

But the forms of unsupervised learning currently most prominent in the humanities (like topic modeling) take a principled rather than ad hoc approach to the problem of dimensionality. Instead of simply clustering data points (using the same measure of "distance" for every cluster), they rely on a hierarchical strategy that allows each cluster-like pattern to be associated with a different set of parameters. In a sense, multiple models are inferred simultaneously from the data. This makes intuitive sense (since different patterns may be organized by different principles), and it also reduces problems of dimensionality, because each pattern is shaped in practice by a subset of variables (not by a measure of distance that combines them all). For instance, in topic modeling, different words have different degrees of influence over different topics (Blei, Ng and Jordan, 2003).

This approach is "principled" in the sense that it is based on explicit theories about the nature of the patterns to be looked for. But this also makes unsupervised algorithms a bit more reliant on a priori assumptions than their supervised cousins. In supervised learning, human guidance is provided by labeling examples in a case-by-case way. But unsupervised learning algorithms draw equivalent guidance from a general mathematical description of the patterns we expect to find.

In topic modeling, for instance, topics are typically modeled as distributions over a vocabulary of possible words, and documents are modeled as distributions over the space of possible topics. So a "topic" is essentially a group of words that tend to occur together in a particular group of documents. The technique is open-ended, in the sense that it can find any pattern of this general form; we do not need to seed the algorithm by telling it, for instance, which words or documents we expect to be related. But it is also less flexible than a supervised model, because it will reveal only and all patterns of this general mathematical shape. In practice, topic modeling is very useful, because many interesting discursive phenomena (genres, subjects, styles) can be understood as groups of words that tend to consort with each other in the same documents. But we do not have a great deal of control over the metadata schema: there is no guarantee that the patterns revealed will turn out to be subject categories rather than, say, genres or styles (Goldstone and Underwood, 2014). Although for convenience we say that this technique models "topics," it is actually finding patterns that are defined quite simply by the mathematics of the algorithm.

Unsupervised learning can be understood as a return to something more like Leo Breiman's data modeling culture, in the sense that it tends to be strongly shaped by assumptions about the underlying generative mechanisms that are imagined to have produced the data. Instead of embodying those assumptions in specific variables, it may express them in the structure of a hierarchical model, where many parameters are being estimated at every level.

Unsupervised algorithms can be configured to search for many different kinds of patterns: they can find multiple styles of gendered expression, for instance, or model character types in fiction (Bamman, Eisenstein and Schnoebelen, 2014; Bamman, Underwood and Smith, 2014). But a set of algorithms that model loosely defined discursive patterns called "topics" have attracted most discussion so far. Topic modeling is a flexible strategy that turns out to be very useful, both as an exploratory tool and as a foundation for argument (Meeks and Weingart, 2012; Jockers, 2013, pp. 122–53; Mohr and Bogdanov, 2013; Goldstone and Underwood, 2014). It can be easier to use than supervised learning, since researchers do not need to label training examples. It is thus possible to package topic modeling as a tool that merely needs to be pointed at a collection of documents (McCallum, 2002). By contrast, supervised algorithms are better understood as a library of problem-solving resources that need to be adapted to a specific task (Pedregosa et al., 2011).

But it may be unfortunate that humanists are being introduced to unsupervised learning algorithms before supervised ones. Although unsupervised methods can be relatively easy to apply, their epistemological foundations are delicate. In particular, it can be difficult to explain how we validate an unsupervised model. In supervised learning, predictive accuracy provides a criterion of success. But there may be no ground truth for an unsupervised algorithm to predict. One can measure the model's internal consistency in various abstract ways, but domain experts have no reason to trust those measures. In practice, we may need to show that the algorithm is useful by showing that it dovetails meaningfully with the results of more familiar methods.

Humanities disciplines have skipped over several decades of debate about statistical modeling in order to borrow unsupervised learning algorithms that are particularly flexible and easy to use. This may partly explain humanists' frequently expressed concern that data-mining algorithms will be inscrutable "black boxes." Unsupervised algorithms are, as a matter of fact, a bit inscrutable: they depend on abstract assumptions that may only seem reasonable if you have used them in other contexts. I suspect topic modeling will make more sense to humanists after more of us have had a chance to experiment with supervised algorithms, which adapt flexibly to a wide range of data models, and have a clearer empirical justification.

5 Conclusion

This chapter has presented statistical models shaped by learning algorithms as a solution to a familiar humanistic problem: the suspicion that we may not yet have an appropriate way to represent our material (or that there may be more than one appropriate way to represent it). Humanists are certainly steeped in this suspicion. Historicism begins with the insight that our apparently universal categories may not provide an appropriate framework for understanding all places and periods. Critical theory often works by subjecting verbal distinctions to skeptical pressure: how solid, actually, is the boundary between "form" and "genre," or "elite" and "mass" culture? But while humanists have long been familiar with these skeptical questions, we do not have many ways of addressing them fruitfully in large collections. Since we need a map to explore the collection in the first place, circularity can be a problem.

Learning algorithms address this humanistic problem by permitting researchers to start with a relatively unstructured data model that may include hundreds or thousands of variables, each separately uninformative. The goal of algorithmic modeling is to translate that uninformative representation, provisionally, into something more meaningful. The algorithm does not guarantee objectivity: there is no neutral starting point or blank slate here. But it does provide interpretive leverage: we can start with a small number of labeled examples and explicit assumptions, and turn them into a probabilistic gradient that organizes a whole collection.

Learning algorithms are not suited to every problem. These methods rarely find much useful purchase on a single text. Nor will they usually replace traditional forms of data modeling. A topic model, for instance, becomes much easier to interpret if we can relate it to subject headings assigned by human catalogers; supervised modeling may even require manually labeled data as a starting point.

Algorithmic modeling is not, in short, an alternative to existing research practices. It is better understood as creating a new bridge between the philosophical modes of argument already common in the humanities (definition and categorization, for instance) and the looser, relational, probabilistic hypotheses explored in quantitative social science. The idea of bridging these modes of inquiry is not new. Humanists have long realized that our categories have fuzzy boundaries and change over time. But the methods that other disciplines use to study questions of degree have been inapplicable in the humanities, because our material was difficult to represent quantitatively. Algorithmic models matter for humanists above all because they address this problem: they are capacious enough to handle unstructured data, and very naturally translate categorical questions into gradients of similarity. This will allow humanists to frame questions we have long wanted to ask: how blurry are the boundaries of this genre, relative to others? How rapidly did artistic standards change in this period? Adoption of algorithmic methods may take some time, because they require a level of computational training that is not yet common in the humanities. But this is only a practical obstacle: philosophically, algorithmic modeling supports the existing aims of humanistic scholarship.

References

Algee-Hewitt, M., Heuser, R., Kraxenberger, M., Porter, J.D., Senenbaugh, J., and Tackett, J., 2014. In: The Stanford Literary Lab Transhistorical Poetry Project Phase II: Metrical Form, *Digital Humanities*, Lausanne, Switzerland, July 11, 2014. Available at: http://dharchive.org/paper/DH2014/Paper-788.xml.

Allison, S., Heuser, R., Lockers, M., Moretti, F., and Witmore, M., 2011. *Quantitative Formalism: An Experiment*. Available through: Stanford Literary Lab: http://litlab.stanford.edu/LiteraryLabPamphlet1.pdf.

Bamman, D., Eisenstein, J., and Schnoebelen, T., 2014. Gender Identity and Lexical Variation in Social Media. *Journal of Sociolinguistics*, 18(2), pp. 135–60.

Bamman, D., Underwood, T., and Smith, N., 2014. A Bayesian Mixed Effects Model of Literary Character. *ACL*. Available at: www.ark.cs.cmu.edu/literaryCharacter/.

Blei, D.M., Ng, A.M., and Jordan, M.I., 2003. Latent Dirichlet Allocation. *Journal of Machine Learning Research*, 3, pp. 993–1022.

Breiman, L., 2001. Statistical Modeling: The Two Cultures. *Statistical Science*, 16(3), 199–231.

Digman, J.M., 1990. Personality Structure: Emergence of the Five-Factor Model. *Annual Review of Psychology*, 41, pp. 417–40.

Ghahramani, Z., 2004. *Unsupervised Learning*. Available at: http://mlg.eng.cam.ac.uk/zoubin/papers/ul.pdf.

Gilens, M. and Page, B.I., 2014. Testing Theories of American Politics: Elites, Interest Groups, and Average Citizens. *Perspectives on Politics*, 12(3), pp. 564–81.

Goldstone, A. and Underwood, T., 2014. The Quiet Transformations of Literary Studies: What Thirteen Thousand Scholars Could Tell Us. *New Literary History*, 45(3), pp. 359–84.

Hastie, T., Tibshirani, R., and Friedman, J., 2009. *The Elements of Statistical Learning: Data Mining, Inference, and Prediction*. New York: Springer-Verlag.

Jockers, M., 2013. *Macroanalysis: Digital Methods and Literary History*. Urbana, IL: University of Illinois Press.

Manning, C., Raghavan, P., and Schütze, H., 2008. *Introduction to Information Retrieval*. New York: Cambridge University Press.

McCallum, A.K., 2002. MALLET: A Machine Learning for Language Toolkit. Available at: http://mallet.cs.umass.edu.

Meeks, E. and Weingart, S.B., 2012. The Digital Humanities Contribution to Topic Modeling. *Journal of Digital Humanities*, 2(1). Available at: http://journalofdigitalhumanities.org/2-1/dh-contribution-to-topic-modeling/.

Mohr, J.W. and Bogdanov, P., 2013. Introduction: Topic Models and Why They Matter. *Poetics*, 41(6), pp. 545–69.

O'Connor, Brendan, 2012. The $60,000 Cat: Deep Belief Networks Make Less Sense for Language than Vision. *AI and Social Science*, July 4. Available at: http://brenocon.com/blog/2012/07/the-60000-cat-deep-belief-networks-make-less-sense-for-language-than-vision/.

Parsons, L., Haque, E., and Liu, H., 2004. Subspace Clustering for High-Dimensional Data: A Review. *SIGKDD Explorations*, 6(1), pp. 90–105.

Pedregosa, F., et al., 2011. Scikit-learn: Machine Learning in Python. *Journal of Machine Learning Research*, 12(28), pp. 25–30.

Rabiner, L.R. and Juang, B.H., 1986. An Introduction to Hidden Markov Models. *IEEE ASSP Magazine*. January. Available at: http://ai.stanford.edu/~pabbeel/depth_qual/Rabiner_Juang_hmms.pdf (accessed September 1, 2014).

Shmuéli, G., 2010. To Explain or to Predict? *Statistical Science*, 25(3), pp. 289–310.

Underhill, D.G., McDowell, L.K., Marchette, D.J., and Solka, J.L., 2007. Enhancing Text Analysis via Dimensionality Reduction. In: *Information Reuse and Integration, 2007 IEEE International Conference on*. Las Vegas, United States of America, August 13–15. Las Vegas: IEEE.

Underwood, T., 2014. *Understanding Genre in a Collection of a Million Volumes*. Available at figshare: http://dx.doi.org/10.6084/m9.figshare.1281251.

Underwood, T. and Sellers, J., 2015. *How Quickly Do Literary Standards Change?* Available at figshare: http://dx.doi.org/10.6084/m9.figshare.1418394.

Witten, I., Frank, E., and Hall, M.A., 2011. *Data Mining: Practical Machine Learning Tools and Techniques* (3rd ed.) Amsterdam: Elsevier.

Wordsworth, W., 1800. Preface. *Lyrical Ballads, with Other Poems*. London: Longman.

14 Modeling the actual, simulating the possible[1]

Willard McCarty

1 Introduction

Pages hence I will have argued my way—our way, if you stay with me—to a point at which Elaine Scarry's road-sign provides compelling direction. She writes:

> Art, as though getting ready for an emergency, holds in steady readiness the intellectual equipment of creation in case (as seems now to be the case) there is a need to begin to look for and make recognizable the act of creating in the many other previously unacknowledged sites . . . Art is our starting place.
>
> (1992, p. 245)

But not yet. We ourselves need to get ready for it by expanding our technological focus outward, step by step, into the surrounding disciplines.

Where else to begin but with a common word? Raymond Williams began with "culture" (1983/1976, 12), I begin with "model"—not just common but infamously polysemous. Trim the rampant growth of meanings back however much you wish, the idea in this age of digital representation is everywhere. It is not merely commonplace, it is fundamental to computing, in consequence ubiquitous, hence largely unnoticed, therefore a topic of considerable importance. The previous chapters of this book and the long essay on the subject in *Humanities Computing* (2014/2005) testify to Brian Cantwell Smith's observation that nothing useful can be done with a computer otherwise. "In fact that's really what computers are (and how they differ from other machines): they run by manipulating representations, and representations are always formulated in terms of models" (1985, p. 20).

But "model" is not adequate. As mere hardware, computers do nothing at all; as abstract formulations and their translations into code, neither do computational models. It is in the manipulating, in the enacting of the encoded model by hardware, that a model becomes a way of probing the known. Thus, there are deep reasons for centering not on "model," but on the recursive *process* of exploring an idea of something by manipulating a digitally operationalized representation of it, changing that representation as results dictate, manipulating the altered representation, and so on. This process is what I mean by "modeling."

In my earlier treatment, I noted that the word is commonly used for the process of designing and building a software model, but that sense emphasizes the engineering and suggests long-term stability of its result (McCarty, 2014/2005, p. 22). My emphasis is on what the scholar sees and does in the recursion of use, rethinking and re-engineering.

I also noted earlier that Clifford Geertz's two kinds, analytic "modeling of" an existing object and synthetic "modeling for" one to be made (1993/1973, pp. 93–4), blur into each other in practice (2014/2005, p. 24). But they differ and develop differently. As I will explain, the synthetic kind is, we might say, the logical precursor of simulation, which is my focus in this chapter.

Modeling *is* fundamental to everything we do with computing. But as we own up to the genuine complexity of that which we study, we face the stark limits of analysis and so need a different approach. My purpose here is twofold. First, it is to suggest how simulation might answer to the limitations of analysis in digital humanities by recalling what earliest users of digital computing did when they faced essentially the same problem, though in very different contexts. Second, by showing what simulation has done and is doing within the sciences, I want to come up with a means of identifying the most promising of futures for digital humanities.

But when we try to say what simulation is, in particular how it differs from modeling, difficulties spring up on every side. Disentangling the two sufficiently is no easy task. Usage in the sciences does suggest that they are quite different, that modeling is analytic, simulation synthetic. Nevertheless, coming to grips with specific differences, and so clearing a space for simulation in digital humanities, is difficult. I must struggle against the infamous polysemy of "model," against the protean nature of simulation in the various disciplines where it has developed over the last 70 years, and against widespread uncertainty of what simulation might signify for and do to the humanities, in which it has received scant critical attention until recently.

From the earliest days of digital humanities, simulation has been harnessed in much maligned experiments with automated writing and in pedagogical applications, though rarely by name or with awareness of its maturity elsewhere. My project here is to bring available knowledge to bear, triangulating on something like a common meaning or tendency detectable from its very different disciplinary forms. Then I will be able to return to the question of where and how simulation parts company with modeling—how it is *new*, at least for us, why it deserves to be called by its proper name. This is not to diminish "modeling," rather to be clearer about what we mean by it.

Clarity *will* prove elusive in the end, though not for want of effort. We, inheritors of Thomas Spratt's "plain style," working in the context of computing, tend to want clear-cut techniques to speed things up, get more done. But that is not what either simulation or modeling delivers. Simulation's mutagenic powers are ways of reasoning that evolve as they travel from discipline to discipline, altering the intellectual landscape wherever they find receptive ground, co-evolving with it.

2 Continuities of reasoning and practice

Definitions of "simulation" from the early period of digital computing frequently emphasize its dynamic, generative nature, sometimes explicitly contrasting it with the static model on which it is based—hence the popular term, "simulation model" to describe a basic design before it is put "in operation" (Lehman, 1977, p. 5). Furthermore, I have suggested that simulation co-evolves with the disciplines that take it up. Thus, its spread through the sciences has led to shifts in the meanings of basic terms, including "science," in the latter half of the twentieth century, as part of greater cultural disturbances. I will argue that now the dust has settled, we can see in simulation a common ground for the sciences and the humanities where "fact" (*factum*, something made) and "fiction" (*fictio*, the act of making) delimit a continuum rather than define an opposition.

The basic meaning of "simulation" is traceable from primeval ideas of similitude, analogy and figuration (Shepard, 1997; Foucault, 1989/1996, pp. 19–28), its technical history from devices in antiquity used or specifically contrived as analogies to physical objects, their functions, processes and later the equations describing them (Canguilhem, 1963, p. 510). Unfortunately, our common division of computing machinery into analogue (whose data varies continuously) and digital (which operates by discrete steps) has by a confusion of referents for "analogue" obscured the fact that both kinds of hardware implement analogical reasoning, though in different ways (Care, 2012, p. 98). As a result, the "continuity of practice" they share has been obscured (Care, 2010, p. vii), and so our view of simulation's history blinkered.

The *Oxford English Dictionary*'s earliest entry for "simulation" in a positive sense does not help: it suggests that before the likely-seeming date of 1947 the word "invariably implied deceit" (Keller, 2003, p. 198), as it continued to do in other contexts. But a closer look reveals straightforward uses of the term in early twentieth-century descriptions of electrical circuits and of mechanics to simulate flight.[2] There can be no question that de facto simulations—Babbage notably describes one (Bullock, 2000)—go back as far as one cares to look, but positive use of the word to denote them would appear to originate near the beginning of the last century. This usage became dominant with the growth of digital computing.

Nevertheless, a redolence of deceit lingers, indeed is crucial to the total meaning of the word. Thus, RAND scientist David G. Hays remarked that "What goes on in a simulation . . . is a sham and a pretense: imaginative play" (1965/1962, p. 412). On one hand, the analogical, figurative nature of simulation makes it troublesome to believers in strict, objectivist realism, for whom it stands in much the same dubious position as figurative, poetic language. On the other hand, its technoscientific basis makes it equally disturbing to those for whom such belief is the enemy. Its dependence on skill and tacit knowledge moves it away from the theoretical to the practical, gives it the ambiguous status of an art or craft—for one ecologist "more akin to making wine than building a machine" (Peck, 2008, p. 394). Comparison to artistic practice is commonplace.

The telling point is simulation's defining moment: when it becomes the only way to know something or to form a coherent picture from fragmentary knowledge. But at that point we must ask, what kind of knowledge does the inferential bridge of simulation offer? How far can we go without it crumbling? I will return to these questions.

3 Continuity of intent

Simulation was intellectually compelling from the outset. Within the first decade of digital computing, publications grew rapidly in number and applications spread into widely diverse contexts. By the end of the 1960s, simulation had spread throughout the social sciences (Dutton and Starbuck, 1971, pp. 3–102). Today, hardly any corner of the sciences remains untouched (Gramelsberger, 2011; Winsberg, 2010; Keller, 2003).

Rapid uptake into such diverse contexts tempts us to look for a common aim or continuity of intent. I raise the question for a specific reason: if continuity could be found, it would give some indication of how those disciplines of the humanities that have not found a use for it might put simulation to innovative work. Evelyn Fox Keller cautions, however: no one taxonomy fits the variety of applications. The dilemma is this: while the "differences in aims, interests, and tradition" from discipline to discipline suggest distinct kinds of simulation, "the extensive cross-disciplinary traffic" that has characterized its history cannot be ignored (2003, p.199). She suggests following quasi-disciplinary lines of development while paying attention to the cross-talk. In the following, I heed her advice as much as limited space allows. But with an eye on the least likely humanities and the future of digital humanities in particular, I attempt two shortcuts: an argument for a continuity of simulation's effect on the sciences, at which I have already hinted, and the continuity of intent I am about to venture.

Consider to that end John von Neumann's "preoccupations with a question that might be regarded as the oldest and most fundamental of all questions about simulation, namely, how closely can a mechanical simulacrum be made to resemble an organism?" (Keller, 2003, p. 209). Among von Neumann's many distinctions, we know him as the father of Artificial Life. Since then A-Life has become an attempt to demonstrate via *in silico* simulation that "*life-as-we-know-it* [can be located] within the larger picture of *life-as-it-could be*" (Langton, 1989/1987, p. 1). But von Neumann's aim was different. In 1949, working on the cellular automata from which A-Life arose, he warned that, "By axiomatizing automata in this manner, one has thrown half of the problem out of the window, and it may be the more important half" (1966, p. 77). We know from his final set of lectures (1958) that his ultimate target was that other half, the problem of simulating the human organism in its physical totality. Elsewhere, I have argued that the implications for human self-understanding and the expressions of these in works of art and literature are central to the humanities (McCarty, 2014). So it begins to look like simulation belongs. But it is an indefatigable trouble-maker.

4 Cybernetics and nuclear weapons research

Between Turing's abstract *analogical* machine of 1936[3] and von Neumann's 1945 translation of it into a design for hardware, World War II intervened. The war-effort resulted in two research programs important here: Norbert Wiener's cybernetics and nuclear weapons development.

Wiener named cybernetics after the Greek word for "steersman" (*kubernētēs*), whose intimate relationship with the tiller of a boat provides a telling metaphor of its aims (Wiener, 1961/1948). Cybernetics began in efforts to improve anti-aircraft artillery during World War II by integrating human with machine (Galison, 1994; Mindell, 2002). It succeeded, but it also resulted in a comprehensive theoretical vision, which for a time seemed to promise a universal science. Cybernetics did far more than is usually remembered: it had deep and long-lasting influence, bringing together common interests in the medical, social, psychological and physical sciences toward an integrative view of the human (Dupuy, 2009/1994; Heims, 1991). It provided a home for attention to kinaesthetic and cognitive human-machine integration, which surfaced later in the work of J.C.R. Licklider (who attended the Macy Conferences on cybernetics), Douglas Engelbart and others, in the fields of robotics, human-computer interaction and user-interface design. But I am getting ahead of myself.

Nuclear weapons development figures here for two reasons. First, digital simulation started there and proved itself to be a practical medium. The thermo-nuclear bomb would otherwise not have been possible. Second, in making the bomb, real simulation led directly to circumstances so unprecedented and otherwise unknowable in their outcome that military and civilian planners had to turn to simulation as the sole way of knowing how to plan for a probable, hauntingly immediate, terrifying future—and so to understand the world they and everyone else were in (Freedman, 2013, pp. 148–9). Simulation showed itself to be a means of realizing the imagined and imagining the real. With such traffic between the one and the other, can we be surprised that leading intellectuals of the time engaged in widespread questioning of what it meant to be rational (Erickson et al., 2013)?

During the research on the atomic bomb and then on the thermonuclear "Super," so much was unknown, yet by military and political imperatives had to be known that action could not be stalled for want of theory. The urgent need to make something that worked without knowing precisely how it might be done transformed the practical work of engineers and ordnance experts on the one side and the theoretical research of physical scientists and mathematicians on the other. Thus came about

> a mode of inquiry to address problems too complex for theory and too remote from laboratory materials for experiment. Christened "Monte Carlo" after the gambling mecca, the method amounted to the use of random numbers (*à la* roulette) to simulate the stochastic processes too complex to calculate in full analytic glory.
>
> (Galison, 1996, pp. 119f.)

Von Neumann was brought in to help with the practical, theoretically messy problems in continuum dynamics such as the behavior of shock-waves, flows of intense energy and other phenomena "too far from the course of ordinary terrestrial experience to be grasped immediately or easily" (Hawkins, 1946, p. 76; Aspray, 1990). Hence, the instrumental innovation required. Monte Carlo simulation thrived, first as a means of advancing the design and refinement of the atomic bomb in concert with laboratory experiments, then with the Super as the reality to be studied. Here we see a decisive shift: "bit by bit (byte by byte), computer designers deconstructed the notion of a tool itself as the computer came to stand not for a tool, but for nature" (Galison, 1996, p. 157; 1997, p. 777).

Let me underscore three things: that shift from tool to nature; the extension of the graspable by means of computationally imagined scenarios; and the Cold War culture of the Super, which simulation made possible. These three converge in a practical epistemology shared, for example, by military strategist Herman Kahn in *On Thermonuclear War* (2007/1960), by environmentalist Donella Meadows and others in *Limits to Growth: A Report for the Club of Rome's Project on the Predicament of Mankind* (1972) and, bridging them in his involvements on both sides, by systems scientist Jay Forrester in *World Dynamics* (1973/1971). What united these very different people and their very different communities of belief was the conviction that global knowledge is simultaneously an absolute imperative and something acquired only by simulating an otherwise "unobtainable referent" (Ghamari-Tabrizi, 2000, p. 163). For Kahn, this referent was the future of warfare; for Meadows, the future of the world's livelihood; for Forrester, the future of organizational systems; for everyone, simply the future.

Kahn argued likewise: all manner of fantasies had to be worked through *very* quickly (2007/1960, p. 125). A new language in which to conceive a practical response to an unprecedented military situation was needed. This the first postwar US defense planners seem to have found in Wiener's *Cybernetics*. In the final report to the Scientific Advisory Committee of the Air Force in October 1950, the Air Defense Systems Engineering Committee (ADSEC) proposed *in these terms*, more than a decade before "cyborg" (Clynes and Kline, 1960, p. 27), a hybrid "organism" with coordinated animate and inanimate components: in effect, a great military anthropomorph comprised of men, mechanical "effectors" analogous to human sensory organs and the communications apparatus or artificial "nervous system" that would connect them (ADSEC, 1950, pp. 2ff.). (Anyone of television-watching age in the late 1980s within range of *Star Trek* will likely think immediately of the Borg.) ADSEC's report was taken seriously, adopted immediately and acted on. From its imaginings evolved in time, the Semi-Automatic Ground Environment (SAGE), "an integrated information and control system on a continental scale" with which Forrester was intimately involved (Edwards, 2000, p. 230; Redmond and Smith, 2000). SAGE in turn led to various forms of "a world-encompassing surveillance, communication and control system" (Edwards, 2000, p. 230), including Ronald Reagan's Strategic Defense Initiative, or "Star Wars." "The President's proposal did not seem bizarre to a public used to science fiction and conditioned by long exposure to Buck Rogers, Star Trek, and Darth Vader to regard outer space as a natural environment for war and counterwar," George Ball commented in the *New York Review of Books*. "The President had told us that the Soviet Union is an 'evil empire' and he was now warning America that the 'empire' might 'strike back'" (Ball, 1985).

Thus, a real world and the simulated one blurred into each other.

5 Climatology

Paul Edwards asks a crucial question: "How did 'the world' become a system?" (2000, p. 221). He draws attention to the close parallel between SAGE and early climate modeling: both had to know the world globally and both to devise solutions for the problems of data-gathering and interpretation (2000, p. 230). Both turned to and developed large-scale computing equipment on which the necessary simulations could be run. Both were indebted to nuclear weapons research.

First efforts in climate modeling *c.* 1949–50 sprang from von Neumann's insight that the nonlinear hydrodynamics of the climate would provide "a crucial test" of the digital machine's potential for scientific research (Aspray, 1990, p. 121). Rapid progress followed: by the 1960s, circulation of the Earth's atmosphere was being simulated, and by the end of that decade "global, three-dimensional climate models had emerged as the central tool of climate science" (Edwards, 2000, p. 234). But "as meteorologists sought to model the entire globe," the lack of uniform, reliable data became the problem. Hence, the computer "now also became a tool for refining, correcting, and shaping data to fit the models' needs" (Edwards, 2000, p. 229). Again, tool blurred into nature. Likewise, in current oceanographic, ecological, agricultural and other global sciences with ambitions beyond ordinary reach the debates quickly became to a large degree "*about* the model/data relationship" (Edwards, 1999, p. 439). Then, too, the models were and are themselves highly interpretative, employing differing techniques, influenced by differing scientific and political agendas, and aimed more at sensitivity to variable human activity and its consequences than non-human phenomena (Dalmedico, 2007). The emergence of the term "scenario" in climatology and other sciences affected by simulation tells the tale: of movement from the theory-like model that converges on and formalizes a singular, agreed-upon understanding of an objective world to narratives expressing the modelers' assumptions, interests and agendas. In consequence, "a different conception of the nature of scientific work" is required (Edwards 1999, p. 439; Galison, 1997, p. 778).

How differently must we conceive the science? Ian Hacking's argument about microscopy (1983, pp. 186–209) suggests to me that simulation does not so much provoke a new epistemological question as rewrite an old one: in what sense do we know when we look by means of a simulation? I will return to this question.

People turn to simulation when direct knowledge of something is blocked by matters of scale or accessibility: in the amount or complexity of the data to be considered, the size of the phenomenon to be known, its distance in time or space, its unfamiliarity or its ethical prohibition. At one end of the realist's scale, a simulation is *of* something relatively near at hand and so at least comparable—for example, how people vote in an election; further away, it is *of* something the reality of which we are persuaded but cannot see, such as interactions at the core of the sun; at the far end it becomes an medium for imaginative projections and their exploration, or as Daniel Dennett has said of Artificial Life, "the creation of prosthetically controlled thought experiments of indefinite complexity" (1998, p. 261).

The idea of complexity, which I have postponed dealing with until now, is important here because it sharpens our grasp of what can be known through simulation. Complexity is a fundamental characteristic of a system in Robert Jervis's sense: an entity made up of interconnected parts that affect each other and that "exhibits properties and behaviors that are different from those of the parts." No ghostly component is needed: a system, he emphasizes, is *"different from*, not *greater than*, the sum of the parts" (1997, pp. 6, 12–13). Examples are common enough—for example water (hydrogen plus oxygen, both gases) and table salt (sodium plus chloride, both toxic). As these suggest the properties and behaviors of a system are from the perspective of those parts *new* and *surprising*; they cannot be derived or inferred from the parts individually because these properties and behaviors are a result of the structural organization of the system. As the number of interconnections in the system increases, so does its complexity. Beyond a certain threshold (again, the matter of scale) a system is thus knowable only in performance. Hence a complex simulation, built from just such interoperable components of code, is necessarily a "black box." How a complex simulation does what it does cannot be verified in detail, and so at its verisimilar best it parallels the object of study, arriving at resemblance (if that can be seen) by a different route that is unknowable move for move. As a modeling device, it invites experiment but weakens analogies between the artificial process and its target's processes, and so weakens the claim of the former to truthfulness, or requires a different conception of being truthful (Hacking, 2005).

6 Biology

What does the dominant science of the twenty-first century and quite possibly the most powerful disciplinary influence of all tell us about simulation? Biologists' uses of simulation to probe entities like us, not merely complex but also adaptive, self-organizing, self-replicating and *alive*, promise closer, or at least usefully different, analogies to simulation on a human scale than the sciences I have considered to this point. The refusal in experimental or field practices to identify theorizing with abstract laws (Keller, 1998, p. S76) makes biology a closer relation to a computationally experimental humanities. Furthermore biology raises the bar by focusing on entities that become "by a rather mysterious process of self-organization . . . more ordered and more informed" than physical law suggests that they should be (Cowan, Pines and Meltzer, 1994, p. 1).

From the nineteenth century to the present time, "the Riddle of the Universe" (as Benjamin Gruenberg called the phenomenon of life in 1911) has been pursued in two directions: first, from the assumption that life could be explained by reduction to physics and chemistry, "to make live matter out of the non-living materials lying all about us," that is, "an artificial system or 'machine' which behaves more or less like a living body;" and second, to create new life artificially from living tissue (1911a, p. 231; 1911b, p. 272). Simulation has been applied to both from the last quarter of the twentieth century and in both shows the same tendency to erode distinctions, formerly thought secure, between living and non-living.

Keller cites Sigmund Freud's work on the uncanny to gloss the admiration and wonder elicited in Gruenberg's time by biologist Stéphane Leduc, who attempted "synthetic biology" and "artificial life" (his terms) by fashioning inorganic materials so that they moved and seemed to grow (Keller 2002, pp. 11–49). Deceitful simulation, yes, but, she argues, "a positive virtue, not a negative one: it made possible that 'willing suspension of disbelief' that permits uncertainty to remain out of focus, that allows the 'as if' to do the remarkable work it has so often done in the past" (2002, p. 49). She quotes James Clerk Maxwell from the heartland of the factual on the usefulness of ideas known not to be true. Roboticist Masahiro Mori, whom she quotes elsewhere, makes a different though related point with his now popular idea of the "uncanny valley": that the uncertainty created by resemblance which does not quite replicate, though it frightens us and so is to be avoided in designing robots, nevertheless promises understanding of "what makes us human" (Mori, 2012/1970, p. 100; Kageki, 2012). But, I have argued elsewhere, this promise comes at a cost: the gap (or valley) between close resemblance and what as a result of it becomes an *inhuman* difference foregrounds uncertainty of a most disturbing kind (McCarty, 2014). Thus biology's basic question—What is life?—becomes existentially fearful.

At the first workshop on A-Life at Los Alamos—the place of the Bomb—in 1987, Christopher Langton shifted the old question of how organic life arose out of inorganic elements to "how lifelike behaviors emerge out of low-level interactions within a population of logical primitives" (Langton, 1989/1987, p. 15). The persuasiveness of Langton's efforts to answer that question, Keller notes, stems from the uncertainty they evoke about their authenticity: "Might not nature, at its most fundamental, really be constituted of cellular automata?" (2005, p. 209). Thus, slippage from hard but comfortable reality into soft but disturbing simulation, as before. However, Langton's "life-as-it-could-be" also runs back to "life-as-we-know-it," and stirs biologists to take up Gruenberg's second direction of research, into creation of new life, then new kinds of life, from biological materials. Keller notes further slippage in the appeal of DIY life to those "who have themselves spent a significant proportion of their real lives inhabiting virtual worlds—as it were, coming of age in cyberspace" (2002, p. 276). The slippage continues in the blurring of analogies into realities— algorithm to genome, program code to body (Hayles, 1996)—and in Thomas Ray's return back from *in silico* simulations to organic life as a model (Ray, 1998). "Life moves out of the domain of the given into the contingent, into quotation marks, appearing not as a thing-in-itself but as something in the making in discourse and practice . . . a shadow of the biological and social theories meant to capture it" (Helmreich, 2011, p. 674).

"Without doubt," Keller comments, "these entities are real. But another question immediately arises: are they 'alive'? This is a question that worries many philosophers, but . . . it may well be a question that belongs more properly in the realm of history than in that of philosophy" (2003, p. 213). Thus, Helmreich's "What was life?" (2011).

If we come to regard these things as alive, then we find ourselves alongside Dr. Frankenstein and so find ourselves with the question of the human. This is why the biological example is so important. We may contemplate with curious equanimity the blurring of many boundaries—it is the fashion now, is it not?—but the boundary between human and non-human is not one so easy to be calm about. And this brings simulation properly into the humanities. Simulation is "just a tool" if all it does is to produce more compelling representations or mechanical simulacra that generate objects of study from simple rules to a surprising degree of fidelity. It is of the humanities when it becomes a tool for raising the questions humans ask about human things and for bringing forth "the alternativeness of human possibility" (Bruner, 1986, p. 53).

7 The interpretative disciplines

Within the last half-dozen years, simulation has begun to receive widespread attention in the humanities, though it is hardly new to these disciplines. By the mid 1980s, when Robert Tannenbaum included it in his taxonomy of basic techniques for the humanities and social sciences (1987a, 1987b), work had been in progress in several fields for a quarter century (Lancashire and McCarty, 1988; Hymes, 1965). In history, the first applications were on the social scientific side of the discipline, in demographic, economic and geographical projects. In addition to yielding new knowledge of their subjects, these contributed methodologically by emphasizing the counterfactual qualities of simulation (Plakans, 1980, p. 140). The alternative-world, as-if status thus underscored made simulations attractive for the classroom (Oakman, 1987; Lancashire and McCarty, 1988), where counterfactual explorations could be enacted without fear of conservative scholarly disapproval.

Surprisingly, perhaps, the earliest simulations in the humanities themselves were of poetry-writing, not of phenomena studied for their law-like behavior, such as language—for example, by Kirby (2013), or Kretzschmar and Juuso (2013). Like the social sciences, the first efforts in poetry generation date to the late 1950s, followed by simulations of folktales and short fiction (Lancashire and McCarty, 1988, p. 2). From that time, experiments with poetry went on to chart an almost unbroken chronology, intermixed with experiments in the arts, into this century (Funkhouser, 2007 and 2012). In 1964, pioneer computational linguist and philosopher Margaret Masterman noted the serious purpose of such work, "to throw light both on the habits of language users and on the nature of conceptual thought itself" (1964, p. 690). But, like other seriously playful efforts in computing, hers proved controversial. F.R. Leavis's outrage at the thought "That any cultivated person should *want* to believe that a computer can write a poem!" (1970, p. 442) and Howard Nemerov's gloomy warning of a mind "simplified (and brutalized) . . . in obeisance to its idol the [behavioristic] machine" (1967, p. 414), register the significance of such work (cf. Drucker, 2009, p. xix), though unraveling that significance is itself a major undertaking.

It may seem odd, then, that Tannenbaum's "Matrix of Applications and Disciplines" records a blank for simulation in literary studies (1987b, pp. 221–2). Simple oversight seems unlikely. I would like to read this blank as the response of someone who, noticing (as he must have) the stalemate repeatedly attested in literary computing from the early 1960s onward, found nothing much to report. In 1976, two years before Susan Wittig argued that text-analysis was theoretically bankrupt (Wittig, 1978), William Benzon and David Hays took up the question of what a theory adequate to the intersection of computing and literature might look like. "Man is self-aware," they wrote. "Consequently, it seems likely that any attempt to develop a computable model of literary texts will have to include a simulation of self-awareness if it aspires to deep results" (1976, p. 267). Are we, then, stuck waiting for adequate artificial intelligence? I will come back to this question.

It seems safe to infer—for example, from the release of *The Matrix* in 1999 and Jean Baudrillard's work on simulation (a must-read from the early 1980s), that by the beginning of this century scholars were familiar with the term, even if it was not widely understood in practice (Ryan, 2001). Since then, the relevant techniques and equipment have grown in speed, flexibility and intelligence, and dramatically shrunk in cost. Now they are within reach attractively for immersive enactment and study of whatever can be visualized.

The most popular simulations in the interpretative disciplines today are of groups or societies of people represented as autonomous agents populating a complex system—thus, "agent-based modeling" (Troitzsch, 2009). Unsurprisingly, these simulations avoid the unique, particular and inconsistent phenomena of human life so as to be able to reduce social behavior to the actions of algorithmic agents. Surprisingly, agent-based modeling from simple rules has proven quite effective at that level of generality, matching the regularities we observe in real societies—thus, Joshua Epstein's "generative social science" (1999). Such work dates from Thomas Schelling's classic papers on race-relations (1969–1978), in which he used a simple model to suggest that quite color-blind preferences could result in segregated neighborhoods (Epstein and Axtell, 1996, p. 3). The best known social generative simulation is of the Anasazi or Ancient Pueblo people, who simply vanished for no apparent reason from their ancestral homeland *c*. twelfth–thirteenth centuries CE (Axtell et al., 2002; Janssen, 2009). Based on all available evidence, the simulation closely matches the growth and partial decline of the Anasazi until their sudden disappearance, but suggests no reason why the civilization vanished: environmental evidence implies that they could have continued. Thus, explanation from purely environmental causes is ruled out. But a tantalizing puzzle remains: did failure occur precisely at the point at which something other than such causes intervened—something, such as a shared crisis of the mind or spirit, that left no computationally tractable data behind?

Grüne-Yanoff convincingly argues that the problem with such work in the social sciences is that a simulation can only be said to explain something in the full sense if its model can be validated; his example is an automobile crash, for which the physical principles and equations are known (2009). In circumstances for which well-confirmed laws are unavailable, a simulation can at best aspire to "articulating the ways in which a phenomenon *could* possibly have been produced" (2009, p. 546, my emphasis). The less law-like a domain is taken to be, the more a simulation reveals not actualities but possibilities.

So far, simulation in the humanities has been a minority pursuit, despite affordances for imaginative exploration and play. There are likely several reasons for this, including mismatches of knowledge, skills and understanding on both sides of the technical divide. A crucial reason—indeed, the one that motivates this essay—is the misunderstanding of what simulation is for, or, more carefully stated, insufficient attention to how its protean capabilities and the disciplines that adopt it adapt to each other. I have argued that the history of simulation in the sciences and the subsequent effects it has had there demonstrate clearly enough a strong tendency away from the known toward the imagined unknown, even the otherwise unknowable. In the sciences, simulation has tended to start, as Elaine Scarry says, with the "made-up" but to finish with the "made-real" (1992). What happens, what could happen in the humanities?

The most likely places to look for plausible simulations are in the historical disciplines. In a recent study, Marten Düring draws on simulations of the Battle of Trafalgar, a Canadian influenza epidemic and the Anasazi to illustrate how the technique is being used in history (2014). His examples show simulation not deployed to explain, as in generative social science, but to test hypotheses and rule out competing explanations. The biggest challenge, he notes, is the degree to which (significantly not whether) historical events can be reduced to rule-based behavior. With Epstein, he observes that it is precisely the struggle with rules that tends to yield the most important insights, not subsequent work with the simulation. Could this amount to the difference between close engagement and distant observation? (Remember this possibility; I will return to it.)

The range and number of the historical simulations we have are also impeded by resistance within history to counterfactual research—a disciplinary problem but one that implicitly recognizes the fictive trajectory of simulation, away from history as usually conceived. It is difficult not to conclude that little has changed fundamentally since those early social-scientific applications in history. "The use of simulation modelling in history and archaeology is still regarded as something of a 'dark art' in many quarters," Stuart Dunn comments in a recent review (2012).

Düring finds no current historical simulation that allows both collective and deviant individual behavior in its model. That fact, if it is one, leads to his most telling point (and recalls Benzon's and Hays's challenge from 1976), which he makes by quoting archaeologist Jim Doran's observation of a "deep difficulty," which in turn suggests a very different response of the social sciences to simulation:

> Distinctive human social structures and social processes emerge from distinctive human cognition. But we do not yet know how to model human cognition on a computer in other than relatively superficial and oversimplified ways. Thus we cannot yet experiment with the models that really matter: those that capture more than simple routine cognitive behavior. Archaeology faces this challenge as do all the social sciences.
>
> (Düring, 2014, p. 133)

Again, the question of artificial intelligence. What is to be done?

8 From the actual to the possible

Before going further, from history into literary studies, let me sum up by returning to a question I raised at the beginning: what is the difference between modeling and simulation? I turn again to the words and to the meanings we make with them. "Modeling" literally insists on "model"—that is, on a representation which however unachievably true and inescapably false is always in mind. Anthony Giddens's description of modernity—the condition of "going on being" in which moment by moment we *do* everyday life, selecting, revising and discarding as we go the lifestyles available to us (1991)—suggests that we find irresistible the pull of "modeling" toward thoughts of an ideal form. Thus, in grammatical terms "modeling" is indicative. Simulation, on the other hand, is subjunctive. It also proceeds from a model; it also can be and is used to approximate an unreachable truth, but (again literally) it insists at root on alternatives to the truth—true lies, if you will. Such alternatives, if they are to be true to simulation's dual character, must preserve the "as-if"—the willing *suspension* of disbelief, not its dismissal. Modeling does not tend toward alternative worlds. It is a struggle with the model ever better to construe the modeled.

Virtual reconstructions of archaeological and historical sites are germane to the distinction I am making and help qualify it. Almost all of such reconstructions take simulation in a different direction than I have been describing, toward the visualized model. These unsurprisingly fit the interests of their disciplines: to make an absent part of the historical world digitally present—best not "as if that which returned were the same" but with conjectural elements marked and documented.[4] These reconstructions move closer to simulation in my sense with the introduction of avatars displaying verisimilar behaviors and appearance, closer yet with the introduction of an avatar controllable by the participant-observer (Bogdanovych, Ijaz, and Simoff, 2012). I will return very briefly to simulations of this kind at the end.

For literary studies, Edward Versluis wrote thirty years ago, the problem is to describe "the dynamic structures we associate with literature," expressing them "in very explicit terms" (1984, p. 230). Simulation, we expect, would operationalize these structures. How? Sack, for example, has described a generative simulation of narrative (2011) in broadly the same vein as earlier experiments in poetry-generation. I want to focus, however, on participant-observer simulation of literature.

Versluis pointed to the "emotionally rich thinking experience" of game-playing (1984, p. 225) and to Joseph Weizenbaum's psychoanalytic simulation *Eliza*, with its striking ability to induce "powerful delusional thinking," as Weizenbaum wrote (1976, p. 7). Versluis rejected Weizenbaum's worry, imagining instead an *Eliza* reconfigured in the service of teaching and research, delusion reconceived as imaginative fantasy exercised in order to elicit and make real Bruner's alternativeness. But note: *Eliza*'s quite surprising power was not the result of sophisticated artificial intelligence, rather the product of a *non-autonomous, cooperative human-machine simulation*. It was a trick but also a clue to what could be done in much less constricted settings, were the artificial intelligence to be devised.

A similar set of ideas about computer-human cooperation underlies experiments like Jerome McGann's *Ivanhoe Game*, in which human players make algorithmic changes to a shared text as a way of exploring the effects of those changes on the literary ecology of that text (McGann, 2014, pp. 100–1; Drucker, 2009, pp. 65–97). The game thus teasingly suggests what could be done cooperatively with a machine capable of adapting to other players' moves. Note the term "player," which suggests not merely connection with gaming, but also *Ivanhoe*'s strategy of "serious play." In such play, the imaginative material on which it focuses—"fictional, counterfactual, hypothetical, heterocosmic"—functions with the force of as-if to keep players "*very* seriously" both unattached and committed to the game (Berger, 1988/1969, pp. 74–80; 1972, pp. 261–5; Wind, 1968/1958, pp. 222ff.). This is simulation achievable in every sense with the technology we have, though with better computer science it could go much further, as I will suggest.

There are other ways of thinking about these examples, other preliminary sketches with which to inspire our infant computer sciences—for example, as creative staging of improvisational performance (Laurel, 2014); as dynamically unfolding conversation (Soules, 2002; McCarty, 2013)—a common metaphor among jazz musicians; as ritual; and as resonance (Erlman, 2010). I must leave it at that for now: a clue, just as it is in Mori's thoughts on the uncanny valley and Keller's on Freud, pointing to the inescapable non-autonomous embodied (and so aesthetically present) other of simulation.

Where does this leave us? I will answer that question with a single project chosen for the clarity with which it poses the core dilemma of simulation: literary scholar John Wall's *Virtual Paul's Cross* (2016). This simulation digitally re-creates the poet and divine John Donne's sermon at the Paul's Cross preaching station in London on November 5, 1622, which celebrated the failure of a plot to blow up the British Parliament with James I inside it. As it stands, it is, like other historical reconstructions, more a visual model than a simulation in my sense. But it points a way forward.

We begin with facts mixed uncertainly with uncertainties. The title-page of the printed edition is sole evidence, published years after Donne's death, that contrary to normal practice, the sermon took place inside the Cathedral because of rain. The simulation locates it outside where Donne would have planned it to happen and where the drama of improvisational performance for which he was noted would have been more in demand to hold listeners' attention against the distractions of an outdoor gathering—the freer social interactions, the dogs, horses and the many unsynchronized bells of nearby churches, not just St Paul's, ringing cumulatively on the quarter-hour. The text itself is a poor thing, without the drama. We know that Donne spoke from notes, writing out the text some time later. As for the solid stones, timbers, plaster, tiles, metal and glass, Paul's Cross and the Gothic Cathedral beside it perished in the Great Fire of 1666. Four centuries of social change and urban development far less reverent of the past than we are have intervened.

I said that *Paul's Cross* and other reconstructions are not quite simulations. But they become much more so once we understand that the kinds of conjectures that they offer us must be understood in the context of "simulation": the kind of counterfactuality or misleadingness deployed here must be understood (in Keller's terms) as "a positive virtue, not a negative one," as would be to an historical positivist. The hermeneutic of suspicion and critical awareness that such simulations call forth can also be understood from a different perspective as a kind of intellectual bravery.

In its current state, *Paul's Cross* is an experiential, *Eliza*-like simulation—cooperative, in resonance between scholar and tool—only for the maker, over whose shoulder the rest of us must look and listen. The next step is to bring us onlookers inside the modeler's head. Technically, that will take significant advances in immersive, participatory VR, but that alone is not enough. It will also take intimate collaboration between computer science and literary studies.

We are left, then, not just with big ideas but with big questions and projects, concerning the roles these two fundamental things you can do with a computer—modeling and simulating—play or are to play in our practices of enquiry, how we are to become self-aware practitioners of them and how they change these practices *and are changed by them*. "[T]he use of computers," Fr Roberto Busa wrote in 1976, "is not aimed towards less human effort, or for doing things faster and with less labor, but for more human work, more mental effort" (1976, p. 3). The question is, to what is that effort directed? Not, as modeling and simulating both make clear, what the bereaved call "closure" but (once again) Bruner's "alternativeness of human possibility," William Blake's "expanding eyes." Simulation returns us to Aristotle's function of poetry (*Poetics*, 1451b), to describe not the thing that has happened (*genómena*) but a kind of thing that might happen (*génoito*), something more philosophical and worthy of serious attention, he thought, even than history.

Notes

1   I am deeply indebted to the editors, especially to Julia Flanders, for the immense patience, intelligent resistance, helpful suggestions and even, in two places, wording that said what I wanted to say but couldn't.
2   Early uses of "simulation" in circuitry are attested by journals in the IEEE Xplore Digital Library; in aeronautics by the US Patent and Trademark Office patent database. Available at: www.uspto.gov.
3   "Turing's 'Machines'. These are *humans* who calculate." Wittgenstein, 1980, p. 191e.
4   Derrida, 1996, p. 182. Note the recommendations of the London Charter, especially 4.6 and 4.10. Available at: www.londoncharter.org (June 3, 2018).

References

ADSEC (Air Defense Systems Engineering Committee), 1950. *Final Report of the Air Defense Systems Engineering Committee, 24 October 1950.* Available at: https://archive. org/details/ADSECFinalReport24October1950.

Aspray, W., 1990. *John von Neumann and the Origins of Modern Computing.* Cambridge, MA: MIT Press.

Axtell, R.L., Epstein, J.M., Dean, J.S., Gumerman, G.J., Swedlund, A.C., Harburger, J., Chakravarty, S., Hammond, R., Parker, J., and Parker, M., 2002. Population Growth and Collapse in a Multiagent Model of the Kayenta Anasazi in Long House Valley. *Proceedings of the National Academy of Sciences,* 99(3), pp. 7275–9.

Ball, G.W., 1985. The War for Star Wars. *New York Review of Books,* 32(6).

Benzon, W. and Hays, D.G., 1976. Computational Linguistics and the Humanist. *Computers and the Humanities,* 10(5), pp. 265–74.

Berger, H., Jr., 1969. Pico and Neoplatonist Idealism: Philosophy as Escape. *The Centennial Review,* 13(1), pp. 38–83.

Berger, H., Jr., 1972. Conspicuous Exclusion in Vermeer: An Essay in Renaissance Pastoral. *Yale French Studies,* 47, pp. 243–65.

Bogdanovych, A., Ijaz, K., and Simoff, S., 2012. The City of Uruk: Teaching Ancient History in a Virtual World. In: Y. Nakano, M. Neff, A. Paiva, and M. Walker (Eds.) *Intelligent Virtual Agents. Proceedings of the 12th International Conference, IVA 2012, Santa Cruz, CA, USA, September 2012.* LNAI 7502. Heidelberg: Springer-Verlag.

Bruner, J., 1986. *Actual Minds, Possible Worlds.* Cambridge MA: Harvard University Press.

Bullock, S., 2000. What Can We Learn from the First Evolutionary Simulation Model? In: M.A. Bedau, J.S. McCaskill, N.H. Packard, and S. Rasmussen (Eds.) 2000. *Artificial Life VII. Proceedings of the Seventh International Conference on Artificial Life.* Cambridge MA: MIT Press, pp. 477–86.

Busa, R., SJ, 1976. Why Can a Computer Do so Little? *Bulletin of the Association for Literary and Linguistic Computing,* 4(1), pp. 1–3.

Canguilhem, G., 1963. The Role of Analogies and Models in Biological Discovery. In: A.C. Crombie (Ed.) 1963. *Scientific Change: Historical Studies in the Intellectual, Social, and Technical Conditions for Scientific Discovery and Technical Invention, from Antiquity to the Present.* London: Heinemann. pp. 507–20.

Cantwell Smith, B., 1985. The Limits of Correctness. *ACM SIGCAS Computers and Society* 14–15.1–4: 18–26.

Care, C., 2010. *Technology for Modelling: Electrical Analogies, Engineering Practice, and the Development of Analogue Computing.* Dordrecht: Springer-Verlag.

Care, C., 2012. Early Computational Modelling: Physical Models, Electrical Analogies and Analogue Computers. In: C. Bissell and C. Dillon (Eds.) *Ways of Thinking, Ways of Seeing: Mathematical and other Modelling in Engineering and Technology*. Berlin: Springer-Verlag, pp. 95–119.

Clynes, M.E. and Kline, N.S., 1960. Cyborgs and Space. *Astronautics* (September), pp. 26–7, 74–6.

Cowan, G.A., Pines, D., and Meltzer, D., 1994. *Complexity: Metaphors, Models, and Reality*. Bolder, CO: Westview Press.

Dalmedico, A.D., 2007. Models and Simulations in Climate Change: Historical, Epistemological, Anthropological, and Political Aspects. In: A.N. Creager, E. Lunbeck, and M.N. Wise (Eds.) *Science without Laws: Model Systems, Cases, Exemplary Narratives*. Durham, NC: Duke University Press, pp. 125–56.

Dennett, D., 1998. Artificial Life as Philosophy. In: D. Dennett (Ed.) *Brainchildren: Essays on Designing Minds*. Cambridge MA: MIT Press, pp. 261–3.

Derrida, J. 1996. By Force of Mourning. Trans. Pascale-Anne Brault and Michael Naas. *Critical Inquiry* 22.2, pp. 171–92.

Drucker, J., 2009. *Digital Aesthetics and Projects in Speculative Computing*. Chicago: University of Chicago Press.

Dunn, S., 2012. Review of ORBIS. *Journal of Digital Humanities*, 1(3). Available at: http://journalofdigitalhumanities.org/.

Dupy, J.-P., 1994. *On the Origins of Cognitive Science: The Mechanization of the Mind*. Translated by M.B. DeBevoise, 2009. Cambridge, MA: MIT Press.

Düring, M., 2014. The Potential of Agent-Based Modelling for Historical Research. In: P.A. Youngman and M. Hadzikadic (Eds.) 2014. *Complexity and the Human Experience: Modeling Complexity in the Humanities and Social Sciences*. Boca Raton, FL: Pan Stanford Publishing, pp. 121–37.

Dutton, J.M. and Starbuck, W.H., 1971. *Computer Simulation of Human Behavior*. New York: John Wiley & Sons.

Edwards, P.N., 1999. Global Climate Science, Uncertainty and Politics: Data-laden Models, Model-filtered Data. *Science as Culture*, 8(4), pp. 437–72.

Edwards, P.N., 2000. The World in a Machine: Origins and Impacts of Early Computerized Global Systems Models. In: T.P. Hughes and A.C. Hughes (Eds.) 2000. *Systems, Experts, and Computers: The Systems Approach in Management and Engineering, World War II and After*. Cambridge, MA: MIT Press, pp. 221–54.

Epstein, J.M., 1999. Agent-Based Computational Models and Generative Social Science. *Complexity*, 4(5), pp. 41–60.

Epstein, J.M. and Axtell, R., 1996. *Growing Artificial Societies: Social Science from the Bottom Up*. Washington, DC: The Brookings Institution.

Erickson, P., Klein, J.L., Daston, L., Lemov, R., Sturm, T., and Gordin, M.D., 2013. *How Reason Almost Lost its Mind: The Strange Career of Cold War Rationality*. Chicago: University of Chicago Press.

Erlmann, V., 2010. *Reason and Resonance: A History of Modern Aurality*. New York: Zone Books.

Forrester, J.W., 1973. *World Dynamics* (2nd ed.). Cambridge MA: Wright-Allen Press.

Foucault, M., 1966. *The Order of Things: An Archaeology of the Human Sciences*. Trans. 1989. London: Routledge.

Freedman, L., 2013. *Strategy: A History*. Oxford: Oxford University Press.

Funkhouser, C.T., 2007. *Prehistoric Digital Poetry: An Archaeology of Forms, 1959–1995*. Tuscaloosa, AB: University of Alabama Press.

Funkhouser, C.T., 2012. First-Generation Poetry Generators. In: H.B. Higgins and D. Kahn (Eds.) 2012. *Mainframe Experimentalism: Early Computing and the Foundations of the Digital Arts*. Berkeley, CA: University of California Press, pp. 243–65.

Galison, P., 1994. The Ontology of the Enemy: Norbert Wiener and the Cybernetic Vision. *Critical Inquiry*, 21(1), pp. 228–66.

Galison, P., 1996. Computer Simulations and the Trading Zone. In: P. Galison and D.J. Stump (Eds.). *The Disunity of Science: Boundaries, Contexts, and Power*. Stanford, CA: Stanford University Press, pp. 118–57.

Galison, P., 1997. *Image and Logic: A Material Culture of Microphysics*. Chicago: University of Chicago Press.

Geertz, C., 1993/1973. *Interpretation of cultures: Selected essays*. London: Fontana Press.

Ghamari-Tabrizi, S., 2000. Simulating the Unthinkable: Gaming Future War in the 1950s and 1960s. *Social Studies of Science*, 30(2), pp. 163–223.

Giddens, A., 1991. *Modernity and Self-Identity: Self and Society in the Late Modern Age*. London: Polity Press.

Gramelsberger, G. (Ed.) 2011. *From Science to Computational Sciences: Studies in the History of Computing and its Influence on Today's Sciences*. Zurich: Diaphanes.

Gruenberg, B.C., 1911a. The Creation of "Artificial Life": The Making of Living Matter from the Non-living. *Scientific American*, 105(11), pp. 222–39.

Gruenberg, B.C., 1911b. Artificial Life: II. Making the Non-Living Do the Work of the Living. *Scientific American*, 105(13), pp. 272–86.

Grüne-Yanoff, T., 2009. The Explanatory Potential of Artificial Societies. *Synthese*, 169(3), pp. 539–55.

Hacking, I., 1983. *Representing and Intervening: Introductory Topics in the Philosophy of Natural Science*. Cambridge: Cambridge University Press.

Hacking, I., 2005. Truthfulness. *Common Knowledge*, 11(1), pp. 160–72.

Hawkins, D., 1946. Inception until August 1945. In: *Manhattan District History: Project Y, The Los Alamos Project*. Vol. 1. LAMS-2532. Los Alamos, NM: Los Alamos Scientific Laboratory.

Hayles, N.K., 1996. Narratives of Artificial Life. In: G. Robertson, M. Mash, L. Tickner, J. Bird, B. Curtis, and T. Putnam (Eds.) *FutureNatural: Nature, Science, Culture*. London: Routledge, pp. 147–64.

Hays, D.G., 1965. Simulation: An Introduction for Anthropologists. In: D. Hymes (Ed.) 1965. *The Use of Computers in Anthropology*. The Hague: Mouton & Co. pp. 402–26.

Heims, S.J., 1991. *The Cybernetics Group*. Cambridge, MA: MIT Press.

Helmreich, S., 2011. What Was Life? Answers from Three Limit Biologies. *Critical Inquiry*, 37(4), pp. 671–96.

Hymes, D., (Ed.) 1965. *The Use of Computers in Anthropology*. The Hague: Mouton & Co.

Janssen, M.A., 2009. Understanding Artificial Anasazi. *Journal of Artificial Societies and Social Simulation*, 12(4). Available at: jasss.soc.surrey.ac.uk/12/4/13.html (accessed July 9, 2015).

Jervis, R., 1997. *System Effects: Complexity in Political and Social Life*. Princeton, NJ: Princeton University Press.

Kageki, N., 2012. An Uncanny Mind. *IEEE Robotics and Automation Magazine*, June, pp. 112, 106, 108.

Kahn, H., 1960. *On Thermonuclear War*. Revised ed. 2007. New Brunswick, NJ: Transaction Publishers.

Keller, E.F., 1998. Models of and Models for: Theory and Practice in Contemporary Biology. *Philosophy of Science*, 67 (suppl.), pp. S72–S86.

Keller, E.F., 2002. *Making Sense of Life: Explaining Biological Development with Models, Metaphors, and Machines*. Cambridge, MA: Harvard University Press.

Keller, E.F., 2003. Models, Simulation, and "Computer Experiments". In: H. Radder, (Ed.) *The Philosophy of Scientific Experimentation*. Pittsburgh, PA: University of Pittsburgh Press, pp. 198–215.

Keller, E.F., 2005. Marrying the Premodern to the Postmodern: Computers and Organisms after World War II. In: S. Franchi and G. Güzeldere (Eds.) *Mechanical Bodies, Computational Minds: Artificial Intelligence from Automata to Cyborgs*. Cambridge, MA: MIT Press, pp. 203–28.

Kirby, S., 2013. Language, Culture, and Computation: An Adaptive Systems Approach to Biolinguistics. In: C. Boeckx and K.K. Grohmann (Eds.) *The Cambridge Handbook of Biolinguistics*. Cambridge: Cambridge University Press, pp. 460–77.

Kretzschmar, W.A. and Juuso, I., 2014. Simulation of the Complex System of Speech Interaction: Digital Visualizations. *Literary and Linguistic Computing*, 29(3), pp. 432–42.

Lancashire, I. and McCarty, W., 1988. *The Humanities Computing Yearbook 1988*. Oxford: Clarendon Press.

Langton, C.G., 1987. Artificial Life. In: C.G. Langton (Ed.) 1989. *Artificial Life. Proceedings of an Interdisciplinary Workshop on the Synthesis and Simulation of Living Systems held September, 1987 in Los Alamos, New Mexico*. Vol VI. Redwood City CA: Addison-Wesley, pp. 1–47.

Laurel, B., 2014. *Computers as Theatre* (2nd ed.). Boston, MA: Addison-Wesley.

Leavis, F.R., 1970. "Literarism" versus "Scientism": The Misconception and the Menace. *Times Literary Supplement*, 3556 (23 April), pp. 441–44.

Lehman, R.S., 1977. *Computer Simulation and Modeling: An Introduction*. Hillsdale, NJ: Lawrence Erlbaum Associates.

Masterman, M., 1964. The Use of Computers to Make Semantic Toy Models of Language. *Times Literary Supplement*, August 6, pp. 690–91.

McCarty, W., 2013. The Future of Digital Humanities is a Matter of Words. In: J. Hartley, J. Burgess, and A. Bruns (Eds.) *A Companion to New Media Dynamics*. Chichester: Wiley-Blackwell, pp. 33–52.

McCarty, W., 2005. *Humanities Computing*. Revised ed. 2014. Houndmills, Basingstoke: Palgrave.

McCarty, W., 2014. Getting There from Here: Remembering the Future of Digital Humanities. Robert Busa Award Lecture 2013. In: P.L. Arthur and K. Bode (Eds.) *Advancing Digital Humanities: Research, Methods, Theories*. Basingstoke: Palgrave Macmillan, pp. 291–321.

McGann, J., 2014. *A New Republic of Letters: Memory and Scholarship in the Age of Digital Reproduction*. Cambridge, MA: Harvard University Press.

Meadows, D.H., Meadows, D.L., Randers, J., and Behrens III, W.H., 1972. *Limits to Growth. A Report for the Club of Rome's Report on the Predicament of Mankind*. New York: Universe Books.

Mindell, D.A., 2002. *Between Human and Machine: Feedback, Control, and Computing before Cybernetics*. Baltimore, MD: Johns Hopkins University Press.

Mori, M., 2012/1970. The Uncanny Valley. Translated by K.F. McDorman and N. Kageki, 2012. *IEEE Robotics and Automation Magazine*, 19(2), pp. 98–100.

Nemerov, H., 1967. Speculative Equations: Poems, Poets, Computers. *The American Scholar*, 36(3), pp. 394–414.

Oakman, R.L., 1987. Perspectives on Teaching Computing in the Humanities. *Computers and the Humanities*, 21(4), pp. 227–33.

Peck, S.L., 2008. The hermeneutics of ecological simulation. *Biology and Philosophy*, 23, pp. 383–402.

Plakans, A., 1980. Rev. of B. Dyke and J.W. MacClure, *Computer Simulation in Human Population Studies*; R.D. Lee, R.A. Easterlin, P.H. Lindert, and E. van de Walle, *Population Patterns in the Past*; N. Howell, *Demography of the Dobe!Kung*; K.W. Wachter, E.A. Hammel, and P. Laslett, *Statistical Studies of Historical Social Structure. Computers and the Humanities* 14(2), pp. 139–42.

Ray, T.S., 1998. Selecting Naturally for Differentiation: Preliminary Evolutionary Results. *Complexity*, 3(5), pp. 25–33.

Redmond, K.C. and Smith, T.M., 2000. *From Whirlwind to Mitre: The R&D Story of the SAGE Air Defense Computer.* Cambridge, MA: MIT Press.

Ryan, M.-L., 2001. *Narrative as Virtual Reality: Immersion and Interactivity in Literature and Electronic Media.* Baltimore, MD: Johns Hopkins University Press.

Sack, G.A, 2011. Simulating Plot: Towards a Generative Model of Narrative Structure. In: M. Hadzikadic and T. Charmichael (Eds.) *Complex Adaptive Systems: Energy, Information, and Intelligence. Papers from the 2011 AAAI Fall Symposium.* Menlo Park CA: AAAI Press, pp. 127–36.

Scarry, E., 1992. The Made-Up and the Made-Real. *Yale Journal of Criticism*, 5(2), pp. 239–49.

Shepard, P., 1997. *The Others: How Animals Made Us Human.* Washington, DC: Island Press.

Smith, B.C., 1985. The Limits of Correctness. *ACM SIGCAS. Computers and Society*, 14.15(1–4), pp. 18–26.

Soules, M., 2002. Animating the Language Machine: Computers and Performance. *Computers and the Humanities*, 36(3), pp. 319–44.

Tannenbaum, R.S., 1987a. Humanizing the Computer: A Course for Non-Science Faculty. *Journal of Computing Sciences in Colleges*, 3, pp. 123–48.

Tannenbaum, R.S., 1987b. How Should We Teach Computing to Humanists? *Computers and the Humanities*, 21(4), pp. 217–25.

Troitzsch, K.G., 2009. Multi-Agent Systems and Simulation: A Survey from an Application Perspective. In: A.M. Uhrmacher and D. Weyns (Eds.) *Multi-Agent Systems: Simulation and Applications.* Boca Raton, FL: CRC Press, pp. 53–75.

Versluis, E.B., 1984. Computer Simulations and the Far Reaches of Computer-Assisted Instruction. *Computers and the Humanities*, 18(3–4), pp. 225–32.

von Neumann, J., 1958. *The Computer and the Brain.* New Haven, NJ: Yale University Press.

von Neumann, J., 1966. *Theory of Self-Reproducing Automata.* Arthur W. Burks (Ed.) and completed. Urbana, IL: University of Illinois Press.

Wall, J.N., 2016. Gazing into Imaginary Spaces: Digital Modeling and the Representation of Reality. In: L. Estill, D.K. Jakacki and M. Ullyot (Eds.) *Early Modern Studies after the Digital Turn. New Technologies in Medieval and Renaissance Studies 6.* Toronto, ON: Iter Press, pp. 283–317. See also the Virtual St. Paul's Cathedral Project, available at: vpcp.chass.ncsu.edu/.

Weizenbaum, J., 1976. *Computer Power and Human Reason: From Judgment to Calculation.* San Francisco: W.H. Freeman.

Wiener, N., 1948. *Cybernetics, or Control and Communication in the Animal and the Machine* (2nd ed. 1961). Cambridge, MA: MIT Press.

Williams, R., 1983/1976. *Keywords: A Vocabulary of Culture and Society*. New York: Oxford University Press.

Wind, E., 1958. *Pagan Mysteries in the Renaissance*. Revised and enlarged ed., 1968. New York: W.W. Norton.

Winsberg, E.B., 2010. *Science in the Age of Computer Simulation*. Chicago: University of Chicago Press.

Wittgenstein, L., 1980. *Bemerkungen über die Philosophie der Psychologie*. Remarks on the Philosophy of Psychology. Ed. and translated by G.E.M. Anscombe and G.H. von Wright. Vol. I. Oxford: Basil Blackwell.

Wittig, S., 1978. The Computer and the Concept of Text. *Computers and the Humanities*, 11, pp. 211–15.

Youngman, P.A. and Hadzikadic, M. (Eds.) 2014. *Complexity and the Human Experience: Modeling Complexity in the Humanities and Social Sciences*. Boca Raton, FL: Pan Stanford Publishing.

15 Playing for keeps

The role of modeling in the humanities

C.M. Sperberg-McQueen

1 Modeling as a humanistic activity

Modeling, it is sometimes said, lies at the very heart of the digital humanities, perhaps constitutes the core of the field.[1] Whether this is so or not, modeling certainly has deep roots. In 1973, Wilhelm Ott described the possible application of data processing tools to humanistic research problems this way (Ott, 1973, p. v):

> *Ihr [d.i. der EDV] Einsatz ist überall dort möglich, wo Daten irgendwelcher Art, also auch Texte, nach eindeutig formulierbaren und vollständig formalisierbaren Regeln verarbeitet werden müssen.*

> [Data processing can be applied wherever data of any kind, including texts, must be processed according to unambiguously formulatable and completely formalizable rules.]

It may be noted that in Ott's formulation the completely formalizable rules are not those of a computer system but those immanent in the humanities research being pursued and in the nature of the information to be processed; the drive for unambiguous formulation and formalization comes from the humanistic research objectives, and not from the demands of computers. Unambiguous formulation is, after all, a traditional goal of humanistic learning, and formalization has a long history in philosophy and elsewhere.

The use of computers introduces into humanities scholarship no demands for clarity or formality that have not already been made there long before the invention of digital stored-program devices.[2] But the availability of computers makes it far easier, in principle, to meet those demands. Computers make it easier to test our ideas for logical consistency, to survey our collections of data for errors, patterns, typical examples, outliers, and exceptions to a proposed generalization. They make it easier, that is, to locate evidence for or against any proposition we can formulate, provided that it is a proposition for which evidence for or against can be marshalled in the first place.

2 What is modeling?

The word *modeling* denotes a variety of practices so varied that they appear to defy lexicography; they do not necessarily share any essential core that distinguishes them from other practices, and most attempts at definition can politely be described as disappointing. Perhaps the most useful general description available is that offered by Marvin Minsky:[3] "To an observer B, an object A* is a model of an object A if B can use A* to answer questions that interest [B] about A."

As a definition, this is too broad: books about A can also be used to answer questions about A, without being models of A in any useful sense. But it does accurately describe all the kinds of modeling that concern us here (and many that do not). The model A* is not identical to the object A of which it is a model, but there must be some similarity, correspondence, or analogy between the two, to allow questions about the one to be answered by examining the other.

One might usefully categorize models based on the nature of the similarity or correspondence between the model and the modeled, but it may be more helpful here to consider the goals or attitudes of the modeler. The paragraphs below distinguish what for want of better terms will be called utilitarian, pedagogical, and self-reflexive modeling.

One common reason to use a model instead of studying an object directly is that direct study of the object A is expensive, or inconvenient, or impossible, while study of A* is cheaper, or easier, or at least possible. In these situations, the model serves a wholly utilitarian function. As Rosenblueth and Wiener say (1945, pp. 317f.):

> Sometimes the relation between the material model and the original system is merely a change of scale, in space or time. As an example of a change of a spatial scale, at any proving ground experiments on shells will not be carried out with large, expensive, and unwieldy calibers, but with handy, cheaper, small calibers. Another example is the use of small animals, instead of large ones, for biological experiments: certainly any physiologist will work as much as possible on a dolphin rather than on a sulphur-bottom whale.

For such utilitarian purposes, it is not important that the model A* answer all questions about A; it suffices if some questions of interest at the moment can be asked about the model A* and the answers extrapolated to A without unacceptable loss of precision or accuracy.

One reason for the prominence of modeling in the digital humanities is that models are useful for anyone interested in building things. And digital humanists, as has often been noted, do build things. Like architects' models, models in general can be used for checking a design before it is too late to change it. Builders build models in order to reduce the cost of design exploration and of mistakes. The closer the model comes to the particularities of a design, the more informative it can be. And, on the other hand, the simpler and rougher a model is, the less expensive it is. In the digital humanities, this can lead to tension between competing goals. On one hand, the use of standardized models can improve the longevity of data, and the use of common (often standardized) models can make it easier to compare data from different collaborating sources, easier to reuse data, and easier to achieve economies of scale and automation. So when a project involves long-term work or collaboration with other projects, there will be some pressure to use pre-existing standard models. But if a project can tailor its models to the needs of the individual project and the idiosyncrasies of the period or region from which a given body of data has been collected, the model is likely to be helpful and informative in the short -run and within the scope of the project. In the long run, the community at large normally benefits the most from reusability, interoperability and longevity of data, and thus from appropriate standardization. But in the short run, almost any project will benefit in some ways from using a model tailored to their data and goals rather than a standardized one, just as tailor-made clothing tends to fit better than off-the-rack clothing. It is no surprise, and should not occasion excessive regret, that many projects end up favoring the short run over the long run, at least in some ways. Before anyone, any project, or any body of data reaches the long run, it must first survive the short run. Before a common data model can ensure the reusability of data, it must first be able to ensure the initial usability of the data for the initial project. Data never used or gathered cannot be reused.

Models used widely and long will, under normal circumstances, eventually need revision as the knowledge and beliefs they reflect change with new research, new experience, or new social values. For this reason, utilitarian models often require clear rules for maintenance, a clear revision policy, and other infrastructure of the kind familiar from large-scale software development projects. Examples include the kind of widely applicable models of prosopographic, geographic, or bibliographic data mentioned below.

Not all models in the digital humanities are utilitarian in this way; some are instead motivated pedagogically. A widely held view holds that modeling provides a useful form of mental discipline, beneficial to the student regardless of any direct utility of the model itself. Nancy Ide expresses this view succinctly in the Preface to her book on Pascal programming (1987, p. x):[4]

> No, humanists don't need to write their own programs ... But experience with computer programming provides an understanding of fundamental computing concepts, familiarity with the principles of algorithmic thought, and a grasp of the ways in which information is stored, accessed, and manipulated ...
> So, yes, humanists need to learn how to program, not in order to write their own software but to learn how to look at the materials within their disciplines in new ways and intelligently utilize (and perhaps develop) tools that help them do it.

In this view, models provide the kind of intellectual challenge and rigor sometimes ascribed to the study of Greek and Latin. The act of modeling and the struggle to learn to do it well are more important here than the models actually produced. Pedagogical concerns correspondingly rise in importance, and calls may be heard for modeling to be made more accessible, less technical, and more easily learnable.

Often, the pedagogical view of modeling as a form of intellectual discipline shades over by imperceptible degrees into a third attitude towards modeling, in which the construction of a model becomes an end in itself. In this self-reflexive approach, as we may call it, the model serves to illuminate a thing by identifying what we take to be its essential parts and characteristics; it thus serves to capture as completely as possible our current understanding of the thing being modeled. Here, for obvious reasons, the completeness of the model becomes more important than in either the utilitarian or the purely pedagogic approach.

A classic formulation of this view of modeling is that offered by Noam Chomsky in the Preface to his book *Syntactic Structures* (1957, p. 5):

> Precisely constructed models for linguistic structure can play an important role, both negative and positive, in the process of discovery itself. By pushing a precise but inadequate formulation to an unacceptable conclusion, we can often expose the exact source of this inadequacy and, consequently, gain a deeper understanding of the linguistic data. More positively, a formalized theory may automatically provide solutions for many problems other than those for which it was explicitly designed.

Here, modeling is not just an exemplary form of clear thinking. The model is itself one goal of our thinking, and serves as a tool for discovery. A correct model is not a tool for building something, but an end in itself.

In teaching descriptive markup to novices, Lou Burnard used to say that markup is a way of making explicit our interpretation of a text. This comes very close to treating text markup as a form of self-reflexive modeling, for which a model is a way of making explicit our understanding of the thing being modeled, our assumptions and beliefs about it. As Julia Flanders has put it, models here become the reflection of our convictions, rather than (solely) a recipe for things to do or build.

The varying attitudes towards modeling just described can help to explain some tensions and disagreements among digital humanists. The long-standing discussion among textual humanists of the best way to model overlapping textual structures, for example, seems interminable and pointless to those who assign to models a purely utilitarian function. For some, overlap constitutes a technical hurdle for the construction of, say, a corpus-linguistic toolkit; it must be modeled in order that the tools can handle it, but it is not an object of study in its own right. For others, the modeling of overlap has become (or has always been) an end in itself, not a preparation for the building of software.

3 Desiderata

The differences among utilitarian, pedagogical, and self-reflexive models, however, can easily be exaggerated. While the modeler may place different weights on properties like completeness, simplicity, brevity, or high levels of accuracy, depending on the goals of the effort, the fact is that the similarities among these ways of thinking outweigh the differences. This is especially true when computers are used.

One striking fact about modeling by computer is that some implications of models become visible more quickly and clearly than is typically the case when computers are not involved. The thesis of some French structuralists—for example, that texts are not distinct, stable objects but interacting manifestations of a vast sea of textuality—formulated concretely in the suggestion that *text* should be a non-count noun (*il n'y a pas des textes; il y a du texte*), may seem remote from any practical implications. But the (contrary) idea that texts are distinct unitary objects with firm boundaries is reflected in the decision of SGML and XML to assign document scope to unique identifiers, which has the direct practical consequence that hypertext references to objects or passages within the same text and references to objects outside the text have different forms (as may be seen, for example, in the <ptr> / <xptr> distinction of TEI P3 and TEI P4). This contrasts with the view reflected in HTML (and TEI P5) that the boundaries of documents are porous and that there should be no structural difference between document-internal and document-external references.

The phenomenon known to markup practitioners as tag abuse is another simple instance of the general rule that models can have perceptible computational consequences. Tag abuse is the inappropriate application of a markup construct (typically an element type) to text passages which do not have the specified semantics. The use of a <technical-term> element to mark words that are to be italicized but that are not, in fact, technical terms would constitute tag abuse. Such abuse reduces the reusability of textual data and makes automatic processing (e.g., the construction of a draft glossary of technical terms) harder. Tag abuse amounts to conscious inaccuracy in the model; it is the modeling of a thing (in the example, an italicized phrase) as if it were a different thing (a technical term). The problems caused by tag abuse illustrate a general principle: lying to one's software turns out almost always to be bad engineering. The principle applies as well to models of other sorts: a model which achieves simplicity or some other desirable property at the cost of an inaccurate representation of the domain being modeled is likely to have less utility than a more accurate model.

The work put in on a model regarded as an end in itself, conversely, may be repaid by utilitarian applications of that model. And in just the way described by Chomsky and illustrated by hyperlinking in TEI and HTML, a model created for purely utilitarian ends can illuminate, by the behavior of things built using it, the intellectual flaws or virtues of the model and thus also of the domain being modeled.

When we identify desiderata for models created by digital humanists, therefore, we need not carefully distinguish between models serving purely utilitarian ends and models regarded as ends in themselves. From any model, we may hope for similar virtues. From any tool or approach to modeling, we may demand that it encourage models with these virtues and discourage models with the corresponding vices.

- Our models should help us to make our assumptions and beliefs visible and explicit. This is a prerequisite to fully self-critical work.
- They should make it easy to test what consequences would follow from a change in our premises.
- They should help us to disagree productively with each other, by helping to identify more precisely the roots and extent of agreement and disagreement.
- They should allow us to work at an appropriate level of abstraction, without forcing the modeler to add inessential details or premises, or to omit essential ones.
- They should ideally make it easier to identify testable consequences of our premises.

By making our assumptions and beliefs explicit and formally manipulable, models that meet these demands will allow us to test our assumptions and beliefs more thoroughly and to consider alternative assumptions and beliefs more systematically. In consequence, by building explicit machine-processable models digital humanists have the capability to perform the core tasks of every humanities discipline more rigorously and more thoroughly than is feasible for non-digital humanists.

4 Formality

We can achieve such results, however, only if we formulate our models in appropriate ways. Many forms of modeling are possible, and each may be used to good effect. But the goals outlined above will more easily be met by the definition of rigorous models with no hand-waving over details. Formal models will be more help than informal models, if we wish to exploit the full potential of modeling. And the best results will be achieved if models use some form of logic for which formal rules of inference have been defined and for which model-checking tools are available.

In the extreme case, the term *modeling* can be used to describe simple prose accounts of the essence of some thing or situation, or even for metaphors like the desktop metaphor of many graphical user interfaces. At another extreme, computer programs are often (rightly) regarded as embodying models of their application domain and by metonymy may be described as being, rather than embodying, a model.

Models not expressed in formal terms can be light-weight and convenient. No formal machinery slows down the modeler with its demands for careful distinctions or bookkeeping detail. But non-formal models[5] make it easy for modelers to deceive themselves as to the completeness, explicitness, and correctness of a model; handwaving, vagueness, and ambiguity find a convenient home in non-formal models expressed only in natural language.

Some examples may be helpful here. A prose description of the information to be included in an edition, or a document to be processed by a given piece of software, or a configuration file for that software, can easily be incomplete, subtly contradictory, or ambiguous; none of these problems can be detected automatically. A formal document-type declaration or schema for the edition, document input, or configuration file, on the other hand, can be tested for consistency and completeness, and the notation rules out ambiguity. And the schema allows a mechanical test to see whether a given document conforms to the schema or not. On a smaller scale, text-critical variants in a text may be given by a formal apparatus criticus or by prose comments in footnotes. The formality of the apparatus makes it possible to check the completeness and the consistency of the information mechanically (have any witnesses been omitted inadvertently? have any witnesses been listed twice with contradictory readings?); an informal apparatus can only be checked by hand. It is quite possible for a non-formal description of variants to be correct and complete, but it cannot be tested or processed automatically; a more formal representation can.

Above all, non-formal models resist refutation: if any part of the model appears to lead to an undesirable consequence (in the kind of argument described by Chomsky above), it is always easy to insist that that part of the model was not meant to be interpreted that way, but must be taken in some other sense which evades the undesirable consequence. If another part of the model proves to lead to a different undesirable consequence, it too can be defended as having been meant in another sense. Whether the sense insisted on for the second passage is logically compatible with that offered in the first case is a question easily overlooked. With non-formal models, moreover, it may be difficult or impossible to build chains of logical inference in the first place, so non-formal models are often difficult to test. For all of these reasons, non-formal models seem to have no consequences which anyone would deem necessary to face or to be held accountable for. Modeling non-formally is like playing poker with the proviso that the losers never have to pay off on their IOUs.

Non-formality in models may make it easier for an author to persuade a reader of an argument, but the argument of which the reader is persuaded may or may not be the one the author had in mind. Non-formality makes it disastrously difficult to achieve clear disagreement; for this reason, non-formal models often merit the dismissive response often attributed to the physicist Wolfgang Pauli: they are not even wrong.

Computer programs, on the other hand, tolerate no vagueness or ambiguity; they will, for any implementable programming language, have a deterministic meaning. Observers will seldom disagree on whether a given behavior or proposition follows or does not follow from the text of the program. (Exceptions may arise when two implementations of the language have interpreted the language specification differently.) This is perhaps why so many digital humanists, like Nancy Ide in the passage quoted above, believe that computer programming will encourage students to think differently, and perhaps more clearly.

Only after some time does it become clear to some practitioners that programs are not always an ideal medium for the expression of assumptions and beliefs about the application domain, or even for the expression of algorithms as they are developed and discussed by computer scientists. Almost always, making an executable program that implements a given algorithm or reflects a given model of the application domain involves making additional decisions that go well beyond the details fixed in the algorithm or the model. A model intended for a collection of prosopographic data, for example, may say that human beings may have both a given name and a family name, but a computer program will typically need to specify further that each of these names is (or is represented as) a sequence of characters, identify the set of characters which may appear in the names, and often lay down a limit to the length of the names. None of this is directly relevant to the plausibility or adequacy of the given name + family name model; none of it helps identify the ways in which that model differs from or resembles a different model involving praenomen, nomen gentilicium, and cognomen. A model may intentionally leave some details of the domain unspecified; a computer program will often force those details to be fixed after all. This is why very few formal specifications intended for wide use take the form of a computer program, or are accompanied by a normative reference implementation. Faced with the daunting wealth of details needed to specify completely in prose the behavior of a correct implementation of a given programming language, some language designers in the 1960s experienced a brief infatuation with the idea of a reference implementation of the language, which could answer with its behavior any question one might put to it as to the meaning of any given language construct. It soon became clear, however, that a reference implementation invariably required the fixing of details which the language designers desired to leave unfixed and open to variation among implementations, such as the underlying representation of numbers or characters. It also became clear that normative reference implementations were just as hard to get right as normative prose specifications and were undesirable unless the community was prepared to accept every bug in the reference implementation as a feature.

Between the absence of detail characteristic of non-formal models and the excess of undesired detail in executable models in the form of programs in conventional programming languages, there is a middle ground. Models can be expressed in formal notations which (like ordinary prose) allow the subject to be treated at any desired level of abstraction, which (like programming languages) have a formally defined syntax, and which have a defined logic, so that the inferences of a model can be identified. For some domains of interest to digital humanists, there are already suitable notations in more or less wide use. XML document type definitions are written in a variety of formal notations, of which the native XML notation for document type definitions (DTD), Relax NG (RNG), and the XML Schema Definition Language (XSD) are most widely used. Database models may be defined using entity-relationship (ER) diagrams. The details of individual statistical models seem generally to be hidden within the statistical tool being used, but the basic properties of any statistical model are consistently described using standard mathematical notation. For work on the many topics that fit none of these domain-specific languages, or when the domain-specific languages do not capture all the relevant aspects of the model to be formulated, however, another solution is needed. Models can be expressed in some variant or other of formal logic; in the current state of the art, I believe that models formulated in some variety of first-order predicate calculus are probably the best vehicles for the modeling efforts of digital humanists.[6] The prescription made here will involve some changes of practice and some learning of new tools and techniques. The use of symbolic logic is not currently unknown in the digital humanities, but it is not particularly widespread. But the basics of logic will be familiar to most humanists, and symbolic logic is probably easier to learn for most digital humanists than programming.

The use of first-order logic for modeling has a number of consequences.

- Because formal logic supports inference, consequences of the model can be identified unambiguously. Examples and counterexamples can (sometimes) be generated automatically. In some cases, the predictions or consequences of a model can be tested against observed reality.
- Because the model is wholly declarative, the modeler need not specify how a given proposition should be instantiated or checked. The proposition can be formulated in the clearest available way, without regard for execution or implementation difficulties.
- Although many tools currently available for working with formal logic are designed primarily to support software development, they can nevertheless be applied to any domain about which we can make useful statements in first-order logic.

No extraneous information need be supplied. The model defines various classes of individuals, various relations on them, and various constraints on the individuals and their relations. There is no requirement to specify how individuals should be represented in memory, as there would be in conventional programming languages, nor to specify where they fit in some global ontology, as there can be in knowledge-representation languages.

The last point is worth stressing: making models formal by using symbolic logic does not entail making them complete in the sense of specifying all details of the domain being modeled, grounding them in some larger ontology, or building them up from some system- or user-defined set of semantic primitives.[7] The modeler can build castles in the air, placing their foundations at any chosen altitude. The mechanism for doing this is simple: one assumes whatever one wishes to assume, and the logical consequences are worked out from there. The only requirement is to make assumptions explicit. This allows the applicability of the model, or the plausibility of the assumptions, to be considered and discussed separately from the question of what follows from the assumptions once they are granted.

The expression of models using formal logic thus achieves more or less automatically the second, fourth, and fifth of the desiderata identified above.

The other desiderata are not guaranteed to follow from the use of logic. In itself, logic can do nothing to ensure that the modeler records all of the relevant assumptions and beliefs (although the failure of an expected consequence to follow from a set of assumptions can call attention to an omitted premise), nor that they are explained clearly. But, if writing the model down in logical form is set as the expected standard of explicitness, it is at least likely to be clear to any observer whether a given assumption has or has not been recorded.

Logic also does not guarantee productive disagreement; many other factors enter into making disagreements clear and useful. Logic does encourage the explicit identification of both premises and conclusions, and systematic distinction between them, which may make it easier to trace a disagreement to its source: perhaps a disputed premise, perhaps a contested inference, perhaps a disagreement over whether a given formalization applies to the domain in question. When models are expressed only non-formally and lack explicit distinction between premises and conclusions, the same level of clarity can be harder to achieve.

5 Examples

A simple illustration of the use of formal modeling in clarifying concepts is offered at the end of this chapter. It shows a model of the overlap relation posited by Nelson Goodman's calculus of individuals (an alternative to conventional set theory), formulated using the Alloy tool for working with logical specifications,[8] and illustrates how the model can be used to discover that Nelson's definition of the relation has consequences not immediately obvious to the reader (in particular that the overlap relation as Goodman defines it is necessarily symmetric and reflexive: if one object overlaps another, the other object also overlaps the first, and every object overlaps itself). The model says nothing about individuals, their nature, or their interrelations other than overlap; it is thus open to and compatible with many different accounts of those topics. The model specifies only that in the universe of discourse, individuals may exist and may overlap, that a given axiom may hold, and that rules about symmetry and reflexiveness may hold.

Some other examples of the utility of formality in modeling may be mentioned. Some concern the nature and structure of text or of its representation in digital form, others the transmission and preservation of texts, or the (metaphoric or literal) codes in which cultural artifacts are expressed. Finally, several concern the referents of our discourse in real and fictive worlds, as recorded in prosopographic and geographic databases.[9]

Perhaps the most striking step forward in the digital representation of textual structure since the introduction of punched cards was the suggestion, in the Standard Generalized Markup Language (SGML – ISO, 1986), that texts have structure and properties which can be marked up explicitly, and that those textual structures can be partially described by document grammars.[10] Both of these ideas involve an increase in formality in document representation. First, by assigning names to textual properties and structural units, the creator of an SGML vocabulary identifies salient concepts explicitly and formally; by using the names declared in the vocabulary to associate those properties and structural units with specific locations in the text, the creator of an SGML document explicitly identifies portions of the document as instantiating the conceptual structures reflected in the document grammar. Both of these stand in striking contrast to the implicit association of conceptual structures with passages in the text found in other methods of document representation. The formality of SGML element declarations is a key contributor to the independence of SGML documents from any one piece of software. Second, by defining explicitly the relations that hold between elements (in particular, the parent-child dominance relations and sibling precedence relations), an SGML document grammar makes possible a purely formal validation of the document, which allows automatic detection of a wide variety of errors in the preparation of the document.

Many SGML users found the explicit identification of textual structures exhilarating and liberating. Inspired, it seems, by the experience of using SGML, a classic paper by DeRose et al. poses the question "What is text, really?" and proposes the answer that text is an "ordered hierarchy of content objects" (1990), which the authors (and many others) associate with SGML.[11] This claim, although later relativized and refined (and in some respects retracted) by several of the same authors, has elicited numerous reactions from digital humanists. Some reactions have limited themselves to denying that text is hierarchical in structure,[12] pointing to overlapping phenomena like paragraphs and pages. Most of the objectors seem not to notice the Platonic focus announced by the final word of the question, and thus neglect to mount any argument that the overlapping structures they identify are essential and not merely phenomenal.

Other reactions have included a long series of proposals describing alternative models of document structure, with a view towards allowing better representation of non-hierarchical phenomena in real-world documents (Sperberg-McQueen and Huitfeldt, 2000; Tennison, Piez, and Cowan, 2002–2008?; Schonefeld, 2007; Stührenberg and Goecke, 2008). The discussion has benefited in more or less direct proportion to the formality of the proposals; non-formality in the description of document structure correlates highly with ambiguity and vagueness.

Allen Renear and Karen Wickett have explored the consequences of the commonly expressed view that SGML and XML documents are, by nature, trees (or graphs) of elements, and shown that if this is so, some unexpected consequences must follow (2009, 2010). Claus Huitfeldt and others have countered with a model of documents as functions from points in time to trees (Huitfeldt, Vitali, and Peroni, 2012).[13]

Like most specifications of machine-processable languages since Algol 60, SGML provides an explicit and formal definition of the syntax of SGML documents; the semantics of those documents are left informal. This may have purely pragmatic causes: there is no universally acceptable basis for a formal semantic description. But it may equally likely have programmatic significance: the meaning of SGML documents is to be specified by the creators of SGML vocabularies and SGML documents, not by the SGML specification; this is consistent with SGML's principled assignment of power and authority to the users of SGML rather than to its creators or to the creators of SGML software.

However, the absence of any formal method of defining the meaning of markup has been felt as a gap by many. Huitfeldt and collaborators have used formal modeling to clarify some aspects of markup semantics (Sperberg-McQueen, Huitfeldt, and Renear, 2001) and the logical structure of transcription (Huitfeldt and Sperberg-McQueen, 2008), at least negatively, by showing some untenable consequences of some simple models (the definition of more satisfactory models for these phenomena is still a desideratum).

Other work worth mentioning here concerns the transmission and preservation of texts. A landmark in this area are the Functional Requirements for Bibliographic Records (FRBR), produced after years of effort in 1998 by the International Federation of Library Associations and Institutions (IFLA). FRBR attempts to disentangle the tightly interrelated concepts surrounding books (and similar cultural objects) and proposes explicit distinctions among the abstract concepts of work, expression, and manifestation which may be embodied by a particular concrete bibliographic item. By proposing an explicit set of fundamental concepts with defined relations among them, which allows a clear analysis for many simple and complex cases, FRBR makes a great step forward in the understanding of the relations between books as physical objects and the cultural artifacts embodied in them.

It can be argued, however, that FRBR would be more useful, and more effective, if it were defined more formally than it now is. Allen Renear's critique of the FRBR model elsewhere in this volume illustrates the point. Renear argues that FRBR's account of inherited properties (properties of works, expressions, or manifestations which are attributed to bibliographic items which instantiate those works, expressions, or manifestations) is self-contradictory. Is FRBR's useof the concept of inheritance in fact wrong or contradictory? Or are the authors of the specification merely guilty of careless wording and sloppy draftsmanship? It will seem to some readers, at least, that Renear is insisting on a particular sense for the word which is not the sense in which the FRBR documents use it, so that instead of an interesting discussion of substantive points the critique risks degenerating into a not very interesting argument about lexicography. The difficulty here is that the FRBR specification neither formalizes its model nor provides binding definitions for terms like *inheritance*, so that it is impossible to tell whether Renear and the authors of FRBR disagree substantively, or agree on the substance of the matter but use different words.

Other examples of the utility of increased formality in modeling are offered by the history of textual criticism. The explicit identification of relations of manuscript descent made possible and necessary by the construction of a stemma, such as became more or less universally expected in editions of medieval and ancient works in the nineteenth century, marked a large step forward. It made it possible to formulate earlier methodological issues on a more systematic basis, and understand more clearly than before the conditions under which different competing positions had a claim to be right, and when not.

It also made it possible to disagree systematically and productively with the model of textual transmission exhibited by the stemma, whether in a particular case (by arguing that the stemma should have a different shape) or in general (by arguing that the methods used for creating the stemma were intrinsically flawed). A general attack of the latter kind was launched in 1913 by the French medievalist Joseph Bédier (1928). He compared the manuscript diagrams in a number of critical editions and observed that they showed a preponderance of stemmas with two main branches, rather than three or more. Bédier found it implausible that historical forces should so systematically seek out representatives of the third branch of descent, if any, for destruction: in reality, he argued, trees of manuscript descent should have far more cases of three branches than are shown in the editions he examined. From this he inferred that the method used to construct the stemmas (what was and is known as Lachmann's method) must be fatally flawed. And he promptly abandoned it, in a move subsequently emulated by virtually all later editors of Old French texts.

Regardless of the merits of Bédier's claims, his formulation of the problem has the advantage of being concrete and clear. What proportion of the family trees for the extant manuscripts of ancient and medieval works should be expected to have two main branches, and what proportion should have three or more? Are the proportions of two and three branches found in editions consistent with plausible expectations, or not? Bédier's attack on the stemmatic method led to rejoinders that criticized his assumptions and proposed different assumptions, which were in turn criticized by later authors. The precise form of Bédier's argument is sometimes obscured by the heat of his prose, but on the whole the later participants in the discussion have had unusual success is identifying the points on which they agree and disagree, and the discussion over the past century has shown something like progress toward greater clarity.[14] This illustrates, if illustration be needed, that formality is an aid to clarity and explicitness, but not a necessary prerequisite. One of the most useful contributions, however, is indeed one of the most formal: Michael Weitzman's construction of a statistical model of manuscript copying and destruction, which showed that random processes will produce many more bipartite stemmas than tripartite stemmas (1982, 1985, 1987).

A third class of example concerns the preservation, or reconstruction, of the codes in which cultural artifacts are expressed. Metaphorically, *code* can be thought of as denoting the language used in artifacts of the past; the efforts of historical linguists and philologists to understand and document the lexicon, grammar, and pragmatics of the languages of the past would all come under this rubric.

Another and altogether more literal sense of the word "code" arises in work on digital preservation. If we wish people in the future to have access to today's video games, we will need an explicit and complete model of the operational semantics of the code in which they are written, as executed by the originally targeted machines. That model must be precise at a very low level; hand-waving about the world-view expressed by video games will not help decipher the code that drives the video screen. It must be complete, or risk having the game crash for a viewer of the future, because there were gaps in the model. It must be formal enough for a machine to process; if it is not, there is no prospect of actually running the game in an emulator on a future machine.

Some of the most striking recent efforts in modeling for the digital humanities are concerned with identifying and describing cultural artifacts and the referents of discourse in cultural artifacts, on a large scale. These are utilitarian models in the sense described above, intended to ease large-scale exchange and integration of data. Because they are concerned with cultural artifacts, however, for which nuance and detail are regarded as very important, they share some properties with the self-reflexive models also described above.

The Europeana Data Model, for example, defines a loosely constrained set of entity types and relations to serve as the target for translation of metadata from heterogeneous sources into a common framework (Europeana, 2013). The Canonical Text Services model (Smith, 2009; Berti et al., 2014) provides a simple but concrete model of the structure of canonical texts that allows references to such texts to be resolved automatically. The SNAP project (Standards for Networking Ancient Prosopographies) similarly seeks to render explicit the assumptions implicit in our knowledge of people, in such a way as to allow different sources of information about people in the ancient world to be interconnected automatically (Bodard et al., 2014).

Perhaps the highest level of formality is achieved by the Conceptual Reference Model (CRM) prepared and maintained over many years by the International Committee for Documentation (CIDOC) of the International Council of Museums/Conseil international des Musées/Consejo internacional de museos (ICOM) is focused on information needed in museum documentation, but necessarily includes many things of broader relevance. It defines some 90 types of entity (Place, Place Name, Man-Made Object, Material, . . .) and 150 relations among entities (is identified by, is composed of, . . .). Subset/superset relations are defined for the entities (the set of Man-Made Objects is subset of Physical Man-Made Things, and also of Physical Objects). Each entity and relation is defined and examples are given; the logical relations specified are expressed in symbolic notation as well as in prose.

6 The limits of first-order logic

There are, it should be said, some limits to what can be done with standard formal logic.

First, there is no effective procedure guaranteed to decide, in finite time, whether a given statement is or is not a consequence of a given model described in logical terms. In 1930, the Austrian logician Kurt Gödel showed (in his so-called completeness theorem) that every valid statement in first-order logic—that is, every statement which is true on every possible interpretation—can be proved. This sounds hopeful, and in principle provides an algorithm for generating a proof for any valid statement. Any valid statement has a finite proof, so one could in principle generate all possible proofs in ascending order of length: eventually, for any valid statement, a suitable proof must inevitably appear, and must do so after a finite (albeit perhaps long) period of time. But this method does not provide an algorithm for distinguishing between valid statements and others— that is, for telling whether a given statement S is valid or not: having generated all possible proofs of length n or less, one may be able to confirm that no proof of S has thus far appeared, but there are always an infinite number of longer proofs still to be considered. For a non-valid statement, the procedure described will never terminate. This means that there can, in principle, be some uncertainty about what consequences follow from a given model: to tell for certain whether a given inference follows from a model expressed in logic, a more sophisticated algorithm than grinding out all possible proofs in length order would be needed. Later work by Turing and Church proved that no such algorithm can exist.

Second, and even more alarming on the face of it, there will in any sufficiently powerful logical system be sentences which are true in the intended domain but cannot be proven in that system, unless (what would be even worse) the system is logically inconsistent, in which case there will be false sentences which can be proven in the system. Nor is it possible to prove the consistency of conventional logic without resorting to some other, non-conventional logic. These results are also due to Gödel (his two incompleteness theorems, for which he is best known).[15]

It follows that at least some models involving first-order logic will be intractable: they cannot be handled successfully by machine. If the use of formal logic seems nevertheless the most fruitful form for digital humanities modeling to take, it is for several reasons. First, despite its limits formal logic remains one of the most effective tools known to humanity for clarifying the meaning of propositions and reasoning about them. Second, as the history of computing since the 1940s illustrates, there is ample room for interesting and useful work even within the bounds set by Gödel, Church, and Turing. And third, one of the most dramatic developments in computer science in the last decades has been the progress of new techniques for model checking and for the solution of Boolean satisfiability problems, which have made possible significant advances in theorem proving and other tools for working with logical specifications.

Practical tools deal with the limits imposed by Gödel in various ways. Theorem provers often require guidance from a human user (which means that they are often rather temperamental and that it may take a good while before a user can use them effectively). Some tools devoted to "light-weight formal methods" (such as the Alloy Analyzer whose use is illustrated at the end of this article) impose various limitations on the first-order logic they support (e.g., limited recursion, or no recursion at all) and do not attempt to prove theorems, limiting themselves to searching for examples or counterexamples for a given proposition, which they can do successfully without requiring any guidance from the user.

Both theorem provers and tools for lightweight formal methods can make it dramatically easier to explore the consequences of a given set of assumptions; they have no serious competition as a tool for making our models more complete and precise. Because they have a gentler learning curve, lightweight tools are probably the best place for most users to begin.

Some scholars may object that the issues studied by humanists are not reducible to simple logical formulae, that any attempt to reduce scholarship to such terms does violence to its nature. There is, I suppose, no way to persuade such scholars to share my view of scholarship; they appear to seek, in Northrop Frye's words, an understanding too occult for syntax. But such scholars are perhaps unlikely to be interested in modeling of any kind, and so unlikely to be reading this volume in the first place.

7 Try again

Three centuries ago, Gottfried Wilhelm Leibniz observed that nature might set limits to human knowledge (1685, p.1). However, he argued, nature does not require that we make so many mistakes in reasoning, or that we spend so much time in fruitless controversy due to lack of clarity in our arguments and premises.

> *Est vero in nostra potestate, ut in colligendo non erremus*, si scilicet quoad argumentandi formam rigide observemus regulas Logicas, [. . .] Quam methodi secuti sunt Mathematici, admirando cum successu.
>
> *Est etiam in potestate nostra, ut controversias finiamus*, si scilicet argumenta quae afferuntur in formam accurate redigamus, non syllogismos tantum formando atque examinando, sed et prosyllogismos, et prosyllogismorum prosyllogismos, donec vel absolvatur probatio, vel constet quid adhuc investigandum probandumve argumentanti supersit, ne scilicet inani circulo priora repetat, et Diogenis dolium volvat.

> [*But it is in our power not to err in logical inference*, namely if we rigidly observe the rules of logic, with respect to the form of argument [. . .] Which is the method that the mathematicians have followed with admirable success.
>
> *It is also in our power to put an end to controversies*, namely if we put the arguments brought forward accurately into a form, in which we not only formulate and examine the syllogisms of the argument, but the prosyllogisms, and the prosyllogisms of the prosyllogisms, until finally the proof is completed, or else it is established what parts of the argument must be further investigated in order to avoid falling into an empty circle repeating what has already been said, and rolling the tub of Diogenes.]

What Leibniz said then still holds now: formal representations of our ideas can help clarify them and can help us identify the points on which different views agree and disagree. For digital humanities, formally expressed models offer an unparalleled opportunity to make our understandings explicit, to observe and test the consequences of our ideas, and to clarify the nature of our agreements and disagreements with each other.

Two hundred years after Leibniz, the work of Frege (explicitly working on the lines sketched by Leibniz) and the *Principia Mathematica* of Russell and Whitehead raised the expectation (the hope, one could say, in some quarters) that there might in principle be a formal proof or disproof of every imaginable mathematical statement. Kurt Gödel proved that this is not so: although the logical system of Russell and Whitehead is complete in the sense mentioned above, it is also incomplete when applied to elementary arithmetic: we can construct statements about elementary arithmetic which we know to be true, for which there are no formal proofs or disproofs. Many have taken Gödel's work as a dark, even an ominous symbol of the limits of rationality, or of humanity. Gödel himself, interestingly, took the opposite view: since the mathematical statement in question (the "Gödel sentence") cannot be proved within the logical system of *Principia Mathematica*, but can be proved by human reasoning, Gödel viewed his theorem as illustrating that mathematics could not be reduced to any purely mechanical or mechanizable system: the limits suggested by his theorem are on his account limits of mechanical processes, but not limits of the human spirit or rationality.

Formal models will not ensure that we always agree with each other on substantive issues, nor that we will always find the same questions important or interesting. They can, however, help us avoid confusing non-substantive questions with substantive ones, and identify both the areas where we disagree and (perhaps not less important) the areas where we agree. We will not always succeed; our understanding of what we want to model may exceed our ability to capture it in formal terms. We will make mistakes, we will fail as well as succeed.

But failure is not unique to those who try to use formal models to understand the world and to record our understanding. Nor is possible failure necessarily a reason not to undertake the effort. As the unnamed narrator of Samuel Beckett's novel *Worstward Ho* says: "Ever tried. Ever failed. No matter. Try again. Fail again. Fail better."

A. Excursus: modeling Goodman's overlap relation

This simple example is offered for those readers who would like a better understanding of what formal models in a logical notation might look like in practice.

It uses the Alloy modeling tool mentioned in the text and developed by Daniel Jackson and others. For a more thorough treatment of Alloy, the reader is referred to Jackson, 2006, and to the various helpful tutorials on the Alloy website.[16] Other examples of Alloy usage may be found by searching the internet.

(One example that may be of interest to some readers of this essay is an Alloy model of the XPath 1.0 data model, which uncovers some unexpected gaps in the W3C specification along the way (Sperberg-McQueen, 2010.)

In his book *The Structure of Appearance* (Goodman, 1966), the philopher Nelson Goodman constructs a careful account of the properties of individuals, and of the meta-properties of those properties. Some properties, for example, have the (meta-)property that if they are true of a thing, they are true of every part of that thing. (The property "is located in Indiana" is an example.) These and several other meta-properties (dissective, expansive, collective, nucleative) are defined by Goodman in terms of a primitive notion he calls overlap (abbreviated "o"), which he describes thus (p. 34): "Two individuals overlap if they have some common content, whether or not either is wholly contained in the other. The predicate 'o' is symmetric and reflexive but not transitive."

As a primitive notion, overlap is not strictly speaking defined by Goodman, but he does characterize it in part with the following description and its translation into symbolic form:

If and only if two individuals x and y overlap is there some individual z (viz., any individual wholly contained within x and within y), such that whatever overlaps z also overlaps both x and y; that is:[17]

2.41 $x \text{ o } y \mathrel{.\equiv} (\exists z)(w)(w \text{ o } z \supset \mathrel{.} w \text{ o } x \mathrel{.} w \text{ o } y)$

A simple translation of the notion of overlap into Alloy may be used to model Goodman's notion of overlap and its properties. We can use the Alloy model to test our understanding of the notion and the implications of its definition.

We define *Individual* as an Alloy signature (a class of objects). Each Individual overlaps with some set of Individuals.

```
sig Individual { overlaps : set Individual }
```

Already at this point, the user can ask Alloy to show instances of the model: universes of discourse in which the constraints imposed by the model all apply. Here, the only constraint is that there may (or may not) be objects of the class Individual, and any two Individuals may (or may not) be related by the relation *overlaps*. One of the first instances shown takes the form shown in Figure 15.1.

The universe shown in this figure has two individuals. Individual1 overlaps Individual2, but not vice versa; this seems intuitively implausible (given the natural language meaning of *overlap*) as well as inconsistent with Goodman's statement that the relation *overlaps* is symmetric. Also, neither Individual overlaps itself, which contradicts Goodman's statement that the relation is reflexive.

To ensure that overlap is symmetric and reflexive, as specified by Goodman, we can add explicit rules to this effect, using Alloy facts (propositions which hold in all instances of the model). To simplify the notation, we first define a predicate *overlap* which holds of Individuals x and y if the pair $x \rightarrow y$ is a member of the relation *overlaps*. Using that predicate, we can conveniently specify that for any

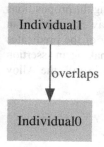

Figure 15.1 Two objects of the class Individual with the relation overlaps.

x and y, if x overlaps y then y overlaps x and vice versa (overlap is symmetric) and that for any x, x overlaps itself (overlap is reflexive).[18]

```
pred overlap[x, y : Individual] {
   x -> y in overlaps
}

fact overlap_is_symmetric {
   all a, b : Individual
      | overlap[a, b] iff overlap[b,a]
}

fact overlap_is_reflexive {
   all a : Individual | overlap[a,a]
}
```

The axiom 2.41 can also be expressed as a fact.

```
pred Axiom2_41 {
   all x, y : Individual
   | overlap[x,y]
     iff
     some z : Individual
   | all w : Individual
      | overlap[w, z] implies
        (overlap[w,x] and overlap[w, y])
}
```

What may not be obvious to the reader of Goodman (or of this exposition) is that the symmetry and reflexiveness of the overlap relation are not independent axioms, but are in fact consequences of Axiom 2.41.

The Alloy user can test for such redundancies by reformulating the propositions in question not as facts but as predicates (which may or may not hold in an instance of the model), and then checking to see whether any of the predicates follows from the others (is always true when they are true), by making an assertion to that effect and asking Alloy to check the assertion. Given in full, the Alloy model now reads as shown below.

```
/* Individuals may overlap.  That's the only
 * property we are currently interested in.
 */
sig Individual {
  overlaps : set Individual
}

pred overlap[x, y : Individual] { x -> y in overlaps }

pred overlap_is_symmetric {
   all a, b : Individual
      | overlap[a, b] iff overlap[b,a]
}

pred overlap_is_reflexive {
   all a : Individual | overlap[a,a]
}

/* Goodman's axiom 2.41:
If and only if two individuals x and y overlap is
there some individual z (viz., any individual
wholly contained within x and within y), such that
whatever overlaps z also overlaps both x and y;
that is:
2.41 (x o y) iff (some z)(w)(w o z => w o x and w o y)
*/
pred Axiom2_41 {
   all x, y : Individual
      | overlap[x,y]
        iff
        some z : Individual
        | all w : Individual
            | overlap[w, z] implies
                (overlap[w,x] and overlap[w, y])
}

/* N.B. this assertion is false; Alloy finds
counter-examples. */
```

```
assert rs_iff_241 {
  (overlap_is_symmetric and overlap_is_reflexive)
  iff Axiom2_41
}


/* N.B. this assertion is true and provable. */
assert rs_if_241 {
  Axiom2_41
  implies
  (overlap_is_symmetric and overlap_is_reflexive)
}


/* N.B. this assertion is false; Alloy finds a
counter-example. */
assert rs_onlyif_241 {
  (overlap_is_symmetric and overlap_is_reflexive)
  implies
  Axiom2_41 }

check rs_iff_241 for 4
check rs_if_241 for 10
check rs_onlyif_241 for 4
```

When the Alloy Analyzer executes the command `check rs_iff_241 for 4` it looks for instances of the model that contradict the assertion that overlap is both reflexive and symmetric if and only if axiom 2.41 also holds. It looks for counterexamples in all instances of the model containing up to four Individuals, and finds one. When the mutual implication is broken into parts to be checked separately, the Analyzer finds a counterexample for one direction (an instance in which overlap is reflexive and symmetric but axiom 2.41 does not hold), but not in the other (even when the scope of the assertion is raised to ten Individuals, which involves checking millions of instances).

The presence of a counterexample to two of the three assertions establishes conclusively that they are not, in the general case, true.

Alloy's failure to find a counterexample for the third assertion, by contrast, does not constitute a proof that the assertion always holds. (It does, in fact, always hold, but to know this with certainty it is necessary to prove it as a theorem.) Alloy's utility here is not in providing the proof of the theorem, but in its ability to show that if there is a counterexample, it must involve more than ten distinct individuals.[19] In practice, many false assertions prove to have small counterexamples (just as programming folklore holds that most bugs in software can be exposed by small test cases, if one can only find the test case), as indeed the two erroneous assertions in this case do.[20] Some users of theorem provers make it a practice to check every candidate theorem in Alloy before attempting a proof with the theorem prover; this helps avoid the frustrating experience of spending substantial time trying without success to lead the software to a proof, only to discover that there is no proof, because the proposition in question is not a theorem.

Notes

1 For example, McCarty (2004), who "argue[s] for modeling as a model" of digital-humanities practice.

2 This view is not universally shared; some humanists regard demands for clarity and explicitness arising in digital humanities as rooted solely in computing technology and essentially foreign to humanistic scholarship. See, for example, the opposition of "computational methods" and "formal logic" to "humanistic tools" in the introduction to Drucker (2009), elaborated more fully in chapter 1.

3 In Minsky, 1968, quoted in McCarty, 2004.

4 Unspoken here is the premise that computer programming is a form of modeling, which I take to be in no need of justification here. But on computer programs as models see further below.

5 I use the term *non-formal* rather than the *informal* often used by logicians and mathematicians, to try to avoid some of the extraneous images raised by the latter term.

6 By *first-order predicate calculus* or equivalently *first-order logic* is meant a set of rules (a calculus; etymologically, a system for calculating by means of small stones) for constructing and manipulating formulas denoting logical values (a predicate calculus), in which the expressions of the language denote objects and their properties, but not sets of objects or properties of properties (a first-order predicate calculus, as opposed to second- and higher-order calculi in which it is possible to quantify over and ascribe properties to properties of objects, properties of properties of objects, and so on in increasingly abstract concepts). The idea that logical reasoning can proceed by means of formal rules dates back in the West at least to Aristotle's rules for the use of syllogisms; those rules were formulated as a mathematical-style calculus in the course of the nineteenth century. The rigorous modern distinction between first- and higher-order predicates and their logics is a consequence of Bertrand Russell's discovery of Russell's Paradox. Less formally, first-order predicate calculus is, roughly, what is usually taught in a first-semester university course in symbolic logic.

Some may prefer to specify the use of description logics, rather than first-order logic, which have been widely promoted as being more tractable than first-order logic; they may have a point. If a given description logic is powerful enough to express the model in question, there is no reason not to use it. But the most satisfactory tools I am familiar with typically use stronger logics.

All of the domain-specific notations mentioned in the text can be translated without too much difficulty into first-order logic, although not all definitions of domain-specific notations specify a canonical translation in to logical notation, and such a translation is not always particularly convenient to work with (that is, of course, why the domain-specific notations exist).

7 Some theorem provers embedded in programming languages—for example, ACL2—do require that objects be defined in terms of a set of available primitives. Fortunately for ACL2 users, Common Lisp makes it relatively easy to work fairly abstractly and avoid irrelevant implementation details, or at least hide them behind suitable abstractions.

8 The Alloy Analyzer is developed by a research group at MIT under the leadership of Daniel Jackson, and described in Jackson's book (2006).

9 Not all of these examples actually use formal logic to formulate their models; the overall level of formality in digital humanities is not currently high enough to allow such a restriction. But the models proposed in these examples are, on the whole, clear enough that they could without excessive effort be translated into logical form. The examples given are concentrated in the areas of textual criticism and markup theory; whether this reflects a greater focus on formality there or merely the author's greater familiarity with the literature in those areas must be left for others to judge.

10 The discussion focuses on SGML, since that is where the crucial concepts originated. In all respects relevant to this discussion, the Extensible Markup Language (XML) defined in 1996–8 as a subset of SGML follows the older specification.

11 The reality is somewhat more complex. SGML makes it easier than any other notation before or since to identify hierarchical structures in documents, but nowhere does SGML claim that only hierarchical structures are relevant to document processing. By providing explicit means for assigning identifiers to elements and referring (pointing) to those elements from others, SGML goes beyond hierarchical structures and allows the representation of arbitrary directed graphs. If the creators of SGML had subscribed to the view that textual structures are exclusively hierarchical, the ID/IDREF mechanism built into SGML would have been unnecessary and irrelevant. Similar remarks apply to SGML's provisions for concurrent markup (the CONCUR feature).

12 None that I am aware of have objected to the claim that text is essentially ordered, although that claim can also be problematic. Nor has there been much discussion of the problematic fact that the authors define none of the terms in their slogan.

13 Renear and Wickett's observations and arguments apply equally well to the common account of relational databases as representing a domain by means of relations, each of which is a set of tuples of the same degree, each of which is a sequence of values. Because sets are timeless and do not change, it is impossible for such a collection of tables to be updated. It is perhaps for this reason that more careful descriptions of relational database refer to them as modeling the domain by means of sets of time-varying relations. Similar qualifications would be necessary in a formally coherent account of mutable XML documents. Huitfeldt, Vitali, and Peroni provide an initial sketch of such an account.

14 I will not attempt to summarize the discussion in detail here. A good brief account of the discussion up to that time is given by Whitehead and Pickford (1973); a very full discussion may be found in Timpanaro, 1960 (in later editions brought up to date through the mid-1980s).

15 A more careful but still non-technical formulation of the first incompleteness theorem can be found in Hintikka, 2000, p. 4: "If an axiomatic system containing elementary arithmetic is consistent, then one can find a specific proposition G that is true but unprovable in that system." The second incompleteness theorem addresses the question of consistency: "Gödel's proof itself can be carried out in a system of elementary arithmetic. Hence, if that system could be proved to be consistent in the elementary arithmetic, one could after all prove in the system that G is true. But by [the] first incompleteness theorem, G is unprovable in that system. Hence the initial assumption must be wrong, in other words, the consistency of the system cannot be proved in the system itself." Hintikka's book provides an accessible, non-technical account of Gödel's results and some of its philosophical ramifications; it is marred only by frequent typographic errors. A sympathetic and insightful treatment of Gödel and the significance of his work is offered by Goldstein (2005). Fuller and more technical accounts can be found in any modern introduction to symbolic logic.

16   Available at: http://alloy.mit.edu.
17   Goodman's formula 2.41 uses dots to indicate the relative binding priority of the operators; the notation was introduced by Giuseppe Peano and popularized by Russell and Whitehead. A fully parenthesized equivalent is

$$(x \text{ o } y) \; \exists \; (\forall z)((w)((w \text{ o } z) \supset ((w \text{ o } x) \wedge (w \text{ o } y)))$$

18   The reader will note that Alloy uses a notation similar to that (or those) of standard first-order logic, but one which uses fewer special symbols and is thus easier to type on a conventional keyboard. The two facts given here correspond to the first-order formulae $(\forall \; x)(\forall \; y)(\text{Individual}(x) \wedge \text{Individual}(y) \supset (x \text{ o } y \equiv y \text{ o } x))$ and $(\forall \; x)(\text{Individual}(x) \supset x \text{ o } x)$.
19   Alloy has checked all smaller instances without finding a counterexample; in this case there are approximately 10^{30} such instances, somewhat more than most modelers will be willing to check by hand.
20   It may be noted, however, that neither of the two erroneous assertions has a counterexample involving fewer than four individuals. If we had checked the assertions only within a scope of three individuals, we would have been wrong to assume that all three assertions hold.

References

Bédier, J., 1928. La tradition manuscrite du *Lai de l'Ombre*. *Romania*, 54, pp. 161–96.

Berti, M., Crane, G., Tiepmar, J., Teichmann, C., and Heyer, G., 2014. A New Implementation for Canonical Text Services. In: The 8th Workshop on Language Technology for Cultural Heritage, Social Sciences, and Humanities (LaTeCH 2014), in conjunction with the 14th Conference of the European Chapter of the Association for Computational Linguistics (EACL 2014). Gothenburg, Sweden, April 26. Toronto: University of Toronto Press.

Bodard, G., Cayless, H., Depauw, M., Isaksen, L., Lawrence, K.F., and Rahtz, S., 2014. Standards for Networking Ancient Prosopographies: the SNAP project. Available at: http://snapdrgn.net/wp-content/uploads/2014/02/SNAPall.pdf.

Chomsky, N., 1957. *Syntactic Structures*. The Hague: Mouton.

Coombs, J.H., Renear, A.H., and DeRose, S.J., 1987. Markup Systems and the Future of Scholarly Text Processing. *Communications of the Association for Computing Machinery*, 30(11), pp. 933–47.

DeRose, S.J., Durand, D.G., Mylonas, E., and Renear, A.H., 1990. What is Text, Really?. *Journal of Computing in Higher Education*, 1(2), pp. 3–26. Reprint 1997. ACM/SIGDOC *Journal of Computer Documentation*, 21(3), pp. 1–24.

Drucker, J., 2009. *SpecLab: Digital Aesthetics and Projects in Speculative Computing*. Chicago, London: University of Chicago Press.

Europeana, 2013. Europeana Data Model Primer. Available at: http://pro.europeana.eu/files/Europeana_Professional/Share_your_data/Technical_requirements/EDM_Documentation//EDM_Primer_130714.pdf.

Goldstein, R., 2005. *Incompleteness: The Proof and Paradox of Kurt Gödel*. New York: W.W. Norton.

Goodman, N., 1966. *The Structure of Appearance*. Indianapolis, IN: Bobbs-Merrill.

Hintikka, J., 2000. *On Gödel*. Wadsworth Philosophers Series. Belmont, CA: Wadsworth/Thompson Learning.

Huitfeldt, C. and Sperberg-McQueen, C.M., 2008. What is Transcription? *Literary & Linguistic Computing*, 23(3), pp. 295–310.

Huitfeldt, C., Vitali, F., and Peroni, S., 2012. Documents as Timed Abstract Objects. In: *Proceedings of Balisage: The Markup Conference 2012. Balisage Series on Markup Technologies, vol. 8* (2012). Available at: www.balisage.net/Proceedings/vol8/html/Huitfeldt01/BalisageVol8-Huitfeldt01.html.

Ide, N.M., 1987. *Pascal for the Humanities*. Philadelphia, PA: University of Pennsylvania Press.

ISO (International Organization for Standardization), 1986. ISO 8879-1986 (E). Information processing—Text and Office Systems—Standard Generalized Markup Language (SGML). Geneva: ISO.

ISO (International Organization for Standardization), 2014. ISO 21127:2014 Information and Documentation—A Reference Ontology for the Interchange of Cultural Heritage Information. Geneva: ISO.

Jackson, D., 2006. *Software Abstractions: Logic, Language, and Analysis*. Revised 2012. Cambridge, MA: MIT Press.

Leibniz, G.W., 1685. *De logica nova condenda* (On the new logic to be established). In: F. Schupp and S. Weber (Eds.) 2000. *Die Grundlagen des logischen Kalküls*. Translated by F. Schupp and S. Weber. Hamburg: Meiner, pp. 1–15.

McCarty, W., 2004. Modeling: A Study in Words and Meanings. In: S. Schreibman, R. Siemens, and J. Unsworth (Eds.) *A Companion to Digital Humanities*. Oxford: Blackwell, pp. 254–70. Available at: www.digitalhumanities.org/companion/view?docId =blackwell/9781405103213/9781405103213.xml&chunk.id=ss1-3-7.

McGann, J., 2004. Marking Texts of Many Dimensions. In: S. Schreibman, R. Siemens, and J. Unsworth (Eds.) *A Companion to Digital Humanities*. Oxford: Blackwell, pp. 198–217. Available at: www.digitalhumanities.org:3030/companion/view?docId= blackwell/9781405103213/9781405103213.xml&chunk.id=ss1-3-4.

Minsky, M.L., 1968. Matter, Mind, and Models. Revised version of an essay first published in *Proceedings of the International Federation of Information Processing Congress 1965*, vol. 1, pp. 45–49, and reprinted in *Semantic Information Processing*, ed. Marvin Minsky. Cambridge, MA: MIT Press. Available at: http://web.media.mit.edu/~minsky/papers/MatterMindModels.html.

Ott, W., 1973. *Metrische Analysen zu Vergil: Aeneis Buch VI*. Tubingen: Niemeyer.

Renear, A.H., Mylonas, E., and Durand, D., 1992. Refining our Notion of What Text Really Is: The Problem of Overlapping Hierarchies. In: N. Ide and S. Hockey, (Eds.) 1996. *Research in Humanities Computing 4: Selected Papers from 1992 ALLC/ACH Conference*. Oxford: Clarendon Press.

Renear, A.H. and Wickett, K.M., 2009. Documents Cannot Be Edited. In: *Proceedings of Balisage: The Markup Conference 2012. Balisage Series on Markup Technologies, vol. 3* (2009). Available at: www.balisage.net/Proceedings/vol3/html/Renear01/BalisageVol3-Renear01.html.

Renear, A.H. and Wickett, K.M., 2010. There are No Documents. In: *Proceedings of Balisage: The Markup Conference 2012. Balisage Series on Markup Technologies, vol. 5* (2010). Available at: www.balisage.net/Proceedings/vol5/html/Renear01/BalisageVol5-Renear01.html.

Rosenblueth, A. and Wiener, N., 1945. The Role of Models in Science. *Philosophy of Science*, 12(4), pp. 316–21.

Schonefeld, O., 2007. XCONCUR and XCONCUR-CL: A constraint-based approach for the validation of concurrent markup. In: G. Rehm, A. Witt, and L. Lemnitzer (Eds.) 2007. *Data Structures for Linguistic Resources and Applications – Proceedings of the Biennial GLDV Conference 2007*. Tübingen: Gunter Narr Verlag. pp. 347–56.

Smith, D.N., 2009. Citation in Classical Studies. *Digital Humanities Quarterly*. Available at: www.digitalhumanities.org/dhq/vol/3/1/000028/000028.html.

Sperberg-McQueen, C.M., 2010. Alloy version of XPath 1.0 data model. Black Mesa Technologies LLC. Available at: http://blackmesatech.com/2010/01/xpath10.als (accessed February 6, 2016).

Sperberg-McQueen, C.M. and Huitfeldt, C., 2000. GODDAG: A Data Structure for Overlapping Hierarchies. In: P. King and E.V. Munson (Eds. 2004). DDEP-PODDP 2000, *Lecture Notes in Computer Science 2023*. Berlin: Springer, pp. 139–60. Available at: www.w3.org/People/cmsmcq/2000/poddp2000.html.

Sperberg-McQueen, C.M., Huitfeldt, C., and Renear, A., 2001. Meaning and interpretation of markup. *Markup Languages: Theory & Practice* 2(3), pp. 215–34. Available at: http://cmsmcq.com/2000/mim.html.

Stührenberg, M. and Goecke, D., 2008. SGF – An integrated model for multiple annotations and its application in a linguistic domain. In: *Proceedings of Balisage: The Markup Conference 2012. Balisage Series on Markup Technologies, vol. 1* (2008). Available at: www.balisage.net/Proceedings/vol1/html/Stuehrenberg01/BalisageVol1-Stuehrenberg 01.html.

Tennison, J., Piez, W., and Cowan, J., 2002–2008?. LMNL Data Model. *LMNL markup dot org*. Available at: http://lmnlmarkup.org/specs/archive/LMNL_data_model.xhtml.

Timpanaro, S., 1960. *The Genesis of Lachmann's Method*. Translated by W. Glenn, 2005. Chicago: University of Chicago Press.

Tukey, J.W., 1977. *Exploratory Data Analysis*. Reading, MA: Addison-Wesley.

Weitzman, M.P., 1982. Computer simulation of the development of manuscript traditions. *Bulletin of the Association for Literary and Linguistic Computing*, 10, pp. 55–9.

Weitzman, M.P., 1985. The Analysis of Open Traditions. *Studies in Bibliography*, 38, pp. 82–120.

Weitzman, M.P., 1987. The Evolution of Manuscript Traditions. *Journal of the Royal Statistical Society*, Series A (General), 150(4), pp. 287–308.

Whitehead, F. and Pickford, C.E., 1973. The introduction to the Lai de l'Ombre: Sixty years later. *Romania*, 94, pp. 145–56.

Part III

Back matter

Glossary

Julia Flanders and Fotis Jannidis

This glossary provides basic definitions, explanations, and historical context for a set of key terms central to the topic domain of the volume. The focus is on explaining the significance of these terms for an understanding of data modeling in a digital humanities context, rather than on providing a comprehensive reference. Our hope is that readers of the volume will be able to use this glossary as a starting point to help elucidate references in the main narrative, and will then be able to consult standard resources such as standards, documentation, Wikipedia, and the like for further detail as needed. Some links and references for further reading are provided.

Annotation

Although the term "annotation" has a wide range of meanings in common usage, from a data modeling perspective the most salient use concerns the annotation of data: the addition of metadata, comments, markup, or other information that supplements the original data and renders it richer or more usable. The term "annotation" in this sense is quite broad and makes no assumptions concerning whether the annotation is embedded in the data or separate from it, or whether the annotation is expressed through a formal language or as natural-language commentary. It also does not make any assumptions about specific markup systems or about the kind of information the annotation contains. In linguistic corpora, for example, annotations may provide part-of-speech information, named entity identification, time code, and other information that explicates or enriches the raw language data. In scholarly editing, one might consider the representation of variants and editorial apparatus as a form of annotation; in image databases, the use of tags to identify people and locations can also be considered annotation. See OADM.

CIDOC Conceptual Reference Model

CIDOC is the International Committee for Documentation of the International Council of Museums (ICOM), and it develops and promulgates good practice in documentation for the museum community. Its Conceptual Reference Model

(CRM) is an object-oriented ontology of concepts required for documenting the holdings of galleries, libraries, archives, museums, and other cultural heritage institutions. In addition to representing concepts specific to this subject domain (such as provenance, authorship, materials, and so forth), it also provides a model of more general concepts (an "upper ontology") necessary to reason inferentially upon the more specific concepts: for instance, CRM includes a model of temporality so that systems using the reference model can work with concepts of sequencing, nested timespans and historical periods, and other temporal relationships that obtain in the curatorial world.

Conceptual model

The term "conceptual model" is used in the context of database design to refer to the first step of data modeling: the identification of entities, their attributes, and their relations on the basis of a close analysis of the universe of discourse which is supposed to be modeled. Conceptual modeling is often carried out by means of an intellectual procedure such as the creation of [see] entity–relationship diagrams that use an abstract graphical notation for the model in question. Although a conceptual model is already an important step in the direction of abstraction and selection, it is meant to be independent of the way the model is implemented at the end and what kind of formal model is the basis of the data model. One of the main functions of conceptual modeling is to provide those participating in the modeling process with a common ground and a basis for communication. Subsequent steps in data modeling create a [see] logical model and a [see] physical model, each of them being less abstract and more determined by aspects of the implementation of the model. The notion of a conceptual model has been transferred to other areas of data modeling and beyond to software design, to process modeling, and to user interface design. In these contexts it usually refers to a level of analysis which is close to the way the user understands and perceives the segment of the world which is modeled. Sometimes the [see] Unified Modeling Language is used to represent these kinds of conceptual models.

Constraint

Constraint is a fundamental condition of the intelligibility of data. At small scale, constraint operates through mechanisms like data typing, specification of units of measurement, and the establishment of controlled vocabularies, all of which help ensure that individual data elements have a consistent and appropriate format and semantics. At a higher level, constraint operates through formal schemas that express a full theory of the data set. At both levels, constraints typically operate in one of two modes. One approach, typified by various types of XML schema and by relational database design, states explicitly what data elements are permitted or required, such that documents diverging from the pattern are considered invalid. In the other approach, the constraint system instead consists of tests for specific patterns or faults (such as omitted elements or values that fall outside of designated bounds), which allow the data to be open-ended in areas not covered by the constraints. The most obvious expression of constraint is the formal test provided by schema validation, or the restrictions imposed by data entry forms—for instance, through the provision of drop-down menus of permitted values, or the verification of data formats such as dates. But constraint may also be expressed, more subtly, through the design processes and conceptual tools that frame the work spaces within which data is created and used. For example, an entity-relationship diagram is an important expression of such constraint, operating not on the data itself (which may not yet have been created) but on the design of the logical and physical models of the data, and also (less directly) on downstream tasks like interface design and planning for data reuse.

Database

A database is a collection of structured data allowing fast and complex queries, different views and failsafe updates. A database management system (DBMS) is the software enabling these forms of access to the data. There are different types of databases, based on the way the data is structured. Since the 1980s, the [see] relational database is the dominant form of DBMS with SQL as a common data management and query language. In the last years, NoSQL databases are playing also an important role, either because they cater to specific data formats like object stores, triple stores or XML databases, or because the amount of data and the required speed can be better served by a database management system with key-value pairs that are swifter to process.

Data curation

Data curation comprises the activities through which data is managed throughout its horizon of use, so as to maximize its continued value. Effective data curation is strongly enhanced by good data modeling practices; explicit and well-documented data models can help data curators align related data sets, and make it possible to handle forward migration in a way that respects the semantics of the data and the intentions behind its design.

Data model

A data model is an abstract structure describing a universe of discourse—that is, some segment of reality—under a functional perspective, by identifying important entities and their relation to each other. It conforms to an underlying mathematical model that specifies the possible operations with the data. Complex data models usually provide information about the structure of the data and also specify the [see] data types for all or some of its components. A data model can be described on a [see] conceptual level, which is quite similar to the way users conceptualize the segment of the world which is modeled, or on a [see] logical level, which is already expressed in a way that conforms fully to the underlying mathematical model, or on a physical level which includes all aspects of the specific implementation of a model. Today, a model is usually expressed using an existing metamodel suited for the task at hand—for example, [see] entity relationship modeling for databases, or XML for textual data. The same model can be applied to many instances ([see] modeled instance)—for example, a specific XML schema represents a markup language that can be used to mark up many different texts. Data models serve different functions. They provide all participants with a common basis for communication, and they may serve as the basis for constraints that ensure data consistency, by both filtering the data at the input and validating the existing data. Via the underlying mathematical model, they also enable a set of functions—for example, the relational model makes use of relational algebra with functions like UNION (creating a new set containing all members of the unified sets), or NATURAL JOIN (creating a new set of all combinations of tuples in the joined sets that are equal on their common attribute names). These functions allow powerful operations on the data, making use of the structure highlighted by the data model.

Data type

A data type is a property of a data component (such as a database field, or an XML element or attribute) that specifies what kind of data the component is expected to contain: for instance, a Boolean value, or a date in ISO format, or an integer. The data type may be used both to constrain data creation, and also to specify the anticipated processing—for instance, a field whose data is assumed to be a call number will be sorted quite differently from one that is assumed to be a decimal number. There are some data types that are common across almost all programming and modeling environments, such as integers and Boolean values, but others may be defined within a specific data modeling system, and still others may be defined by users. For example, the TEI defines a specialized data type called "data.xTruthValue" (extended truth value) to express "a truth value which may be unknown"; this data type is defined as a choice between a Boolean value as defined by the XML Schema Definition ("true" or "false") or the values "unknown" or "inapplicable." And the TEI customization mechanism permits users to define their own datatypes in their [see] ODD file.

Descriptive markup

The term "descriptive markup" is used to identify forms of markup that focus on describing the properties of objects being represented (such as documents or data sets) rather than specifying the intended processing of that representation. The term arose in connection with the emergence of SGML and its precursors, languages that were designed to operate outside the domain of any specific processing system and hence permitted a clear separation between the general description of textual features (such as headings or lists) and the system-specific instructions for how to process and format such features (through indentation, font shifts, and so forth). The use of descriptive markup assumes that the specification of formatting and processing will be given separately—for instance, through a stylesheet or processing guide. From a data modeling perspective, descriptive markup is a crucial milestone and has particular importance for the digital humanities, since it treats markup as an instrument for describing the ontology of documents—their content, structure, and other features of interest to scholars—rather than as a tool for achieving a single practical outcome. As a result, it also supports the idea that the data being modeled will have value for many different users and for an extended period of time, and thus must operate outside the context of specific processing environments.

Document type definition (DTD)

A document type definition is a set of explicit declarations that define the components of an SGML or XML markup language, including its elements, attributes, entities, and other features. A DTD is a form of schema; in the digital humanities world, DTDs are now less commonly used than other methods of expressing schemas (such as RelaxNG, which is the language in which the TEI schema is most commonly expressed).

Encoded Archival Description (EAD)

The Encoded Archival Description is an XML language developed by the Society of American Archivists and the Library of Congress, for the purpose of representing archival finding aids in digital form. It is used both for capturing existing paper finding aids, and also for creating new finding aids; as a result, it combines a transcriptional approach to data modeling (in which the structure of the original document is considered significant and is retained), and a more architectural approach in which consistency and automated processing are the primary goals.

Entity-relationship model (ERM)

The entity-relationship model is a way to describe the structure and semantics of data which was first proposed in a now famous paper by Peter Chen (Chen, 1976) and since then developed—with some important changes and additions – into a widely used design tool especially for relational databases. Its basic assumption is that "the real world consists of entities and relationships" (Chen, 1976, p. 9). An entity usually has one or more attributes—for example, the entity "employee" could have the attributes "employee number", "name" and "age." A relationship describes the relation between entities—for example, between employees and projects—and can have attributes on its own—for example, the time an employee is working on the project. Chen also proposed a graphical model for the ERM which became very popular, because it provides a relatively easy and accessible way to visualize ERMs. Entities are referenced by rectangles and relationships by

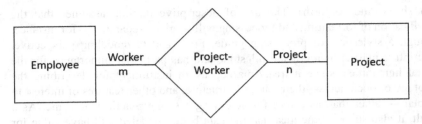

Figure 16.1 The relationship between employee and project.

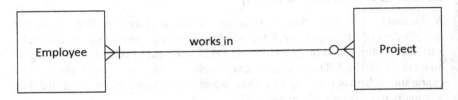

Figure 16.2 Use of the "crow-foot" notation to describe a relationship.

diamonds. The lines between these building blocks contain additional information —for example, the possible number of entities being part of the relationship. The relationship between employee and project would be modeled like this ("m" and "n" indicate any positive integer) (please see Figure 16.1).

Modern variations of Chen's ER diagram often substitute the relationship symbol with a line. The so-called "crow-foot" notation, which is especially widespread, would describe the relationship in this way (please see Figure 16.2).

The vertical line indicates "at least one," the triangle with a middle line is the notation for "many" and the circle means "zero." So this diagram says: "One or many employees work in a project, and a project has zero or many employees working in it." There is no real standard for ER diagrams (the existing ISO standard hasn't established itself as such) and there are many more or less similar implementations. Many of the basic ideas of the ERM and the ER diagram are also part of [see] UML.

Functional Requirements for Bibliographic Records (FRBR)

FRBR describes an entity-relationship model for bibliographic records. It comprises three groups of entities: 1) products of intellectual or artistic endeavour, 2) agents responsible for the content, dissemination, or the custodianship of these products, and 3) subjects of intellectual or artistic endeavour. The first group in particular has been adapted by other attempts to model cultural heritage.

In describing bibliographic items it distinguishes between four levels: the work (for example, Schubert's *Trout Quintet*), the expression (the composer's score or a specific performance, such as, for example, by the Amadeus Quartet with Emil Gilels), the manifestation (the performance on CD-ROM or on Spotify) and the item (a specific CD-ROM). The relationship between these levels can be expressed in the following way: the expression is a realization of the work, while the manifestation is an embodiment of an expression, and an item is an exemplar of a manifestation. Under the label of FRBRoo, there exists a proposal to merge FRBR (which is already [see] object-oriented) and [see] CIDOC-CRM into a common model.

Geographic information systems (GIS)

Geographic Information Systems are technologies for representing, managing, and expressing geospatial information (now typically in digital form). In GIS, data is modeled such that each item of data (on climate, population, epidemiology, human culture, and so forth) also contains a co-ordinate-based representation of where the item is located. This allows the data to be mapped and explored spatially.

Graph theory

Graph theory is a field mostly studied by mathematics, computer science, sociology and network science; its main object are graphs. Graphs consist of nodes, often also called vertices, and links, formally known as edges or arcs. Graph theory describes and classifies graphs, from very simple graphs consisting only of "plain" nodes and links, to very complex structure where the links are directed and have values attached, and where nodes have information assigned to them and are connected by more than one link. The following shows a visualization of a multigraph where the nodes are connected by more than one directed link with weights attached (please see Figure 16.3).

Graphs are an important data model for many kinds of relational structures, especially for network science which analyses anything from computer networks to streets and for its important subfield, social network theory, which describes social networks like families or facebook users. Graph theory also provides many algorithms for the description and analysis of networks—for example, centrality measures to determine important nodes or algorithms to find effectively the shortest path from one node to another.

Internet Engineering Task Force (IETF)

The IETF is an international standards body that creates standard documents in form of requests for comments (RFC). Well-known and widely used standards published as RFCs include POP3, SMTP and IMAP (email), TCP and IP (basic internet protocol), URLs and URIs (internet addressing schemes) and many more.

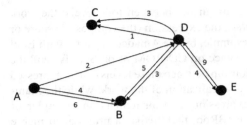

Figure 16.3 A visualization of a multigraph with weights attached.

International Organization for Standardization (ISO)

The International Organization for Standardization (ISO) is an international institution dedicated to developing and curating standards. A total of 162 countries are members of ISO. In cooperation with over 3,000 technical bodies more than 20,000 standards have been developed since 1949. Not all of these standards are IT related, but many important information standards are ISO standards. An ISO standard promises to be especially sustainable.

Linked open data

Linked open data is structured data that has been openly published (without access restrictions or usage limitations) in a manner that permits it to be queried, interlinked, and processed using automatable web technologies. In practical terms, this means that the individual entities being represented must be addressable via a URI—that is, a unique, universal identifier that can be used to locate and link to the resource. Linked open data resources are becoming an increasingly important component of the digital humanities infrastructure, since they provide access to authoritative forms of information concerning entities like people, bibliographic items, and geographic locations, which can then be recombined into useful research tools and systems. Although linked, open data can in principle be published in a variety of different formats and from a variety of different platforms. It is most commonly represented using RDF and the family of related standards that support the creation and querying of ontologies, because these technologies provide for semantically aware processing.

Logic

Logic is a very general term and covers different related concepts. While logic in general can be understood as a very old endeavor to establish principles of sound reasoning, in computer science and digital humanities especially, formal logic plays an important role, because it offers a frame to consistently understand the mechanics of information processing starting from the components of central processing units like logic gates up to the underlying principles of programming languages, and of process and data modeling. Some areas of logic are especially relevant in this regard: Boolean algebra offers an abstract way to describe the truth value of propositions connected by operators like conjunction, disjunction or negation, and it is the basis to describe the logic of hardware circuits, is used in all programming languages and is the foundation of all data modeling activities. Statements in classical propositional logic can be expressed in Boolean algebra. Predicate logic adds quantifiers to the logical calculus ("for all" and "there exists"), and provides the basis for relational databases and schema languages. Other forms of logic—for example, fuzzy logic or probabilistic logic, are applied in areas like natural language processing or machine learning to model concepts in ways that are more similar to human usage.

Logical model

In data modeling a logical model is—in contrast to the [see] conceptual model —a more formalized version of the model that conforms to all rules and constraints of the underlying mathematical model (which in turn conforms to the [see] metamodel for relational data). In distinction from the [see] physical model, the logical model is expressed independent of any specific details of the implementation of a model.

Markup language

Broadly speaking, a markup language is a system for representing the structure, content, and other aspects of a document or data object, using some form of embedded markup. In the digital humanities, the most common markup languages are all applications of XML, and thus the structures of XML (its tag structure and notation, its structural constraints) are treated as synonymous with "markup," but non-XML languages have been used in the past and still exist—for example, TeX, COCOA, and LMNL. Although XML markup is very commonly used in digital humanities for the representation of textual data, many text encoding languages are capable of modeling various kinds of non-textual data, including geospatial information, images, and musical notation. The most commonly used markup languages in the digital humanities are TEI, HTML, EAD (the Encoded Archival Description, used for finding aids), METS (the Metadata Encoding and Transmission Standard), MODS (the Metadata Object Description Schema), SVG (Scalable Vector Graphics, used for representing vector images) and MEI (the Music Encoding Initiative). See also the entry on annotation.

Metamodel

If a model is a representation of a specific set of relations between entities in an information system—for instance, a relationship between personnel names, addresses, and human resource data—a metamodel stipulates the possible structuring mechanisms for such a model. The metamodel defines the possible meaningful relations between entities in a given modeling system, and the informational properties entities can possess, such as hierarchy, inheritance, one-to-one vs. many-to-one relationships, cyclicality, nesting, sequencing, and so forth. For example, XML is a metamodel that supports a hierarchically organized set of data elements with inheritance, sequentiality, attributes, and other features; all XML models (such as TEI, MODS, EAD, etc.) reflect this architecture. Similarly, the relational model can be understood as a metamodel that defines the general architecture of relational databases, which is shared by all specific relational database systems.

Metadata

Metadata is, colloquially, "data about data": information that operates at the level of the file or data set to provide information necessary to the management, interpretation, or use of the data. Some of the most broadly required metadata elements have been identified and formalized as a vocabularry called "Dublin Core," which covers information such as title, creator, subject, creation date, format, language, and rights, and is widely used for basic description of web resources and digital objects. More specific metadata standards are appropriate for cases where more detail and more domain-specificity are required. In some cases, metadata is contained within the digital object itself (as in the case of the TEI header or the EXIF data embedded in a JPEG image). In other cases, the metadata may stand outside the entity being documented (as in the case of a METS record).

Modeled instance

In data modeling, the modeled instance is a specific data object that has been represented using a specific data model—for example, a network graph of familial relationships in *War and Peace*, or a TEI-encoded letter, or a database table of mortality records. In cases where the data model is entirely prescriptive and contains no optional or omissible features, the modeled instance may serve as a representation of the model itself, demonstrating its specific provisions, field names, sequencing requirements, and so forth. In cases where the data model contains features that may vary, it may take a large number of modeled instances (in some cases, an infinite number) to demonstrate the full set of possibilities permitted by the model.

Namespace

At a basic level, namespaces are a mechanism for avoiding name collisions—that is, cases where the same name is used for two different objects in the same information space. They operate by supplementing the local name of an object ("head," "table," readMe.txt, etc.) with a namespace that indicates the domain within which the local name operates. In computer programming, that domain might be the scope of a particular code package; in a file system, that domain might be the specific directory within which a data object is located.

In XML, the namespace identifies a specific XML vocabulary within which a given element or attribute is defined, and thus provides a way of formally distinguishing one XML language from another. This provision permits a given modeled instance to use elements from more than one model while making it clear which language—and hence which set of semantic and structural constraints—apply in each case. From a data modeling perspective, namespaces are crucial as a way of situating a data object within an appropriate interpretive context, and as a way of managing the interactions between multiple vocabularies and data representation regimes that are increasingly common in the universe of linked open data—thus, for example, enabling the reuse of existing specialized standards.

Natural language

A natural language is a human language (written or spoken) that arises from human culture and use; the term is used in contradistinction both to programming languages and also to invented human languages, like Esperanto or Klingon. Because natural language is generated out of human contingency, its vocabulary and other structures are open-ended; while grammars and lexicons can be created that assist in artificial processing of natural languages, those languages exhibit irregular and unpredictable features that pose ongoing challenges to natural language processing. Natural language processing is a subfield at the intersection of computer science and linguistics, which is developing tools to extract information from unstructured speech or text. Some of the core tasks of NLP are part-of-speech tagging, named entity recognition, parsing—that is, the identification of sentence structures—machine translation, and speech recognition. One important ultimate goal is understanding human language.

Open Archives Initiative (OAI)

The Open Archives Initiative is an international organization aimed at developing standards for disseminating and discovering digital content, with particular emphasis on information resources used by research institutions (such as digital repositories, digital scholarly publications, and digital cultural heritage resources). OAI has developed several standards of particular importance for data modeling in digital humanities, including OAI-PMH (the Open Archives Initiative Protocol for Metadata Harvesting), which specifies standards and methods for exposing and harvesting metadata; and OAI-ORE (Open Archives Initiative Object Reuse and Exchange), which specifies standards for the exchange of complex digital objects between repositories.

Open Annotation Data Model (OADM)

The Open Annotation Data Model provides a formal specification that describes both the internal structure of annotations and also the ways in which they are connected to the object or objects they annotate. This data model treats the concept of "annotation" as covering essentially any kind of association between resources (or parts of resources), including cases where the assertion of an association is the entire content of the annotation. The OADM does not supersede the models that have been developed for more specific purposes, such as specific languages for linguistic annotation, or TEI markup for scholarly editions. Its contribution is rather that it provides a standard data model for the broad set of generically conceptualized "annotations" that currently are supported ad hoc, including things like user comments on web-based resources, user-generated topic keywording, personal note-taking, and the like. Since OADM operates at a very high level of generality, it can also accommodate some of the terrain covered by more specific standards (such as TEI), but with a corresponding loss of efficiency and situational functionality.

Object-oriented modeling

Object-oriented modeling is an approach to modeling made popular by object-oriented programming (OOP). OOP is a programming paradigm like procedural programming, functional programming or declarative programming. Its basic goal is to identify the essential entities of the target domain and their functions. These entities are then modeled as self-contained data structures that also include the related procedures as methods. The abstract blueprints of these entities, consisting of data structures and methods, are called classes. From a data modeling perspective, the most important concept of OOP and object-oriented modeling is inheritance. A class can be defined as the subtype of another class. The subclass inherits the properties and methods of the superclass. This allows the construction of class relationships that are easy to understand and that map naturally to the way humans organize entities. In the digital humanities, object-oriented modeling is used in some of the established standards like [see] CIDOC-CRM or the object-oriented version of the [see] Functional Requirements of Bibliographic Records. Often [see] UML diagrams are used to depict object-oriented models.

ODD (One Document Does it all)

An ODD file is a TEI file used as part of the TEI schema customization process that expresses the selection of modules, elements, attributes, and other components that make up a specific TEI schema. The ODD format is a specialized module of the TEI language that contains elements specifically oriented towards schema-writing. When an ODD file is processed by an ODD processor, such as the TEI's Roma tool, the main output is a customized TEI schema reflecting the selections expressed in the ODD file. The significance of the name "ODD" (One Document Does it all) has to do with the fact that the ODD format combines formal schema specifications with documentation in a single file (inspired by the concept of "literate programming" pioneered by Donald Knuth), enabling the schema designer's modeling choices to be made explicit in a manner closely tied to the schema itself. From a data modeling perspective, the role of the ODD file in the overall TEI schema customization process reflects a distinctive and culturally significant approach to the management of divergence within a community of practice. Because the ODD file expresses a schema customization as a set of explicitly documented divergences from a standard model—i.e. the comprehensive TEI schema—customizations can be meaningfully compared and their commonalities and differences made visible. The ODD file is thus a key component in a system of intersecting and dialogic modeling, governed by the larger shared rubric of the TEI standard.

Ontology

An ontology is a formal expression and definition of the entities and concepts that make up a particular information domain. The purpose of an ontology is to provide a formally processable set of declarations concerning the different types of entities that exist within the domain, and their relationships to one another, such that the ontology can support inferencing processes. Ontologies also perform an important social function in relation to data representation, by providing a formal expression of a community consensus with respect to a specific information domain. By stating the axioms and information classes that the community agrees upon, they lay a foundation for data interchange and make it possible to reason programmatically with the information resources the community creates. For a very simple example, imagine an ontology for describing art works that includes entities representing physical materials (paper, metal, ceramic, leather, silk, paint, glue, and so forth) and the concept of "being made of" a material (in the sense that a painting "is made of" canvas and paint, or a book "is made of" paper and leather and glue). The ontology might also represent the concept of "being vulnerable to" or "being damaged by," and might include representation of entities that are risk agents (fire, water, acid, humidity, light, etc.). Using this ontology, we can express the fact that a given art work is made of a certain set of materials, and we can also express the fact that a given material is vulnerable to damage by a certain set of risk agents; from these statements, we can infer what the risk agents are for each art work. As new risks become known, we might expand the ontology—for instance, to reflect research showing that certain ceramics are vulnerable to acid. Ontologies are typically constructed with the goal of rendering a domain formally intelligible so as to coordinate and mediate between different applications of that information. If two projects are both creating databases to manage museum records, having a shared ontology will enable them to express the commonalities between those records even if the field names are in different languages or use different terminology. With the rise of linked data, this kind of curation-driven approach to ontologies is becoming increasingly important as a way of attempting to anchor the meaning of linked data entities so that the linkages produced can be used appropriately.

Parser

A parser, broadly speaking, is that part of a software system that transforms (usually human-readable) input data into some other data structure for further analysis and transformation. Such components, which can take a variety of forms, have wide applicability in computing. In the case of programming languages, a parser is typically used to translate programming code into a data structure more suitable for providing lower-level instructions to the computer. Regular expression "engines" are likewise tools that generate parsers for matching text. Systems for processing markup languages also involve parsers, since the generated data structures can be used either to check for syntactic validity or else (as in the case of HTML) directly transformed into a data structure that a program (like a browser) can render to the screen. Parsing is typically preceded by the more basic task of separating the individual parts of the input into individual atomic units, and checking to make sure that that those units represent valid input for the parser (a step variously referred to as "tokenization" or "lexing"). This division is important in all areas where parsing is involved, since an XML document or a program might represent a valid set of tokens (hence "well-formed," in the case of XML), but invalid as a usable data structure.

Physical model

In contrast to the [see] conceptual and logical model, a physical model specifies the model including all aspects of its implementation in a specific programming language or system. Usually, the physical model is not part of the data modeling process.

Process model

In modeling a universe of discourse, process modeling entails modeling entities and their relations as they move either in a linear or in a cyclic form in time, including the different states in time and the related requirements at each state. For example, one might develop a process model describing an editorial workflow for a class of digital objects, specifying the schema and other constraints to be applied at each stage, the agents who have responsibility for modifying and approving each stage, and the stylesheets and other publication processes to be applied to each form of the data.

Prototype

In general terms, a prototype is a preliminary version of something being built, usually on a small-scale or simplified form, for purposes of testing the feasibility, development process, or usability of the object. In these respects, a prototype resembles a model in several ways. It serves as a model of an idea: an incomplete, provisional realization or exploration of the idea's potential, permitting the discovery of flaws or unseen opportunities. It also serves as a kind of proleptic model of the thing to be built: a surrogate that is typically cheaper and easier to create, and less wasteful to destroy in the testing process.

Query language

A query language is a computer language specifically designed for requesting information from a database or other data structure. Its terminology typically includes language for specifying the scope of the query, what data fields are being addressed, and how the results should be reported or scoped. Specific query languages are designed to work with specific types of data resources—for instance, SQL is designed for use with relational databases, while XQuery is designed for use with XML data sources, and RDQL and SPARQL are designed for use with RDF.

Resource Description Framework (RDF)

The Resource Description Framework is a language to express statements about entities in the digital and real world. RDF is a recommendation of the W3C and is part of its semantic web agenda, which aims to enable more complex automatic forms of retrieval and analysis over the web, moving towards increasing the availability of web-based data formatted for consumption by machines rather than humans. RDF defines a syntax to express statements in three parts: subject, predicate and object. These RDF triples use uniform resource identifiers (URI) to refer to entities and predicates making use of existing ontologies, such as Friend of a Friend (FOAF) and many others. Each triple is a small directed [see] graph and the triples together describe huge information networks which can be queried using a query language like [see] SPARQL and which allow inferences about the objects described by the triples. In digital humanities, one of the most important applications of RDF is [see] linked open data.

Relational model/relational database

A relational database is a database that uses the relational model as the principal way to structure the data. According to the relational model, which was proposed in 1970 by E.F. Codd, information about an entity is expressed as a relation (in the logical model represented as a table). So, in the context of a cultural heritage model, there could be an entity "Artist," which in the relation model is denoted as the relation ARTIST and is represented by a table called ARTIST. A relation is defined by its attributes—for example, could the relation ARTIST have the three attributes NAME – YEAR_OF_BIRTH – YEAR_OF_DEATH. In the table, ARTIST, these attributes would be represented as column headings. A relation consists of a set of tuples; in a table, each tuple is represented as a row—for example, Goethe – 1749 – 1832. Each element of the tuple is an attribute value for one of the attributes defining the relation: "Goethe" is the attribute value for NAME etc. A relation has at least one attribute which is a primary key, that is, the value of this attribute is unique for each tuple and can serve as an identifier. In a table there is at least one column with unique values; it is also called the primary key. Relational databases usually support more commonalities than just the relational model. [see] SQL provides a common interface for data management and queries to relational databases. The [see] entity-relationship model is used to create a model on the conceptual level.

Resource Description and Access (RDA)

Resource Description and Access is a recently developed standard for the description of bibliographic resources, based on and replacing the Anglo-American Cataloguing Rules (AACR2). Initially developed jointly by library organizations in the US, Canada, and the UK, RDA is now supported by two international bodies with increasing support outside the English-speaking world. RDA is based on the conceptual models defined by the Functional Requirements for Bibliographic Records (FRBR) and the Functional Requirements for Authority Data (FRAD), both of which are designed to facilitate meaningful interconnections between data resources and effective discovery and retrieval beyond the boundaries of a single library catalog.

Schema

In broad terms, a schema is a set of rules and constraints that govern a specific data resource or class of data resources by expressing the data elements or fields that the resource is permitted or required to include, and the relationships between those elements (containment, ordering, omissibility, and so forth). These constraints come into play in specific ways that are determined by the specific type of resource in question. In XML data, a schema may be considered from two different perspectives. It can be understood as the definition of a specific XML language (representing its vocabulary and grammar), so that the act of confirming validity against the schema makes a statement concerning the overall intelligibility of the data as an expression in that language, to those who use the language for data exchange. But a schema can also be used in a practical sense as a way of checking for the presence or absence of specific features in the data—for instance, to check for compliance with the requirements of a particular tool or work process—and for this kind of purpose there may be many schemas that can be usefully applied to the data.

Semantics

In data modeling, the semantics of a data element are what constitute its meaning: both its significance as distinct from other data elements within the same data system, and its connection to the world of human concepts. If we think of data representation systems entirely in formal terms—that is, as systems whose significance can only be derived through formal operations—then we must understand them as systems of difference in which the meaning of a given element exists only as a function of the other elements in the same system from which it is distinguished. The question of how the meaning that circulates within such systems can be formally connected with, or grounded in, systems of human meaning is one of the large ongoing challenges in data modeling with particular significance for the digital humanities.

SPARQL Protocol and RDF Query Language (SPARQL)

SPARQL is a declarative language to express queries for data stored in [see] RDF. SPARQL, which is modeled on [see] SQL, is a [see] W3C recommendation and part of W3C's semantic web activity adding a common query language to RDF, the intended way to express semantic content and relations on the web. Basically RDF graphs are stored in triple stores and SPARQL is used to query them. Large triple stores—for example *DBpedia* containing the structured information from Wikipedia—are accessible via public SPARQL endpoints.

Structured Query Language (SQL)

The Structured Query Language is a programming language for database manipulation and retrieval. It defines a declarative language with commands to manage and query relational databases, thus shielding the user from the details how the database is implemented. The queries make use of the data model expressed in the database, embodying the knowledge about the entities, their attributes and the relationships between them. SQL is based on the [see] relational model, described by Codd in one of the most influential papers in computer science, "A Relational Model of Data for Large Shared Data Banks" (1970). SQL is an ANSI and an ISO standard and is widely supported.

Standard

In the digital world, where almost everything is contingent and could be different, standards have developed as fundamental intellectual endeavors to provide a common operational basis for all participants. Thus, standards bodies like the [see] International Organisation for Standardization, the [see] W3C, or the [see] Internet Engineering Task Force play an important role in the organization of the creation, publication and promotion of standards.

From a digital humanities perspective, while the direct role of international standards may seem remote or even somewhat problematic (since the humanities tend to see their methods and objects of study as individualized and not subject to standardization), there is an important deeper role for such standards. By establishing agreement on informational practices whose consistent handling is essential to the creation of tools and the transmission of information, standards like SGML or HTTP enable the creation of infrastructure that works across platforms and systems.

Stylesheet

A stylesheet is a formal specification of the processing to be applied to specific data elements within a given context, most typically when producing output of some kind. In a data ecology where the data modeling describes information structures and content elements in a general way, the stylesheet is the place where details of formatting and presentational behavior are expressed, often in different ways for different situations. For example, a digital edition represented in XML might contain information about different documentary witnesses, editorial conjectures, annotations, spelling regularization, and other features. A stylesheet for publishing this edition on the web might describe one set of output behaviors for a school audience (perhaps displaying a modernized reading copy of the text with basic annotations) and another set for an audience of specialists (showing variant readings from all witnesses, original spellings, and full editorial notes). Another stylesheet for the same data might produce camera-ready copy in PDF for print publication. The term "stylesheet" also applies more generally to programs such as XSLT stylesheets that manipulate XML data in some manner, not only to produce output but also to convert from one data format to another.

Table

A table is a simple way to organize data that has a clear structure in rows and columns. Each column typically contains the same kind of information and a column header specifies in a human-readable form the semantics of the column. Each row contains a set of attributes (the individual fields in the row) concerning a single entity. In relational databases tables underlie additional constraints, because they are understood as a relation ([see] relational model/ relational database). One of these constraints is the requirement that each row in a table must contain a unique identifier in a column that is the primary key of the table.

Tag abuse

Tag abuse is a colloquial and humorous term that describes the use of a modeling construct in a way that disregards its intended purpose, most often to achieve some desired effect of output. A classic example of this in the markup world would be the use of <title> to encode a foreign-language word so as to italicize it in the output. From a data modeling perspective, tag abuse is problematic for practical reasons, since it produces misleading modeling information: it hides information that could be useful (the title) and it creates false information (a text full of spurious "foreign" words). Additionally, tag abuse reflects a disregard for the goals of the modeling enterprise itself, since it treats it as a means to a single short-term practical end within a very narrow set of circumstances, rather than as the basis for a shared understanding of the data.

Text Encoding Initiative (TEI)

The Text Encoding Initiative is an international consortium that maintains and develops the TEI Guidelines for Electronic Text Encoding and Interchange, a community standard for representing a wide variety of research materials in digital form. The TEI Guidelines are currently realized as a markup language expressed in XML, but at a deeper level they represent a data model that could in principle be expressed using other modeling systems. Because they are so complex, so thoroughly documented, and so widely used in digital humanities, the TEI Guidelines are a useful entry point into humanities data modeling. They demonstrate many of the core principles and challenges, such as the strategic advantages of narrowly or broadly defined semantics, or of tightly or loosely formalized data structures. To a significant degree they also support the kinds of self-reflexive modeling and attention to ambiguity, provenance, editorial perspective, and transcriptional complexity that are characteristic of data modeling in digital humanities.

Tree structure

If in the context of graph theory an information structure is described as a tree, it is usually understood to be an undirected, connected graph without cycles in which two nodes are connected by only one edge. The underlying structure of XML documents is often described as a tree; in the language of graph theory, it is more exact to describe it as a rooted tree—that is, a tree where one node is special and ordered (because the sequence of the subgraphs matters). Because XML documents have an orientation—the root node is the only node without a parent and every other node has a parent and (potentially) one or more child nodes—they are also described as directed acyclic graphs with a root. Trees in this more specific sense as directed acyclic ordered rooted graphs, where two nodes are only connected by one edge, are a widely used and well-understood data structure, which made the development of XML tools much easier than more complex data models like SGML. The XML data model, which is so important for text encoding in the digital humanities, has a tree structure but is also defined by additional features, [see] XDM.

Unified Modeling Language (UML)

UML, developed by Grady Booch, Ivar Jacobson and James Rumbaugh, is an ISO standard. From the many diagram options, UML offers especially the way to describe classes and their relationship is in wider use, although it also includes diagramming conventions for describing relationships among larger components of software systems and interactions among entities (including the user).

World Wide Web Consortium (W3C)

The World Wide Web Consortium is an international standards body focusing on internet-related standards like HTML, XHTML, CSS, SVG, XML and the group of related standards including XSLT, XSL:FO etc. It was founded by Tim Berners-Lee, known for the invention of HTML, and has over 400 members from businesses, universities and other institutions. The W3C and Tim Berners-Lee have played a pivotal role in developing the necessary standards for the semantic web like RDF, OWL and SKOS. RDF has been especially important for libraries and other public institutions that offer their metadata and data in the form of linked open data.

XML (eXtensible Markup Language) and Standard Generalized Markup Language (SGML)

SGML (the Standard Generalized Markup Language) is a metalanguage for representing markup languages. It is an ISO standard, and is entirely platform- and software-independent. It represents data as a tree structure, a directed, acyclic graph whose data elements are bounded by tags and whose grammar is defined by a schema. Because SGML is expressed in plain text, it is human-readable and highly portable across systems and tools. XML (the eXtensible Markup Language) is a subset of SGML that retains these crucial features but eliminates much of SGML's complexity, with the goal of making it easier (and hence cheaper) to develop software tools that can process XML data. Compared with XML, SGML permits greater flexibility—for instance, it permits the language creator to specify what delimiters will be used to structure the markup (rather than requiring angle brackets and quotation marks); it permits end-tags to be omitted in cases where their presence can be inferred from the surrounding structure; and it provides for the possibility of overlapping hierarchies. As a result, while any given SGML document represents essentially the same modeled information as an equivalent XML document, the choices that take place in the metamodeling constitute an additional processing burden on any SGML software, making such software much more difficult to develop and more costly to run. XML was designed as a data format that could be used to exchange information over the web, and as a result it assumes that the software tools used to process XML data will need to be cheap and ubiquitous. The design of XML also assumes that control over the grammar and semantics of data— while still important as an option—are not essential features as they are in SGML. XML thus permits the creation of XML data without a schema, and does not require the presence of a schema to process the data, thereby permitting XML to be read and processed by lightweight tools such as web browsers. While XML as a metalanguage is defined by a relatively slim standard, it is the basis for some of the more complex standards in the digital humanities which provide data models for cultural entities like material objects or texts, for example [see] TEI.

XPath, Extensible Stylesheet Language for Transformations (XSLT), and XQuery

XPath, XSLT and XQuery are standards that describe how to address, manipulate and query XML documents. They are recommendations by the W3C and part of its larger XML activities. XPath is an expression language used for selecting nodes in an XML document, and for representing paths to XML nodes in the context of other programming, schema, and query languages. XSLT (the eXtensible Stylesheet Language for Transformations) is a programming language designed for manipulating and transforming XML data. It is widely used in the digital humanities as a way of converting XML data into other formats, either to create output for display and publication (e.g. HTML, PDF, JSON) or to assist in data curation activities such as migrating data to a new version of the TEI. XSLT uses XPath to identify nodes in the XML tree. XQuery is a functional programming language designed for querying and transforming XML data. Like XSLT, it uses XPath to search and to manipulate XML data, but it does so in a way that draws on the structure and logic of query languages like SQL. From a data modeling perspective, XSLT and XQuery are of interest because they permit the creation of well-modeled data without requiring the modeler to anticipate all future formats in which the data will need to be expressed. With XSLT and XQuery, details of element naming, sequencing, and structuring can be altered fairly straightforwardly as long as the underlying intellectual modeling is sound. These languages also make it possible to automate the down-translation of data from a strongly modeled format (such as TEI) into the more weakly modeled formats like HTML or RTF that are used for publication, so that the strongly modeled data may be treated as an archival format from which many different outputs can be automatically derived.

XQuery and XPath Data Model (XDM)

The XQuery and XPath Data Model is an XML-related standard created and curated by the [see] W3C. XDM describes the data model underlying all XML documents and XML query languages. It provides an overall structure for XML data and a set of building blocks to fill this structure, which includes seven different node types (such as elements, attributes, processing instructions), and additional atomic elements. XDM provides an important extension for the XML infoset, which was only intended to describe the data model for XML documents. XDM is a rather abstract model that provides a common ground for a large family of XML-related standards.

References

Chen, P., 1976. The Entity-Relationship Model—Toward a Unified View of Data. *ACM Transactions on Database Systems*, 1(1), pp. 9–36.

Index

Note: page references in *italics* indicate figures, in **bold** indicate tables, and with 'n' indicate chapter notes.

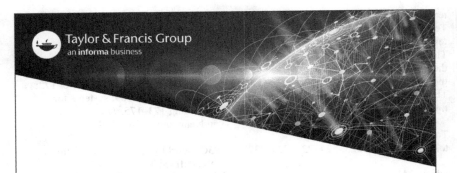

Printed in the United States
by Baker & Taylor Publisher Services